HE███████████ LIBRARY
P9-EDM-149   98948

WITHDRAWN
From Heritage University Library

History
of the
Concept of Time

Studies in Phenomenology and
Existential Philosophy

GENERAL EDITOR
J A M E S M. E D I E

CONSULTING EDITORS

David Carr
Edward S. Casey
Stanley Cavell
Roderick M. Chisholm
Hubert L. Dreyfus
William Earle
J. N. Findlay
Dagfinn Føllesdal
Marjorie Grene
Dieter Henrich
Don Ihde
Emmanuel Levinas
Alphonso Lingis

William L. McBride
J. N. Mohanty
Maurice Natanson
Frederick Olafson
Paul Ricoeur
John Sallis
George Schrader
Calvin O. Schrag
Robert Sokolowski
Herbert Spiegelberg
Charles Taylor
Samuel J. Todes
Bruce W. Wilshire

CONSULTANTS FOR HEIDEGGER TRANSLATIONS
Albert Hofstadter
Theodore Kisiel
John Sallis
Thomas Sheehan

Martin Heidegger

History
of the
Concept of Time

Prolegomena

TRANSLATED BY

Theodore Kisiel

Heritage University Library
3240 Fort Road
Toppenish, WA 98948

Indiana University Press
Bloomington

NEH
115
H 362h
1985

Preparation of this book was aided by a grant from the Program
for Translations of the National Endowment for the Humanities,
an independent federal agency.

A translator's introduction to this volume, by Theodore Kisiel, is published
separately as "On the Way to *Being and Time*: Introduction to the Translation
of Heidegger's *Prolegomena zur Geschichte des Zeitbegriffs*," *Research in
Phenomenology* XV (1985).

Published in German as *Prolegomena zur Geschichte des Zeitbegriffs*

© 1979 by Vittorio Klostermann

© 1985 by Indiana University Press

All rights reserved

No part of this book may be reproduced or utilized in any form
or by any means, electronic or mechanical, including photocopying
and recording, or by any information storage and retrieval system,
without permission in writing from the publisher. The Association
of American University Presses' Resolution on Permissions constitutes
the only exception to this prohibition.

Manufactured in the United States of America

Library of Congress Cataloging in Publication Data

Heidegger, Martin, 1889–1976.
History of the concept of time.

(Studies in phenomenology and existential philosophy)
Translation of: Prolegomena zur Geschichte des Zeit-
begriffs.
1. Time—Addresses, essays, lectures. 2. Phenome-
nology—Addresses, essays, lectures. I. Title.
II. Series.
B3279.H48P7613 1985 115 84-47703
ISBN 0-253-32834-9

1 2 3 4 5 89 88 87 86 85

Heritage University Library
3240 Fort Road
Toppenish WA 98948

88H0588

Contents

Contents

MAIN PART

Analysis of the Phenomenon of Time and Derivation of the Concept of Time

FIRST DIVISION

Preparatory Description of the Field in Which the Phenomenon of Time Becomes Manifest

Contents

TRANSLATOR'S FOREWORD

History of the Concept of Time: Prolegomena is a translation of *Prolegomena zur Geschichte des Zeitbegriffs*, which constitutes the text of a lecture course delivered by Martin Heidegger at Marburg University in the summer semester of 1925. The German edition, edited by Petra Jaeger, first appeared in 1979 as volume 20 of Heidegger's *Gesamtausgabe* (Collected Edition), the series of volumes currently being put together for publication by the publishing house of Vittorio Klostermann in Frankfurt. This Collected Edition is not intended to be a critical edition but seeks to provide readable working texts within the comprehension of the lay reader while still being of use to the scholar. This translation seeks to do the same for the English reader.

The scholar would do well to consult the Editor's Epilogue following the text on the mechanics and hermeneutics of composing the German edition from the extant documents in accordance with a few general guidelines for editing the lecture courses of the Collected Edition. Dr. Jaeger would be the first to admit that this is only one possible rendition of the 1925 lecture course. Another editor might have made many a different decision in weaving together the two basic documents, Heidegger's handwritten manuscript of lecture notes and Simon Moser's transcript of the lecture course as delivered. The task is complicated not only by the differences in these two stages in the composition of the course but also by the emendations and remarks added by Heidegger to the Moser transcript after the lectures were delivered. There is more than one indication in the emendatory trail thus left behind suggesting that the Moser transcript was put to direct use by Heidegger in the final drafting of his magnum opus of 1927, *Sein und Zeit*. The resulting edition thus includes a few formulations which postdate the lecture course itself. At any rate, Dr. Jaeger is to be lauded for her valiant and enormous labor in transcribing Heidegger's minuscule and sometimes almost illegible handwriting in order to incorporate the original manuscript into this edition, a labor which for other lecture courses had already been realized during Heidegger's lifetime by his brother Fritz. Her unstinting effort has thus given us this important lecture course much sooner than we might have expected.

In keeping with the intent of the Collected Edition, I have sought to provide a readable working text of this lecture course for the English reader. For one thing, giving primacy to the standard of readability in translation is in keeping with the lecture format of the text. In prac-

tical terms, this resulted not only in the proliferation and amplifica-
tion that come, for example, in recasting the typically long German
sentence into several shorter English sentences; it also on occasion
(but as sparingly as possible) led to the strategy of a 'sliding' translation of such key Heideggerian terms as *vorhanden* (both 'extant' and
'on hand') and occasionally even the use of a hendiadys ('extant and
on hand'). A Glossary of German Terms is provided for the scholar
interested in how I have translated key Heideggerian and Husserlian
terms. Regarding my overall approach to this translation, let me state
at least the following: When the means of illumination are available, I
do not believe that a translator has the 'right' (which is quite often a
disguise for timidity or indolence) to let ambiguous and opaque passages stand in the name of a purportedly 'literal' translation. I have
made the words of Gadamer my own here: "A translator must understand that illumination is part of his task. He therefore cannot leave
open whatever is unclear to him. He must show his colors and lay his
cards on the table. . . . He must state clearly how he understands."[1]
In this regard, I am especially grateful to Dr. Hermann Heidegger,
Martin Heidegger's literary executor, for permitting me to examine
photocopies of the manuscripts from which the German edition was
composed. First, this allowed me to verify and correct the errors that
cropped up in the first German edition.[2] This additional dimension of
illumination also assisted me enormously in clarifying a number of
ambiguous and obscure passages and in avoiding many an error in
interpretation. There is no doubt in my mind that this has contrib-
uted substantially to the clarity and accuracy of this English rendition
of the lecture course.

The present translation reproduces the notes and note numbering
of the German edition, but I have corrected errors and added biblio-
graphical information as needed; in particular, I have included references to extant English translations of the texts actually cited in the
body of the lecture course, though the translations of such passages
are always my own. The numbered footnotes are translations of those
appearing in the German edition; additional remarks by the translator are appended in square brackets, which also set off translator's
insertions—e.g. the German word, translations from the Latin, clarifying phrases and numerals—in the body of the text. The numbers in
the running heads refer to the pagination of the German edition. The
rare additional remark by Heidegger or by the German editor incorporated into the body of the text, typically in the citations, is indicated
by braces: {   }. Notes added by the translator are indicated by asterisks.

Only the briefest of commentaries on the translated text itself now
follows in order to provide the most indispensable guides and caveats

for the English reader. The task in this Foreword is simply to situate
this text within the larger context of Heidegger's development, especially within the earlier phases of what he himself liked to call his
Denkweg. This I have sought to do to the best of my knowledge of the
material and documents available to me at this time. A more extensive
introduction to this text is presented in my paper "On the Way to
Being and Time: Introduction to the Translation of Heidegger's *Prolegomena zur Geschichte des Zeitbegriffs*," *Research in Phenomenology* XV
(1985). I often refer to this separately published introduction within
the translator's footnotes to this volume. Among other things, this
paper provides a unified account of my translation decisions regarding the most problematic Heideggerian terms peculiar to this text and
shows how they are dictated by the matter of this text understood precisely as a phase of Heidegger's development.[3] As a text that is clearly
in transition toward *Being and Time*, it includes some central 'concepts
in transition' that pose special problems for the translator, especially
Appräsentation, *Jeweiligkeit* (temporal particularity), *Zu-sein* (to-be), and
Bewandtnis (standing, deployment). The critical reader is advised to
consult this paper for an explanation of how I have dealt with these
problems.

The announced title of this lecture course for the summer semester
of 1925, "History of the Concept of Time," reflects the titles of two
earlier lectures given by Heidegger at significant turning points in his
career. Heidegger's demonstration lecture at the beginning of his
teaching career in 1915 was entitled "The Concept of Time in Historical Science"; it is concerned with that concept as it is developed in both
historical and natural science. The more famous lecture given by
Heidegger to the Marburg Theological Faculty on July 25, 1924, was
entitled simply "The Concept of Time" and has been called by one
who was there[4] the 'Urform' of Heidegger's magnum opus, *Being and
Time* (1927). Some of the concepts and theses sketched out in this ger-
minal lecture are worked out in far greater detail, probably for the
first time in the general form they were to assume in *Being and Time*, in
the lecture course of 1925 presented here.

But the lecture course of 1925 falls far short of a re-examination of
the traditional concepts of time, the task implied in its announced title
and divided into three historical stages in the Second Part of the announced outline for the course (11).[5] In fact, only the First Division of
the First Part of that outline, "the preparatory description of the field
(namely Dasein) in which the phenomenon of time becomes manifest," is developed in any great detail.

Instead, it is the theme of *phenomenology* itself which predominates
in the early weeks of the course. The so-called Preliminary Part is in
effect a phenomenological reflection upon the history of phenome-

xvi   Translator's Foreword

nology designed to demonstrate the necessity within phenomenology
itself for the consideration of Dasein in its relation to being and time.
On the opening day, the outline for the course is introduced through
its announced subtitle, "Prolegomena to the Phenomenology of History and Nature"; in short, the course is designed to provide what is
first needed "in order to be able to do a phenomenology of history
and nature" (3). Later in the course, Heidegger notes that Husserl's
quest for a personalistic psychology then took the form of a course
given repeatedly and entitled "Nature and Spirit" (121). Here, in the
context of some personal remarks about his relationship to Husserl,
Heidegger reveals that earlier in that year he had received from Husserl the then unpublished manuscript of *Ideas II*, which is devoted to
the problem of the constitution of the domains of nature and spirit
that underlie natural and historical science. It is accordingly this fundamental distinction plaguing the early phenomenologists which Heidegger's own course from the outset is designed to overcome. From
the start, he suggests that the separation of these two domains may
well be hiding an original and undivided context which underlies them.

There is more than one indication here that Heidegger studied the
newly acquired text of *Ideas II* intensively in preparation for his own
course. The new text appears to have driven Heidegger to a renewed
detailed examination of Husserl's work, especially the Sixth Logical
Investigation, the Logos-Essay, and *Ideas I*. The result is the most sustained and specific confrontation of phenomenology in general and
Husserl in particular that we are likely to get from Heidegger. It is
therefore not without reason, no mere case of pedagogical dawdling,
that the so-called Preliminary Part on the history and nature of phenomenology grows far beyond the "short introductory orientation"
(10) which it was initially intended to be. Here we find the fruit and
climax of the close working relationship which Heidegger then enjoyed with Husserl, more than two years before the celebrated 'falling
out' between the two began. Here Heidegger specifies in precise philosophical detail what it was in Husserl's breakthrough book, *Logical Investigations*, that so 'fascinated'[6] him, and how he interprets its central
discoveries (intentionality, categorical intuition, and the ensuing new
sense of the apriori) in the direction of his more hermeneutical version of phenomenology. Here he repeatedly takes sharp issue with
Husserl's placing of primacy on the 'bodily presence' of perceived
things in favor of how the world 'appresents' things. In short, this
1925 course gives us Heidegger's most profound appreciation and
criticism of Husserl's founding contributions to phenomenology during the period when Heidegger was still immersed in the struggle to
go beyond his teacher.

Heidegger later notes that the "hermeneutic of facticity" in *Being and Time* was already developing in his courses as early as the winter semester of 1919–20.[7] Phenomenology is to take as its subject matter not just the theoretical but also the practical and, most basically, the factical life, the great 'fact of life.' It is this relation to the pretheoretical 'matters themselves' which makes phenomenology the science of origins and the original science, serving to revolutionize the idea of philosophy as a strict science and setting it off from all the other sciences: the course given in the 'war emergency semester' (February–April 1919) was entitled "The Idea of Philosophy and the Problem of World Views." All of the courses of this period were given under the banner of phenomenology as Heidegger understood it, for example, in the summer semester of 1920: "Phenomenology of Intuition and Expression: Theory of Philosophical Concept Formation." The course in the winter semester of 1921–22, "Phenomenological Interpretations of Aristotle," was in subtitle and in content really an introduction to phenomenological research on the basis of Aristotle. The first course at Marburg in 1923–24, purportedly on Descartes and modern philosophy, is actually entitled "Introduction to Phenomenological Research" and contains Heidegger's first overt critique of Husserl's turn toward the consciousness, along with the first detailed clarification of the term phenomenology, and a history of the breakthrough and initial development of phenomenology. All of these themes are again taken up in the 1925 lecture course.

What is therefore novel and unique to this course is the detailed treatment of the three 'breakthrough' discoveries of phenomenology (intentionality, categorial intuition, and a concomitant new sense of the apriori) in the Preliminary Part, and a number of hints in the Main Part on how these Husserlian themes are subsumed by the terminology of *Being and Time*. For the Main Part is by and large a first draft of the First Division of *Being and Time* and, in view of its organic continuity with the preceding Part, a phenomenological draft. Correlatively, it is a far less existentialistic draft. In fact, upon closer inspection, the lecture course itself is not an existentialistic draft at all; it is a pure phenomenological draft. The scattered allusions in this published version of the 1925 course to *Existenz* and the 'existential-ontological' (162, 216, 228, 238, 243, 246, 282, 291, 292, 295) are later additions superimposed upon the stenographic typescript of the lecture course 'aus letzter Hand Heideggers,'[8] apparently in the process of drafting the final version of *Being and Time*. In fact, at one point in the course itself, Heidegger mocks '*Existenz*' and 'decision' as the mode-words of his day which had replaced the pre-war mode-words of *Erleben* and *Erlebnis* (lived experience) in the philosophical fashion show (272). In view of how completely the terminology of 'existence' dominated *Being and Time* itself, it is in fact surprising how diligently he avoided this language in the first draft of 1925. (The technical term *Existenz* and the problem of developing special categories called the existentials, however, are mentioned as early as 1923 in Heidegger's lecture courses). The 1925 course thus provides dramatic proof of Heidegger's repeated contention that the way to *Being and Time* passes through phenomenology rather than through existentialism, contrary to decades of commentators who have chosen to ignore his disclaimers of existentialism.

Acknowledgment has already been made of substantial aid from the National Endowment for the Humanities, which enabled me to take a semester's leave to work on this project and, later, to return to Germany for another look at the manuscripts. Special thanks are due to Susan Mango of that organization for her understanding and unflagging support of this work. Additional significant financial support for various phases of this project came from the Alexander von Humboldt Foundation and Northern Illinois University. The latter also provided the secretarial assistance essential to such an endeavor. Inter Nationes has also promised financial support.

For their generous and unselfish help in countless ways in making my stays in Germany much easier, I am forever obligated to Walter and Marly Biemel and Monika Brand. For their hospitality and assistance during my stays at the German Literature Archive in Marbach am Neckar, I am grateful to the entire staff of the Archive, but especially to Dr. Joachim W. Storck who, despite a busy and often hectic schedule, helped me to decipher many questionable passages in the Heidegger manuscripts and advised me on a number of other linguistic problems.

I am especially grateful to Albert Hofstadter, that master of Heidegger translation, for a meticulous scrutiny of my translation. He caught a surprising number of residual errors at a late stage in the work and forced me back to the ideal of accuracy in that delicate balance with readability.

Support for such an international project over an extended period of time comes from numerous and sometimes unexpected quarters. To name only a few who have given me various forms of material assistance and professional advice at different stages of the project: Walter Biemel, Hartmut Buchner, Klaus Held, Petra Jaeger, Otto Pöggeler, John Sallis, Andre Schuwer, Tom Sheehan and Ernst Tugendhat. My family, forced to put up with my absences even in those times when I am 'bodily present,' has been patient throughout.

Theodore Kisiel

NOTES

1. Hans-Georg Gadamer, *Wahrheit und Methode* (Tübingen: Mohr, 1965), pp. 363–364. Though the translation is my own, cf. *Truth and Method* (New York: Seabury, 1975), p. 348.

2. An errata list for this edition has recently been published and is available upon request from the Klostermann Verlag. A few apparent errors not listed there and corrected in the body of this translation are usually indicated by a translator's note.

3. This understanding is what Heidegger would have called the *Vorhabe* of the translation (i.e., interpretation). Heidegger himself was acutely aware that every translation is already an interpretation, and spent many a page explaining his own translation decisions, say, of Anaximander's fragment. Cf. Martin Heidegger, *Der Satz vom Grund* (Neske: Pfullingen, 1957), p. 164; *Was Heisst Denken?* (Tübingen: Niemeyer, 1954), p. 107: English translation by J. Glenn Gray, *What Is Called Thinking?* (New York: Harper & Row, 1968), p. 174: "But every translation is already an interpretation." The same observation can be found as early as Heidegger's course on Aristotle in the summer semester of 1922 with respect to the then extant translations of Aristotle and his own.

4. Hans-Georg Gadamer, "Martin Heidegger und die Marburger Theologie," in Otto Pöggeler (ed.), *Heidegger: Perspektiven zur Deutung seines Werks* (Köln und Berlin: Kiepenheuer & Witsch, 1970), p. 169. For a summary of this lecture, cf. Oskar Becker, "Mathematische Existenz," *Jahrbuch für Philosophie und phänomenologische Forschung* VIII (1927), esp. pp. 660–666; Thomas J. Sheehan, "The 'Original Form' of Sein und Zeit: Heidegger's *Der Begriff der Zeit* (1924)," *Journal of the British Society for Phenomenology* X (1979), 78–83. In the latter essay, Sheehan misleadingly translates "Dasein" as "existence" without explicitly informing the reader. It is important for our purposes to note that the technical term *Existenz* does not appear in Heidegger's 1924 lecture.

5. Numbers in parentheses here refer to the pagination of the translated text below.

6. "Yet I remained so struck by Husserl's work that in the following years I read it again and again without sufficient insight into just what fascinated me." Martin Heidegger, "My Way to Phenomenology," *On Time and Being,* trans. Joan Stambaugh (New York: Harper & Row, 1972), p. 75.

7. Martin Heidegger, *Being and Time,* translated by John Macquarrie and Edward Robinson (New York: Harper, 1962), p. 490, Heidegger's note to page 72 of the German edition. This period preceding the publication of *Being and Time* is probably the most productive and most influential period of Heidegger's career.

8. Apparently all six Moser-transcripts in Heidegger's personal possession during these years pose this problem of editorial exegesis. Cf. Friedrich Wilhelm von Herrmann, "Die Edition der Vorlesungen Heideggers in seiner Gesamtausgabe letzter Hand," *Freiburger Universitätsblätter* 78 (December 1982), esp. p. 88.

History
of the
Concept of Time

Introduction

The Theme and Method
of the Lecture Course

§1. Nature and history as domains of objects
for the sciences

The first thing we must do is to come to an understanding of the theme of this lecture course and the way in which it is to be approached. We shall do this by clarifying its subtitle, "Prolegomena to the Phenomenology of History and Nature." Taken strictly, the expression refers to that which must be stated and stipulated in advance. In this case, it is a matter of what must be put forward in the beginning in order to be able to do a phenomenology of history and nature. We learn what the prolegomena are from what a phenomenology of history and nature is supposed to be.

In naming history and nature together, we are reminded first of all of the domains of objects which are investigated by the two main groups of empirical sciences (natural science and human science, the latter sometimes being called cultural science or historical science). We tend to understand history and nature by way of the sciences which investigate them. But then history and nature would be accessible only insofar as they are objects thematized in these sciences. But it is not certain whether a domain of objects necessarily also gives us the actual area of subject matter out of which the thematic of the sciences is first carved. To say that the science of history deals with history does not necessarily mean that history as this science understands it is as such also the authentic reality of history. Above all, no claim is made as to whether historiological knowledge of historical reality ever enables us to see history in its historicity. It might well be that something essential necessarily remains closed to the potentially scientific way of disclosing a particular field of subject matter; indeed, must remain closed if the science wishes to perform its proper function. In the case before

1

us, the separation of the two domains may well indicate that an original and undivided context of subject matter remains hidden and that it cannot be restored by a subsequent effort to bring the two, nature and spirit, together within the whole of human Dasein.

The separation comes first from the sciences, which reduce history and nature to the level of domains of objects. But the phenomenology of history and nature promises to disclose reality precisely as it shows itself *before* scientific inquiry, as the reality which is already given to it. Here it is not a matter of a phenomenology of the sciences of history and nature, or even of a phenomenology of history and nature as objects of these sciences, but of a phenomenological disclosure of the original kind of being and constitution of both. In this way, the basis for a philosophy of these sciences is first created, serving 1) to provide the foundation for their genesis from pretheoretical experience, 2) to exhibit the kind of access they have to the pregiven reality, and 3) to specify the kind of concept formation which accrues to such research. Because reality—nature as well as history—can be reached only by leaping over the sciences to some extent, this prescientific—actually philosophical—disclosure of them becomes what I call a *productive logic*, an anticipatory disclosure and conceptual penetration of potential domains of objects for the sciences. Unlike traditional philosophy of science, which proceeds after the fact of an accidental, historically given science in order to investigate its structure, such a logic leaps ahead into the primary field of subject matter of a potential science and first makes available the basic structure of the possible object of the science by disclosing the constitution of the being of that field. This is the procedure of the *original logic* put forward by Plato and Aristotle, of course only within very narrow limits. Since then, the idea of logic lapsed into obscurity and was no longer understood. Hence phenomenology has the task of making the domain of the subject matter comprehensible *before* its scientific treatment and, on this basis, the latter as well.

Our path to the fields of subject matter is therefore not by way of the theory of the factually available sciences. This is shown by the sense of the present *crisis of the sciences*, if we truly understand what this means. Nowadays, we speak of a crisis of the sciences in a twofold sense. First, there is the sense in which contemporary man, especially among the young, feels that he has lost an original relationship to the sciences. Recall the discussion evoked by Max Weber's lecture on this subject, which was so despairing over the sciences and their meaning. Taking Weber's standpoint to be that of despair and helplessness, one wanted to restore meaning to science and scientific work and sought to do so by cultivating a world view of science and constructing from it a mythical conception of the sciences.

But the real crisis is internal to the sciences themselves, wherein their basic relationship to the subject matter which each of them investigates has become questionable. The basic relationship to the subject matters is becoming insecure, which activates the tendency to carry out a propaedeutic reflection on their basic structure. Such a reflection seeks to dispel the insecurity over the fundamental concepts of the science in question or to secure those concepts in a more original understanding of its subject matter. Genuine progress in the sciences occurs only in this field of reflection. Such crises do not take place in the historiological sciences only because they have not yet reached the degree of maturity necessary for revolutions.

The present crisis in all the sciences therefore stems from the burgeoning tendency in them to reclaim their particular domain of objects originally, to forge their way back to the field of subject matter which is thematizable in their research.

What task is incurred in this comprehensive crisis? What is to be accomplished? How is that possible?

The crisis can be directed in ways which are fruitful and secure for the sciences only if we are clear about its scientific and methodological sense and see that the exposition of the primary field of subject matter calls for a mode of experience and interpretation in principle different from those which prevail in the concrete sciences themselves. In crisis, scientific research assumes a philosophical cast. Sciences thus say that they are in need of an original interpretation which they themselves are incapable of carrying out.

We can demonstrate this succinctly and concretely by way of the following series of particular sciences, chosen here to suit our purpose. Characteristic is the crisis in contemporary *mathematics*, which is emphatically characterized as a *crisis of foundations*. In the dispute between *formalism* and *intuitionism*, the question is whether the fundaments of the mathematical sciences are based upon formal propositions that are simply assumed and that constitute a system of axioms from which all the other propositions can be deduced. This is Hilbert's position. The opposing direction, essentially influenced by phenomenology, asks whether or not in the end what is primarily given is the specific structure of the objects themselves (in geometry the continuum which precedes scientific inquiry, for example, in integral and differential analysis). This is the doctrine of Brouwer and Weyl. Thus, what is *prima facie* the most firmly established science manifests the tendency toward a transposition of the entire science onto new and more original foundations.

In *physics* the revolution came by way of relativity theory, which has no other sense than the tendency to exhibit the original interconnectedness of nature insofar as this is independent of any analysis and inquiry. Relativity theory is a theory of relativities, a theory of the conditions of access and modes of conception, which are to be arranged so that in this access to nature, in a specific mode of space-time measurement, the invariance of the laws of motion is preserved. Its aim is not relativism but just the opposite. Its real aim is to find the in-itself of nature by way of the detour through the problem of gravitation, concentrated as a problem of matter.

In *biology*, likewise, the effort is being made to reflect upon the basic elements of life. It seeks to free itself from the presuppositions which take the living being as a bodily thing and so define it mechanistically. Even *vitalism* is caught up in these presuppositions in trying to define the life-force with mechanistic concepts. For the first time, there are now attempts to get a clear sense of "living being" and "organism" in the hope of finding a clue to guide concrete research.

The *historiological sciences* are currently troubled by the question of historical reality itself. In the history of literature we now have a key expression from Unger: history of literature as a history of problems. Here the attempt is being made to go beyond a merely historiological, literary, and artistic presentation to a history of the state of affairs thereby presented.

Theology wishes to go forward from a revival of belief, its basic relationship to the reality which it thematizes, so that it may arrive at an original explication of the being of man toward God, which involves the disengagement of the fundamental question of man from the traditional systematic approach of dogmatics. For this systematic approach is based upon a philosophical and conceptual system which has created confusion in both the question of man and the question of God and all the more in the question of the relationship of man to God.

Everywhere we see advances being made toward an original relationship* to the matters themselves. The laws of progress by which a scientific revolution occurs differ in the individual sciences because the mode of being of the experience and what is experienced is different, because the states of affairs stand in definite fundamental relationships to man himself, and because sciences themselves are nothing but concrete possibilities of human Dasein speaking out about the world in which it exists and about itself. Therefore, if the sciences are not to be regarded as a spurious enterprise, founding their justification merely by invoking the prevailing currents of the tradition, but instead are to receive the possibility of their being from their meaning in human Dasein, then the decisive question, and the place where an

---

*Reading *Verhältnis* here instead of *Verständnis*.

answer to the crisis is to be found, is in bringing the subject matters under investigation to an original experience, before their concealment by a particular scientific inquiry. Here we restrict ourselves to the domains of history and nature, which are to be exhibited in their original mode of being.

§2. *Prolegomena to a phenomenology of history and nature under the guidance of the history of the concept of time*

We have come to an initial understanding of this task simply by way of the sciences of these two domains. But such an extrinsic understanding is not the true entry to the thematic object. We wish to exhibit history and nature so that we may regard them *before* scientific elaboration, so that we may see both realities in their reality. This means that we wish to arrive at a *horizon* from which history and nature can be originally contrasted. This horizon must itself be a *field of constituents* against which history and nature stand out in relief. Laying out this field is the task of the "prolegomena to a phenomenology of history and nature." We shall approach this task of laying out the actual constituents which underlie history and nature, and from which they acquire their being, by way of a *history of the concept of time*.

At first sight, this seems to be a strange sort of an approach, or in any case a detour. But it loses its strangeness as soon as we recall, even quite superficially, that both historical reality and natural reality are continuities that run their course *in time* and are traditionally understood as such. In natural science, especially in its basic science of physics, the *measurement of time* plays a fundamental role in defining its objects. The investigation of historical reality is completely incomprehensible without a *chronology*, an ordination of time. Viewed simply from the outside, history and nature are temporal. To the totality of temporal reality we tend to juxtapose the *extratemporal* constituents which, for example, are the topic of research in mathematics. In addition to these extratemporal constituents in mathematics we are familiar with *supratemporal* constituents in metaphysics or theology, understood as eternity. In a very schematic and crude way, time already announces itself as *one* 'index' for the differentiation and delimitation of domains of being as such. The concept of time discloses particulars about type and reality for such a demarcation of the universal realm of entities. It becomes, according to the particular stage of its development as a concept, a guide for the question of the being of entities and their potential regions. This occurs without an expressly fundamental consciousness of such a role, which is thus fulfilled in a correspondingly crude way, without bringing to the fore the possibilities which are implied in such an orientation. The concept of time is therefore not an arbitrarily posited concept but is linked to the *basic question of philosophy*, if indeed this asks about the *being* of entities, the actuality of the actual, the reality of the real.

But then *the history of the concept of time* is the *history of the discovery of time* and the *history of its conceptual interpretation*. In other words, it is the *history of the question of the being of entities*, the history of the attempts to uncover entities in their being, borne by the particular understanding of time, by the particular level of conceptual elaboration of the phenomenon of time. Hence, in the end, the history of the concept of time is more accurately *the history of the decline* and *the history of the distortion of the basic question* of scientific research into the being of entities. It is the history of the incapacity to pose the question of being in a radically new way and to work out its first fundaments anew—an incapacity which is grounded in the being of Dasein. But over against this wholly external characterization of the fundamental role of the concept of time we will in the course of our considerations be confronted with the question: What after all makes time and the concept of time, the comprehending regard to time, appropriate for this peculiar function, hitherto always assumed as self-evident, of characterizing and dividing the domains of reality—temporal, extratemporal, supratemporal reality?

Commensurate with the fundamental significance of time and its concept, the history [*Geschichte*] of the concept of time is in turn no arbitrary historiological [*historische*]* reflection. This distinction in turn suggests the manner of this fundamental reflection on the history of the concept of time. The historiology of the time concept could be carried out as a gathering of opinions about time and a summary of its conceptual formulations. Through such a doxographical survey of the concept of time, one might expect to obtain an understanding of time itself and thus the basis for characterizing the special temporal realities 'history' and 'nature.' But even the most meticulous collections of opinions remain blind so long as one does not first have a clear idea of just what is constantly being sought in gathering such information. The understanding of time itself will never be obtained from the historiology of the time concept. Instead, it is precisely the understanding of the phenomenon of time, worked out in advance, which first permits us to understand earlier concepts of time.

But in that case would not the *plain and simple discussion of the concept of time* suffice for a determination of history and nature as temporal

---

* *Geschichte* is the history that actually happens (*geschieht*) while *Historie* is the explicit thematization of that happening and so, usually, the science of history or 'historiology.' Cf. *Being and Time*, §§6 and 76.

realities? Then why the history of the concept as well? This is plainly an additional orientation in regard to what was thought in earlier times, but has no bearing upon what is called the 'systematic' discussion of time and temporal reality. This attitude makes sense as long as the belief persists that a systematic philosophical discussion is possible in a radical sense *without being historiological in its innermost grounds.* But if on the contrary that should be the case, if it should turn out that precisely the basic question of philosophical research, the question of the being of entities, compels us to enter into an original arena of research which *precedes* the traditional partition of philosophical work into historiological and systematic knowledge, then the *prolegomena* to the investigation of entities in their being are to be won only by way of *history.* This amounts to saying that the manner of research is *neither* historiological *nor* systematic, but instead *phenomenological.*

One of the goals of this lecture course is to demonstrate the necessity and the sense of such a fundamental form of research. Indeed, this is to be demonstrated from the thematic content of the subject matters to be explored and not from an arbitrarily concocted idea of philosophy or on the basis of what is called a philosophical standpoint. This original mode of research which *precedes* the historiological mode and the so-called systematic mode we shall come to understand as the *phenomenological* mode. The kind of object and even more the kind of being of that which is the theme of philosophy demands just this kind of research.

But at first we shall proceed in the traditional manner [and utilize the separation which we now regard as a purely didactic device]. The historiological clarification of the history of the concept of time is only didactically separated from the [systematic] analysis of the phenomenon of time. The latter in turn is the preparation for the possibility of historiological understanding.*

---

*Whence the justification for the first two words added to the German title for this edition, *Prolegomena zur Geschichte des Zeitbegriffs,* inasmuch as the course stops short in the middle of the systematic analysis. (Cf. Editor's Epilogue below). The distinction between the systematic and the historiological is likewise the basis for the two Parts of the original plan of *Being and Time* (§8). Both the systematic and the historiological are in turn the "Prolegomena to the Phenomenology of History and Nature."

The summer semester course of 1927, *The Basic Problems of Phenomenology* (§5), develops a threefold distinction within the phenomenological approach. The move away from beings and the ontic (for example, the empirical sciences) to their being (to their regional ontologies and then to fundamental ontology) is called *reduction*; the actual projection of beings onto their ontological structures is *construction* (= the systematic); and the dismantling of the historically transmitted concepts in which their being is customarily described in order to get back to the experiential sources from which they are drawn, is *destruction* (= the historiological). These three elements of the phenomenological method are regarded as co-original or equiprimordial, that is, as belonging essentially together in reciprocal equality.

§3. Outline of the lecture course

To summarize: the basic question of the reality of history and nature is the basic question of the reality of a particular domain of being. For the question of being, the concept of time is our guide. Accordingly, the question of the being of entities, if it is to be regarded as radical, is tied to a discussion of the phenomenon of time. This discussion of the phenomenon of time is neither systematic in the traditional sense nor historiological, but phenomenological.* This results in the following outline for the entire course, which is divided into three parts.

First Part: Analysis of the phenomenon of time and derivation of the concept of time.

Second Part: Disclosure of the history of the concept of time.

Third Part: On the basis of the first and second parts, the elaboration of the horizon for the question of being in general and of the being of history and nature in particular.

These three parts will be preceded by a short introductory orientation {Preliminary Part} regarding the general methodological character of the investigations, that is, a specification of the sense of phenomenological research and its tasks. It is divided into three chapters:

Chapter One: Emergence and initial breakthrough of phenomenological research.

Chapter Two: The fundamental discoveries of phenomenology, its principle, and the clarification of its name.

Chapter Three: The initial development of phenomenological research and the necessity of a radical reflection in and of itself.

The *First Part*, "The Analysis of the Phenomenon of Time and the Determination of the Concept of Time," is divided into three divisions:

First Division: The preparatory description of the field in which the phenomenon of time becomes manifest.

Second Division: The exposition of time itself.

Third Division: The conceptual interpretation.

The *Second Part*, "The History of the Concept of Time," begins in the present and works backwards:

First: Bergson's theory of time.

Second: The concept of time in Kant and Newton.

---

*This sentence added to complete the summary. This entire summary paragraph is cited from the Moser transcript by Walter Biemel, "Heideggers Stellung zur Phänomenologie in der Marburger Zeit," E. W. Orth (ed.), *Phänomenologische Forschungen*, Volume 6/7 (Freiburg/Munich: Alber, 1978), p. 144.

Third: The initial conceptual discovery of time in Aristotle.

Why these three major stages of the history of the concept of time are explored will become evident from the investigation itself, inasmuch as these three stages constitute the stations at which a relative transformation of the concept of time has occurred. I say 'relative' because basically the concept of time as Aristotle conceived it is retained throughout. Bergson in fact makes an attempt to go beyond this concept to a more original one. This justifies our treating him separately within the question of the historical concept of time. Basically, when we consider the categorial fundaments which he presupposes, namely, quality and succession, Bergson does not advance the matters at issue and so remains traditional.

The *Third Part* deals with the exposition of the "Question of Being in General and the Being of History and Nature in Particular." It at the same time paves the way for a more lucid determination of the sense and the task of phenomenological research, on the basis of the elucidated material content of the theme reached by then.

PRELIMINARY PART

The Sense and Task of Phenomenological Research

Chapter One

Emergence and Initial Breakthrough
of Phenomenological Research

§4. *The situation of philosophy in the second half of the 19th century. Philosophy and the sciences.*

We must first get a clear sense of the history of phenomenological research as it emerged from the historical situation of philosophy in the last decades of the 19th century. This situation in turn is determined by the transformation of the scientific consciousness in the 19th century which took place after the collapse of the idealistic systems, a transformation which affects not only philosophy but all sciences. This transformation allows us to understand the way in which a fresh attempt was made in the course of the second half of the 19th century to bring scientific philosophy into its own. This attempt came about in the tendency to grant the particular sciences their independent right and at the same time to secure for philosophy its own field in relation to these sciences. This leads to a philosophy which has the essential character of a *theory of science*, a *logic of the sciences*. This is the first distinctive feature of the philosophical renewal in the second half of the 19th century.

The second is that the renewal takes place not in an original return to the matters at issue but by going back to a historically established philosophy, that of Kant. Philosophy is thus traditionalistic; it assumes a well-defined complex of a well-defined line of questioning and thus in turn comes to a well-defined position toward the concrete sciences.

The scientific situation around the middle of the 19th century will be characterized only in terms of the main features relating to the manner and scope of the renewal of philosophical science. It is defined in all the sciences by the watchword *empirical facts*, as opposed to speculation and empty concepts. The prevalence of this watchword has many causes, first of all the collapse of the idealistic systems. The sciences brought their full weight to bear upon the empirical domains, and in fact upon the two domains of the historical world and of nature, even then becoming dissociated from one another. On the whole, the dominant force operative in philosophical reflection at the time took the form of an arid and crude materialism, what was then called the *world view of natural science.*

The historiological sciences generally dispensed with any philosophical reflection. In their overall intellectual orientation they lived in the world of Goethe and Lessing. But what alone mattered, what was decisive for them, was concrete work, and that meant the *propensity toward 'facts.'* Accordingly, the first task to be carried out in history was to disclose and to secure the sources. This was accompanied by the cultivation of philological criticism, the technique of interpretation. The interpretation of the subject matter, what was then called the 'reading' of the material given in the sources, in its methodological direction and its principles was left to the particular mental-set of the historian; the reading varied according to the impulses operative in him. These were diverse; since the seventies they were essentially nourished by politics. This was paralleled by a trend toward cultural history. This confluence erupted in the eighties into a discussion over whether history is cultural history or political history. No headway was made in the area of fundamentals since all the means to do so were lacking. But it indicates that the basic relationship of the historian to his objects was uncertain and was left to general considerations which were cultural and popular in nature. This condition still prevails today, even if the two are now brought together under the title of *history of the spirit.* Historical sciences thus concentrated strictly on their concrete work, where they have accomplished important things.

The natural sciences of that time were defined by the great tradition of Galileo and Newton. Most notably, the domain of the natural sciences was expanding into the physiological and biological sphere. Thus, on the heels of the physiological, psychic life entered into the horizon of inquiry of the natural sciences. It entered first through those areas most closely associated with the physiological, through life as it expresses itself in the sense organs. To the extent that psychic life is explored by means of the methods of natural science, such an exploration is a psychology of the senses, sensation, and perception, and is intimately associated with physiology. Psychology became *physiological psychology*, as Wundt's major work shows. Here domains were found in which even psychic life, mind, could be disclosed by the investigative means of natural science. One should also keep in mind that the task of psychology then, under the influence of *British em-*

piricism (and going back to Descartes) was conceived as a *science of consciousness*. In the middle ages and in Greek philosophy, the whole man was still seen; inner psychic life, what we now so readily call consciousness, was apprehended in a natural experience which was not regarded as an inner perception and so set off from an outer one. Since Descartes the concept of psychology, in general the science of the psychic, is altered in a characteristic manner. The science of the mental, of reason, is a *science of consciousness*, a science which arrives at its object in what is called inner experience. Even for physiological psychology the approach to the theme of psychology is from the start taken for granted. Its conception was given a purely external formulation by way of a contrast: *not a science of the soul as a substance but of the psychic manifestations of that which gives itself in inner experience*. Characteristically, the natural sciences, in their methodological import, here entered into a domain which was traditionally reserved for philosophy. The tendency of a scientific psychology is to transpose itself into the domain of philosophy itself, indeed even to become, in the course of further development, the *basic science of philosophy itself*.

a) The position of positivism

All the scientific disciplines are dominated by *positivism*, the tendency toward the *positive*, where "positive" is understood in terms of *facts*, and facts are understood in terms of a particular interpretation of *reality*. Facts are facts only if they can be enumerated, weighed, measured, and experimentally determined. In history, facts are those movements and events which are in the first instance accessible in the sources.

Positivism is to be understood not only as a maxim of concrete research but in general as a theory of knowledge and culture. As a theory, positivism was developed concurrently in France and in England through the work of Auguste Comte and John Stuart Mill. Comte distinguishes three stages in the development of human existence: religion, metaphysics, and science. The stage of science is now in its initial phases. Its goal is a *sociology* developed by the methods of natural science into a general theory of man and his human relations.

John Stuart Mill conceives positivism philosophically as a universal theory of science. The Sixth Book of his *System of Deductive and Inductive Logic* deals with the logic of the moral sciences, which was the old name for what we call historical science or human science. This English-French positivism soon found its way into Germany and in the decade of the fifties initiated reflection in the philosophy of science. Within this movement of positivism in the sciences themselves and positivism as a philosophical theory stands Hermann Lotze, to some extent all by himself. He kept the tradition of German idealism alive and at the same time tried to give the positivism of the sciences its due. He played a noteworthy transition role not without significance for subsequent philosophy.

b) Neo-Kantianism—the rediscovery of Kant in the philosophy of science

In the sixties Mill's *Logic* was known far and wide. The possibility of an investigation of the structure of the particular sciences offered the prospect of an autonomous task for philosophy while at the same time preserving the inherent rights of the particular sciences. This task recalled Kant's *Critique of Pure Reason*, which itself was interpreted as an exercise in the philosophy of science. The return to Kant, the renewal of Kantian philosophy, the founding of neo-Kantianism all take place from a very particular line of questioning, that of philosophy of science. This is a narrow conception of Kant which we only now are again trying to overcome. This reflection in the philosophy of science and the return to Kant also exposed a fundamental omission in prior philosophy of science. In considering the second major group of empirical sciences alongside the natural sciences, namely, the historical disciplines, philosophy of science found itself confronted with the task of supplementing the Kantian endeavor with a "critique of historical reason." This is how Dilthey formulated the problem already in the seventies.

The rediscovery of Kant, with a very pronounced bias toward philosophy of science, was first concentrated upon a positivistic interpretation of Kantian philosophy. This work was done by Hermann Cohen, the founder of the so-called *Marburg School*, in his *Kant's Theory of Experience*. One can see from the title just how Kant is fundamentally regarded: *theory of experience*, experience understood as scientific experience as it was concretely realized in mathematical physics, thus a theory of the positivism of the sciences oriented along Kantian lines. To be more exact, this philosophy of science is carried out as the investigation of the structure of knowledge wholly within the Kantian horizon, working out the constitutive moments of knowledge in the form of a *science of consciousness*. Thus, even here, in the philosophy of science, there is a return to consciousness, in line with the trend in psychology. Even though consciousness became a theme in scientific psychology and in epistemology in completely different ways, it nevertheless remained and until now has remained the tacit thematic field of consideration. It is the sphere which Descartes, in his pursuit of very particular objectives, made into the basic sphere of philosophical reflection.

c) Critique of positivism—Dilthey's call for an independent method for the human sciences

In the Sixth Book of his *Logic*, "On the Logic of the Moral Sciences," J. S. Mill sought to carry the method of the natural sciences over into the human sciences. From his early years, Dilthey saw the impossibility of such a transposition as well as the necessity of a positive theory of the sciences drawn from the sciences themselves. He saw that the task of understanding the historical disciplines philosophically can succeed only if we reflect upon the object, the reality which is the actual theme in these sciences, and manage to lay open the basic structure of this reality, which he called *life*. It was in this way, from this positively novel and independently formulated task, that he came to the necessity of a *psychology*, a *science of consciousness*. But this was not to be a psychology fashioned after a natural science nor one invested with an epistemological task. Its task is rather to regard 'life' itself in its structures, as the basic reality of history. The decisive element in Dilthey's inquiry is not the theory of the sciences of history but the tendency to bring the reality of the historical into view and to make clear from this the manner and possibility of its interpretation. To be sure, he did not formulate the question so radically. He continued to operate in the interrogative ambience of his contemporaries. Accordingly, along with the question of the reality of the historiological sciences, he also discussed the question of the structure of knowledge itself. This line of inquiry was for a time predominant, and the text, *Introduction to the Human Sciences* (1883), is essentially oriented toward a philosophy of science.

d) The trivializing of Dilthey's inquiry by Windelband and Rickert

The initiatives of the Marburg School and of Dilthey were then taken up by Windelband and Rickert, who leveled and trivialized them and twisted their problems beyond recognition. In other words, inquiry understood as the theoretical clarification of science is reduced by this school to an empty methodology. The structure of knowledge itself, the structure of research, of the access to the realities in question, are no longer investigated, much less the structure of these realities. The sole theme is the question of the logical structure of scientific representation. This is carried to such an extreme that in Rickert's philosophy of science the sciences under study are no longer even recognizable. Mere schemes of sciences are laid down and taken as basic. This distortion and trivialization had the dubious consequence of covering up the authentic meaning of Dilthey's inquiry and rendering its positive effect impotent to the present day.

But the positive element in Dilthey's endeavor is its tendency toward the reality which the historiological sciences thematize. Because of this line of questioning, Dilthey holds an outstanding place within philosophy in the second half of the 19th century; likewise because, in contrast to the Marburg School, he stayed clear of a *dogmatic Kantianism* and, with his proclivity for radicalism, sought to philosophize strictly out of the matters themselves. To be sure, the weight of the tradition and the philosophy of his contemporaries proved to be too powerful for him to remain true to his special bent and to keep it on a sure and steady path. He often wavered. There were times when he viewed his own work purely in terms of the traditional philosophy of his time, which was moving in a completely different direction. But time and again the elementary instinct of his own way of questioning broke through. This insecurity indicates that he never found his own method or a true formulation of the question. At any rate, his sally into the authentic domain in the face of traditional inquiry remains decisive. This can only be appreciated if we free ourselves from the traditional standards prevalent nowadays in scientific philosophy, if we see that what is decisive in philosophy is not what characterized scientific philosophy at the end of the 19th century, namely, the battle of trends and schools and the attempts to bring one standpoint to prevail over another. It is not decisive, in philosophy, to deal with the things once again by means of traditional concepts on the basis of an assumed traditional philosophical standpoint, but instead to disclose new domains of the matters themselves and to bring them under the jurisdiction of science by means of a productive concept formation. This is the criterion of a scientific philosophy. The criterion is not the possibility of constructing a system, a construction which is based purely on an arbitrary adaptation of the conceptual material transmitted by history. Nowadays, a tendency toward system is once again stirring in philosophy, yet it is devoid of any sense that would be dictated by an in-depth treatment of the problems. The tendency is purely traditionalistic, like the renewal of Kantian philosophy. Now, one merely goes beyond Kant to Fichte and Hegel.

e) Philosophy as 'scientific philosophy'— psychology as the basic science of philosophy (the theory of consciousness)

To summarize: In the middle of the 19th century a well-defined scientific philosophy gained prevalence. The expression '*scientific philosophy*' has a threefold sense. This philosophy characterizes itself as scientific:

　　1. Because it is a philosophy of the sciences, that is, because it is a

theory of scientific knowledge, because it has as its actual object the fact of science.

2. Because by way of this inquiry into the structure of already given sciences it secures its own theme which it investigates in accordance with its own method, while it itself no longer lapses into the domain of reflection characteristic of the particular sciences. It is 'scientific' because it acquires its own domain and its own method. At the same time, the method maintains its security by its constant orientation to the factual conduct of the sciences themselves. Speculation aimed at world views is thereby avoided.

3. Because it seeks to give a foundation to the various disciplines which are directed toward consciousness through an original science of consciousness itself, a *psychology*.

Neo-Kantianism has, it is true, launched a very strong opposition to psychology regarded as a natural science. That has not prevented the elevation of psychology to the basic science of philosophy both by the natural sciences themselves (Helmholtz) as well as through philosophy. If knowledge is an act of consciousness, then there is a theory of knowing only if psychic life, consciousness, is first given and has been investigated 'scientifically,' which means by the methods of natural science.

It should be noted that psychology today, with its various directions, is on a completely different level from this natural-scientific psychology. Under the essential influence of phenomenological work the manner of inquiry in psychology has been altered.

At the end of the 19th century, 'scientific' philosophy in all of its directions was pervaded by the theme of *consciousness*. It has an explicit awareness of its connection with Descartes, who was the first to identify consciousness, *res cogitans*, as the basic theme of philosophy. It is difficult to see through this philosophy of the turn of the century to all of its particulars. This is not the place to pursue the particular connections; it is irrelevant for our inquiry. Let us note only that since 1840 an *Aristotelian tradition* has been an active force within this movement. It was founded by Trendelenburg. It arose from the opposition to Hegel and began as a way of assimilating the historical research by Schleiermacher and Böckh into the field of Greek philosophy. Dilthey and Brentano are students of Trendelenburg.

α) Franz Brentano

Franz Brentano was a student in Berlin at the end of the sixties, where he first studied Catholic theology. His first work was on Aristotle. He sought to interpret Aristotle against the horizon of medieval philosophy, above all that of Thomas Aquinas. Such an interpretation is the distinguishing mark of this work, which is not to say that this is really the way to understand Aristotle. On the contrary, through this kind of interpretation Aristotle essentially undergoes a drastic reinterpretation. But that is not the crucial issue. What is important is that Brentano himself, through his preoccupation with Greek philosophy, arrived at some more original horizons for his philosophical inquiry. Personal difficulties with Catholic belief, in particular the mystery of the Trinity and, in the seventies, the declaration of the infallibility of the Pope, forced him to leave this intellectual world. But he took with him some well-defined horizons and a reverence for Aristotle, and now moved into the current of a free and unrestricted philosophical science.

The way out of the tradition was traced for him by Descartes. Brentano's work thus reveals a unique blend of *Aristotelian-Scholastic* philosophizing and modern *Cartesian* inquiry. He makes the philosophical goal of a science of consciousness his own. But the decisive move is to be found in Brentano's *Psychology from the Empirical Standpoint* (1874). Here for the first time he detaches himself from the tendency to transpose the methods of natural science and physiology into the exploration of psychic life. Characteristic for the direction of his thought is the thesis of his inaugural dissertation (1866): *Vera methodus philosophiae non alia est nisi scientiae naturalis* ("The true philosophical method is none other than that of the natural sciences"). It would be wrong to interpret this thesis as a call to transpose the methods of natural science into philosophy. The thesis rather means that philosophy has to proceed in its field exactly as the natural sciences do in theirs, namely, it has to draw its concepts from *its own* matters. This thesis is not a proclamation in favor of a brute transfer of scientific methodology into philosophy but the opposite: the exclusion of the methodology of natural science and the call to proceed in philosophy as the natural sciences do in their field—with a fundamental regard for the character of the subject matters in question.

For the task of a psychology this means that, prior to all theories about the connection of the psychic with the bodily or of sense life with the sense organs, what really matters first is to accept the actual elements of psychic life as they are immediately accessible. The first and foremost task is a 'classification of psychic phenomena,' a division of psychic phenomena not on the basis of an arbitrary principle imposed from without, but a division and order which follows the nature of the psychic, an order—which would include the formation of basic concepts—drawn from the essence of the matters being considered here, from the essence of the psychic itself.

Brentano thus tried to provide the foundations for the science of consciousness, of lived experiences, of the psychic in the broadest sense, by accepting the actual elements just as they are given in this field. He did not begin with theories about the psychic, about the soul itself, about the connection of the psychic with the physiological and biological. Instead, he first clarified what it is that is given when one speaks of the psychic, of lived experiences. His major work, *Psychology from the Empirical Standpoint* (1874), is divided into two books. The first book discusses psychology as a science and the second addresses psychic phenomena in general. 'Empirical' here does not mean inductive in the sense given to it by the natural sciences, but rather drawn from the subject matter, without constructions. The first thing, therefore, is to characterize the psychic phenomena themselves, to order their multiplicity according to basic structures; hence the task of a 'classification.' *'Classification'* means dividing and ordering actual elements which are already given. Ordering is always done from a point of view, as everyone says. Point of view is that toward which I look, with regard to which I make certain distinctions in a domain of subject matter. This regard or point of view can vary in kind. I can order a given manifold of objects with regard to a devised scheme; I can imagine that there are very general processes which run from within to without and others which proceed from without to within, and order the psychic phenomena from this point of view. Second, the point of view can be taken from the objective context which bears a connection with that which is itself to be ordered, in the manner that I order psychic processes with regard to physiological relationships. The attempt was accordingly made to define even thinking and willing in terms of phenomena of neural kinetics. Third, the point of view can itself be drawn from the actual elements to be ordered. No principle is superimposed upon them; it is rather drawn from the actual elements themselves. This is the real maxim which Brentano follows in his classification: "The order of lived experiences must be natural." An experience must be assigned to a class to which it belongs in accordance with its nature. 'Nature' here means that which is what it is, as seen from itself. When it is genuine, a classification can be made only "from a prior familiarity with the objects," "from the study of the objects."[1] I must have prior familiarity with the objects, their basic structures, if I am to order them properly, in accord with the subject matter or object. The question therefore arises, what is the nature of psychic phenomena compared with the physical? This is the question posed by Brentano in the first book on psychology. He says that psychic phenomena differ from all physical phenomena by nothing so

---

1. Franz Brentano, *Psychologie vom empirischen Standpunkt*, 1874; editor's note: Cited according to the edition of 1925, Vol. 2, p. 28. [There is an unaltered later printing of this 1925 edition edited by Oskar Kraus in the series *Philosophische Bibliothek*, Vol. 193 (Hamburg: Meiner, 1959). English translation: *Psychology from an Empirical Standpoint*, edited by Linda L. McAlister (New York: Humanities, 1973), p. 194.]

much as by the indwelling in them of something objective. Accordingly, if there are to be distinctions within the field of psychic phenomena, they must be distinctions with respect to the basic structure of this indwelling, distinctions in the way in which something is objective in these lived experiences. These differences in how something is objective in the various lived experiences, the represented in representing, the judged in judging, the willed in willing, accordingly form the principal distinctions of classes among the psychic phenomena. This basic structure of the psychic, whereby something objective inheres in each lived experience, is called *intentional inexistence* by Brentano.

Intentio is a Scholastic expression which means *directing itself toward*. Brentano speaks of the intentional inexistence of the object. Each lived experience directs itself toward something in a way which varies according to the distinctive character of the experience. To represent something after the manner of representing is a different self-directing than to judge something after the manner of judging. Brentano expressly emphasizes that Aristotle already made this point of view the basis for his treatment of psychic phenomena, and that the Scholastics took over this phenomenon of intentionality.

Regarding this basic structure of psychic phenomena, Brentano divides the various ways of self-directedness toward their particular objects into three basic classes of psychic comportment: representation, judgment, and interest. "We speak of a representing wherever something appears," [1a] wherever something is simply given and the simply given is perceived. Representing in the broadest sense is the simple having of something. Brentano interprets judging as "an accepting as true or a rejecting as false." [2] In contrast to merely having something, judging is taking a definite position toward the represented as represented. Brentano designates the third class with different titles: interest, love, emotion. "This class for us shall include all psychic appearances which are not contained in the first two classes." [3] He emphasizes that a proper expression for these acts of taking an interest in something is lacking. It was later also called 'valuing,' or better yet, 'worthtaking.'

Using this basic division of psychic experiences as a guide, Brentano seeks to exhibit the basic structure of representing, judging, and emotions. Regarding the relationship of these phenomena, Brentano laid down the following *basic thesis*: *Every psychic phenomenon is itself either a representation or is based upon representations.* "This representing

1a. Brentano, *Psychologie vom empirischen Standpunkt* (Leipzig: Duncker and Humblot, 1874), p. 261 [1925 ed., p. 34; Eng. tr., p. 198. Note especially here that the exact note numbering from the German edition is being preserved in this translation.]
2. Ibid., p. 262 [1925 ed., p. 34; Eng. tr., p. 198].
3. Ibid. [1925 ed., p. 35; Eng. tr., p. 199].

forms the basis of judging just as it does of desiring and every other psychic act. Nothing can be judged, but also nothing can be desired, nothing can be hoped or feared, if it is not represented."[4] Hence the simple having of something assumes the function of a basic comportment. Judging and taking an interest are possible only if something is represented, which gets judged, in which an interest is taken. Brentano operates not only in mere description but tries to set off this division from the traditional one in a critical examination which we will not pursue any further.

Thus a completely new movement was initiated in psychology and philosophy, a movement which already had an effect upon the American psychology of that time, upon William James, who gained influence in Germany and all of Europe, and from James back upon Henri Bergson, whose theory of the immediate data of consciousness (*Essai sur les données immédiates de la conscience*, 1889) accordingly goes back to the ideas of Brentano's psychology. His idea of a *descriptive psychology* had a profound impact upon Dilthey. In his Academy essay of 1894, "Ideas toward a Descriptive and Analytic Psychology," Dilthey sought to make such a psychology the basic science among the human sciences. The truly decisive aspect of the development of Brentano's way of questioning is to be seen in the fact that Brentano became the teacher of Husserl, the subsequent founder of phenomenological research.

β) Edmund Husserl

Husserl himself was originally a mathematician. He was a student of Weierstrass and wrote a mathematical dissertation for his degree. What he heard of philosophy did not go beyond what any student picked up in the lecture courses. What Paulsen said was reliable and clear, but nothing apt to inspire Husserl to regard philosophy as a scientific discipline. It was only after he graduated that Husserl attended the courses of the man who was then much discussed. Brentano's passion for questioning and reflection impressed Husserl so strongly that he remained with Brentano for two years, from 1884 to 1886. Brentano provided the decisive turn to the scientific direction which Husserl's work was to take. His wavering between mathematics and philosophy was resolved. Through the impression which Brentano as teacher and researcher made upon him, Husserl espied, within the unproductive philosophies of the time, the possibility of a scientific philosophy. Characteristically, Husserl's philosophical efforts did not begin with some contrived and far-fetched problem. Rather,

---

4. Ibid., p. 104 [Eng. tr., p. 80].

in accord with the course of his own scientific development, he began to philosophize upon the foundation which he already had. Accordingly, his philosophical reflection, now guided by Brentano's methodology, turned toward mathematics.

At first, he was concerned with what was traditionally called the logic of mathematics. For Husserl, this meant not only the theory of mathematical thought and knowledge. The first theme of his reflections was the analysis of the structure of the objects of mathematics— number. A work on the concept of number[5] written under Stumpf, Brentano's very first student, in Halle at the end of the eighties qualified Husserl as an academic lecturer. This work, understood as an actual investigation of the matters at issue, became possible upon the basis provided by Brentano's descriptive psychology. But soon Husserl's questioning extended into matters of principle and his investigations advanced to the *fundamental concepts of thinking as such* and of objects in general. It grew into the problem of a *scientific logic* in close conjunction with reflection upon the methodological ways and means for the correct exploration of the objects of logic. This meant a more radical conception of what was already advanced in Brentano's descriptive psychology, as well as a basic critique of the contemporary confusion of psychological-genetic inquiry with logical inquiry. This work on the fundamental objects of logic occupied Husserl for more than twelve years. The initial results of this effort form the content of the work which appeared in two volumes in 1900–1901 under the title *Logical Investigations*. This work marks the initial breakthrough of phenomenological research. It has become *the basic book of phenomenology*. The personal history of its origin is a story of continual despair, and does not belong here.

The first to immediately recognize the central significance of these investigations was Dilthey. He described them as the first great scientific advance in philosophy since Kant's *Critique of Pure Reason*. Dilthey was seventy years old when he became acquainted with Husserl's *Logical Investigations*, an age at which others have long since become secure and complacent in their systems. Dilthey immediately embarked upon semester-long studies of the book within a circle of his closest students. To be sure, an inner kinship with its basic direction made it easier for Dilthey to see the significance of this book. In a letter to Husserl, he compared their work to boring into a mountain from opposite sides until they break through and meet each other. Dilthey here found an initial fulfillment of what he had sought for decades and formulated as a critical program in the Academy essay of 1894: a fundamental science of life itself.

---

5. Edmund Husserl, *Uber den Begriff der Zahl. Psychologische Analysen* (Halle: Heynemann, 1887).

The book also influenced Lipps and his students in Munich but here *Logical Investigations* was regarded simply as an improved descriptive psychology.

The Marburg School took a characteristic position. In an extensive review, Natorp praised only the first volume, which included a critique of the logic of the time and showed that logic cannot be grounded in psychology. He observes that the Marburgers did not have all that much to learn from this work; what it has to say they had already discovered for themselves. The second volume, which contains the decisive elements, was not examined. There is only the blanket assertion that the second volume is a relapse into psychology, whose transference into philosophy had been explicitly rejected by Husserl in the first volume.

This misunderstanding is due to some extent to the self-interpretation which Husserl himself gives in the introduction to this volume: "Phenomenology is descriptive psychology." This self-interpretation of his own work is quite incongruous with what is elaborated in it. In other words, when he wrote the introduction to these investigations, Husserl was not in a position to survey properly what he had actually presented in this volume. Two years later, he himself corrected this mistaken interpretation in the journal *Archiv für systematische Philosophie* (1903).

These "Logical Investigations," as fundamental as they are, do not bring us any in-depth knowledge for the mastery of emotional needs and the like. Rather, they deal with very special and arid problems: with object, concept, truth, proposition, fact, law. The subtitle of the positive second volume is "Investigations into the Phenomenology and Theory of Knowledge." It includes six extensive special investigations whose connection is not immediately clear: I. "Expression and Meaning"; II. "The Ideal Unity of Species and the More Recent Theories of Abstraction"; III. "On the Doctrine of Wholes and Parts"; IV. "The Distinction between Independent and Dependent Meanings and the Idea of Pure Grammar"; V. "On Intentional Experiences and their 'Contents'"; VI. "Elements of a Phenomenological Elucidation of Knowledge." These are unusual themes for a logic and theory of knowledge. The choice of the subtitle, "Theory of Knowledge," came about solely in deference to the tradition. The Introduction states that, strictly speaking, theory of knowledge is not a theory at all but a "reflection which comes to an evident understanding of what thinking and knowing as such are in their generically pure essence."[6] Calling it a theory is still a covert form of naturalism, for which any theory

---

6. Edmund Husserl, *Logische Untersuchungen* (Halle: Niemeyer, 1900/1901) [Introduction] Vol. II/1, §7, p. 19 [English translation by J. N. Findlay, *Logical Investigations* (New York: Humanities, 1970), Vol. I, p. 263].

is a deductive system whose goal is to explain given facts. Husserl expressly rejects this customary sense of a theory of knowledge.

Even more unusual than the subject matter and totally contrary to the customary way of philosophizing is the kind of penetration and appropriation which the work demands. It proceeds in a thorough-going investigative fashion. It calls for a step-by-step, expressly intuitive envisaging of the matters at issue and a verifying demonstration of them. Accordingly, one cannot, without subverting the entire sense of the investigations, simply pull out results and integrate them into a system. Rather, the whole thrust of the work serves to implicate the reader into pressing further and working through the matters under investigation. If the impact of the work were compared to what it demands of us, then it would have to be said that its impact has been minimal and superficial, in spite of the major revolutions initiated by it in the last two decades.

It is of the essence of phenomenological investigations that they cannot be reviewed summarily but must in each case be rehearsed and *repeated* anew. Any further synopsis which merely summarizes the contents of this work would thus be, phenomenologically speaking, a misunderstanding. We shall therefore try an alternate route by providing an initial orientation concerning what is actually accomplished here. This will also serve as an initial preparation and elaboration of the working attitude which we shall assume throughout this lecture course.

Chapter Two

The Fundamental Discoveries of Phenomenology, Its Principle, and the Clarification of Its Name

We shall detail these discoveries and then supplement this account with an elucidation of the principle of phenomenological research. On this basis we shall try to interpret the name given to this research and thus define 'phenomenology.'

Of the decisive discoveries, we intend to discuss three: 1) *intentionality*, 2) *categorial intuition*, and 3) the *original sense of the apriori*. These considerations are indispensable in their content as well as in the way it is considered. Only in this way can *'time'* be brought into view phenomenologically. Only in this way is the possibility given for an orderly procedure in the analysis of time as it shows itself.

§5. *Intentionality*

We want to consider intentionality first, precisely because contemporary philosophy then and even now actually finds this phenomenon offensive, because intentionality is precisely what prevents an immediate and unprejudiced reception of what phenomenology wants to do. Intentionality was already alluded to in our account of how Brentano sought to classify the totality of psychic phenomena in strict accord with it. Brentano discerned in intentionality the structure which constitutes the true nature of a psychic phenomenon. Intentionality thus became for him the criterion for the distinction of psychic from physical phenomena. But at the same time this structure is the criterion and principle of a natural division among psychic phenomena themselves, inasmuch as it is already found in the essence which appears in these phenomena. Brentano expressly emphasizes that he is only tak-

27

ing up what Aristotle and the Scholastics were already acquainted with. It was through Brentano that Husserl learned to see intentionality.

But by what right do we then still speak of the discovery of intentionality by phenomenology? Because there is a difference between the rough and ready acquaintance with a structure and the understanding of its inherent sense and its implications, from which we derive the possibilities and horizons of an investigation directed toward it in a sure way. From a rough acquaintance and an application aimed at classification to a fundamental understanding and thematic elaboration is a very long road calling for novel considerations and radical transpositions. On this point Husserl writes: "Nevertheless, from an initial apprehension of a distinction in consciousness to its correct, phenomenologically pure determination and concrete appreciation there is a mighty step—and it is just this step, crucial for a consistent and fruitful phenomenology, which was not taken."[1]

In the popular philosophical literature, phenomenology tends to be characterized in the following manner: Husserl took over the concept of intentionality from Brentano; as is well known, intentionality goes back to Scholasticism; it is notoriously obscure, metaphysical, and dogmatic. Consequently, the concept of intentionality is scientifically useless and phenomenology, which employs it, is fraught with metaphysical presuppositions and therefore not at all based upon immediate data. Thus, in "The Method of Philosophy and the Immediate," H. Rickert writes:

> Especially where the concept of 'intentionality,' Scholastic in origin but mediated by Brentano, plays a role, there the concept of the immediate still seems to be left largely unclarified and the train of thought of most phenomenologists seems steeped in traditional metaphysical dogmas, which make it impossible for its adherents to see impartially what is before their very eyes.[2]

This article contains a fundamental polemic against phenomenology. Elsewhere also, and right in the Introduction to the new edition of Brentano's *Psychology* by O. Kraus,[3] it is stated that Husserl had simply

---

1. Edmund Husserl, *Ideen zu einer reinen Phänomenologie und phänomenologischen Philosophie*, in the *Jahrbuch für Philosophie und phänomenologische Forschung*, Vol. 1, Part 1 (Halle: Niemeyer, 1913), p. 185. Editor's note: cited as *Ideen I*; cf. Husserliana Vol. III, First Book, ed. Walter Biemel (The Hague: Nijhoff, 1950), pp. 223f. [English translation by Fred Kersten, *Ideas Pertaining to a Pure Phenomenology and to a Phenomenological Philosophy. First Book: General Introduction to a Pure Phenomenology* (The Hague/Boston/London: Nijhoff, 1982), §90, p. 218.]

2. Heinrich Rickert, "Die Methode der Philosophie und das Unmittelbare. Eine Problemstellung," *Logos* XII (1923/24), p. 242 n. [Cf. note 2 in §9 below.]

3. Cf. the *Philosophische Bibliothek* edition (Hamburg: Meiner, 1925). [Cf. note 1 above, chapter one.]

taken over Brentano's concept of intentionality. For the Marburg
School as well, intentionality remained the real stumbling block, ob-
structing its access to phenomenology.

We expressly reject such opinions, not in order to preserve Husserl's
originality against Brentano, but to guard against having the most elementary considerations and steps necessary for the understanding of
phenomenology thwarted in advance by such characterizations.

a) Intentionality as the structure of lived experiences: exposition and initial elucidation

We will try to show that intentionality is a structure of lived experiences as such and not a coordination relative to other realities, something added to the experiences taken as psychic states. It should first
be noted that this attempt to make intentionality clear, to see it and in
so doing to apprehend what it is, cannot hope to succeed in a single
move. We must free ourselves from the prejudice that, because phenomenology calls upon us to apprehend the matters themselves, these
matters must be apprehended all at once, without any preparation.
Rather, the movement toward the matters themselves is a long and
involved process which, before anything else, has to remove the prejudices which obscure them.

Intentio literally means *directing-itself-toward*. Every lived experience,
every psychic comportment, directs itself toward something. Representing is a representing of something, recalling is a recalling of something, judging is judging about something, presuming, expecting,
hoping, loving, hating—of something. But, one will object, this is
a triviality hardly in need of explicit emphasis, certainly no special
achievement meriting the designation of discovery. Notwithstanding, let us pursue this triviality a bit and bring out what it means
phenomenologically.

The following considerations call for no special talent. They do demand that we set aside our prejudices, learn to see directly and simply
and to abide by what we see without asking, out of curiosity, what we
can do with it. In the face of the most obvious of matters, the very fact
of the matter is the most difficult thing we may hope to attain, because
man's element of existence is the artificial and mendacious, where he
is always already cajoled by others. It is erroneous to think that phenomenologists are models of excellence who stand out in their resolve
to wage an all-out war with this element, in their positive will-to-
disclose and nothing else.

Let us envisage an exemplary and readily available case of 'psychic
comportment': a concrete and natural perception, the perception of a
chair which I find upon entering a room and push aside, since it

stands in my way. I stress the latter in order to indicate that we are after the most common kind of everyday perception and not a perception in the emphatic sense, in which we observe only for the sake of observing. Natural perception as I live in it in moving about my world is for the most part not a detached observation and scrutiny of things, but is rather absorbed in dealing with the matters at hand concretely and practically. It is not self-contained; I do not perceive in order to perceive but in order to orient myself, to pave the way in dealing with something. This is a wholly natural way of looking in which I continually live.

A crude interpretation tends to depict the perception of the chair in this way: a specific psychic event occurs within me; to this psychic occurrence 'inside,' 'in consciousness,' there corresponds a physically real thing 'outside.' A coordination thus arises between the reality of consciousness (the subject) and a reality outside of consciousness (the object). The psychic event enters into a relationship with something else, outside of it. But in itself it is not necessary for this relationship to occur, since this perception can be a delusion, a hallucination. It is a psychological fact that psychic processes occur in which something is perceived—presumably—which does not even exist. It is possible for my psychic process to be beset by a hallucination such that I now perceive an automobile being driven through the room over your heads. In this case, no real object corresponds to the psychic process in the subject. Here we have a perceiving without the occurrence of a relationship to something outside of it. Or consider the case of a deceptive perception: I am walking in a dark forest and see a man coming toward me; but upon closer inspection it turns out to be a tree. Here also the object supposedly perceived in this deceptive perception is absent. In view of these indisputable facts which show that the real object can in fact be missing in perception, it can *not* be said that every perception is the perception of something. In other words, intentionality, directing itself toward something, is not a necessary mark of every perception. And even if some physical object should correspond to every psychic event which I call a perception, it would still be a dogmatic assertion; for it is by no means established that I ever get to a reality beyond my consciousness.

Since Descartes, everyone knows and every critical philosophy maintains that I actually only apprehend 'contents of consciousness.' Accordingly, the application of the concept of intentionality to the comportment of perception, for example, already implies a double presupposition. First, there is the metaphysical presupposition that the psychic comes out of itself toward something physical. With Descartes, as everyone knows, this became a forbidden presupposition. Second, there is in intentionality the presupposition that a real object always corresponds to a psychic process. The facts of deceptive perception and hallucination speak against this. This is what Rickert maintains and many others, when they say that the concept of intentionality harbors latent metaphysical dogmas. And yet, with this interpretation of perception as hallucination and deceptive perception, do we really have intentionality in our sights? Are we talking about what phenomenology means by this term? In no way! So little, in fact, that use of the interpretation just given as a basis for a discussion of intentionality would hopelessly block access to what the term really means phenomenologically. Let us therefore clear the air by going through the interpretation once again and regarding it more pointedly. For its ostensible triviality is not at all comprehensible without further effort. But first, the base triviality of spurious but common epistemological questions must be laid to rest.

Let us recall the hallucination. It will be said that the automobile here is in reality not present and on hand. Accordingly, there is no coordination between psychic and physical. Only the psychic is given. Nonetheless, is not the hallucination in its own right a hallucination, a presumed perception of an automobile? Is it not also the case that this presumed perception, which is without real relationship to a real object, precisely as such is a directing-itself-toward something presumably perceived? Is not the deception itself as such a directing-itself-toward, even if the real object is in fact not there?

It is not the case that a perception first becomes intentional by having something physical enter into relation with the psychic, and that it would no longer be intentional if this reality did not exist. It is rather the case that perception, correct or deceptive, is in itself intentional. Intentionality is not a property which would accrue to perception and belongs to it in certain instances. As perception, it is *intrinsically intentional*, regardless of whether the perceived is in reality on hand or not. Indeed, it is really only because perception as such is a directing-itself-toward something, because intentionality constitutes the very structure of comportment itself, that there can be anything like deceptive perception and hallucination.

When all epistemological assumptions are set aside, it becomes clear that comportment itself—as yet quite apart from the question of its correctness or incorrectness—is in its very structure a directing-itself-toward. It is not the case that at first only a psychic process occurs as a nonintentional state (complex of sensations, memory relations, mental image and thought processes through which an image is evoked, where one then asks whether something corresponds to it) and subsequently becomes intentional in certain instances. Rather, the very being of comporting is a directing-itself-toward. Intentionality is not a relationship to the non-experiential added to experiences, occasion-

ally present along with them. Rather, the lived experiences themselves
are as such intentional. This is our first specification, perhaps still
quite empty, but already important enough to provide the footing for
holding metaphysical prejudices at bay.

b) Rickert's misunderstanding of phenomenology and intentionality

In the reception of intentionality as well as in the way in which
Brentano was interpreted and developed, everyone saw not so much
the exposition of this composition of the structure of lived experience
as what they suspected in Brentano: metaphysical dogmas. The decisive thing about Husserl was that he did not look to the dogmas and
presuppositions, so far as these were there, but to the phenomenon
itself, that *perceiving is a directing-itself-toward*. But now this structure
cannot be disregarded in the other forms of comportment as well.
Rickert makes this the basis of his argument and disputes seeing such
a thing in these comportments. He reserves intentionality for the
comportment relating to judgment but drops it for representing. He
says representing is not knowing. He comes to this because he is
trapped in dogmas, in this case the dogma that my representing involves no transcendence, that it does not get out to the object. Descartes in fact said that representing (*perceptio*) remains in the consciousness. And Rickert thinks that the transcendence of judging,
whose object he specifies as a *value*, is less puzzling than the transcendence which is in representing, understood as getting out to a real
thing. He comes to this view because he thinks that in judgment something is acknowledged which has the character of value and so does
not exist in reality. He identifies it with the mental which consciousness itself is, and thinks that value is something immanent. When I
acknowledge a value, I do not go outside of consciousness.

The essential point for us is not to prove that Rickert is involved in
contradictions, that he now uses the phenomenological concept of
representing and now a mythical one from psychology. The point is
rather that he lays claim to intentionality in his own starting point to
the extent that it fits his theory but casts it aside when it contravenes
his theory that representing is not knowing. What is characteristic is
that, in spite of all the sagacity, the most primitive of requirements is
nevertheless missing: admission of the matters of fact as they are
given. The thinking thus becomes groundless. The constraint of
the facts cannot in one case be heeded and in others not; heeded
when they fit into a preconceived theory and not heeded when they
explode it. A typical example of this kind of thinking is Rickert's theory of knowledge and of judgment as it takes its starting point from

Brentano. We shall review it in order to see how judgments depend
upon the apprehension of the matters themselves.

Rickert takes from Brentano the definition of judgment as *acknowledging*. We can trace the exact place where he makes use of intentionality as exhibited by Brentano and at the same time shuts his eyes
to it and falls into theory construction. Let us briefly recall the theory
which he bases upon Brentano's account of judgment.

When we judge, Rickert says, we concur with the representations or
we reject them. Invested in the judgment as its essential element is a
'practical' comportment. "Since what is valid for judgment must also
be valid for knowing, it follows, from the kinship that judgment has
with willing and feeling, that also *in pure theoretical knowing what is involved is taking a position toward a value. . . .* Only in relation to values
does the alternative comportment of approval and disapproval make
any sense."[4] Rickert thus arrives at his theory that *the object of knowledge is a value*. When I perceive a chair and say, "The chair has four
legs," the sense of this knowledge according to Rickert is the *acknowledging of a value*. Even with the best of intentions one cannot find anything like this in the structure of this perceptual assertion. For I am
not directed toward representations and less still toward value but instead toward the chair which is in fact given.

Acknowledging is not imposed upon representations; representing
is itself directing-itself-toward. Representing as such gives the potential about-which of judging, and the affirmation in judging is founded
in representing. There is an intentional connection between representing and judging. If Rickert had seen the intentionality of representing, he would not have fallen into the mythology of the connection between judgment and representation, as though judgment comes
as an 'aside.' *The relations between intentionalities are themselves intentional.*

Hence Rickert arrived at this theory not from a study of the matters
themselves but by an unfounded deduction fraught with dogmatic
judgments. The last vestige of the composition of this matter is solely
what Rickert took from Brentano. But even here it is questionable
whether it is brought to bear upon the full composition of judgment.
"When we characterize judgment as a comportment which is not like
representation, this does not mean that, with Brentano, we see in it
another kind of relation of consciousness to its objects than the kind
involved in representation. This claim is for us far too full of presuppositions."[5] Here Rickert rejects intentionality, in Brentano's sense, as

---

4. Heinrich Rickert, *Der Gegenstand der Erkenntnis. Ein Beitrag zum Problem der phi-
losophischen Transzendenz* (Freiburg i. Br.: Wagner, 1892), p. 57. Editor's note: 2nd Edition, 1904, p. 106.
5. Ibid., p. 56; 2nd ed., p. 104.

a criterion distinguishing the comportments of representation and judgment. What does he put in its place? How does he define and ground the distinction?

We are investigating

> in what genus of psychic processes the complete judgment belongs when we generally distinguish those states in which we comport our-selves impassively and contemplatively from those in which we take an interest in the content of our consciousness, as a content *of value* to us. . . . We thus simply wish to establish a fact which even a pure sen-sualistic theory cannot dispute.[5a]

One would have to be blind not to see that this is word for word the position of Brentano, who wanted nothing other than to subdivide the genus of psychic processes according to the mode of our comport-ment, whether we contemplate them impassively or take an active in-terest in them. Rickert first takes his theory from a basis which is ex-posed by Brentano's description but does not see that he lays claim to intentionality as the foundation of his theory of judgment and knowl-edge. The proof for this is that while he lays claim to this descriptive distinction Rickert at the same time employs a concept of representa-tion which runs counter to that which he uses as a basis for securing the definition of judgment, here impassive directing-itself-toward— accordingly representing as the manner of representing—and there
· representation as the represented, where the represented is in fact the content of consciousness. Wherever Rickert refutes the idealism of representation and wants to prove that knowing is not represent-ing, he does not restrict himself to the direct and simple sense of rep-resenting but bases himself upon a mythical concept. Rickert says that as long as the representations are only represented, they come and go.[6] Representing is now not direct representational comportment; the representations now get represented. "A knowing that represents needs a reality independent of the knowing subject because with rep-resentations we are capable of apprehending something independent of the knowing subject only by their being images or signs of a real-ity."[7] In such a concept of representation it can of course be shown that representing is not a knowing if the directing-itself-toward can tend only toward signs.

But how does it stand with the concept of representation which Rickert uses when he differentiates the judgment from representing understood as a comportment that simply contemplates? Why does

---

5a. Ibid., 2nd ed., p. 105.
6. Ibid., p. 57; 2nd ed., p. 105.
7. Ibid., p. 47; 2nd ed., p. 78.

Rickert not take the concept of representation in a descriptive sense as he does the concept of judgment, which has accrued to description? Why does he not go straight to the sense of its implication, namely, a comportment which contemplates impassively?

It is because Rickert is guided by the presumption, the thesis that *knowing cannot be representing*. For if it were, then his own theory that knowing is acknowledging and the object of knowledge is a value would be superfluous and perhaps wrong. Representing cannot be knowledge. This prejudice is given further weight by an appeal to Aristotle's thesis that knowing is judging. Knowledge is always true or false, and according to Aristotle only judgments are true or false. In this appeal to Aristotle, Rickert supposes that Aristotle means the same by judgment—whereas Aristotle means precisely that which Rickert is not willing to see in the simple composition of representing as such—"*letting something be seen.*" Rickert does not see that the simple sense of representing actually includes knowing.

He is prevented from seeing the primary cognitive character of representation because he presupposes a mythical concept of representing from the philosophy of natural science and so comes to the formulation that in representing the representations get represented. But in the case of a representation on the level of simple perception a representation is not represented; I simply see the chair. This is implied in the very sense of representing. When I look, I am not intent upon seeing a representation of something, but the chair. Take for example mere envisaging or bringing to mind, which is also characterized as a representation of something which is not on hand,* as when I now envisage my writing table. Even in such a case of merely thinking of something, what is represented is not a representation, not a content of consciousness, but the matter itself. The same applies to the recollective representation of, for example, a sailboat trip. I do not remember representations but the boat and the trip itself. The most primitive matters of fact which are in the structures themselves are overlooked simply for the sake of a theory. Knowing cannot be representing, for only then is the theory justified that the object of knowledge is and must be a value, because there must be a philosophy of value.

What makes us blind to intentionality is the presumption that what we have here is a theory of the relation between physical and psychic, whereas what is really exhibited is simply a structure of the psychic itself. Whether that toward which representing directs itself is a real material thing or merely something fancied, whether acknowledging

---

*Reading *was nicht vorhanden ist* here in this sentence rather than two lines earlier, in the preceding sentence.

acknowledges a value or whether judging directs itself toward something else which is not real, the first thing to see is this directing-itself-toward as such. The structure of comportments, we might say, is to be made secure without any epistemological dogma. It is only when we have rightly seen this that we can, by means of it, come to a sharper formulation and perhaps a critique of intentionality as it has been interpreted up to now. We shall learn that in fact even in phenomenology there are still unclarified assumptions associated with intentionality which admittedly make it truly difficult for a philosophy so burdened with dogmas as Neo-Kantianism to see plainly what has been exhibited here. As long as we think in dogmas and directions, we first tend to assume something along the same lines. And we hold to what we assume all the more so as the phenomena are not in fact exhaustively brought out into the open.

When it comes to comportments, we must keep a steady eye solely upon the structure of directing-itself-toward in them. All theories about the psychic, consciousness, person, and the like must be held in abeyance.

c) The basic constitution of intentionality as such

What we have learned about intentionality so far is, to put it formally, empty. But one thing is already clear: before anything else, its structural coherence must be envisaged freely, without the background presence of any realistic or idealistic theories of consciousness. We must learn to see the data as such and to see that relations between comportments, between lived experiences, are themselves not complexions of things but in turn are of an intentional character. We must thus come to see that all the relations of life are intrinsically defined by this structure. In the process we shall see that there are persistent difficulties here which cannot be easily dispelled. But in order to see this, we must first take a look at intentionality itself. From this point on we can also fix our terminology in order to come to understand an expression which is often used in phenomenology and is just as often misunderstood, namely, the concept of *act*. The comportments of life are also called acts: perception, judgment, love, hate. . . . What does act mean here? Not activity, process, or some kind of power. No, act simply means *intentional relation*. Acts refer to those lived experiences which have the character of intentionality. We must adhere to this concept of act and not confuse it with others.

As fundamental as intentionality is, it also seems empty at first glance. We are simply saying that representing is the representing of something, judging is judging about something, and the like. It is hard to see just how a science is to be made possible from such structures. This science is evidently at its end before it has really begun. In fact, it seems as if this phenomenological statement of intentionality is merely a tautology. Thus Wundt early on observed that all phenomenological knowledge can be reduced to the proposition A = A. We will try to see whether there is not very much to say and whether in the end most of it has not yet even been said. By holding to this first discovery of phenomenology that intentionality is a structure of lived experiences and not just a supplementary relation, we already have an initial instruction on how we must proceed in order to see this structure and constitution.

α) The perceived of perceiving: the entity in itself (environmental thing, natural thing, thinghood)

In maintaining that intentionality is the structure found in comportments, we have in any case avoided the danger of lapsing into construction and into a theory which goes beyond what is before us. But at the same time the necessity of this structure, in order to be equally impartial in our pursuit of it, is decided within it. We shall now try to shed some light upon the basic structure of intentionality. The preliminary designation of directing-itself-toward is only an initial moment in this structure, far removed from its full constitution as well as wholly formal and empty.

In order to clarify the basic constitution of intentionality, let us turn once again to the exemplary case of naturally perceiving a thing. By intentionality we do not mean an objective relation which occasionally and subsequently takes place between a physical thing and a psychic process, but the structure of a comportment as comporting to, directing itself toward. With this, we are not just characterizing this one particular perception (of the chair) here and now, but the *perceived as such*. If we are after the basic constitution of intentionality, the best way to do it is to go after it itself—directing-itself-toward. Let us now focus not on the directing-itself but on the *toward-which*. We will not look at the perceiving but at the perceived, and in fact at the *perceived of this perception*. What is this?

If I answer without prejudice, I say the chair itself. I see no 'representations' of the chair, register no image of the chair, sense no sensations of the chair. I simply see *it*—it itself. This is the most immediate sense that perceiving offers. More precisely, I must ask: *What* do I see in my 'natural' perception, in which I now live and dwell and am here in this room; what can I say about the chair? I would say that it stands in Room 24 next to the desk, and it is probably used by lecturers who prefer to sit while they lecture. It is not just any chair but a very particular one, the desk chair in Room 24 at Marburg University, perhaps somewhat worse for wear and poorly painted in the factory from which it evidently came. Something like this could be said of the chair when I describe it quite naturally, without elaborate constructions and advance preparations. What would I then be saying? I would simply be recounting the very particular as well as trivial story of the chair as it is here and now and day after day. What is perceived in this 'natural' perception we shall designate as a thing of the environing world, or simply the *environmental thing*.

I can dwell upon this perception and further describe what I find in it, the chair itself, and can say: it is so heavy, so colored, so high, and so wide; it can be pushed from one place to another; if I lift it and let go, it falls; it can be chopped into pieces with a hatchet; if ignited, it burns. Here again we have plain statements in which I speak of the perceived itself and not of representations or sensations of the chair. But now it is a matter of other determinations of the chair than those we began with. What we have just said of the perceived can be said of any piece of wood whatsoever. What we have elicited in the chair does not define it as a chair. Something is indeed asserted about the chair, not qua chair-thing, but rather as a thing of nature, as *natural thing*. The fact that what is perceived is a chair is now of no account.

The perceived is an environmental thing, but it is also a natural thing. For this distinction, we have in our language very fine distinctions in the way in which language itself forms its meanings and expressions. We say, "I am giving roses." I can also say, "I am giving flowers," but not "I am giving plants." Botany, on the other hand, does not analyze flowers but rather plants. The distinction between plant and flower, both of which can be said of the same rose, is the distinction between natural and environmental thing. The rose as flower is an environmental thing, the rose as plant is a natural thing.

The perceived in itself is both. And still the question arises whether this description eliciting what is given in the perceived thing itself already gives us what phenomenology strictly means by the perceived. When we consider that these two thing-structures—environmental thing and natural thing—apply to one and the same chair, one obvious difficulty already arises: how are we to understand the relationship of these two structures of a thing? We shall arrive at a more precise knowledge of this later in other contexts. At the moment, I only maintain that when I say in ordinary language and not upon reflection and theoretical study of the chair, "The chair is hard," my aim is not to state the degree of resistance and density of this thing as material thing. I simply want to say, "The chair is uncomfortable." Already here we can see that specific structures belonging to a natural thing and which as such can be regarded separately—hardness, weight—present themselves first of all in well-defined environmental characteristics. Hardness, material resistance, is itself present in the feature of discomfort and even only present in this way, and not just inferred from it or derived through it. The perceived gives itself in itself and not by virtue of points of view, say, which are brought to the thing. It is the specific environmental thing, even when it remains concealed from many.

I can go still further into what is found in perceiving, this natural thing here. By applying an appropriate form of research to it, I can show that, as a natural thing, something like materiality and extension belong to it, that anything extended is as such colored, and further, that every color as color has its extension, and that a material and extended thing is displaceable, subject to change of place. Thus once again I have elicited something found in this thing itself, but now it is no longer in the perceived (chair) as environmental thing or as natural thing. Now I am concerned with *thingness* as such. I speak of materiality, extension, coloration, local mobility, and other determinations of this kind which do not belong to the chair as this peculiar chair but to any natural thing whatsoever. These are structures which constitute the thingness of the thing, structural moments of the natural thing itself, contents which can be read out from the given itself.

In all three cases we were concerned with the perceived entity in itself, with what can be found in it through a cognizance of it. Perceiving is here taken in a broad but natural sense. The typical epistemology as well as psychology will say that these descriptions of the natural thing and environmental thing are quite naïve and as such essentially unscientific. For in the first instance and in actuality, with my eyes I merely see something colored, in the first instance I merely have sensations of yellow, to which I then add other such elements.

In opposition to this scientific account, what we want to precisely naïveté, pure naïveté, which in the first instance and in actuality sees the chair. When we say 'we see,' 'seeing' here is not understood in the narrow sense of optical sensing. Here it means nothing other than 'simple cognizance of what is found.' When we hold to this expression, then we also understand and have no difficulty in taking the immediately given just as it shows itself. We thus say that one sees in the chair itself that it came from a factory. We draw no conclusions, make no investigations, but we simply see this in it, even though we have no sensation of a factory or anything like it. The field of what is found in simple cognizance is in principle much broader than what any particular epistemology or psychology could establish on the basis of a theory of perception. In this broad sense of perceiving and seeing, what is perceived even includes, as we shall see later, all of what I have said about thingness, that this thing itself includes materiality, that to materiality belongs extension as well as coloration, which in turn has its own kind of extension. These are not matters that I discover here

HERITAGE COLLEGE LIBRARY
Toppenish, WA 98948

in this classroom; they are correlations between general features. But they are not invented or constructed. I can also see these structures and their specific correlations in an adequately and sufficiently culti-vated form of simple finding—seeing not in the sense of a mystical act or inspiration but in the sense of a simple envisaging of structures which can be read off in what is given.

β) The perceived of perceiving: the how of being-intended (the perceivedness of the entity, the feature of bodily-there)

But we have still not arrived at what we have called the perceived in the strict sense. The perceived in the strict sense for phenomenology is not the perceived *entity* in itself but the *perceived* entity insofar as it is perceived, *as* it shows itself in concrete perception. The perceived in the strict sense is the perceived as such or, more precisely expressed, the *perceivedness*, of this chair for example, the way and manner, the structure in which the chair is perceived. The way and manner of how this chair is perceived is to be distinguished from the structure of how it is represented. The expression *the perceived as such* now refers [not to the perceived entity in itself but] *to this entity in the way and manner of its being-perceived*. With this we have, as a start, only suggested a com-pletely new structure, a structure to which I cannot now attribute all those determinations which I have thus far attributed to the chair.

The being-perceived of the chair is not something which belongs to the chair as chair, for a stone or house or tree or the like can also be perceived. Being-perceived and the structure of perceivedness conse-quently belong to perceiving as such, i.e., to intentionality. Accord-ingly, we can distinguish along the following lines: *the entity itself*: the environmental thing, the natural thing, or the thingness; and *the entity in the manner of its being intended*: its being-perceived, being-represented, being-judged, being-loved, being-hated, being-thought in the broadest sense. In the first three cases we have to do with the entity in itself, in the latter with its being-intended, the perceivedness of the entity.

What is perceivedness? Is there really anything like this? Can any-thing be said about the perceivedness of the chair? Independent of any theories, we must regard these structures in their distinction from the structures that pertain to the thing and to the entity as an entity. This provisional specification and differentiation from thingness al-ready give us an initial indication as to where we should look: mani-festly not at the chair itself as it is intended in perceiving, but rather at it *in the how of its being-intended*. What shows itself there? The per-ceived as such has the feature of *bodily presence* [*Leibhaftigkeit*]. In other words, the entity which presents itself as perceived has the feature of being *bodily-there*. Not only is it given as itself, but as itself in its bodily

presence. There is a distinction in mode of givenness to be made between the *bodily-given* and the *self-given*. Let us clarify this distinction
for ourselves by setting it off from the way in which something merely
represented is there. Representing is here understood in the sense of
simple envisaging, simply bringing something to mind.

I can now envisage the Weidenhauser bridge; I place myself before
it, as it were. Thus the bridge is itself given. I intend the bridge itself
and not an image of it, no fantasy, but it itself. And yet it is not bodily
given to me. It would be bodily given if I go down the hill and place
myself before the bridge itself. This means that what is itself given
need not be bodily given, while conversely anything which is bodily
given is itself given. *Bodily presence is a superlative mode of the self-
givenness of an entity.* This self-givenness becomes clearer still by setting it off from another possible mode of representing, which in
phenomenology is understood as *empty intending*.

Empty intending is the mode of representing something in the
manner of thinking of something, of recalling it, which for example
can take place in a conversation about the bridge. I intend the bridge
itself without thereby seeing it simply in its outward appearance, but I
intend it in an empty intending [which in this conversation is left intuitively unfulfilled]. A large part of our ordinary talk goes on in this
way. We mean the matters themselves and not images or representations of them, yet we do not have them intuitively given. In empty
intending as well, the intended is itself directly and simply intended,
but merely emptily, which means without any intuitive fulfillment.
Intuitive fulfillment is found once again in simple envisaging; this
indeed gives the entity itself but does not give it bodily.

This distinction between empty intending and intuitive representing applies not only to sense perception but to the modifications of all
acts. Take the sentence: 1 + 2 is 2 + 1. One can repeat it thoughtlessly
but still understand it and know that one is not talking nonsense. But
it can also be carried out with insight, so that every step is performed
by envisaging what is intended. In the first instance it is uttered to
some extent blindly, but in the second it is seen. In the latter case, the
intended is envisaged in an originary envisaging, in that I make
present to myself 2 + 1 . . . , i.e., all determinations in their original
meanings. This mode of intuitive thinking demonstrates the determinations in the matters themselves. But it is only on rare occasions
that we operate in this mode of intuitive thinking. For the most part
we operate in foreshortened and blind thinking.

Another type of representing in the broadest sense is the *perception
of a picture*. If we analyze a perception of a picture, we see clearly how
what is perceived in the consciousness of a picture has a totally different structure from what is perceived in simple perception or what is

represented in simple envisaging. I can look at a picture postcard of
the Weidenhauser bridge. Here we have a new type of representing.
What is now bodily given is the postcard itself. This card itself is a
thing, an object, just as much as the bridge or a tree or the like. But it
is not a simple thing like the bridge. As we have said, it is a picture-
thing. In perceiving it, I see through it what is pictured, the bridge. In
perceiving a picture, I do not thematically apprehend the picture-
thing. Rather, when I see a picture postcard, I see—in the natural attitude—what is pictured on it, the bridge, [which is now seen as] what is
pictured on the card. In this case, the bridge is not emptily presumed
or merely envisaged or originarily perceived, but apprehended in this
characteristic layered structure of the portrayal of something. The
bridge itself is now the represented in the sense of being represented
by way of being depicted through something. This apprehension of a
picture, the apprehension of something as something pictured through a
picture-thing, has a structure totally different from that of a direct
perception. This must be brought home quite forcefully because of
the efforts once made, and once again being made today, to take the
apprehension of a picture as the paradigm by means of which, it is
believed, any perception of any object can be illuminated. In the consciousness of a picture, there is the picture-thing and the pictured.
The picture-thing can be a concrete thing—the blackboard on the
wall—but the picture-thing is not merely a thing like a natural thing
or another environmental thing. For it shows something, what is pictured itself. In simple perception, by contrast, in the simple apprehension of an object, nothing like a consciousness of a picture can be
found. It goes against all the plain and simple findings about the
simple apprehension of an object to interpret them as if I first perceive a picture in my consciousness when I see that house there, as if a
picture-thing were first given and thereupon apprehended as picturing that house out there. There would thus be a subjective picture
within and that which is pictured outside, transcendent. Nothing of
the sort is to be found. Rather, in the simple sense of perception I see
the house itself. Even aside from the fact that this transposition of the
consciousness of a picture, which is constituted in a totally different
way, onto the simple apprehension of an object explains nothing and
leads to untenable theories, we must keep in mind the real reason for
rejecting this transposition: it does not correspond to the simple phenomenological findings. There is also the following difficulty, which
we shall only mention without exploring. If knowledge in general is
an apprehension of an object-picture as an immanent picture of a
transcendent thing outside, how then is the transcendent object itself
to be apprehended? If every apprehension of an object is a consciousness of a picture, then for the immanent picture I once again

need a picture-thing which depicts the immanent picture for me etc. etc. This is a secondary factor which argues against this theory. But the main thing is this: not only is there nothing of the pictorial and picturing in the course of simple apprehension; there is in particular nothing like a consciousness of a picture in the very act of apprehending an object. It is not because we fall into an infinite regress, and so explain nothing, that the infrastructure of the consciousness of a picture for the apprehension of an object is to be rejected. It is not because we arrive at no genuine and tenable theory with this infrastructure. It is rather because this is already contrary to every phenomenological finding. It is a theory without phenomenology. Hence perceiving must be considered totally distinct from the consciousness of a picture. Consciousness of a picture is possible at all first only as perceiving, but only in such a way that the picture-thing is actually apprehended beginning with what is pictured on it.

When we start from simple perception, let us reaffirm that the authentic moment in the perceivedness of the perceived is that *in perception the perceived entity is bodily there*. In addition to this feature, another moment of every concrete perception of a thing in regard to its perceivedness is that the perceived thing is always presumed in its *thing-totality*. When I see a sensibly perceptible object, this familiar chair here, I always see—understood as a particular way of seeing—only one particular side and one aspect. I see, for example, the upper part of the seat but not the lower surface. And yet, when I see the chair in this way or see only the legs, I do not think that the chair has its legs sawed off. When I go into a room and see a cupboard, I do not see the door of the cupboard or a mere surface. Rather, the very sense of perception implies that I see the cupboard. When I walk around it, I always have new aspects. But in each moment I am intent, in the sense of natural intending, upon seeing the cupboard itself and not just an aspect of it. These aspects can change continually with the multiplicity of aspects being offered to me. But the bodily selfsameness of the perceived persists throughout my circling of the thing. The thing *adumbrates*, shades off in its aspects. But it is not an *adumbration* which is intended, but the perceived thing itself, in each case in an adumbration. In the multiplicity of changing perceptions the selfsameness of the perceived persists. I have no other perception in the sense of something else perceived. The content of perception is different, but the perceived is presumed as the same.

In view of the apprehension of the whole and its adumbrations, there is one further structure of the perceived in the narrow sense to be considered in the perception of a picture. What is bodily perceived is the picture-thing itself, but this too is perceived in each instance in an aspect. To some extent, however, the perception of a picture-thing does not come to completion in the normal and natural perception of a picture. Contrariwise, for example, the postman can take the picture-thing (the *picture* postcard) simply as an environmental thing, as a *post*card. Not only does such a perception not come to completion, but it is also not the case that I first merely see a thing and then conclude "it is a picture of. . . ." Instead, I see in a flash something pictured and not really the picture-thing, the strokes and patches of the drawing, in the first instance and in thematic isolation. To see these as pure moments of the thing already calls for a modification of our natural regard, a kind of *depicturization*. The natural tendency of perception in this sense proceeds in the direction of apprehending the picture.

γ) Initial indication of the basic mode of intentionality
as the belonging-together of *intentio* and *intentum*

Within this manifold of modes of representation we have at the same time a specific interrelation. Empty intending, envisaging, apprehending a picture and simple perceiving are not merely juxtaposed, but inherently have a specific structural interrelation. Empty intending, for example, can be intuitively fulfilled in intuitive envisaging. In thoughtless thought, in empty intending, the intended is intuitively unfulfilled, it lacks the fullness of intuition. Envisaging has the possibility of intuitive fulfillment up to a certain level, since envisaging is never capable of giving the matter itself in its bodily givenness.

Instead of talking about it in this way, I can talk about what is envisaged from the simple and persistent envisaging of something, or I can even, if for example a dispute arises over the number of arches and pillars in the bridge, fill the envisaged in a new way through bodily givenness itself. Perception, with its kind of givenness, is a superlative case of intentional fulfillment. Every intention has within it a tendency toward fulfillment and its specifically proper way of possible fulfillment: perception in general only through perception; remembrance never through expectation but through an envisaging that remembers or through perception. There are very specific laws which govern the connections among the possibilities of fulfilling an already given empty intention. This is also true in the realm of perceiving pictures. It is possible to arrange these connections in more complicated ways. I can place, next to the original picture, a copy of it. If I have a copy, that is, a copied picture of something, I have a specific structural continuity running from copy to picture (original) to model [what is pictured], so that what is actually pictured shows through the depicting function of the copy (picture to model). But if the copy is to furnish evidence of its genuineness as a copy, then I cannot compare it to the model. Instead, the intuitive demonstration of the copy is given by the copied picture (original) which, as the picture of the model, is in itself a model. These characteristic structures of demonstration and their possibility run through all acts of apprehending, even if we now totally disregard this specific act of perceptual apprehension. Thus the perceived shows itself in its perceivedness (this is the most important), what we are conscious of as a picture shows itself in its pictoriality, the simply envisaged shows itself in the way of envisaging, the emptily intended shows itself in the way of empty intending. All of these distinctions are different ways in which their objects are intended.

These structural continuities and levels of fulfillment, demonstration, and verification are relatively easy to see in the field of intuitive representation. But they are to be found without exception in all acts, for example, in the domain of pure theoretical comportment, determination, and speech. Without the possibility here of following the structures of every pertinent intention to its intended as such, the scientific elaboration of a genuine phenomenology (drawn from the phenomena themselves) of concept formation—the genesis of the concept from raw meaning—cannot even be considered. But without this foundation every logic remains a matter for dilettantes or a construction.

We thus have an inherent affinity between the way something is intended, the *intentio*, and the *intentum*, whereby *intentum*, the intended, is to be understood in the sense just developed, not the perceived as an entity, but the entity in the how of its being-perceived, the *intentum* in the how of its being-intended. Only with the how of the being-intended belonging to every *intentio* as such does the basic constitution of intentionality come into view at all, even though only provisionally.

Intentio in phenomenology is also understood as the act of presuming [*Vermeinen*]. There is a connection between presuming and presumed, or *noesis* and *noema*. Νοεῖν means to perceive [*vernehmen*] or come to awareness, to apprehend simply, the perceiving itself and the perceived in the way it is perceived. I refer to these terms because they involve not only a terminology but also a particular interpretation of directing-itself-toward. Every directing-itself-toward (fear, hope, love) has the feature of directing-itself-toward which Husserl calls *noesis*. Inasmuch as νοεῖν is taken from the sphere of theoretical knowing, any exposition of the practical sphere here is drawn from the theoretical. For our purposes this terminology is not dangerous, since we are using it to make it clear that intentionality is fully determined only when it is seen as this belonging together of *intentio* and *intentum*. By way of summary let us therefore say: just as intentionality is not a subsequent coordination of at first unintentional lived experi-

ences and objects but is rather a structure, so inherent in the basic
constitution of the structure in each of its manifestations must always
be found its own intentional toward-which, the *intentum*. This provisional exposition of the *basic constitution of intentionality as a reciprocal
belonging-together of intentio and intentum* is not the last word, but only
an initial indication and exhibition of a thematic field for consideration.

How is this analysis of intentionality different from Brentano's? In
intentionality Brentano saw the *intentio*, *noesis*, and the diversity of its
modes, but not the *noema*, the *intentum*. He remained uncertain in his
analysis of what he called "intentional object." The four meanings of
the object of perception—the perceived—already indicate that the
sense of 'something' in the representation of something is not transparently obvious. Brentano wavers in two directions. On the one
hand, he takes the "intentional object" to be the entity itself in its
being. Then again it is taken as the how of its being-apprehended un-
separated from the entity. Brentano never clearly brings out and
highlights the how of being-intended. In short, he never brings into
relief intentionality as such, as a structural totality. But this further
implies that intentionality, defined as a character of a certain entity, is
at one with the entity; intentionality is identified with the psychic.
Brentano also left undiscussed just what intentionality is to be the
structure of, since his theory of the psychic assumed its traditional
sense of the immanently perceptible, the immanently conscious along
the lines of Descartes's theory. The character of the psychic itself was
left undetermined, so that that of which intentionality is the structure
was not brought out in the original manner demanded by intentionality. This is a phase which phenomenology has not yet overcome.
Even today intentionality is taken simply as a structure of consciousness or of acts, of the person, in which these two realities of which
intentionality is supposed to be the structure are again assumed in a
traditional way. Phenomenology—Husserl along with Scheler—tries
to get beyond the psychic restriction and psychic character of intentionality in two very different directions. Husserl conceives intentionality as the universal structure of reason (where reason is not
understood as the psychic but as differentiated from the psychic).
Scheler conceives intentionality as the structure of the spirit or the
person, again differentiated from the psychic. But we shall see that
what is meant by reason, spirit, *anima* does not overcome the approach operative in these theories. I point this out because we shall
see how phenomenology, with this analysis of intentionality, calls for
a more radical internal development. To refute phenomenological
intentionality, one cannot simply criticize Brentano! One thus loses
touch with the issue from the very beginning.

It is not intentionality as such that is metaphysically dogmatic but what is built under its structure, or is left at this level because of a traditional tendency not to question that of which it is presumably the structure, and what this sense of structure itself means. Yet the methodological rule for the initial apprehension of intentionality is really not to be concerned with interpretations but only to keep strictly to that which shows itself, regardless of how meager it may be. Only in this way will it be possible to see, in intentionality itself and through it directly into the heart of the matter, that of which it is the structure and how it is that structure. Intentionality is not an ultimate explanation of the psychic but an initial approach toward overcoming the uncritical application of traditionally defined realities such as the psychic, consciousness, continuity of lived experience, reason. But if such a task is implicit in this basic concept of phenomenology, then "intentionality" is the very last word to be used as a phenomenological slogan. Quite the contrary, it identifies that whose disclosure would allow phenomenology to find itself in its possibilities. It must therefore be flatly stated that what the belonging of the *intentum* to the *intentio* implies is obscure. How the being-intended of an entity is related to that entity remains puzzling. It is even questionable whether one may question in this way at all. But we cannot inquire into these puzzles as long as we cover up their puzzling character with theories for and against intentionality. Our understanding of intentionality is therefore not advanced by our speculations about it. We shall advance only by following intentionality in its concretion. An occasion for this is to be found in our effort to clarify the second discovery of phenomenology, the discovery of *categorial intuition*.

§6. Categorial intuition

What calls for clarification under this heading could be discovered only after the exposition of *intentionality* as a structure. The term 'intuition' corresponds in its meaning to what above was already defined as 'seeing' in the broad sense of that word. *Intuition* means: simple apprehension of what is itself bodily found just as it shows itself. First, this concept carries no prejudice as to whether sense perception is the sole and most original form of intuiting or whether there are further possibilities of intuition regarding other fields and constituents. Second, nothing should be read into its meaning other than what the phenomenological use of the term specifies: *simply apprehending the bodily given as it shows itself*. Intuition in the phenomenological sense implies no special capacity, no exceptional way of transposing oneself into otherwise closed domains and depths of the world, not even the kind of intuition employed by Bergson. It is therefore a cheap characterization of phenomenology to suggest that it is somehow connected with modern intuitionism. It simply has nothing to do with it.

The discovery of categorial intuition is the demonstration, first, that there is a simple apprehension of the *categorial*,* such constituents in entities which in traditional fashion are designated as *categories** and were seen in crude form quite early [in Greek philosophy, especially by Plato and Aristotle]. Second, it is above all the demonstration that this apprehension is invested in the most everyday of perceptions and in every experience. This only clarifies the meaning of the term. What matters is to exhibit this kind of intuition itself, to bring it to givenness as intentionality, and to make clear *what* is intuited in it and *how*.

It was already suggested that categorial intuition is found in every concrete perception (perception of a thing), as it were, as an inclusion. In order to show this we shall return to our exemplary case of the perception of this chair. But in order to see the categorial intuition in it, we must be adequately prepared. This calls for two more general considerations. We shall deal with 1) intentional presuming and its intentional fulfillment and 2) intentional comportments as expressed—*intuition and expression*.

We shall see that our comportments, lived experiences taken in the broadest sense, are through and through *expressed* experiences; even if they are not uttered in words, they are nonetheless expressed in a definite articulation by an understanding that I have of them as I simply live in them without regarding them thematically.

a) Intentional presuming and intentional fulfillment

α) Identification as demonstrative fulfillment

Our account of the interrelation of the modes of representation manifested a distinct sequence of levels ranging from mere empty intending (signitive acts) to originarily giving perception (intuitive act in the narrowest sense). Empty intending is unfulfilled in its sense; what is presumed in it is there in the how of non-fulfillment. Empty intend-

---

*I have underscored these two terms because student notes indicate that Heidegger highlighted their distinction in his summary review of this lecture hour. The basic point is that categories are already 'seen' in perception, for example, though not *as* categories but such that the simple perception of an object is in its way absorbed and engrossed in categorial apprehension. Categorial intuition here is intuition of that which is then conceptually grasped as a category. There is therefore a distinction between the *categorial*, that which can eventually be grasped as a category, and the *category* as a concept. The distinction is important in understanding in what way the discovery of categorial intuition provides the basis for research into the categories and apriori structures of experience (cf. pp. 71ff. below).

ing or what is presumed in it can in a certain sense be fulfilled in intuitive envisaging. The presumed (envisaged) is thus given in greater or
lesser completeness (bridge: columns—railings—type of arches—ar-
rangements of the building stones). But however great the perfection
of the fullness may be, it always manifests a difference from the fullness of perception, which gives the entity bodily. But even here, if we
restrict ourselves to the sense perception of material things, the fullness is not total. Sense perception indeed gives the entity originarily,
but always only from one side. However adequate a perception may
be, the perceived entity always shows itself only in a particular adumbration. There are thus distinctions with regard to the definitiveness
and completeness of the fullness which a fulfilling intuition is capable
of giving. We accordingly speak of a *definitive and thoroughgoing fulfillment* when on the side of presuming *all the partial intentions are fulfilled*
and, on the side of the intuition which bestows fulfillment, that intuition presents the *whole matter in its totality*.

The interrelation of these modes of representations is a functional
interrelation which is always prefigured in their intentionality. Empty
intending, envisaging, sense perception are not simply coordinated as
species in a genus, as when I say that apples, pears, peaches, and plums
are fruits. Rather, these modes stand to one another in functional relation, and the fulfillment itself is of an intentional character. Fulfillment
means having the entity present in its intuitive content so that what is
at first only emptily presumed in it demonstrates itself as grounded in
the matters. Perception, or *what* it gives, *points out, de-monstrates*. The
empty intention is demonstrated in the state of affairs given in intuition; the originary perception gives the demonstration.

The peculiar thing is that there is a correlation in such demonstration or fulfillment. Let us look at this more concretely. I can in an
empty way now think of my desk at home simply in order to talk
about it. I can fulfill this empty intention in a way by envisaging it to
myself, and finally by going home and seeing it itself in an authentic
and final experience. In such a demonstrative fulfillment the emptily
intended and the originarily intuited come into coincidence. This
bringing-into-coincidence—the intended being experienced in the intuited as itself and selfsame—is an *act of identification*. The intended
identifies itself in the intuited; selfsameness is *experienced* [*erfahren*].
Here it is well to note that in this act of identification the identity is not
apprehended thematically as selfsameness. Identification is for its
part not already an apprehension of identity but solely of the identical. Inasmuch as intuition is bodily originary, it gives the entity itself,
the matter itself. The emptily presumed is compared to the matter itself, so that in fulfillment I obtain insight into the matter itself. More
precisely, I obtain insight into the groundedness in the matter of what

was before only presumed. This fulfillment as an act of identification includes obtaining insight into the grounding of what is presumed in the matter. This act of obtaining insight, as identifying fulfillment, is called *evidence*.

β) Evidence as identifying fulfillment

Identifying fulfillment is what we call evidence. Evidence is a specific intentional act, that of identifying the presumed and the intuited; the presumed is itself illuminated in the matter. This elaboration of evidence was for the first time brought to a successful resolution by Husserl, who thus made an essential advance beyond all the obscurities prevalent in the tradition of logic and epistemology. But it has not had much of an effect. Even today we still adhere to the traditional mythological account of evidence in regarding it as a peculiar indicator of certain lived experiences, especially experiences of judgment. It is something like a sign which wells up at times in the soul and announces that the psychic process with which it is associated is true. To some extent, it is as if a psychic datum announces that there is something real outside which corresponds to the judging. As everyone knows, this transcendent reality cannot itself become immanent. So there must be a way in which it can be announced on the 'inside.' This is the so-called "*feeling of evidence*" of Rickert.

But if we see that the acts of identifying apprehension are defined by intentionality, then we do not resort to the mythological account of evidence as psychic feeling or psychic datum, as though a pressure were first exerted and then it dawns on one that the truth is indeed there.

It is further customary to regard evidence as an addition to a specific class of lived experiences, that of judgments. This restriction along with the concept of evidence as a possible addition to [psychic] processes do not correspond to the findings. It is readily seen that evidence in general is comprehensible only if we regard the intentionality in it [now understood as identifying apprehension]. But this at the same time yields a fundamental insight of great significance. Since the act of evidence connotes an identifying vision that selects a state of affairs from the originarily intuited matter, evidence is in its sense always of a sort and rigor which varies according to the ontological character [*Seinscharakter*] of the field of subject matter, the intentional structure of the kind of apprehensive access, and the possibility of fulfillment grounded therein. We therefore speak of the *regionality of evidence*. All evidence is in its sense geared to a corresponding region of subject matter. It is absurd to want to transpose one possibility of evidence, for example, the mathematical, into other kinds of apprehension. The same holds for the idea of rigor of theoretical dem-

onstration, which in its sense is built upon the concept of evidence peculiar to each type: philosophical, theological, physical. With all this
regionality, on the other hand, the *universality of evidence* must again
be stressed. *Evidence is a universal function, first, of all acts which give their
objects, and then, of all acts* (evidence of willing and wishing, of loving
and hoping). It is not restricted to assertions, predications, judgments. In this universality it at the same time varies according to the
region of subject matter and the kind of access to it.

We have thus arrived at 1) the idea of pure and absolute evidence,
'*apodicticity*' as insight into essential states of affairs; 2) the idea of insight into 'individual' states of affairs, 'subject matters,' *assertoric* evidence; 3) the idea of the connection of these two, the insight into the
necessity of an individual state of affairs "being so" [*Sosein*] based
upon the essential grounds of the 'posited individual.'

γ) Truth as demonstrative identification

From what has now been brought out about the supreme and total
fulfillment come two phenomenological concepts, those of *truth* and
being. Definitive and thoroughgoing fulfillment means commensuration (*adaequatio*) of what is presumed (*intellectus*) with the intuited subject matter itself (*res*). We thus obtain a phenomenological interpretation of the old scholastic definition of truth: *veritas est adaequatio rei et
intellectus*. In the context of presuming, this means that there is no
partial intention in what is objectively given which would not be fulfilled intuitively, i.e., from the originarily intuited matter. Phenomenologically understood, *adaequatio* refers to this commensuration in the
sense of bringing-into-coincidence. Now what does the term "truth"
mean in the full structural context of knowledge?

The demonstration of the presumed in the intuited is identification, an act which is phenomenologically specified in terms of intentionality, directing-itself-toward. This means that every act has its
intentional correlate, perception the perceived, and identification the
identified, here the being-identical of presumed and intuited as the
intentional correlate of the act of identification. Truth can be designated in a threefold way. The *first* concept of truth is this *being-
identical of presumed and intuited*. Being-true is then equivalent to this
being-identical, *the subsistence* of this identity*. We obtain this first con-

---

*Bestand, 'subsistence' in the double sense of being and persistence, i.e., continued
existence; it may also etymologically suggest a background presence that 'stands under'
what is overtly present. *Bestand* is a 'stock' word in the vocabulary of Heidegger both
early and late; in general, it serves as his focus on the classical problem of permanence
and change, and the traditional conception of being as constant presence. But the immediate context relevant here is Husserl's anti-psychologistic distinction between the
persistent sameness of ideal being (sense) and the temporal variability of the real acts

cept of truth by referring to the correlate of the act of identification: subsistence of the identity of presumed and intuited. Here it should be noted that in the living act of concrete perceiving and in the demonstration of what is presumed, this perceiving lives in the apprehension of the matter as such, in the performance of the act. In the coming into coincidence of the presumed with the intuited, I am solely and primarily directed toward the subject matter itself, and yet—this is the peculiarity of this structural correlation—evidence is experienced in this apprehension of the intuited matter itself. The correlation is peculiar in that *something is experienced but not apprehended*. So it is really only in apprehending the object as such, which amounts to not apprehending the identity, that this identity is experienced. This act of bringing into coincidence is in touch with the subject matter; it is precisely through this particular intentionality of being-in-touch-with-the-subject-matter [*Bei-der-Sache-sein*] that this intentionality, itself unthematic in its performance, is immediately and transparently experienced as true. This is the phenomenological sense of saying that in evident perception I do not thematically study the truth of this perception itself, but rather live *in* the truth.* Being-true is experienced as a distinctive *relation*, a *comportmental* relation [*Verhalt*] between presumed and intuited specifically in the sense of identity. We

---

which intend such sense, as is evident from the following semester's course on *Logik: Die Frage nach der Wahrheit*, Gesamtausgabe Volume 21, Marburger Vorlesung Wintersemester 1925-26, edited by Walter Biemel (Frankfurt: Klostermann, 1976) pp. 50-56, 111-113. Here as well as in *Being and Time* (H. 216) Heidegger raises the question of the ontological status of a relation which subsists purportedly between the real and the ideal. Likewise, the reader should bear in mind that in most contexts *Bestand* has been translated as 'composition' or, in the plural, 'constituents.' In some of these contexts, such as the initial description of 'the categorial' as 'constituents in entities' (48 above), *Bestand* seems also to carry the connotation of 'subsistence,' i.e., the type of being proper to the 'ideal being' of categories.

*This formulation serves to link this commentary by Heidegger on the four senses of truth in the *Logical Investigations* (VI, §39)—the fourth is taken into account tacitly in the following subsection—with his own sense of truth in *Being and Time*. To "live *in* the truth" here means to live in the state of identity and continuity between the signified and the intuited, a state which we continually experience but do not grasp. This is indicative of what it means "to be in the truth" (*Being and Time*, H. 221) without knowing it thematically, whereby we understand the structures of our world as 'self-evident,' as a matter 'of course' in a straightforward living of them without considering them thematically. (Cf. my "Heidegger (1907-27); The Transformation of the Categorial," in Hugh J. Silverman, John Sallis, and Thomas M. Seebohm, eds., *Continental Philosophy in America* [Pittsburgh: Duquesne University Press, 1983], pp. 165-188, esp. p. 178.) The formula recurs in the very next semester's course on *Logik: Die Frage nach der Wahrheit* (op. cit., p. 143) but now with regard to the prepredicative structures of handy things in whose *disclosure* "we already live." The habitual realm of 'static unions' of which Husserl speaks on the basis of acts of naming and predication is thus shifted to the prepredicative acts (comportments) of "having to do with" things which *fulfill* their expectations in their functions and so establish a practical network of stable *signifying* relations involving 'for,' 'in order to,' and 'for the sake of.'

call this distinctive relation the *truth-relation*; being-*true* consists precisely in this relation. Truth in this sense is seen with respect to the correlate of the act of identification, that is, by way of intentionality with reference to the *intentum*.

Correlatively, we can obtain a *second* concept of truth commensurate to the *intentio*, not to the content of the act but to the act itself. What is now thematic is not the being-identical of what is intended in presuming and intuiting but *the act-structure of evidence itself as this coincident identification*. Formulated differently, under consideration now is the idea of the structural relationship of the acts of presuming and intuiting, the structure of the intentionality of evidence itself, *adaequatio* understood as *adaequare*. Truth is now taken as a character of knowledge, as an act, which means as intentionality.

The concept of truth as *adaequatio* can be taken in a double sense, as it always has been in history: on the one hand as the correlate of identification, of the bringing into coincidence, and on the other as a specification of this very act of bringing into coincidence. The controversy over the concept of truth goes back and forth between the thesis, *Truth is a relationship of the state of affairs to the subject matter*, and the thesis, *Truth is a specific correlation of acts*, for I can really only assert truth about knowing. Both conceptions try to direct the concept of truth to one side and so are incomplete. Neither the one oriented toward the state of affairs nor the one oriented toward the act captures the original sense of truth.

We obtain a *third* concept of truth by turning once again to the intuited entity itself. The true can also be understood in terms of the very object which is. As the originarily intuited it provides the demonstration, it gives the identification its ground and legitimacy. Here, the true amounts to that which *makes* knowledge *true* [i.e., the true-making matter, the entity itself as an intuited matter]. Truth here comes down to *being, being-real*. This is a concept of truth which also emerged very early in Greek philosophy and was constantly being confused with the first two concepts.

δ) Truth and being

The first concept of truth understood as the subsistence of the identity of the intended and intuited—truth as being-true—at the same time also provides us with a specific *sense of being, being in the sense of being-true*. Let us make this clear in connection with an assertion about a thing made in the simple perception of our chair: "The chair is yellow." What is asserted as such, the asserted content of this assertion, is the being-yellow of the chair, a content which is also called the judged state of affairs. It is subject to a twofold distinction. I can stress the being in the *being*-yellow and so mean that the chair is *really* and *truly* yellow. You may have noted how we can use 'really' and 'truly' interchangeably. Underscoring being means that the truth-relation just discussed subsists, an identity between presumed and intuited subsists. Being here means something like the *subsistence* of truth, of the *truth-relation*, subsistence of identity.

I can now emphasize this formulation of the state of affairs "*being-yellow*" in its opposite pole—this is of course only a schematic consideration—I now underscore being-*yellow*. If I reduce the judgment to the formula S = P, this emphasis refers formally to the being-P of S. This time I do not want to say that the judged state of affairs truly is, but to express the being-P of S, the pertinence of the predicate to the subject. In other words, in the emphasis of being-*yellow* 'being' refers to the *being of the copula*—The chair *is* yellow. This second concept of being does not refer to the subsistence of the truth-relation, as the first does, but to a structural moment of the state of affairs itself. The *state of affairs as a relation of the subject matter* [*Sachverhalt als Verhalt*] has the formal structure S = P. In the expression "The chair is yellow" both meanings of being are meant—*being as relational factor of the state of affairs as such and being as truth-relation*, or more accurately, *the subsistence and the stasis* [*Bestand und Stehen*] *of the state of affairs in the truth-relation*. Since these two meanings have never been worked out phenomenologically, constant confusion reigns in the theory of judgment, in that such theories have been constructed without having separated these two senses of being. Only by way of such a separation can one see how these two senses condition each other in their structure and what possibilities of expression exist in the proposition as proposition. These are questions which belong to a phenomenological logic, including the distinction of these two concepts of being: being in the sense of truth interpreted as the subsistence of identity, and being in the sense of the copula interpreted as a structural moment of the state of affairs itself. The phenomenal connection in the structure is this: a true state of affairs which has this 'is' in its structure, this 'being' within itself, is itself the correlate [of the act of identification, its *intentum*], the single correlate in the state of affairs. Put another way, the state of affairs as merely presumed *is* true as demonstrated in that very state of affairs. The truth-relation thus subsists, the truth-relation *is* true.

These two concepts of truth and the corresponding two concepts of being were established in the initial elaboration of phenomenology and have persisted in further developments. This is important to keep in mind since we shall later raise the *fundamental question of the sense of being* and thus come to face the question of whether the concept of being can really be originally drawn in this context of being-true and the corresponding being-real, and whether truth is primarily a phenomenon which is to be originally conceived in the context of assertions or, in the broader sense, of objectifying acts.

The term "truth" is originally and properly attributed to intentionality, but this is done on the basis of its being composed of both the *intentio* and the *intentum*. Traditionally, it is attributed in particular to acts of assertion, that is, relational acts of predication. But we need only to recall our explication of evidence to see that even non-relational acts, that is, single-rayed monothetic acts of simple apprehension, likewise can be subject to demonstration, that is, can be true or false. Phenomenology thus breaks with the restriction of the concept of truth to relational acts, to judgments. The truth of relational acts is only one particular kind of truth for the objectifying acts of knowing in general. Without being explicitly conscious of it, phenomenology returns to the broad concept of truth whereby the Greeks (Aristotle) could call true even perception as such and the simple perception of something. Since it does not become conscious of this return, it cannot even get in touch with the original sense of the Greek concept of truth. But because of this connection it succeeds for the first time in bringing an understandable sense to the Scholastic definition of truth, which by way of a detour goes back to the Greeks, and in rescuing it from the confusing misreading which instituted the fateful introduction of the concept of image into the interpretation of knowledge.

While truth is traditionally linked to the relational acts of judgment, the term 'being' is readily attributed to the correlate of non-relational, single-rayed acts, as a specification of the object, of the subject matter itself. But just as truth must undergo a 'widening,' so too must 'being,' a widening not only from the subject matter but from the state of affairs—being and being-such-and-such. This may suffice for the characterization of the phenomenological interpretation of *being and truth*. What we have attained with it is first of all a preparation for the understanding of categorial intuition, but it is also of fundamental significance for our broader topical discussions.

b) Intuition and expression

It has already been noted that the fundamental sense of intuition is not necessarily limited to the originary apprehension of the sensory. In addition, the concept does not imply even the slightest assumption as to whether the intuition is realized in a flash and yields isolated pointlike objects. At the same time we have, with the closer examination of the intentional connection of intention and fulfillment and the elaboration of evidence as an identifying act, tacitly introduced phenomena without clarifying them. The determination of truth as a truth-relation, say, of a state of affairs, was accomplished by going back to propositions and assertions in which it was suggested that we consummate these assertions in perceiving the chair as a thing.

Assertions are acts of meaning, and assertions in the sense of a formulated proposition are only specific forms of expressness, where expressness has the sense of expressing lived experiences or comportments through meaning. It is essentially owing to phenomenological investigations that this authentic sense of the expressing and expressedness of all comportments was made fundamental and placed in the foreground of the question of the structure of the logical. This is not surprising when we consider that our comportments are in actual fact pervaded through and through by assertions, that they are always performed in some form of expressness. It is also a matter of fact that our simplest perceptions and constitutive states are already *expressed*, even more, are *interpreted* in a certain way. What is primary and original here? It is not so much that we see the objects and things but rather that we first talk about them. To put it more precisely: we do not say what we see, but rather the reverse, we see what *one says* about the matter. This inherently determinate character of the world and its potential apprehension and comprehension through expressness, through already having been spoken and talked over, is basically what must now be brought out in the question of the structure of categorial intuition.

α) Expression of perceptions

The question now is how we can call an assertion true when we make it within a concrete perception. Can the assertion which I make in a concrete and actual perception be fulfilled in the same way that an empty intention corresponding to the concrete perception is fulfilled?

Let us formulate this sort of case in ordinary language: I give expression to my perception with the assertion "This chair is yellow and upholstered." What are we to understand here by expression? There are two possibilities. First, to give expression to a perception can mean to give notice or *to announce*, announcement of the act of perceiving, announcing that I am now performing it. I communicate that I am now having this perception. This possibility of announcing acts exists not only for perceiving but for any act. There are announcements which confirm the performance of perceiving, representing, judging, wishing, expecting, and the like. When I say to you "I hope you'll take care of that," this implies that I expect you to take care of it. Among other things here it is a matter of communicating to the other that I expect something from him. Or when I say "I wish that . . . ," I give expression to the wish, I announce that I am animated by this wish. Giving expression in this first sense is therefore announcing the presence of an act, my being animated by it. To give expression to a perception then means something like the following: I now communicate that I hear the sound of a car below.

But giving expression to a perception may not signify giving notice of the act but the *communication* of what is perceived in the act. In this second kind of expressing I make no assertion about the act and its presence and I do not confirm the occurrence within me of a perception of a chair. Now the assertion expounds on what is itself apprehended, on the basis of what is perceived in these acts; it expounds on the entity itself. This sense of expression now carries over into all acts which simply give the object. Thus, in emptily intending, merely thinking of something, I can make assertions about it. I then do not make an assertion about a mere representation, about something subjective, but about what is itself presumed, but of course in a way such that I do not intuitively demonstrate in it the individual steps of that about which I say something. Giving expression in the sense of communicating what is perceived in perception becomes a question for us when we speak of perceptual assertions. A perceptual assertion is a communication about the entity perceived in perception and not about the act of perception as such.

Let us stay with our exemplary case of the perception of a particular thing and the assertion made in it. Such an assertion makes certain relations stand out from the matter, which is at first apprehended directly and simply in its unarticulated totality. It draws these relations out of the originarily given intuitive content. It is here that the assertion has its demonstration as coincidence; it is true. There is a tendency toward truth, of being true to itself, in the very sense of the assertion. Only in this way is it really what it is. What was said about truth, adequation, fulfillment in the simple acts of apprehension obviously applies all the more to the acts of assertion. We shall therefore try to see how the perceptual assertion is fulfilled in what is perceived.

Let us therefore return to our exemplary case: we have what the simple perception gives, the complete content of the real subject-matter found before us (chair) as well as the assertion about it: "This chair is yellow and upholstered." This S is P and Q. Our question is whether this assertion finds its complete fulfillment in what is perceived. Is every intention within the full intending and asserting perceptually demonstrable in the subject matter? In short, is the perceptual assertion which gives expression to perception demonstrable perceptually? Put another way, can the idea of truth, gained in connection with evidence, be realized in assertions themselves, which constitute such a broad field among the concrete acts of our comportment? To direct our question more precisely into the particulars of this assertion: Are the 'this,' the 'is,' the 'and' perceptually demonstrable in the subject matter? I can see the chair, its being-*upholstered* and its being-*yellow* but I shall never in all eternity see the 'this,' 'is,' 'and' as I see the chair. There is in the full perceptual assertion a *sur-*

plus of intentions whose demonstration cannot be borne by the simple perception of the subject matter.

But perhaps such a demonstration is still possible in the less complicated expression of a simple naming, a so-called nominal positing of the kind "the yellow upholstered chair." But upon closer inspection we find a surplus even here. I can see the color yellow but not the *being*-yellow, *being*-colored; and the expressive element 'yellow,' that is, the attribute, in its full expression in fact means "the chair being yellow." And this 'being' in this expression and in the one above in the form 'is' cannot be perceived.

'Being' is not a real moment in the chair like the wood, the weight, hardness, or color; nor is it something on the chair like the upholstery and screws. *'Being,'* Kant already said, whereby he meant *being-real, is not a real predicate of the object.* This also holds for being in the sense of the copula. There is obviously no adequation between what is expressed and what is perceived. In content, what is perceived falls short of what the assertion asserts of it. The assertion expresses something which is simply not found perceptually. Accordingly, it seems that we must give up the idea of an adequate fulfillment of assertions and the idea of truth associated with it.

But before we draw conclusions, which is always suspect in philosophy, we first wish to examine the matter a bit more closely. We wish to ask what exactly is here at first left unfulfilled: the 'this,' the 'is,' the 'and.'

We said that color can be seen, but *being*-colored cannot. Color is something sensory and real. Being, however, is nothing of the sort, for it is not sensory or real. While the real is regarded as the objective, as a structure and moment of the object, the non-sensory is equated with the mental in the subject, the immanent. The real is given from the side of the object, the rest is thought into it by the subject. But the subject is given in inner perception. Will I find 'being,' 'unity,' 'plurality,' 'and,' 'or' in inner perception? The origin of these non-sensory moments lies in *immanent perception*, in the *reflection* upon consciousness. This is the argument of *British empiricism* since Locke. This argumentation has its roots in Descartes, and it is in principle still present in Kant and *German idealism*, though with essential modification. Today we are in a position to move against idealism precisely on this front only because phenomenology has demonstrated that the non-sensory and ideal cannot without further ado be identified with the immanent, conscious, subjective. This is not only negatively stated but positively shown; and this constitutes the true sense of the discovery of categorial intuition, which we now want to bring out more precisely.

Because the 'is,' 'being,' 'unity,' 'thisness' and the like refer to the non-sensory, and the non-sensory is not real, not objective, hence is something subjective, we must look to the subject, to consciousness. But when we consider the consciousness, then, as long as its intentionality is not taken into account—and this was the typical way of considering it before—, what we find are acts of consciousness understood as psychic processes. If I study the consciousness, I always find only judging, wishing, representing, perceiving, remembering, in short, immanent psychic events or, to put it in Kant's terms, that which becomes present to me through the *inner sense*. Phenomenological consistency dictates that even those concepts which are demonstrated through the inner sense are basically sensory concepts accessible through the inner sense. When I examine the immanence of consciousness, I always find only the sensory and objective, which I must take as an "immanently real" [*reelles*] component of the psychic process, but I never find anything like 'being,' 'this,' 'and.' Husserl therefore says:

> It is not in the reflection upon judgments nor even upon fulfillments of judgments but rather in these fulfillments themselves that we find the true source of the concepts 'state of affairs' and 'being' (in the copulative sense). It is not in these *acts as objects* but in the *objects of these acts* that we find the abstractive basis for the realization of the concepts in question.[1]

The category "being,' 'and,' 'or,' 'this,' 'one,' 'several,' 'then' are nothing like consciousness, but are correlates of certain acts.

If I want to form the concept of *aggregate*, I find this phenomenon of aggregate not by reflecting upon the psychic process of bringing together a + b + c + d . . . but by referring to what is presumed in this act of assembling, not in the direction of the act but of what the act gives. Likewise, I find the categorial of identity not in the reflection upon consciousness and the subject as a process of ideating comportment, but in reference to what is intended in this comportment as such.

From this fundamental and crucial rectification of an old prejudice, which interprets and identifies 'non-sensory' or 'unreal' with immanent and subjective, we at the same time see that the overcoming of this prejudice is at once linked to the discovery of intentionality. We do not know what we are doing when we opt for the correct conception of the categorial and at the same time think we can dismiss intentionality as a mythical concept. The two are one and the same.

'Allness,' 'and,' 'but' . . . are nothing like consciousness, nothing psychic, but a special kind of objectivity. Here it is a matter of acts which aim to give something in itself, something which does not have the

---

1. Husserl, *Logische Untersuchungen*, Vol. II/2, p. 141. [Eng. tr., Investigation VI, §44, pp. 783–784.]

character of a real sensory thinglike object or a part or moment of such an object. These moments are *not demonstrable through sense perception*. But they are demonstrable by way of an essentially *similar type of fulfillment*, namely, an *originary self-giving* in corresponding dator acts. Since 'allness,' 'number,' 'subject,' 'predicate,' 'state of affairs,' 'something' are objects, we will correspondingly have to understand as intuitions the acts which originarily demonstrate them, if only we adhere to our initial sense of intuition. The moments in the full assertion which did not find fulfillment in sense perception receive it through *non-sensory perception*—through *categorial intuition*. The categorial are the moments of the full assertion whose mode of fulfillment has not yet been clarified.

β) Simple and multi-level acts

We must now 1) sharpen the distinction between the two kinds of intuition and 2) define more precisely categorial acts as such.

We showed that the simple perception, that is, the sense perception of a thing, does not bring about the fulfillment of all the intentions of the assertion. While perception in its intentionality has already been roughly characterized, the feature of the 'simple' has been left undefined. But supplying the missing definition of this feature must at the same time permit its difference from the other kind of acts, so-called categorial acts, to emerge.

What constitutes the feature of *simplicity* in perception? Clarification of this element of simplicity will also lead to the clarification of the sense of the founding and being founded of categorial acts. With the clarification of the founded act, we are concurrently placed in the position of understanding the objectivity both of simple perception and of founded acts as a unified objectivity. It permits us to see how even simple perception, which is usually called sense perception, is already intrinsically pervaded by categorial intuition. The intentionality of perceptual apprehension is in fact simple and straightforward, but this in itself does not rule out a high degree of complexity in its act-structure.

We have already established a number of things about simple perception. For one thing, it implies that its object is bodily given and persists in this state as the same object. In the course of various adumbrations which show themselves in a sequence of perceptions, I see the object as identically the same. I can go through such a sequence of perceptions of one and the same thing, for example, by going around the object. How can the continuity of this sequence be specified? The sequence is no mere demonstration of temporally contiguous acts which are subsequently drawn together and so made into a perception. Rather, it can be phenomenologically established that every single phase of perception in the whole of the continuous sequence is in itself a full perception of the thing. In every moment the whole thing is bodily itself and is this itself as the same. This means that the continuum of the perceptual sequence is not instituted supplementally by a supervening synthesis, but that what is perceived in this sequence is there at *one* level of act. In short, the perceptual continuity is a single perception, merely extended, one might say. It "presents its object in a straightforward and immediate way."[2] We call this feature, whereby the perceptual phases are carried out at *one* level of act and every phase of the perceptual sequence is a full perception, the *simplicity* or *single-level character* of perception. *Simplicity means the absence of multi-level acts, which institute their unity only subsequently.* This feature of the "simple" therefore refers to a way of apprehending and that means a *feature of intentionality*. As a way of apprehending, such a feature does not rule out the highest degree of complexity in the structure of this perception (as we have already said). Simplicity of perception also does not mean simplicity of the act-structure as such. Conversely, the multi-level character of categorial acts does not exclude the simplicity of these acts.

This characteristic manner of apprehension in sense perception and its single-level character also permit a definition of the *real* object. This definition, which certainly has its limits, is first derived strictly within this analysis of perception and its object. For Husserl, this sense of the 'real' signifies the most original sense of reality: a real object is by definition a possible object of a simple perception.[3] This also determines the concept of the real part or, in the broadest sense, of the real portion, the real moment, the real form. "Every part {e.g., form} of a real object is a real part."[4] We must adhere to this definition when we come to the question of how the structural moments of the categorial structures themselves are related to the real object. I expressly emphasize that this concept of 'real,' reality correlative to simple sense perception, is a very particular concept of 'real,' precisely the one that determines the analysis of the reality of the world as Husserl carries it out.

In simple apprehension the totality of the object is explicitly given through the bodily sameness of the thing. The parts, moments, portions of what is at first simply perceived, by contrast, are there implicitly, unsilhouetted—but still given so that they can be made ex-

---

2. Ibid., p. 148. [Eng. tr., §47, p. 789. More accurately, perception *makes* the object *present* (*gegenwärtigt*), a Husserlian word which becomes all-important for Heidegger in this lecture course on time.]

3. Ibid., p. 151 [Eng. tr., p. 791].

4. Ibid. [The insertion within the quote is Heidegger's.]

plicit. This simple perception, or what it gives—the entity itself in the present—can of course on its part now become the basis for acts which are built upon it in its specific intentionality as correlate of its objectivity, and so claim it as the foundation for the construction of new objectivities.

In the foregoing, these new kinds of objects were merely indicated, presumed in the act of presuming the full assertion. This initial indication included a preliminary suggestion of a mode of intuition giving such objects. Now it is a matter of seeing the connection of this new objectivity with that of the real objects, the objectivity of the basic level, in other words, of seeing the structural and constructional relationships of the intentions themselves. From what has been said about the basic constitution of intentionality, the two objectivities cannot be separated. When we now speak of connections between acts, like those at the ground level and those built upon it (simple and founded acts), we are not thereby directing our attention to psychic events and their coupling in the manner of temporal succession. Rather, connections between acts are constructional relationships and modifications of intentionality, that is, structures of the particular directedness toward the objects appropriate to each type. As acts, they always have their possible entity which they themselves intend, and they have it in a specific *how* of givenness. What gives itself as objective in the multilevel acts can never become accessible in the simple acts at the ground level. This means that categorial acts make the objectivity upon which they build—the simply given—accessible in a new kind of object. This new way of making the simply given object accessible is also called the *act of expression*.

Quite generally, the following can be said of the relationships of the founded acts to the simple founding acts: The founded acts, the categorial acts, are indeed directed toward the objectivities co-posited in them from the simple acts, the founding acts, but in a manner which does not coincide with the intentionality of the simply giving act, as if the founded categorial act were only a formalized repetition of the simply giving act. This implies that the founded acts *disclose* the simply given objects *anew*, such that these objects come to explicit apprehension precisely in what they are.

Two groups of such categorial, founded acts shall be considered in order to bring out the essential elements of categorial intuition: 1) *acts of synthesis*, 2) acts of universal intuition, or better, acts of intuition of the universal, or in more rigorous terminology, *acts of ideation*. This consideration of acts of ideation at the same time gives us the transition to the third discovery of phenomenology we shall discuss, the *characterization of the apriori*. We shall consider categorial acts from three points of view: 1) in regard to their founded character; 2) in regard to their character as giving acts; in short, they are intuitions, they *give* objectivity; 3) in regard to the way and manner in which the objectivity of simple acts are given with them.

c) Acts of synthesis

In the simple perception of an entity, the perceived entity itself is first there simply [in "onefold," as it were] without complication. This simplicity means that the real parts and moments included in it do not stand out in relief. But inasmuch as they are present in the unity of the whole object which is apprehended simply, they can also be brought out explicitly. This bringing into relief takes place in new and special acts of explication. Consider, for example, the simple accentuation of the q, of the 'yellow' in the perceived chair, in the S, that is, in the whole of the subject matter perceived as a unity. Simply drawing out the color as a specific property in the chair first makes the q, the 'yellow,' present as a moment, [that is, in a form] which was not present before in the simple perception of the thing. Accentuating q as something which is in S however also involves accentuating S as a whole containing the q within itself. Accentuating q as part of the whole and accentuating the whole which contains q as a part are one and the same act of accentuating S as a whole. Moreover, this accentuation of q as something situated in S basically accentuates this relation of q and S. In other words, the being-yellow of the chair, the previously unarticulated subject matter, now becomes visible through the articulation, through the arrangement which we call the state of affairs. However, even though this accentuation of the state of affairs is grounded in the perceived subject matter, it cannot be said that the state of affairs itself, the composition brought out in the subject matter, is a real part or portion of this matter. The being-yellow of the chair, this state of affairs as such, is not a real moment in the chair like the arms or the upholstery. This state of affairs is rather of an ideal nature. The chair does not contain its being-yellow as a real property. What is real is the yellow, and in the state of affairs only the quality is accentuated as something real, objective. Drawing out the state of affairs thus transforms nothing in the given matter; nothing happens to the chair and its simply given reality. Yet through this new objectivity of the accentuated state of affairs, the chair becomes expressly visible precisely in what it is. Its presence, its being present, becomes more authentic through this assertion, through the accentuation of q as situated in S, the accentuation therefore of the relation of the state of affairs. In this accentuation, we have a form of more authentic objectification of the given matter. We should bear in mind here that the sequence of accentuating steps which proceeds from q to S and then to the relation does not ultimately and authentically depict how such an accentuation of a state of affairs is carried out. We shall see later that what is primary is not first drawing q out, then S as the whole, and finally taking them together, as if the relationship of the state of affairs were assembled from elements already given. Instead, the reverse is the case: what is primary is the relating itself, through which the members of the relation as such first become explicit.

Another observation: the direction in the accentuation of the state of affairs as just described is not the only one possible. We just went from q to S, or from part to whole. But we can also go in the opposite direction, from the simple apprehension of the whole to the part. In other words, we can say not only that q is situated in S but also that S contains q. We are thus discussing a relation which can be taken in two ways. This double direction belongs to the very sense of the structure of a state of affairs.

The acts of accentuating and giving the relationship are not next to and after one another but are unified in the unity of intending the very relation of the state of affairs. They constitute an original unity of acts which, as an overarching unity, brings the new objectivity, more precisely, the entity in this new objectivity, to givenness—primarily presumed and as such present. The new objectivity, the state of affairs, is characterized as a specific relation whose members give what is articulated in them in the form of subject and predicate.

The act of relating, in which the subject matter becomes present in the how of the state of affairs now so founded, can be understood according to the double analysis of regarding whole or part, both as *synthesis* and as *dihairesis* [taking together and laying apart]. This Aristotle already saw. The sense of these acts must now be properly understood. Synthesis is not so much a matter of connecting two parts which are at first separated, as we glue two things together and fuse them. Instead, σύνθεσις and διαίρεσις are to be understood intentionally; in other words, their sense is one which gives an object. Synthesis is not a connecting of objects, but σύνθεσις and διαίρεσις give objects. The crucial feature in this synthesis is that q shows itself as belonging to S, the simple wholeness of S shows itself explicitly. It thus becomes clear that the accentuation and presentation of the state of affairs as a whole is possible only on the basis of the already given subject matter, and in fact takes place so that this matter and this alone shows itself explicitly in the state of affairs. The founded act of relating gives something which is inconceivable through simple perception as such.

A further observation: the accentuated state of affairs is itself not a real part of the subject matter but a categorial form. The non-real, categorial character of the specific relation 'state of affairs' is brought

home most vividly by envisaging an explicating assertion in which a
real relation is thematically asserted. This will also give us an opportunity to describe a new kind of categorial objectification.

Suppose we are asked simply to look at two platelets of different
hues.[5] We find that we can plainly see that a is 'brighter than' b. This
particular *real relation* is given with the intuitive presentation of the
two. We must take the sense of the real here in its most natural and
familiar meaning and not talk of, say, physical or physiological objectivity. This given matter of fact can now be made expressly present in
the assertion "a is brighter than b." This means that a is specified by its
being-brighter than b. In a formal abridgment: a has o in itself, where
o does not merely signify "brighter" but "brighter than b." In other
words, within the presently accentuated state of affairs as a relational
whole, there is a relation which is itself included in one of the relational members, the predicate-member. The one *relatum* of the state
of affairs, which is a categorial relation, is itself a relation, in fact a real
one. Brighter-than is already there at the ground level of perception
as a content of the real subject matter [the two platelets]. *Being-*
brighter-than, however, is accessible only in a new act, namely, in the
first founded act of predicative relating. The real relation brighter-
than is presented in the new objectivity of the predicate-member, and
that means in the whole of a non-real relation. This presentation of
the real relation in the whole of the ideal relation of the state of affairs
now however does not imply that the real relation itself is thematically
apprehended here. This is indeed the case in a somewhat differently
constructed assertion of the form: This relationship of brightness between a and b is easier to notice than that between c and d. Now, on
the one hand, the brighter-than is apprehended thematically specifically by way of a naming, a nominalization; at the same time, as named,
thus simply considered (and no longer merely simply perceived), it
stands in the objectivity of the subject-member of an assertion. Any
state of affairs posited explicitly in the full assertion "a is brighter than
b" can be nominalized. Nominalization is the form in which we thematically grasp a state of affairs itself, here, the being-brighter of a
with respect to b. But this nominalization is to be distinguished from
the simple accentuation of brighter-than. The possibility thus exists
that a real relation, that of brighter-than, can be accentuated in the
matters themselves into an ideal relation, that of a state of affairs "a is
brighter than b," in which the real relation forms a relation of the
ideal one. The two do not coincide. For the real relation of brighter-

---

5. Editor's note: Cf. the example given by Husserl in the *Logische Untersuchungen,*
Vol. II/2, §50, p. 159. [Eng. tr., pp. 797-798.]

than is merely the content of one *relatum* in the whole of the state of affairs. Here it is clear that the state of affairs itself must be understood as a relation of a very special kind.

When we say that the relation of state of affairs is ideal and not real, this certainly does not mean—and this is the decisive point—that it is not objective or even the least bit less objective than what is given as real. Rather, by way of understanding what is present in categorial intuition, we can come to see that the objectivity of an entity is really not exhausted by this narrow definition of reality, that objectivity in its broadest sense is much richer than the reality of a thing, and what is more, that the reality of a thing is comprehensible in its structure only on the basis of the full objectivity of the simply experienced entity.

Some other kinds of synthetic acts within the group of categorial intuition are the *acts of conjoining and disjoining*, whose objective correlates are the conjunction and disjunction, the 'and' and the 'or.' A simply given multiplicity of objects can become expressly objective in the act of conjoining by my assertion of "a + b + c . . . ." In this act of comprising, the plus always appears objectively too. In such acts the 'and' appears and with it the objective basis for the formation of the concept of *aggregate*. The 'and' institutes a new objectivity which is founded in the initial one but which makes this first objectivity more explicit. The 'and' always includes, with structural necessity, the cointention of that of which it is this particular relation 'and.' Accentuation is most clearly seen in the distinction of the simple perception of a matter in its figural moments as against the express presentation of the multiplicity as an enumerated plurality. I can in a single act of perception simply see a flock of birds or a row of trees. Such given wholes are self-contained. The unity of a row, a swarm, a flock of wild ducks is not based upon a prior act of counting. It is an intuitive unity which gives the whole simply. It is figural. Husserl saw the figural quite early in his mathematical investigations. It has now also entered psychology under the name of *Gestalt*. This discovery forms the basis for a new psychology, *Gestalt psychology*. It has already become a world view.

d) Acts of ideation

We have been discussing the founded acts of synthesis, which necessarily cointend their founding objectivity. These differ from the *act of ideation*, which is also based upon a founding objectivity but does *not* actually intend this founding objectivity. These acts of ideation, *of the intuition of the universal*, are categorial acts which give their object. They give what is called an idea, ἰδέα, *species*. The Latin term *species* is the translation of εἶδος, *the outward appearance of something*. The acts of universal intuition give what is seen in the matters first and simply.

When I perceive simply, moving about in my environmental world, when I see houses, for example, I do not first see houses primarily and expressly in their individuation, in their distinctiveness. Rather, I first see universally: this is a house. This "as-what," the universal feature of house, is itself not expressly apprehended in what it is, but is already coapprehended in simple intuition as that which to some extent here illuminates what is given. Ideation is that act of dator intuition which actually gives the species, that is, the universal of individuations. In ideating abstraction, the species house is brought into relief within the multiplicity of individual houses. From a multitude of individuations of red I see *the* red. This "seeing from" of the idea is a founded act, since it is based upon an already given apprehension of individuation. But the objective here, which ideation allows us to see anew, the idea itself, the identical unity red: this objective is not the individuation, this particular red. The individual is indeed founding, but in such a way that it is precisely not cointended, as it is in the 'and' of conjunction, which cointends both this and that, raises this 'a and b' up into the new objectivity. Here, however, the founding objectivity is *not* taken up into the content of what is intended in ideation. The founding act of individual representation intends the this-here or a multiplicity of them in a particular regard: these red balls insofar as they are alike. This being-alike can be seen at a glance or can be established in a comparative survey of the balls. But in all these cases the likeness as such is not thematically objective. In other words, it is not that in-itself with regard to which the balls are compared. The to-which of the regard is the ideal unity of likeness as such and not the likenesses of the balls as real objects. Each concrete apprehending thus also already includes the ideal unity of the species, although not explicitly as that toward which the regard of comparative consideration looks. That toward which I look in comparing, the regard of the comparable, can in its own right be isolated in its pure state of affairs. I thus acquire the idea. The state of affairs of red as such is thereby totally indifferent to any particular individuation. As far as the content of the idea is concerned, it makes absolutely no difference in which concrete objects, in which nuances the red is realized in the particular individuation. But the fact that a fundament is there at all belongs in turn to the act of ideation, which like all categorial acts is a founded act.

We have thus made four points about the sense of the object of categorial intuition in the form of ideation: 1. The new objectivity, the species, in general requires a fundament in some kind of individuation, the exemplary foundation which gives something but is not itself intended. 2. The extent of the concrete individuations is arbitrary. 3. Even the relation of the material content of the idea to the possible extent of its individuations is secondary. 4. The ideal unity of the species, of the universal, as it is also called, is a unity of immutable or invariant identity. The unity of the species is one and the same in every concrete red.

We have accordingly set forth two groups of categorial acts. In the latter group, we have seen that there are categorial acts which in their sense naturally need founding objects, and yet do not themselves intend them.

The distinction between simple acts of intuiting and founded acts of intuiting should now be clear, at least in a provisional form. The former are called sense intuition and the latter categorial intuition. The full composition of the intentions of the assertion "This S is p and q" certainly does not get fulfilled in the domain of sense intuition, but even the categorial acts of 'is' and 'and' as such cannot in isolation provide the possible fulfillment of this assertion. The full composition of the intentions of this assertion instead takes place intuitively only in a founded act, in a sense perception pervaded by categorial acts. This means that concrete intuition expressly giving its object is never an isolated, single-layered sense perception, but is always a multi-layered intuition, that is, a categorially specified intuition. It is just this full, multi-layered, categorially specified intuition which is the possible fulfillment of the assertion giving expression to it. If we look for the composition wholly in acts which give their objects and do not reduce categorial acts to subjective additions and functions of a mythical understanding, just because their correlate as ideal being is not found in the real, in the sensory, then the field of assertions also contains the idea and the possibility of adequate fulfillment. To put it more accurately, the discussion of the idea of truth as a unity of coincidence of the presumed and intuited was for us but the occasion for clarifying the compositive existence [*Bestand*] of categorial acts as such in the act of asserting itself.

α) Averting misunderstandings

Before we summarize the significance of this discovery of categorial intuition and secure its positive scope for ourselves, we should first correct certain misunderstandings which easily creep into the phenomenological concept of categorial intuition. This happens all the more readily because this discovery is itself obtained in a traditional horizon of inquiry and interpreted with traditional concepts. This is also an indication that the discovery has perhaps not yet really been exploited in its true possibilities. In order to proceed in this direction, however, the discovery first had to be made. In other words, we must first gain control of it. It is very easy and pleasant to make great projections after the barricades of prejudice have been breached, after the horizon has been laid open, but then one forgets that the crucial work in the field of philosophical research is always this first step, namely, the work of laying open and disclosing as such. Such research, which, one might say, works invisibly below the surface and is itself buried when the prejudices collapse, yields meager results. And practical results in logical and ontological work are unusual enough, even in Aristotle. But this is precisely our guide and direction: in order to arrive at the ground and horizon, the way must be followed in that direction; the radical and perhaps not yet explicit line of questioning must be undertaken.

Categorial intuition itself and its manner of elaboration have exercised a positive influence especially on the works of Scheler, particularly in his investigations on the *material ethics of value*. Lask's investigations into the logic of philosophy and the theory of judgment are also determined by these investigations into categorial intuition.

Categorial acts are founded acts; in other words, everything categorial ultimately rests upon sense intuition. This thesis must be correctly understood. It does not say that the categories ultimately can be interpreted as sensory. Rather, "resting" here means that they are founded. We can formulate the import of the sentence in this way: Everything categorial ultimately rests upon sense intuition, no objective explication floats freely but is always an explication of something already given. The thesis that everything categorial ultimately rests upon sense intuition is but a restatement of the Aristotelian proposition: οὐδέποτε νοεῖ ἄνευ φαντάσματος ἡ ψυχή[6]; "The soul can presume nothing, apprehend nothing objective in its objectivity, if nothing at all has been shown to it beforehand." A thought without a founding sensuousness is absurd. The idea of a 'pure intellect' could only be conceived "*before* an elementary analysis of knowledge in the irrevocable evidence of its composition."[7] While the idea of a pure intellect is also absurd, the concept of a pure categorial act still has a valid sense.

Acts of ideation indeed rest upon individual intuition but do not directly intend what is intuited in it as such. Ideation constitutes a new objectivity: *generality*. Now, intuitions which exclude not only everything individual but also everything sensory from their objective content are *pure categorial intuitions*, in contrast to those which still include sensory components, *categorially mixed intuitions*. In contrast to these two groups—pure and mixed categorial intuitions—there is *sense in-*

6. Editor's note: *De anima*, 431a16f. (Oxford 1956). ["... the soul never thinks without an image." English translation by J. A. Smith in Richard McKeon (ed.), *The Basic Works of Aristotle* (New York: Random House, 1941), p. 594.]

7. *Logische Untersuchungen*, Vol. II/2, p. 183. [Eng. tr., Investigation VI, §60, p. 818.]

tuition, sense abstraction, the abstractive seeing of a pure sensory idea. Ideation in the field of the sensory yields objects such as color in general,
house in general; in the field of inner sense, it yields judgment in general, wish in general and the like. Mixed categorial ideations yield
ideas like coloration in the sense of *being*-colored, where 'being' constitutes the specifically non-sensory categorial moment. The axiom
of parallels, every geometric proposition, is certainly categorial but is
still defined by sensuousness, by spatiality in general. Examples of
pure categorial concepts are unity, plurality, relation. Pure logic, as
pure *mathesis universalis* (Leibniz), does not contain a single sensory
concept. Pure categorial, mixed, and sensory abstraction make it clear
that the concept of sensuousness is a very broad one. One must therefore be very careful about proceeding in the usual way, to impute a
sensualism to phenomenology and to think thereby that it is solely a
matter of sense data.

Sensuousness is a formal phenomenological concept and refers to all material content as it is already given by the subject matters themselves.
This is to be contrasted with the proper concept of the categorial, that
is, of the formal and objectively empty. *Sensuousness is therefore the title
for the total constellation of entities which are given beforehand in their material content.* Materiality in general, spatiality in general are *sensory concepts*, even though there is nothing of the data of sensation in the idea
of spatiality. This broad concept of sensuousness is really at the bottom of the distinction of sense and categorial intuition. Of course, this
had not yet clearly surfaced in the initial elaboration of these connections in the *Logical Investigations*, as it did ten years later.

One sees in the antithesis of the two kinds of intuition a recurrence
of the old contrast of sense and understanding. If one adds to this the
conceptual pair of *form* and *matter*, the issue may be laid out in the following fashion: Sensuousness is characterized as receptivity and understanding as spontaneity (Kant), the sensory as matter and the
categorial as form. Accordingly, the spontaneity of understanding becomes the formative principle of a receptive matter, and in one stroke
we have the old mythology of an intellect which glues and rigs together the world's matter with its own forms. Whether it is metaphysical or epistemological as in Rickert, the mythology is the same.
Categorial intuition is subject to this misunderstanding only as long as
the basic structure of intuiting and of all comportments—intentionality—is not seen or is suppressed. The categorial 'forms' are not constructs of acts but objects which manifest themselves in these acts.
They are not something made by the subject and even less something
added to the real objects, such that the real entity is itself modified by
this forming. Rather, they actually present the entity more truly in its
'being-in-itself.'

Categorial acts constitute a new objectivity. This is always to be understood intentionally and does not mean that they let the things spring up just anywhere. '*Constituting*' does not mean producing in the sense of making and fabricating; it means *letting the entity be seen in its objectivity*. This objectivity, which presents itself in the categorial acts or in perceptions pervaded by categorial acts, is not a result of the activity of intellectual understanding upon the external world. It is not a result of an activity upon an already given mix of sensations or throng of affections, which are ordered to form a picture of the world. Employment of these old terms—matter and form, especially in their traditional exhaustion and impoverished meaning—obviously fosters this misinterpretation. But our remark on the distinction of sensory and categorial concepts already indicates that 'matter' and 'material' do not acquire their sense in relation to the potential transformability of a material by functions and forms of the mind. Instead, materiality refers to the content of a subject matter as against a formally empty something and its structures, which bring out that content. But the prevalence of concepts like matter and form, which one might say belong to the ancestral household effects of philosophy, and the prevalence of the problems embedded in them are too powerful to be overcome neatly in a single stroke here as well, where with their assistance something completely new is emerging.

β) The significance of this discovery

The decisive character of the discovery of categorial intuition [can be summarized in a threefold way]:

[1.] There are acts in which ideal constituents show themselves in themselves, which are not constructs of these acts, functions of thinking or of the subject.

[2.] The possibility of this kind of intuition and of what presents itself in it provides the basis for bringing out the structures of these ideal objects, for working out the categories. In other words, the discovery of categorial intuition for the first time concretely paves the way for a genuine form of research capable of demonstrating the categories.

In a narrower context, this discovery has pointed the way to a real understanding of abstraction (ideation), of the apprehension of the idea. A provisional answer is thus provided to an old dispute, *the problem of the universals, of the being of universal concepts*. The middle ages from the time of Boethius posed the question of whether a universal is a *res* or a mere *flatus vocis*,* what in the 19th century was called a

---

*Literally "breath of the voice," that is, a mere name or sound, which characterizes the position of nominalism in the medieval controversy over the existence of universals.

mere viewpoint, a universal consciousness to which nothing objective corresponds. But the justified denial of the reality of universals in the same sense as the reality of a chair also led to the denial of the objectivity of the universal and so obstructed the path to the understanding of universal objects and of the being of the ideal. This spell was broken by the discovery of categorial intuition, in particular ideation. As a result of this discovery, philosophical research is now in a position to conceive the *apriori* more rigorously and to prepare for the characterization of the sense of its being.

[3.] This objectivity which gives itself in such acts of categorial intuition is itself the objective manner in which reality itself can become more truly objective. The exhibition of categorial structure serves to broaden the idea of objectivity such that this objectivity can itself be exhibited in its content in the investigation of the corresponding intuition. In other words, the phenomenological research which breaks through to objectivity arrives at the form of research sought by ancient ontology. There is no ontology *alongside* a phenomenology. Rather, *scientific ontology is nothing but phenomenology.*

Categorial intuition as intentional comportment was deliberately given only second place in the series of discoveries. With regard to our understanding of the first discovery, categorial intuition is just a concretion of the basic constitution of intentionality announced there. As categorial intuition is possible only on the basis of the phenomenon of intentionality having been seen before it, so the *third discovery* to be discussed now is intelligible only on the basis of the *second* and accordingly on the basis of the *first*. It is first in this way that the sequence of discoveries accounts for itself, and the first manifests its fundamental significance step by step.

§7. The original sense of the apriori

The elaboration of the sense of the apriori is the third discovery which we owe to the beginnings of phenomenology. This discovery may be characterized more briefly 1) because despite some essential insights into phenomenology the apriori itself is still not made very clear, 2) because it is still by and large intertwined with traditional lines of inquiry, and 3) above all because the clarification of its sense really presupposes the understanding of what we are seeking: *time.*

Accordingly, general ideas have no existence except as a word. (Heidegger is here placing the discovery of categorial intuition in the context of traditional philosophy since Plato. It is seldom noted that Heidegger has inaugurated a new chapter in the staid old "problem of the universals" in his search for an ontology of occasional expressions, for the universal structures of 'temporal particularity.' Cf. "On the Way to *Being and Time*.")

The latter is already evident from the clarification of the term: apriori—*prius*—προτερον—earlier; apriori—what from before, from earlier on already is. The apriori to something is that which already always is the earlier. This is a wholly formal definition of the apriori. It has not yet been stated what that something is in regard to which something earlier is found. The apriori is a term which implies a time sequence [the idea of a before and after], although this is left quite vague, undefined, and empty.

The scientific motives for the discovery and development of the apriori, which already begin with Plato,—How was it first conceived? What were the limits within which it could be conceived?—cannot be depicted or clarified now. Our only questions will be: What was understood by this term? How does phenomenology now understand it?

Since Kant, but in its substance since Descartes, the term apriori has been attributed first and foremost to knowing, to that which determines cognitive comportment. Knowledge is apriori when it is not based upon empirical inductive experience, when it is not dependent upon knowledge of the real as its founding authority. Apriori knowledge accordingly has no need of experience. From the interpretation of knowing given by Descartes, apriori knowledge is accessible first and only in the subject as such, insofar as it is self-enclosed and remains within its own sphere. Apriori knowledge is in this way always already included in all knowledge of the real, in all transcendent knowledge.

The opposite to apriori knowing is now called knowing *aposteriori*, the later, that is, that which comes after the earlier and pure subjective knowing. It is the knowledge of the object. Underlying this classification of the sense of the apriori and aposteriori of knowledge is the thesis of the priority of the knowledge of subjectivity, a thesis which Descartes based on the *cogito sum, res cogitans*. Thus even today, the apriori is still identified as a feature belonging specifically to the subjective sphere, and apriori knowledge is also called *inner knowledge, inner vision*. This concept of the apriori can be broadened to include any subjective comportment as such—whether it be knowing or any other comportment—*before* it oversteps the bounds of its immanence.

In conjunction with this Kantian concept of the apriori, the attempt is now also being made to interpret the apriori in Plato in the same way. For Plato speaks of how the true being of entities is known when the soul speaks to itself in the λογος ψυχης προς αυτην (*Sophist* 263e). The identification of ψυχη in the Greek sense with consciousness and the subject now supports the view that already in Plato, the discoverer of the apriori, apriori knowledge means immanent knowledge. This interpretation of Plato is absurd. It has no basis in the matters at issue, as we shall now show more precisely.

The apriori in Kant's sense is a feature of the subjective sphere.

This coupling of the apriori with the subjectivity became especially pertinacious through Kant, who joined the question of the apriori with his specific epistemological inquiry and asked, in reference to a particular apriori comportment, that of synthetic apriori judgments, whether and how they have transcendent validity. Against this, phenomenology has shown that the apriori is not limited to the subjectivity, indeed that in the first instance it has primarily nothing at all to do with subjectivity. The characterization of ideation as a categorial intuition has made it clear that something like the highlighting of ideas occurs both in the field of the ideal, hence of the categories, and in the field of the real. There are sensory ideas, ideas whose structure comes from the subject matter's content (color, materiality, spatiality), a structure which is already there in every real individuation and so is apriori in relation to the here and now of a particular coloration of a thing. All of geometry as such is proof of the existence of a material apriori. In the ideal as in the real, once we accept this separation, there is in reference to its objectivity something ideal which can be brought out, something in the being of the ideal and in the being of the real which is apriori, structurally earlier. This already suggests that the apriori phenomenologically understood is not a title for comportment but a *title for being*. The apriori is not only nothing immanent, belonging primarily to the sphere of the subject, it is also nothing transcendent, specifically bound up with reality.*

Thus the first thing demonstrated by phenomenology is *the universal scope of the apriori*. The second is *the specific indifference of the apriori to subjectivity*. The third is included in the first two: the way of access to the apriori. Inasmuch as the apriori is grounded in its particular domains of subject matter and of being, it is in itself demonstrable in a simple intuition. It is not inferred indirectly, surmised from some symptoms in the real, hypothetically reckoned, as one infers, from the presence of certain disturbances in the movement of a body, the presence of other bodies which are not seen at all. It is absurd to transpose this approach, which makes sense in the realm of the physical, to philosophy too and to assume a stratification of bodies and the like. The apriori can in itself be apprehended much more directly.

This leads to a fourth specification of the apriori. The 'earlier' is not a feature in the ordered sequence of knowing, but it is also not a feature in the sequential order of entities, more precisely in the sequential order of the emergence of an entity from an entity. Instead, the apriori is a *feature of the structural sequence in the being of entities, in the ontological structure of being*. Taken formally, the apriori prejudges nothing at all in regard to whether this earlier refers to a knowing or a

---

Ergo, it is indifferent to the distinction of immanent and transcendent.

being-known or some other kind of comportment to something, or whether it refers to an entity or to being, not even whether it means being in the traditional form of the Greek concept of being transmitted to us. This cannot be drawn from the sense of the apriori. Toward the end of the course, it will become clear that the discovery of the apriori is really connected or actually identical with the discovery of the concept of being in Parmenides or in Plato. In view of the prevalence of this particular concept of being, the apriori even within phenomenology still stands in this traditional horizon, so that there is some warrant for speaking of Platonism within phenomenology itself.

The *threefold** exposition of the apriori—1) its universal scope and its indifference to subjectivity, 2) the way of access to it (simple apprehension, originary intuition), and 3) preparation for the specification of the structure of the apriori as a feature of the being of entities and not a feature of entities themselves—revealed the original sense of the apriori to us. It is of essential significance that this exposition depends in part on the clearer formulation of ideation, that is, on the discovery of the genuine sense of intentionality.

When we take these three discoveries—intentionality, categorial intuition, and the apriori—together as they are connected among themselves and ultimately grounded in the first, in the discovery of intentionality, we arrive at the goal which has been guiding us and gain an understanding of phenomenology as a *research endeavor*. In the first chapter, we described the breakthrough of phenomenology and its prehistory. In this second chapter, we have now delineated its decisive discoveries. We must now complete this account by inquiring into the sense of the phenomenological principle and then using this as a basis to make clear to ourselves what the self-characterization of this research under the rubric of '*phenomenology*' means. Accordingly, on the basis of our account of the three discoveries, we shall now discuss the principle of phenomenology.

§8. *The principle of phenomenology*

a) The meaning of the maxim
"to the matters themselves"

The principle of a research endeavor is the principle of its investigative conduct, and so the principle by which the idea of that research investigation is appropriated and carried out. From what we

---

*Here, the first two in the above list of four are combined into the first point of the following list of three.

have just said* about research work, this means that the *principle of research* is [1] the *principle for securing its field of subject matter*, [2] the *principle for drawing out the regard* by which the subject matter is investigated, and [3] the *principle for developing the way of dealing with it, the method.* Accordingly, the principle of a research endeavor is that by which it constantly orients itself in its execution and that which serves as a constant guideline in directing the actual steps of its execution. The principle of research contains no result, no thesis, no dogma from the material content of the knowledge of this research. What it does contain for research is the guiding direction of its quest.

Insofar as it determines the execution of a possibility of the very existence of Dasein, a principle is also called a *maxim.* And science itself, researching-for, in its very being is nothing but a particular possibility of human existence. The phenomenological maxim *"to the matters themselves"* is addressed against construction and free-floating questioning in traditional concepts which have become more and more groundless. That this maxim is self-evident, that it nevertheless has become necessary to make it into an explicit battle cry against free-floating thought, characterizes the very situation of philosophy. We now want to make this maxim more specific. In its expressed formal generality, it is the principle of *all* scientific knowledge. But our question is really: *what are these matters* to which philosophy must return if it ever is to be scientific research? Back to which matters themselves? In the phenomenological maxim we hear a double demand: 1) to do research that is autochthonously demonstrative, to provide demonstrations rooted in native ground (the demand to do demonstrative work), then 2) to arrive at and to secure this ground once more, which is the way Husserl understood his philosophical effort (the demand to lay open the ground). The second is the demand to lay the foundation, and so includes the first.

What instructions does phenomenology give on the demand to lay open the field? It is easily seen that the determination and demarcation of the field of subject matter of phenomenological research is involved in the idea of philosophy. But we shall now not pursue the path of determining this field from the idea of philosophy. We shall instead examine how the breakthrough of phenomenology and its discoveries have laid open a field of research within contemporary philosophy. So we now ask, while the substance of the three discoveries is fresh in our minds, which matters are taken up here, or, which matters does this

*Namely, that a research endeavor regarded as a whole includes its field of subject matter, the way in which this matter is to be regarded interrogatively, and the way it is to be treated in the course of being interrogated. We have encountered this threefold division in the opening section (p. 2 above) and we shall meet it again in a more hermeneutic formulation as prepossession, preview, and preconception (§31d below).

research tend to take up? This will enable us to specify the first sense of the phenomenological maxim (the demand to do demonstrative work), that is, to ascertain the mode of treatment appropriate to these matters by reading it from the concretion of its principle. We are making no deduction from the idea of phenomenology but are *reading the principle from its concretion in the research work.* The concretion is characterized by the discoveries, and now it is only a question of the extent to which they supply content to the formal sense of the research principle: *What field of subject matter, what regard toward it and what mode of dealing with it* are intended? The clarification of the phenomenological principle according to field and mode of treatment then permits the legitimacy of the designation 'phenomenology' to emerge of its own accord and to set itself off from misinterpretations.

[Let us proceed to the first question: Toward what matters does phenomenology tend?] The initial phenomenological investigations were investigations in logic and the theory of knowledge. They were inspired by the goal of a *scientific logic and epistemology.* The question here is: Do the three discoveries—the elaboration of intentionality, of the categorial and the way of access to it, and of the apriori—give us the ground on which the matters of logic can be located and demonstrated?

Logic is the science of thinking and of the laws of thought, but not of thinking as a psychic occurrence and the laws regulating its course, but instead of thinking as the lawfulness of the object, of that which is thought as such. All thinking is at the same time expression, understood as the meaningful fixation of what is thought. In the area of the objects of logic, this refers to matters like meaning, concept, assertion, and proposition. Traditionally, knowing was conceived in terms of self-contained and finished cognitions formulated in assertions, propositions, judgments, where judgments are composed of concepts and complexes of judgments are syllogisms. All of these and what they intend imply lawful structures. Judging is carried out in representational or generally in intuitive apprehension; it thus involves truth and objectivity. The concepts of these objects are to be genuinely secured, which means that they are to be drawn from themselves and demonstrated in reference to themselves. The objects of logic are meaning, concept, assertion, proposition, judgment, state of affairs, objectivity, fact, law, being, and the like. Where and as what can and must such objects become accessible? Is there a field of objects which in and of themselves are coherent in content? Does the unity of a field of subject matter lead to the unity of a discipline which treats these objects? Or are these objects in the end abandoned to any passing shrewdness, which invents something for them in coarse and loose speculation? Or is a demonstration possible at all for these matters which are so fundamental to all the sciences and to all knowledge as such? Can a unified horizon of a field of subject matter be found in the material content of the three discoveries taken as a whole? Or do these refer to disparate objects? This is the real direction of the line of questioning in search of a scientific logic.

Intentionality now is nothing other than *the basic field* in which these objects are found. [As *intentio* and *intentum*, it is] the totality of comportments and the totality of entities in their being. Now the question is: In the two directions of *intentio* and *intentum*, where the given is either the comportment or the entity in regard to its being, what is it that is structural, what is already there in the given as a structural composition, what is to be found in it as that which constitutes its being? The field of matters for phenomenological research is accordingly *intentionality in its apriori*, understood in the two directions of *intentio* and *intentum*. But this implies that the so-called logical comportments of thinking or objective theoretical knowing represent only a particular and narrow sphere within the domain of intentionality, and that the range of functions assigned to logic in no way exhausts the full sweep of intentionality.

We have thus specified the *field of subject matter* and the *regard* taken toward it—*intentionality* and *apriori*. The second question is, what *mode of treatment* corresponds to this field?

The characterization of the apriori as well as the specification of categorial intuition have already shown that this mode of treatment is a simple originary apprehension and not a kind of experimental substructing in which I construct hypotheses in the field of the categorial. Instead, the full content of the apriori of intentionality can be apprehended in simple commensuration with the matter itself. Such a directly seeing apprehension and accentuation is traditionally called *description. Phenomenology's mode of treatment is descriptive.* To be more exact, description is an *accentuating articulation of what is in itself intuited. Accentuating articulation is analysis. The description is analytical.* This serves to specify the mode of treatment of phenomenological research, although once again only in a formal way.

It is easy to see, or better, we constantly overlook and so fail to see that the general term 'description' still says nothing at all about the specific structure of phenomenological research. The character of description is first specified by the content of the matter to be described, so that description can be fundamentally different in different cases. One should keep in mind that this characterization of the way of treating objects in phenomenology as description first of all refers only to *direct self-apprehension* of the thematic and not to indirect hypothesizing and experimenting. The term 'description' at first implies nothing more. The clarification of the content of the phenomenologi-

cal maxim on the basis of its initial factual concretion in the breakthrough to phenomenology consequently leads to the following definition of such research: *Phenomenology is the analytic description of
intentionality in its apriori.*

b) Phenomenology's understanding of itself as analytic description of intentionality in its apriori

If the sense of this research is explained by defining it in retrospect
from the past situation of philosophy, that is, if we hear in the term
intentionality what this new research combines, namely, intentionality
and the psychic, then phenomenology is description of the psychic,
'*descriptive psychology.*' If in addition we assume the traditional problem-
horizons and their division into fixed disciplines (logic, ethics, aesthetics . . .), then this descriptive psychology deals with all comportments,
the logically cognitive, ethical, artistically creative, appreciative, social,
religious comportments, in short, the comportments which are defined in terms of their laws and norms in the corresponding disciplines of logic, ethics, aesthetics, sociology, philosophy of religion.
From this standpoint we come to regard the descriptive discipline of
phenomenology as a *propaedeutic science* for the traditional philosophical disciplines, where the problems come up for discussion. Phenomenology does not yet discuss problems, it only has to take up the
matters of fact, and is excluded from the actual judicial hearing of
the problems. It also has no desire to be admitted to this trial.

But now let us consider whether this interpretation does not put
this research endeavor and the originality of its principle right back
into the position which it has abandoned and which phenomenology
is designed to overcome. This conception of phenomenology and its
interpretation is like wanting to interpret modern physics from astrology or chemistry from alchemy instead of the other way around,
where astrology is taken as a stage preceding physics and overcome by
it. In other words, the definition of phenomenology which we have
obtained by clarifying its principle is to be understood from its task,
from the positive possibility which it implies, from what guides its
efforts and not from what is said about it.

This understanding and even the realization of this phenomenological task does not bring us to a happy ending but instead to a meager though liberating beginning. If the formal indication defining
this research as analytic description of intentionality in its apriori is
secured expressly, phenomenologically, that is, in the direction of the
material content of what it poses for scientific treatment, then this
provides a hint of a more radical form of this research; it comes
strictly from the research itself, in the direction of its ownmost maxim

"to the matters themselves," and that in turn only puts us on the path of further effort.

We have explained the principle of phenomenological research first by highlighting the major achievements contained in its actual efforts and by trying to view these in a unified way. We have thus determined that intentionality gives us the proper field of subject matter, the apriori gives us the regard under which the structures of intentionality are considered, and categorial intuition as the originary way of apprehending these structures represents the mode of treatment, the method of this research. This serves to bring the task of philosophy since Plato once again to its true ground, inasmuch as it now gives us the possibility to do research into the categories. As long as phenomenology understands itself, it will adhere to this course of investigation against any sort of prophetism within philosophy and against any inclination to provide guidelines for life. Philosophical research is and remains atheism, which is why philosophy can allow itself 'the arrogance of thinking.' Not only will it allow itself as much; this arrogance is the inner necessity of philosophy and its true strength. Precisely in this atheism, philosophy becomes what a great man once called the "joyful science."

§9. Clarification of the name 'phenomenology'

We shall now try to make clear to ourselves what the name 'phenomenology' actually means in relation to the subject matter just identified. We shall develop this clarification in three steps: a) The clarification of the original sense of the component parts of the name; b) The definition of the unified meaning thus obtained for the composite word and comparison of this actual meaning of the name with what it names, with the research so characterized; c) We will briefly discuss several misunderstandings of phenomenology which are connected with the external and aberrant interpretation of the name.

a) Clarification of the original sense of the component parts of the name

The name 'phenomenology' has two components, 'phenomenon' and '-logy.' The latter phrase is familiar from such usages as theology, biology, physiology, sociology, and is commonly translated as 'science of': theology, science of God; biology, science of life, of organic nature; sociology, science of the community. Accordingly, phenomenology is the *science of phenomena*. 'Logy,' science of, varies in its character according to the thematic matter, which is logically and formally undefined. In our case, it is defined by what phenomenon stands for. So, to begin with, the first part of the name must be clarified [in order to see what this particular -logy stands for].

α) The original sense of φαινόμενον

Both parts refer back to Greek expressions, phenomenon to φαινό-μενον, -logy to λόγος. Φαινόμενον is the participle of φαίνεσθαι, the middle voice which means *to show itself*; φαινόμενον is accordingly that which shows itself. The middle voice φαίνεσθαι is a form of φαίνω: to bring something to light, to make it visible in itself, to put it in a bright light. Φαίνω has the stem φα—φῶς, light, brightness, that wherein something can be manifest, visible in itself. We shall adhere to this meaning of phenomenon: φαινόμενον, *that which shows itself*. The φαινόμενα form the totality of that which shows itself, what the Greeks also simply identified with τὰ ὄντα, entities.

Now an entity can show itself in itself from itself in various ways, depending in each case on the kind of access we have to it. There is the noteworthy possibility that an entity may show itself as something which it nevertheless is not. We do not call such an entity a phenomenon, something which shows itself in the authentic sense, but a *semblance [Schein]*. The expression φαινόμενον thus receives a modification in meaning: instead of the ἀγαθόν we speak of a φαινόμενον ἀγαθόν, a good which only looks good but actually is not, it only 'appears' good. Everything now depends upon seeing the connection between the basic meaning of φαινόμενον, the manifest, and the second meaning, semblance. Φαινόμενον can mean semblance only because semblance is a modification of φαινόμενον in the first sense. Formulated more pointedly, only because φαίνεσθαι means "showing itself" can it also mean "merely showing itself as," "only looking like." Only insofar as something in its sense makes a pretense of showing itself can it pass itself off as . . . ; only what makes a pretense to be manifest can be a semblance. In fact, that is the *sense of semblance: pretension to be manifest but not really being it.* Φαινόμενον as semblance thus serves to show that the sense of phenomenon is *the entity itself manifest in itself.* Semblance, on the other hand, is a pretended self-showing. Phenomenon is therefore *a mode of encounter of entities in themselves such that they show themselves.*

We must adhere to this genuine sense of φαινόμενον employed by the Greeks. But we must also see that at first it has absolutely nothing to do with our term 'appearance' or still less 'mere appearance.' Probably no word has caused as much havoc and confusion in philosophy as this one. We cannot trace the history of these errors here. We shall only try to give the main differences of the authentic and original meaning of phenomenon as semblance in contrast to appearance.

We use the term 'appearances,' for example, in the German expression *Krankheitserscheinungen*, "symptoms" [literally, "appearances of a disease"]. In a thing, processes and properties show themselves through which the thing represents itself as this and that. Appearances are themselves occurrences which refer back to other occurrences from which we can infer something else which does not make an appearance. Appearances are appearances of something which is not given as an appearance, something which refers to another entity. Appearance has the distinguishing feature of reference. What distinguishes reference is precisely this: that to which the appearance refers does not show itself in itself but merely represents, intimates by way of mediation, indirectly indicates. The term appearance therefore means a kind of reference of something to something which does not show itself in itself. More precisely, not only does it not show itself in itself, but according to its very sense it does not even pretend to show itself but instead pretends to represent itself. The characteristic feature of the referential function in appearance, in appearing, is the function of *indicating, of the indication or announcement of something*. Indicating something by means of another, however, means precisely not to show it in itself but to represent it indirectly, mediately, symbolically. We have here then, with what we mean by appearance, a very different connection. In the case of the phenomenon, we do not really have a referential connection; the structure peculiar to it is instead that of self-showing. It is now important for us to elucidate the inner connection between phenomenon in this genuine sense and appearance, but in the process we must also differentiate appearance from semblance.

Semblance is a modification of the manifest, of something manifest which it pretends to be but is not. Semblance is *not* phenomenon in this privative sense; it has the characteristic of showing itself, but that which shows itself does *not* show itself as what it is, while appearance is precisely the representation of something which is essentially not really manifest. Semblance thus always goes back to something manifest and includes the idea of the manifest. But now it is also becoming clear that an appearance, a symptom, can only be what it is, namely, reference to something else which does not show itself, through the self-showing of that which appears. In short, that which gives itself as a symptom is a phenomenon. The possibility of appearance as reference of something to something rests on having that something which does the referring show itself in itself. To put it another way, the possibility of appearance as reference is founded in the authentic phenomenon, in self-showing. The structure of appearance as reference already intrinsically presupposes the more original structure of self-showing, the authentic sense of phenomenon. Something can be referential only as a self-showing something.

The concept of appearance now also gets the name of phenomenon. Or phenomenon is defined as the appearance of something which does not appear; it is defined in terms of a state of affairs which already presupposes the sense of phenomenon but which on its part cannot define it. But in addition, appearance implies something which appears and, at the opposite pole, something which does not appear. So there are two entities and it is then maintained that appearances are something and behind them is something else, that of which they are appearances. By and large, we do not learn from philosophy what this standing behind the scenes really means. But in any event this is included in the concept of appearance, so that now appearance and the referential connection included in it are taken ontically, in terms of entities, and the connection between appearance and thing in itself is then a relation of being: one stands behind the other. Add to this the move whereby that which stays in the background and does not show itself but only announces itself in the appearance is now labelled ontically as the real and true entity; this naturally leads to the move of designating that which does appear, the appearance itself, as *mere* appearance. Thus, within the ontic referential context a distinction in grades of being is made between that which shows itself and that which only appears in the sense of announcing itself in the former. We thus come across a double possibility: appearance purely as a referential connection without first conceiving it ontically in any particular way, and then appearance as the name for an ontic connection of reference between φαινόμενον and νούμενον, between essence and appearance in the ontic sense. If we now take this degraded entity, the appearance versus the essence in this sense of mere appearance, then this mere appearance is called semblance. Confusion is then carried to extremes. But traditional epistemology and metaphysics live off this confusion.

By way of summary, the following must be made clear: There are two basic meanings of 'phenomenon'; first the manifest, that which shows itself, and second that which presents itself as something manifest but which only gives itself [out] in this way—semblance. For the most part, we are not at all familiar with the original meaning of phenomenon and dispense with the task of making clear to ourselves what it does mean. We simply call something a 'phenomenon' which here has been identified as 'appearance' and analyzed as such. When phenomenology is criticized, the critic simply takes the concept of 'appearance,' which is convenient for his purposes [but has nothing to do with phenomenology], and uses this word to criticize a research endeavor oriented to the matters themselves. This should suffice for the clarification of the first component part of the term 'phenomenology.'

β) The original sense of λόγος
(λόγος ἀποφαντικός and λόγος σημαντικός)

The term λόγος goes back to λέγειν. In the word combinations already mentioned (theology, biology, etc.), -logy means "science of." Science is understood as an interconnection of propositions and assertions about the unity of a domain of subject matter. But λόγος does not actually mean science; in relation to λέγειν it means discourse, *discourse about* something. The sense of λόγος should not be defined in arbitrary terms that happen to come to mind. We must rather abide by what the Greeks understood by λέγειν.

How did the Greeks define λέγειν, "to discourse," "discoursing"? Λέγειν does not merely mean to form and to recite words. The sense of λέγειν is rather δηλοῦν, making manifest, where what is made manifest includes what the discourse is about and how it should be talked about. Aristotle defines its sense more precisely as ἀποφαίνεσθαι, *letting something be seen in itself and indeed—ἀπό—from itself*. In discourse, to the extent that it is genuine, what is said should be drawn from—ἀπό—what is talked about, so that discursive communication in its content, in what it says, makes manifest what it is talking about and makes it accessible to the other party. This is the strict functional sense of λόγος elaborated by Aristotle.

In its concrete performance, discourse assumes the form of speaking, vocal utterance in words. In this regard λόγος is φωνή, voice. This feature however does not constitute the essence of λόγος. On the contrary, the feature of φωνή is defined from the authentic sense of λόγος as ἀποφαίνεσθαι, from what discourse truly is and does—pointing out and letting something be seen. As Aristotle emphasizes, λόγος is φωνή μετά φαντασίας, so that a making visible and perceptible accompanies the vocal utterance; it includes something φαίνεσθαι, φαντασία, which can be seen. The essential element in the utterance is the φαντασία, the ἀποφαίνεσθαι, what is said in the discourse and, as spoken, is meant and signified. The λόγος is therefore quite generally a φωνή σημαντική, something vocal which shows something in the sense of a *signifying*, which yields something understandable. Ἐστι δὲ λόγος ἅπας μὲν σημαντικός, . . . ἀποφαντικὸς δὲ οὐ πᾶς.[1]

Aristotle now makes the distinction between λόγος taken quite generally insofar as it is σημαντικός, insofar as discoursing in general sig-

---

1. Aristotle, *De interpretatione*, {Ch. 4, 17a1ff.}. ["Every sentence has meaning. . . . Yet every sentence is not a/theoretical/proposition." English translation by E. M. Edghill in McKeon (ed.), *The Basic Works of Aristotle*, op. cit., p. 42.]

nifies, and λόγος insofar as it is ἀποφαντικός. The ἀποφαίνεσθαι, letting the spoken be seen in itself, is a particular meaning of discourse. Not every proposition is a theoretical proposition, an assertion about something. None of the following is a λόγος ἀποφαντικός, in which something is communicated: an exclamation, a request, a wish, a prayer. But each is a σημαντικός, each signifies something. In these instances, however, signifying does not mean the theoretical apprehension of something. But λόγος in all of the combinations like theology, biology, etc., has to be taken in the sense of the special λόγος σημαντικός, namely, that of λόγος ἀποφαντικός, λόγος as θεωρεῖν, discoursing in the sense of communicating the apprehension of a subject matter and only such a communication. This sense of λόγος ἀποφαντικός is accordingly the sense λόγος also has in the combination 'phenomeno-logy.'

b) Definition of the unified meaning thus obtained and the research corresponding to it

Let us now put together these two separately clarified parts of the name "phenomenology." What unified meaning results from this, and to what extent is this unity of meaning, as the name for the kind of research we have described above, a fitting expression of this research? The surprise is that λόγος understood as ἀποφαίνεσθαι has an intrinsic and material relation to φαινόμενον. Phenomenology is λέγειν τὰ φαινόμενα = ἀποφαίνεσθαι τὰ φαινόμενα—letting the manifest in itself be seen from itself. In the same vein, the maxim of phenomenological research—back to the matters themselves—is basically nothing other than a rendition of the name of phenomenology. But this means that phenomenology is essentially distinct from the other names for sciences—theology, biology, etc.—in that it says *nothing about the material content* of the thematic object of this science, but speaks really only—and this emphatically—of the *how*, the way in which something is and has to be thematic in this research! Phenomenology is accordingly a *'methodological'* term, inasmuch as it is only used to designate the mode of experience, apprehension, and determination of that which is thematized in philosophy.

The objects of philosophical research have the character of the phenomenon. In brief, such research deals with phenomena and only with phenomena. Phenomenology in its original and initial meaning, which is captured in the expression 'phenomenology', signifies a way of encountering something. It is in fact the outstanding way: *showing itself in itself*. The expression phenomenology names the way something has to be there through and for λέγειν, for conceptual exposition and interpretation. As our preceding discussion has shown, phenomenology deals with intentionality in its apriori. The structures of intentionality in its apriori are the phenomena. In other words, the structures of intentionality in its apriori circumscribe the objects which are to be made present in themselves in this research and explicated in this presence. The term 'phenomenon' however says nothing about the being of the objects under study, but refers only to the *way they are encountered.* The *phenomenal* is accordingly everything which becomes visible in this kind of encounter and belongs in this structural context of intentionality. We therefore speak of 'phenomenal structures' as of what is seen, specified and examined in this kind of research. *Phenomenological* signifies everything that belongs to such a way of exhibiting phenomena and phenomenal structures, everything that becomes thematic in this kind of research. The *unphenomenological* would be everything that does not satisfy this kind of research, its conceptuality and its methods of demonstration.

Phenomenology as the science of the apriori phenomena of intentionality thus never has anything to do with appearances and even less with mere appearances. It is phenomenologically absurd to speak of the phenomenon as if it were something behind which there would be something else of which it would be a phenomenon in the sense of the appearance which represents and expresses [this something else]. A phenomenon is nothing behind which there would be something else. More accurately stated, one cannot ask for something behind the phenomenon at all, since what the phenomenon gives is precisely that something in itself. Admittedly, what can in itself be exhibited and is to be exhibited can nonetheless be *covered up.* What is in itself visible and in its very sense is accessible only as a phenomenon does not necessarily need to be so already in fact. What a phenomenon is as a possibility is not directly given as a phenomenon but *must first be given. As research work, phenomenology is precisely the work of laying open and letting be seen,* understood as the methodologically directed dismantling of concealments.

Being-covered-up is the *counterconcept to phenomenon,* and such concealments are really the immediate theme of phenomenological reflection. What can be a phenomenon is first and foremost covered up, or known in a tentative form. The concealment can assume various guises. First, a phenomenon can be covered up in the sense that it is *still quite undiscovered,* so that there is no knowledge or clue to its existence. Second, a phenomenon can be *buried.* This means that it was discovered before but once again got covered up. This is not a total concealment. What was discovered before is still visible, though only as a semblance. But so much semblance—so much being; this concealment understood as *disguise* is the most frequent and most dangerous kind, for here the possibilities of deceiving and misleading are especially great. The originally seen phenomena are uprooted, torn from their ground, and are no longer understood in their origins, in their "extraction" from their roots in a particular subject matter.

Concealment itself, whether it is taken in the sense of the undiscovered pure and simple or of burying or disguise, has in turn a twofold sense. There are *accidental concealments* and there are *necessary* ones, given in the very being of their manner of discovery and its possibilities. Every phenomenological proposition, though drawn from original sources, is subject to the possibility of concealment when it is communicated as an assertion. Transmitted in an empty and predisposed way of understanding it, it loses its roots in its native soil and becomes a free-floating naming. This possibility of petrification of what it has drawn out and demonstrated in an original way is implied in the concrete labor of phenomenology itself. Concealment may at times also proceed from it because phenomenology carries this radical principle within itself. The possibility of radical discovery at the same time brings with it the corresponding danger that phenomenology may become hardened in its own results.

The reason why genuinely phenomenological work is difficult is that it must be especially critical of itself in a positive way. The sort of encounter involved in the mode of phenomenon must first of all be wrested from the objects of phenomenological research. This means that the characteristic mode of apprehending phenomena—originarily apprehending interpreting—implies not one iota of an immediate apprehension in the sense in which it can be said that phenomenology is a straightforward seeing which requires absolutely no methodological preparation. Precisely the opposite is the case, which is also why the expressness of the maxim is so essential. Because the phenomenon must first be won, scrutinizing the point of departure for access to the phenomenon and clearing the passage through the concealments already demand a high degree of methodological preparation so that we may be guided and determined by what the phenomenal givenness of intentionality in each instance implies. The demand for an ultimate direct givenness of the phenomena carries no implication of the comfort of an immediate beholding. There can be no disclosure or deduction of essence from essence, apriori from apriori, one from the other. Rather, each and every one of these must come to demonstrative vision. Accordingly, the way to go in each instance begins with the individual phenomenal correlations and varies according to the degree to which the apriori has been uncovered and the tradition has buried it, as well as the kind of obfuscation involved. Since every structure must ultimately be exhibited in itself, phenomenology's way of research at first assumes the character or the aspect of what is called a *picture-book phenomenology*. It gives greater prominence to the exhibition of individual structures which are perhaps very useful for a systematic philosophy, even though the exhibition can only be provisional. As a result, there is a tendency to give philosophical sanction to the prominent displays of particular phenomenological considerations by finding a place for them in some sort of dialectic or the like. Against this tendency, it must be stated that at first nothing at all is to be made of the interconnections of the structures of intentionality. Rather, the interconnection of the apriori is always determined only from the subject matter which is to be explored in its phenomenal structure. Furthermore, at first we need not concern ourselves with these considerations, since they will always remain fruitless as long as the concrete aspect of phenomena is not clear.

c) Correcting a few typical misunderstandings of phenomenology which stem from its name

I now want to deal only very briefly with a few typical misunderstandings of phenomenology, since they are still generally prevalent in philosophy, and since there are only a few who make the effort to elucidate the authentic sense of phenomenology from its concrete work. A typical example, and indeed the best example of what one can get away with today in this regard, is an article by Rickert in the journal *Logos*.[2]

Rickert here wants to show that phenomenology is not and cannot be a philosophy of the immediate and, by way of contrast, makes some suggestions on how a philosophy of the immediate would look. The characteristic attitude is already evident here: there must be a philosophy of the immediate and everything must be organized in accord with it. "To begin with, at least a mediation is needed in order to define the concepts of appearance and phenomenology in such a way that they will be useful for a philosophy of the immediate."[3] In opposition to this, it must first be stated generally that phenomenology does not wish to be either a philosophy of intuition or a philosophy of the immediate. It does not want to be a philosophy at all in this sense, but wants the subject matters themselves.

Rickert's critique is based on his understanding of the word "appearance." He states that the word "appearance" has, in its sense as appearance of something, the orientation toward something which is not appearance, which is therefore not immediately given. And since appearance is always appearance of something which is behind it, the

---

2. Heinrich Rickert, "Die Methode der Philosophie und das Unmittelbare. Eine Problemstellung," *Logos* XII (1923/24), pp. 235-280. [Cf. note 2 in §5 above.]
3. Ibid., p. 242 n.

immediate cannot be apprehended, so that we are always dealing with something already mediated. Phenomenology is accordingly unsuited to be the basic science of philosophy. It is apparent first that the concept of appearance, phenomenon, is merely taken up without any attempt to see what phenomenon originally means and in phenomenology truly means. Instead, the traditional concept of appearance, an empty verbal concept, is taken as a basis for criticizing the concrete labor of a research effort. It is unnecessary to go any further into this article, since nothing of relevance to our topic would be dredged up by such a critique and since it is in fact no great feat to criticize such an objection. It has to be mentioned, however, since Rickert in this essay gives voice to what is otherwise typical in philosophy and in its attitude toward phenomenology. I stress this not to save phenomenology but to make clear how such an interpretation not only deforms the sense of the phenomenological endeavor but above all loses the instinct for sticking to the topic in philosophizing.

Chapter Three

The Early Development of
Phenomenological Research
and the Necessity of a Radical Reflection
in and from Itself

We now come to the third chapter of our introductory considerations of the sense and the task of phenomenological research. The account of the term phenomenology based upon the clarification of its principle and its three main discoveries has accomplished the task, set in the second chapter, of clarifying the sense of phenomenological research. In the first chapter, our topic was the origin and breakthrough of phenomenological research, and in the second it was the fundamental discoveries of phenomenology, its principle and the clarification of its name. In this third chapter, we shall now briefly trace the early development of phenomenological research and examine the necessity of reflecting anew upon its field of objects, out of itself according to its own principle.

This reflection will be directed toward the original, that is, phenomenologically basic, determination of the thematic field, namely, the fundamental determination of intentionality and of what is already given with it. In the light of this new task of securing the thematic field originally, as it is prefigured in the phenomenon of intentionality, the account of the cultivation and development of phenomenological research will also shift its ground. We shall examine the growing elaboration of the thematic field, its determination, and the outlining of the working horizons as they emerge from this determination of the field. In point of fact, we shall pursue this theme in the double orientation of the work of the two leading researchers in phenomenology today, Husserl and Scheler.

We shall then show from this very research that a fundamental problem is left unposed and must remain unposed in it and why it must, what conditions must be fulfilled in order to pose it, and how this leads to a more radical definition of the task of phenomenological research. This problem is the *basic phenomenological question* of the *sense of being*, a question which an ontology can never pose but already constantly presupposes and thus uses in some sort of answer, grounded or otherwise. The immanent critique of the natural trend of phenomenological research itself allows the question of being to arise. A partial answer to this question is in fact the real theme of this course. This third chapter of the Preliminary Part is thus the *exposition* of the material content of the considerations which will now concern us in the following.

§10. Elaboration of the thematic field:
The fundamental determination of intentionality

a) Explication of the demarcation
of the thematic field of phenomenology
and fixation of the working horizons
in Husserl and Scheler

In its initial breakthrough, the phenomenological endeavor concentrated on determining the basic phenomena by which the objects of logic and epistemology are given. In short, it concentrated on the intentional comportments which are essentially theoretical in character, in particular on cognitive comportments which are specifically scientific. Of course, these considerations already included aspects of the description of other comportments which are specifically emotional, especially in connection with the question of how acts as such can be expressed in concepts. The thematic goal of the first investigations was to lay open a particular portion of the field. The primary aim of the initial attempt was not to mark off and bring out the whole field itself in a basic way, even though considerations of this sort are not lacking.[1] Moreover, intentionality, the character of objectifying acts, was naturally expounded in the two main directions of *intentio* and *intentum*, but these two essential structural moments of the basic constitution of intentionality were as such not yet brought to full clarity.

All of this—*the concrete expansion of the field, the fundamental reflection upon its regional character and its demarcation from other regions, the elaboration of the basic directions in which intentionality could be explored*—took place in the decade following the appearance of *Logical Investigations*,

---

1. Cf. esp. the Fifth Investigation of Husserl's *Logische Untersuchungen*, Vol. II.

between 1901 and 1911. Along with the increasingly richer and clearer disclosure of the phenomenal field came the development of the method and its phenomenological theory. This development and the literary output associated with it can only be outlined very briefly, in order to give a brief answer to the questions which I am constantly asked about what is called the phenomenological literature, which does not actually exist.

After the appearance of *Logical Investigations*, Husserl's work was at first concentrated upon the extension of the phenomenology of perception in the broadest sense, not only sense perception but perception in the sense of originary apprehension in the different domains of objects. These investigations were concluded just a year ago, after almost 25 years, but have not been published. In addition, in connection with his new teaching duties at Göttingen, Husserl's work was oriented toward the systematic extension of logic, toward a phenomenology of objectifying knowledge, with special emphasis on the phenomenology of judgment. Despite a series of ever new approaches, this logic is also incomplete. At the same time, work was concentrated on the phenomenology of practical comportment, in a confrontation with Kant's practical philosophy. This period (1913–1914) also included the first attempts toward what is called an apriori axiomatic of values, which Scheler later took up and carried further.

Also in this period, Bergson gradually became known in Germany. This was basically due to Scheler, who recognized Bergson and his significance quite early, and then was influenced by him in return. Scheler was instrumental in having Bergson translated into German. This recognition of Bergson also brought, within Husserl's work, the *investigations of internal time consciousness*, which are in part published in his later works.[2]

Then the influence of Dilthey made itself felt, manifesting his inner kinship with the tendencies of phenomenology. This led to a transposition of Husserl's orientation in the philosophy of science, taken in the broadest sense, from one-sided work on problems relating to the natural sciences to a broader reflection on the specific objectivity of the human sciences. A final essential direction channeling these efforts came from the confrontation with the Marburg School, above all with Natorp's *Introduction to Psychology*.[3] The confrontation with this psychology was naturally nothing other than the dispute over the direction of the question of the structure of consciousness, of the region

2. Editor's Note: Edmund Husserl, *Vorlesungen zur Phänomenologie des inneren Zeitbewusstseins*, edited by Martin Heidegger, offprint from *Jahrbuch für Philosophie und phänomenologische Forschung*, Vol. IX (Halle a.d.S.: Niemeyer, 1928).

3. Paul Natorp, *Einleitung in die Psychologie nach kritischer Methode* (Freiburg: Mohr, 1888); second edition in 1912 under the title *Allgemeine Psychologie*.

in which the totality of comportments, and so all the states of intentionality, are ordered. This period in the development of phenomenology thus saw its work being drawn into the horizon of contemporary philosophy, a tendency which has not remained without influence upon the subsequent inquiries of phenomenology.

No phenomenological publication appeared in the decade between 1900 and 1910. As a result, the effect of the work within the narrow circle of researchers in Göttingen was all the more intensive. Two lectures by Husserl at the Göttingen Mathematical Society in 1902 were especially important. At this time, the so-called collapse of the Lipps School also occurred, so that a number of Lipps's former students then came to Göttingen, discussed fundamental questions in the circle of phenomenologists, and prepared themselves for subsequent publications. Husserl at that time gave away large portions of his ongoing work in the discussion, and much of what was later published under other names is really his. In the phenomenological endeavor, however, this plays no role; who discovered what ultimately makes no difference.

The first published statement by Husserl was an essay in *Logos*, "Philosophy as Strict Science."[4] The essay has a programmatic character, but it is not a program that precedes the work. It emerged from the work, against the background of a labor of ten years. This treatise evoked almost universal opposition among philosophers, while within phenomenology it served to unite the slowly rising generation of younger researchers in a common and secure endeavor. This closing of ranks within phenomenological research led in 1913 to the founding of its own organ, the *Yearbook for Philosophy and Phenomenological Research*. The first volume appeared in 1913 and six more volumes have appeared since, the last in 1923. The first two volumes contain treatises by the editors: Husserl, Scheler, Reinach, Pfänder, and Geiger. The later volumes present in part further works by Pfänder and Geiger, as well as student works of varying quality.

In its first volume, the Yearbook published the treatise by Husserl entitled *Ideas toward a Pure Phenomenology and Phenomenological Philosophy*, First Book.[5] The second book was written immediately after the first and brought to a conclusion, but so far has not appeared.[6]

In the second volume, already in part in the first, the second work

---

4. Edmund Husserl, *Philosophie als strenge Wissenschaft*, in *Logos* I (1910/1911); editor's note: Now available as an offprint in *Quellen der Philosophie*, No. 1, ed. Rudolph Berlinger (Frankfurt: Klostermann, 1965).

5. Husserl, *Ideen I*. [Cf. note 1 in §5 above.]

6. Edmund Husserl, *Ideen zu einer reinen Phänomenologie und phänomenologischen Philosophie*, Second Book. Editor's note: now in Husserliana, Vol. IV, edited by Marly Biemel (The Hague: Nijhoff, 1952).

of fundamental importance appeared, namely Max Scheler's *Formalism in Ethics and the Material Ethics of Value*.[7] It contains large sections of fundamental phenomenological considerations which go beyond the special domain of ethics. Also to be noted are the collected essays of Max Scheler, in particular the treatise *On the Idols of Self-Knowledge*[8] as well as *Toward the Phenomenology and Theory of Sympathy*.[9] These collected essays appeared a few years ago in a second edition, though basically in a poorer version.

These problems of Husserl and Scheler just enumerated serve to define the actual development of phenomenology and the more detailed explication of the problem of demarcating and founding the thematic field of phenomenology. Accordingly, the analysis of the later basic studies will have to keep to these two spheres of problems. Within this concrete development of the phenomenological endeavor, the working horizons were at first also fixed by the purely traditional disciplines of logic, ethics, aesthetics, sociology, and philosophy of law. The horizons of inquiry remained the same as in traditional philosophy. In addition, on the basis of the orientation to the phenomenon of intentionality, which is phenomenologically distinguished into *intentio*, *intentum*, and the correlation between the two, there arose three directions of work which always reciprocally require one another: phenomenology of the act, phenomenology of the subject matter, and the correlation between the two. The same separation is found in Husserl in the terms *noesis*, the specific structure of directing-itself-toward, and *noema*, the subject matter insofar as it is intended in the intention. For Husserl there is no special correlation, since it is given with *noema* and *noesis* and included in them.

b) Fundamental reflection upon the regional structure of the field in its originality: elaboration of pure consciousness as an independent region of being

Our question is: How is the fundamental and explicit elaboration of the thematic field of phenomenology carried out by Husserl?

Phenomenology was characterized as the analytic description of in-

7. Max Scheler, *Der Formalismus in der Ethik und die materiale Wertethik (mit besonderer Berücksichtigung der Ethik Immanuel Kants)*, First Part, 1913, in *Jahrbuch für Philosophie und phänomenologische Forschung*; published along with the Second Part under separate cover, ibid. (Halle: Niemeyer, 1916).

8. Max Scheler, "Idole der Selbsterkenntnis," in *Abhandlungen und Aufsätze* (Leipzig: Verlag der Weissen Bücher, 1915).

9. Max Scheler, *Zur Phänomenologie und Theorie der Sympathiegefühle* (Halle: Niemeyer, 1913); Second Edition under the title *Wesen und Formen der Sympathie* (Bonn: Friedrich Cohen, 1923); Third Edition, 1926.

tentionality in its apriori. Can intentionality in its apriori be singled out as an independent region, as the possible field of a science?

Intentionality was defined as the structure of lived experiences, this in accord with the basic moments of its constitution, *intentio—intentum*. The elaboration of its apriori calls for the exposition of the structures which in advance constitute the individual comportments and their possible contexts, that which already lies in every perceiving or perceived regardless of how perception as perception is concretely individuated in these particular men, or in this particular provenance and form. This discerning of the apriori is called *ideation*. Ideation is an act of categorial intuition, that is, an act founded in a prior envisaging of a concrete individuation. Ideation must always take place on the basis of an intuition of an example. A fundamental accentuation of the apriori field of intentionality will therefore have to give an account 1) of the exemplary ground, the field of concrete individuations of lived experiences from which its structure of intentionality is to be brought into relief ideatively; 2) of the way the apriori structures are brought into relief from this background; 3) of the character and type of being of this region thus brought out and highlighted.

It is easy to see that the crucial consideration is the first, that of securing and specifying the field from which we start. For it is from this field that the field we seek is to be derived and demarcated. The difference of such a fundamental reflection from the procedure followed in the breakthrough phase is plain. In the initial phase of phenomenology, the discussion and description of intentionality still operated wholly within the framework outlined by the disciplines of psychology and logic and their particular questions. Now, however, the discussion no longer deals with these old questions and traditional tasks but is concerned with the reflection, secured in the matters themselves, upon the connection between the phenomenological field to be derived and the field from which we start. In other words, it is concerned with the concrete individuation of intentionality, of comportments and of lived experiences. It is now a matter of defining the field in which the comportments first become accessible.

The question therefore is: How do comportments in which the structure of intentionality is to be read become accessible? How is something like intentionality, the structure of lived experience, lived experience itself, first given? "First given" here means given for a so-called *natural attitude*. In what way, *as what* are lived experiences, comportments, the various modes of the consciousness of something, found in the natural attitude? What is to be seen and traced is how the 'new scientific domain' of phenomenology arises from what is given in the natural attitude.[10] Hence the aim is to discover a new scientific do-

---

10. Husserl, *Ideen I*, p. 56 (Biemel's 1950 ed., p. 67). [Eng. tr., §32, p. 60.]

main. This new region is called the region of *pure lived experiences*, of *pure consciousness with its pure correlates*, the region of the *pure ego*. This region is a new domain of objects and—as Husserl puts it—a region of being which is in principle special, the specifically phenomenological region. Husserl himself characterizes the manner of proceeding in this way:

> We first proceed by way of direct exhibition, and since the being to be exhibited is nothing other than what we, for essential reasons, shall call 'pure lived experiences,' 'pure consciousness' with its pure 'correlates of consciousness' and on the other side with its 'pure ego,' we first proceed from *the* ego, from *the* consciousness, *the* lived experiences which are given to us in the natural attitude. . . . [11]

How am I given in the natural attitude in Husserl's description? I am "a real object like others in the natural world," [12] that is, like houses, tables, trees, mountains. Human beings thus occur *realiter* in the world, among them I myself. I perform acts (*cogitationes*). These acts belong to the "human subject," hence are "occurrences of the same natural reality." [13] The totality of such a continuity of lived experiences in the human or animal subject can be called an *individual stream of lived experiences*. The experiences are themselves 'real occurrences in the world' 'in animal beings.'

We shall persist in this natural attitude in which we find such objects and direct our gaze upon the experiential continuity, and in fact upon our own as it takes its course *realiter*. This self-directedness toward our own experiential continuity is a new act which is called *reflection*. In such acts of reflection we find something objective which itself has the character of acts, of lived experiences, of modes of consciousness of something. In this reflection in which we follow acts, we can describe them as we did earlier in the analysis of representation, of the consciousness of a picture and of empty intending. When we live in acts of reflection, we ourselves are directed toward acts. The peculiar feature of reflection is already evident here, namely, that the object of the reflection, acts, belongs to the same sphere of being as the contemplation of the object. Reflection and reflected object both belong to one and the same sphere of being. The object, the contemplated, and the contemplation are *really* [*reell*] included in one another. The object and the way of apprehending it belong to the same stream of experience. This real inclusion of the apprehended object in the apprehension itself, in the unity of the same reality, is called *immanence*.

---

11. Ibid., p. 58 (70). [Eng. tr., §33, p. 64.]
12. Ibid.
13. Ibid.

Immanence here has the sense of the real togetherness of the reflected and the reflection. It characterizes a particular multiplicity of
an entity, namely, that of the being of lived experiences and acts.
"Consciousness and its object {reflection and act as object of re-
flection} form an individual unity produced purely through lived
experiences."[14]

The state of affairs in so-called transcendent perceptions, the perceptions of things, is obviously totally different. The perception of the
chair as thing does not as lived experience really contain the chair
within itself, in such a way that as a thing it would, so to speak, swim in
and with the stream of experience. As Husserl also puts it, the perception exists "apart from any and all {properly} essential unity with the
thing."[15] A lived experience can "only by joined with lived experiences
into a whole whose total essence comprises the particular essences of
these experiences and is founded in them."[16] The wholeness of consciousness, the wholeness of the stream of experience is such that it
can only be founded in lived experiences as such. The unity of this
wholeness, the continuity of experience, is determined purely by the
particular essences of the lived experiences. The unity of a whole is
after all only one by way of the particular essence of its parts. This
wholeness of the stream of experience as a self-contained totality excludes every thing, that is, every real object, beginning with the entire
material world. Over against the region of lived experiences, the material world is alien, other. This is apparent in any analysis of a simple
perception.

At the same time, however, it already became evident at the beginning of this consideration that the stream of experience understood
as a real occurrence is conjoined with the real world, with the bodies.
For example, it is attached to a concrete unity in the unity of psychophysical animal things. Consciousness, as a name for the experiential
totality, is therefore involved in the real structure in a double manner.
First, consciousness is always a consciousness in a man or animal. It
makes up the psychophysical unity of an *animal* which occurs as a
given real object. "The psychic is not a world for itself, it is given as an
ego or ego-experience . . . , and this turns out to be empirically tied to
certain physical things called organisms."[17]

---

14. Ibid., p. 68 (85). [Eng. tr., §38, p. 79; Heidegger's insertion.]
15. Ibid., p. 69 (86). [Eng. tr., §38, p. 80; Heidegger's insertion is here also reported
to be in Husserl's 'Copy A' of this text.]
16. Ibid.
17. Edmund Husserl, "Philosophie als strenge Wissenschaft," *Logos* I, p. 298. [En-
glish translation by Quentin Lauer, "Philosophy as Rigorous Science," in Edmund Husserl, *Phenomenology and the Crisis of Philosophy* (New York: Harper Torchbook, 1965),
pp. 71–147, esp. p. 85.]

"Every psychological determination is *eo ipso* psychophysical, which is to say in the broadest sense . . . that it has a never-absent physical connotation. Even where psychology—the empirical science—concerns itself with the determination of bare occurrences of consciousness and not with dependences that are psychophysical in the usual narrower sense, those occurrences are still thought of as belonging to nature, that is, as belonging to human and animal consciousness which in turn have an obvious and coapprehended connection with human and animal organisms." [18]

This consciousness as a component part of the animal unity is at the same time consciousness of this real nature, in reality one with the nature in the concretion of every factual living being (man); but at the same time consciousness is also separated from it by an absolute gulf, as every perception of a thing shows in the distinction of immanence and transcendence. Now this separation into two spheres of being is remarkable precisely because the sphere of immanence, the sphere of lived experience, establishes the possibility within which the transcendent world, separated from it by a gulf, can become objective at all. It is now a question of envisaging this double involvement, first in the real unity of concretion of the *animal* and then in the involvement stemming from the relation of immanence and transcendence despite the real gulf. How can it still be said that consciousness has its 'own essence,' an essence particular to it? That it is a self-contained continuity? How is the drawing out and highlighting of consciousness as an independent region of lived experiences, as an independent region of being, still at all possible?

Already in our very first considerations we have seen that the region of lived experience is specified by the character of intentionality. Because of their intentionality, the transcendent world is in a certain sense there in the lived experiences. But it should be noted that just because the transcendent world, beginning with the things, is objective, this is no reason to assume that this is necessarily apprehended. As Husserl expressly emphasizes, apprehending the given things is only one particular mode of act. For example, in the act of love I live 'in' the beloved, in such a way that the beloved in this act is not an object in the sense of an apprehended object. For this, a new modification of attitude is required so that the beloved may be presented objectively in the sense of mere apprehension. In order to avoid narrowing down the concept of intentionality, it must be seen that apprehension is not identical with directing-itself-toward. Apprehen-

---

18. Ibid., pp. 298f. [Eng. tr., p. 86.]

sion is only a very particular and not necessarily even a predominant mode of intending entities. Thus, when in reflection I am directed toward a particular experience, toward a particular act such as that of perceiving a thing, I am thematically focused upon the perception and not upon the perceived. I can of course make the perception itself the theme such that the perceived, what the perception perceives, its object, is itself co-apprehended, but in such a way that I do not *live directly* in the perception, say, of the chair, but rather *live thematically* in the apprehension of the perceptual act and of what is perceived in it. This way of considering the act and its object is not a transcendent apprehension of the thing itself. In considering reflection in this way, I to some extent do "not go along with" the concrete perception, to put it in the vernacular. I do not really live in the perception of the chair but in the attitude of the immanent reflective apprehension of perceiving the chair, not in the thesis of the material world but in the thematic positing of the act apprehending the perception and of its object as it is there in the act. This "not going along with" the thesis of the material world and of every transcendent world is called ἐποχή, refraining.

Every phenomenological analysis of acts considers the act in such a way that the analysis does not really go along with the act, does not follow its thematic sense, but rather makes the act itself the theme, so that the object of the act is also thematized in terms of how it is presumed in the corresponding intention. This implies that the perceived is not directly presumed as such, but in the how of its being. This modification, in which the entity is now regarded to the extent that it is an object of intentionality, is called *bracketing*.

This bracketing of the entity takes nothing away from the entity itself, nor does it purport to assume that the entity is not. This reversal of perspective has rather the sense of making the being of the entity present. This phenomenological suspension of the transcendent thesis has but the sole function of making the entity present in regard to its being. The term "suspension" is thus always misunderstood when it is thought that in suspending the thesis of existence and by doing so, phenomenological reflection simply has nothing more to do with the entity. Quite the contrary: in an extreme and unique way, what really is at issue now is the determination of the being of the very entity.

Such an ἐποχή can now be performed in principle upon all possible comportments of consciousness, so that I now envisage consciousness in such a way that, in the individual acts of perceiving, deliberating, etc., I do not go along with what their object is but perform the ἐποχή uniformly throughout the whole sphere of acts. I thus envisage the acts and their objects in terms of how they are presumed in the acts. This securing of the sphere of acts and its objects in the uniformity of a specific sphere is called *reduction*.

This reduction in the sense of not going along with any transcendent thesis is the first stage within the process of *phenomenological reductions*. When I reduce the concrete experiential continuity of my life in this way, after the reduction I still have the same concrete experiential continuity. It is still my continuity. But now I do not have it in such a way that I am engrossed in the world, following the natural direction of the acts themselves. Now I have the acts themselves present in their full structure. Even after this so-called *transcendental reduction*, the reduced field is the field of a unique singularity, that of my stream of consciousness.

This singular field of my own stream of experience is then subjected to a second reduction, the *eidetic reduction*. The acts and their objects now are not studied as concrete individuations of my concrete being, as this stream of experience. Rather, this unity of the stream of experience is now regarded ideatively. Every moment which specifies this individual stream as individual is now suspended. What is now discerned in the concretely lived experiences is simply the structure belonging to a perception, representation, or judgment as such, regardless of whether this judging or perceiving is mine, regardless of whether it takes place in this moment either in this concrete constellation or in another. This double reduction (the transcendental and the eidetic) draws from the initially given concrete individuation of a stream of experience what is called the *pure field of consciousness*, that is, a field which is no longer concrete and individual but *pure*.

In demarcating the reality of the thing from the reality of the stream of experiences, it was already shown that the transcendent world-reality does not belong to the immanently real whole of the stream of experience. The chair is not a lived experience or an experiential thing. Its kind of being is totally different from that of lived experience. By contrast, everything objective in what is called immanent perception is defined by the same kind of being as immanent perception itself. This implies that the object of immanent perception is *absolutely given*. The stream of lived experience is therefore a region of being which constitutes a sphere of *absolute position*, as Husserl says. It is true that every transcendent perception apprehends what is perceived by it, the thing, in its bodily character, but there is always the possibility that what is perceived cannot be and is not. In immanent apprehension, however, lived experience is given in its absolute self. Immanent perception, the reflection upon the acts, gives entities whose existence cannot in principle be denied. Or as Husserl once put it: "Any bodily given thinglike entity can also not be, but a bodily given lived experience cannot also not be."[19] It thus becomes apparent that the sphere of immanence is distinguished by its mode of givenness, which is called absolute. Combining this with our earlier considerations, we now see that the sphere of pure consciousness obtained by way of transcendental and eidetic reduction is distinguished by the character of being *absolutely given*. Pure consciousness is thus for Husserl the sphere of absolute being.

Nothing is altered in the absolute being of lived experiences by the contingency of the world of things. Indeed, these experiences are always presupposed for all of that. Phenomenological reflection here has come to a climax. "The essential contexts disclosed to us already include the most important premises for the conclusions we wish to draw about the fundamental detachability of the entire natural world from the domain of consciousness, the sphere in which lived experiences have their being;"[20]—detachability of its how with the help of the reductions.

Already here, we can detect a kinship with Descartes. What is here elaborated at a higher level of phenomenological analysis as pure consciousness is the field which Descartes glimpsed under the heading of *res cogitans*, the entire field of *cogitationes*. The transcendent world, whose exemplary index for Husserl as well is to be found in the basic stratum of the material world of things, is what Descartes characterizes as *res extensa*. This kinship is not merely factual. Husserl himself, at the point where he observes that the reflection has come to a climax, refers explicitly to Descartes. He says that what comes to a head is simply what Descartes really sought in the *Meditations*, to be sure with another method and another philosophical goal. This connection with Descartes and the explicit formulation of this connection is important for the critical understanding of the ontological character of this region obtained by these so-called reductive considerations.

We will have to pose a more precise question: How is it at all possible that this sphere of absolute position, pure consciousness, which is supposed to be separated from every transcendence by an absolute gulf, is at the same time united with reality in the unity of a real human being, who himself occurs as a real object in the world? How is it possible that lived experiences constitute an absolute and pure region of being and at the same time occur in the transcendence of the world? This is the line of questioning motivating the elaboration of the phenomenological field of pure consciousness in Husserl.

---

19. *Ideen I*, p. 86 (109). [Eng. tr., §46, p. 102.]
20. Ibid., p. 87 (109f.). [Eng. tr., §46, pp. 103f.]

§11. *Immanent critique of phenomenological research: critical discussion of the four determinations of pure consciousness*

Our question will be: Does this elaboration of the thematic field of phenomenology, the field of intentionality, raise the question of the *being of this region*, of the *being of consciousness*? What does *being* really mean here when it is said that the sphere of consciousness is a sphere and region of *absolute* being? What does *absolute being* mean here? What does being mean when we speak of the being of the transcendent world, of the reality of things? Is there somewhere in the dimension of this fundamental deliberation, in which the elaboration of the field of phenomenology is decided, in turn a clarification of the regard from which the separation of the two spheres of being is considered, namely, the *sense of being*, to which there is constant reference? Does phenomenology anywhere really arrive at the methodological ground enabling us to raise this *question of the sense of being*, which must precede any phenomenological deliberation and is implicit in it?

We are still leaving undiscussed whether this question is or is not a *fundamental question*, whether a radical securing of the field of intentionality is possible and makes sense without raising this question explicitly and answering it. But if the question is necessary, then the reflection upon being as such is phenomenologically even more necessary, and ultimately also the concrete possibility of exploring this question. But then the prior position seems phenomenologically inadequate.

We shall establish the basis for the critical consideration of the field of objects proper to phenomenology by investigating whether the being of the intentional as such is explored within the following three horizons of consideration: [1.] What is the basis upon which this field of objects is secured? [2.] What is the way of securing this thematic field? [3.] What are the determinations of this newly found field of objects, of what is called pure consciousness? We shall start with the latter horizon, the determination of the being of the region 'consciousness.' As the basic field of intentionality, is the region of pure consciousness determined in its being, and how?

The determination obviously aims at a determination of being. Consciousness is plainly identified as a region of absolute being. It is moreover that region from which all other entities (reality, the transcendent) are set off. In addition, this particular distinction is specified as the *most radical distinction in being* which can and must be made within the system of categories.

In view of these determinations regarding pure consciousness, does our particular critical distinction, whereby we ask whether and to what extent the inquiry is directed toward being, still have any sense and basis? We shall discuss in detail the determinations of being which Husserl gives to pure consciousness. There are four of them and they are peculiarly tied together, so that the same designation is often used for two different determinations.

Consciousness is 1) *immanent being*; 2) the immanent is the *absolutely given being*. This absolute givenness is also called *absolute being* pure and simple. 3) This being, understood as absolute givenness, is also absolute in the sense that *nulla re indiget ad existendum* (thus the old definition of substance is adopted): "it needs no *res* in order to be." *Res* is here understood in the narrower sense of *reality, transcendent being*, that is, any entity which is not consciousness. 4) Absolute being in these two significations—absolutely given and needing no reality— is *pure* being, in the sense of being the essence, the ideal being of lived experiences.

We shall ask the following about these four determinations of being: Are they determinations which arise from a regard for the subject matter itself? Are they determinations of being which are drawn from the consciousness and from the very entity intended by this term?

a) Consciousness is immanent being

Formally, *immanence* implies, first of all, to be in another. This property of immanence is said of the region of consciousness, of lived experience, more precisely, in reference to the apprehending acts, to the acts of reflection which in their turn are directed toward acts, toward lived experiences. Immanence is asserted of a relation which is possible between lived experiences themselves, between the reflecting act and the reflected. Between the reflecting experience and the reflected, the objective element in the reflection, there is a relation of real inclusion in one another. Immanence, being in one another, is here asserted of lived experiences insofar as they are a possible object of an apprehension through reflection. Immanence is not a determination of the entity in itself with regard to its being, but a relation of two entities within the region of lived experience or consciousness. This relation is characterized as a *real in-one-another*, but nothing is actually said about the being of this being-in-one-another, about the "immanent reality" [*Reellität*], about the entity in the whole of this region. A relationship of being between entities, and not the being as such, is determined here. Thus the first determination of being which Husserl gives for the region of pure consciousness, either as an originary or a non-originary determination, is not carried out.

b) Consciousness is absolute being
in the sense of absolute givenness

How is it with the second character: Consciousness is absolute being
in the sense of absolute givenness? The reflected experience which is
the object in a reflection is originarily given in itself. In contrast to the
transcendent, lived experiences are there in the absolute sense. That
is, they do not display themselves indirectly, symbolically, but are apprehended in themselves. They are called absolute because of this absolute givenness.

If the lived experiences are called absolute in this sense, this characteristic of being—absolute—once again implies a determination of
the region of lived experiences with reference to its being apprehended. This determination is still based upon the first determination. This determination—absolutely given—does not refer to the
mutual regional pertinence of the apprehended and the apprehending but now to the relation of a lived experience as an object for another lived experience.

The first characteristic, immanence, identified a relationship of
being between acts of the same region. Now what is characterized is
the specific mode of being-an-object by which an entity of the region
of lived experience is an object for another such entity. Once again,
the entity in itself does not become a theme. What does become thematic is the entity insofar as it is a possible object of reflection.

c) Consciousness is absolutely given in the
sense of 'nulla re indiget ad existendum'

The third determination likewise characterizes consciousness as absolute being, but "absolute" is now taken in a new sense. We can make
this new sense clear to ourselves by referring back to the first determination of the region of lived experience, consciousness as immanent being. While all lived experiences are immanently given, every
other sort of being is such that it manifests itself in consciousness. In
principle, therefore, the possibility exists that the continuity of the
flow of lived experiences, of the stream of consciousness, possesses "a
self-contained continuity of being,"[1] a certain univocity, without having anything in reality correspond to what is presumed in this experiential continuity. In other words, in principle the possibility exists that
consciousness itself is "not affected in its own existence" by an "anni-

---

1. *Ideen I*, p. 93 (117). [Eng. tr., §49, p. 112.]

hilation of the world of things"[2]—a consideration which, as is well-known, Descartes had already employed.

Real being can be otherwise or even not be at all, while consciousness is capable of displaying in itself a closed continuity of being. This consideration means that consciousness is absolute in the sense that it is the presupposition of being on the basis of which reality can manifest itself at all. Transcendent being is always given in representation; indeed, it is represented precisely as the object of intentionality.

Consciousness, immanent and absolutely given being, is that in which every other possible entity is constituted, in which it truly 'is' what it is. Constituting being is absolute. All other being, as reality, is only in relation to consciousness, that is, relative to it. "The common way of talking about being is thus reversed. The being which for us is the first is in itself the second, that is, it is what it is only in 'relation' to the first."[3] This first, which must be presupposed, which must already be there so that something real can manifest itself, this first being has the advantage of not needing reality. On the contrary, it is rather reality which has need of the first being. All consciousness is therefore absolute compared to any and every reality.

This determination—absolute—is now obtained with regard to the particular role which consciousness has as constituting consciousness. This means that the character of absolute being is now attributed to consciousness insofar as it is regarded in the horizon of a theory of reason, in terms of the question of the possible demonstration of reality in rational consciousness. The character 'absolute' is now attributed to consciousness to the extent that it is regarded in its potential function as object of constituting consciousness. And in this sense consciousness is that sort of being which for its part is not constituted once again in another consciousness but which, in constituting itself, itself constitutes every possible reality. Absolute being accordingly means not being dependent upon another specifically in regard to constitution; it is the first, that which must already be there in order that what is presumed can be at all. There is something presumed, in the widest sense, only insofar as a presuming, that is, a consciousness, is. Consciousness is the earlier, the apriori in Descartes's and Kant's sense.

Consciousness in this sense of the absolute means the priority of subjectivity over every objectivity. This third determination—absolute being—once again does not determine the entity itself in its being but rather sets the region of consciousness within the order of constitu-

---

2. Ibid., p. 91 (115). [Eng. tr., §49, p. 110.]
3. Ibid., p. 93 (118). [Eng. tr., §50, p. 112.]

tion and assigns to it in this order a formal role of being earlier than anything objective. This determination and conception of consciousness is likewise the place where idealism and idealistic inquiry, more precisely idealism in the form of neo-Kantianism, enter into phenomenology. Thus this determination of being is also not an original one.

d) Consciousness is pure being

The fourth determination of being, which regards consciousness as *pure* being, is even less than the other three a characterization of the being of the intentional, that is, of the entity which is defined by the structure of intentionality. Consciousness is called pure consciousness to the extent that it, as this region, is no longer regarded in its concrete individuation and its tie to a living being. It is not consciousness to the extent that it is *hic et nunc* real and mine, but instead purely in its essential content. At issue is not the particular individuation of a concrete intentional relation but the intentional structure as such, not the concretion of lived experiences but their essential structure, not the real being of lived experience but the ideal essential being of consciousness itself, the apriori of lived experiences in the sense of the generic universal which in each case defines a class of lived experience or its structural contexture. In other words, consciousness is called pure to the extent that every reality and realization in it is disregarded. This being is pure because it is defined as *ideal*, that is, *not real* being.

This character of being, consciousness as pure, shows especially clearly that what matters here is not the ontological characters of the intentional but the determination of the being of intentionality, not the determination of the being of the entity which has the structure intentionality, but the determination of the being of the structure itself as intrinsically detached.

All four determinations of the being of the phenomenological region: immanent being, absolute being in the sense of absolute givenness, absolute being in the sense of the apriori in constitution, and pure being, are in no way drawn from the entity itself. Rather, to the extent that they are brought out as determinations of the being of consciousness, they immediately qualify as obstacles in the path of asking about the being of this entity and so also about the clearer elaboration of this entity itself. The determinations of being are not derived by considering the intentional in its very being, but to the extent that it is placed under scrutiny as *apprehended, given, constituting* and *ideating* taken as an essence. It is from such perspectives, which in the first instance are alien to consciousness, that these determinations of being are derived. It would however be premature, from the absence of the determination of the being of consciousness, from the neglect of the question of being in characterizing consciousness as a region, to jump to the conclusion that the question of being is as such being neglected. Perhaps here, we merely need to determine consciousness as a region, the way in which it is a field for a particular consideration, but not the being of the entity itself, which can [also] be set apart as a possible field for consideration.

In point of fact, all of these determinations of being are derived with a view to working out the *context of lived experience as a region for absolute scientific consideration.* Perhaps precisely here the question of the being of the entity should not be raised. In any case, we must first look into whether the sense of this entity is determined in the process of bringing this region into relief, even if only in the sense that it is suspended as irrelevant for its being a region.

Husserl's primary question is simply not concerned with the character of the being of consciousness. Rather, he is guided by the following concern: *How can consciousness become the possible object of an absolute science?* The primary concern which guides him is the *idea of an absolute science.* This idea, that *consciousness is to be the region of an absolute science,* is not simply invented; it is the idea which has occupied modern philosophy ever since Descartes. The elaboration of pure consciousness as the thematic field of phenomenology is *not derived phenomenologically by going back to the matters themselves* but by going back to a traditional idea of philosophy. Thus none of the characters which emerge as determinations of the being of lived experiences is an original character. We cannot go into more detail here into the motivation for this entire line of inquiry and into its way of posing problems. To begin with, it is enough for us to see that the four characters of being which are given for consciousness are not derived from consciousness itself.

With that, we have gone through only the first stage of our critical reflection. The second is to ask whether, on the way taken to elaborate pure consciousness, we shall not perhaps still come to a genuine determination of the being of lived experience. But if not here, then surely we find it in the starting point of the entire reflection, that is, in securing and preparing the exemplary field, where it is said that phenomenological reflection must start from the natural attitude, from the entity as it first gives itself. With this, we also get a preview of the determination of the being of the entity in which consciousness and reason are concrete, in the determination of the being of the concrete entity called man.

§12. Exposition of the neglect of the question of the being of the intentional as the basic field of phenomenological research

The critical question which emerged in the first detailed and systematic treatment by Husserl is the question of the being of that which is put forth as the theme of phenomenology. Why we place the question of being in the foreground as the critical question, by what warrant we even approach the position of phenomenology with this question, will become clear later. At first, we are presupposing that there must be an inquiry into this being. We are asking whether this question is asked in phenomenology itself.

If we recall the determinations which Husserl himself gives to pure consciousness as the phenomenological region, it becomes apparent that these four determinations—being as immanent being, being as absolute being in the sense of absolute givenness, being as absolute being in the sense of constituting being over against everything transcendent, and being as pure being over against every individuation—are not drawn from the entity itself but are attributed to it insofar as this consciousness as pure consciousness is placed in certain perspectives. If consciousness is regarded as apprehended, then it can be said to be immanent. If it is regarded with respect to the manner of its givenness, it can be said to be absolutely given. With regard to its role as constituting being, as that in which every reality manifests itself, it is absolute being in the sense of *nulla re indiget ad existendum*. Regarded in its essence, its what, it is ideal being, which means that it posits no real individuation in the content of its structure. If these determinations are not originary determinations of being, then on the positive side it must be said that they only determine the region as region but not the being of consciousness itself, of intentional comportments as such; they are concerned solely with the being of the region consciousness, the being of the field within which consciousness can be considered. This consideration is in fact possible. To make this clear with an example, the mathematician can circumscribe the mathematical field, the entire realm of that which is the object of mathematical consideration and inquiry. He can provide a certain definition of the object of mathematics without ever necessarily posing the question of the mode of being of mathematical objects. Precisely in the same way, it can at first be granted with some justification that here the region of phenomenology can simply be circumscribed by these four aspects without thereby necessarily inquiring into the being of that which belongs in this region. Perhaps the being of consciousness should not be inquired into at all. In any case, the final critical position cannot be based upon this initial critical consideration. Moreover, what must be

asked and studied more closely in the whole of this elaboration of consciousness is whether being is explored within it, whether perhaps en
route to the reduction, to the securing and bringing into relief of this
region called consciousness, the question of being is after all raised,
whether perhaps right on the way which leads from what is given in
the natural attitude to what the reduction offers, the question of being is after all under consideration.

Let us recall the sense and methodological task of the *phenomenological reduction*. It seeks to arrive at the pure consciousness starting from
the factual real consciousness given in the natural attitude. This is
done by disregarding what is really posited, by withdrawing from
every real positing. In the reduction we disregard precisely the reality
of the consciousness given in the natural attitude in the factual human
being. The real experience is suspended as real in order to arrive at
the pure absolute experience (ἐποχή). The sense of the reduction is
precisely to make no use of the reality of the intentional; it is not
posited and experienced as real. We start from the real consciousness
in the factually existing human, but this takes place only in order finally to disregard it and to dismiss the reality of consciousness as such.
In its methodological sense as a disregarding, then, the reduction is in
principle inappropriate for determining the being of consciousness
positively. The sense of the reduction involves precisely giving up the
ground upon which alone the question of the being of the intentional
could be based (admittedly with the aim of then determining the
sense of this reality from the region now secured). But the sole question here is whether reduction as such brings out something for the
determination of the being of the intentional. Of course, one must be
careful here, inasmuch as Husserl here would reply: The sense of the
reduction is *at first* precisely to disregard reality in order then to be
able to consider it precisely as reality as this manifests itself in pure
consciousness, which I secure through the reduction. In reply we
would again ask whether this can be sufficient for the question of the
being of the intentional.

What more does the reduction accomplish? It disregards not only
reality but also any particular individuation of lived experiences. It
disregards the fact that the acts are mine or those of any other individual human being and regards them only in their *what*. It regards
the what, the structure of the acts, but as a result does not thematize
their *way to be*, their being an act as such. It is solely concerned with
the what-contents of the structures, the structure of the intentional
as the basic structure of the psychic, the what-contents of the constitution of this structure, the essence of the what of comportments, the
variations of their self-directedness and the what-content of their constructional relationships, but not the essence of their being.

In ideation (eidetic reduction), when we discern the essential content of the acts, only the structure of that content is regarded. The essence of the being of lived experiences is not also taken up ideatively into the essential contexture of pure consciousness. An example may serve to make this clear, although the objects here are completely different. When I seek to distinguish the essence of color from that of sound, this distinction can be made without my asking about the manner of being of these two objects. When I determine the *essentia*, the essence of color and sound, I disregard their *existentia*, their particular individuation, whether the color is the color of a thing, in this or that illumination. I look only at what pertains to every color as color, regardless of whether it exists or not. I disregard its existence, and so all the more the essence of its existence.

Likewise, in the consideration and elaboration of pure consciousness, merely the *what-content* is brought to the fore, without any inquiry into the being of the acts in the sense of their existence. Not only is this question not raised in the reductions, the transcendental as well as the eidetic; it *gets lost precisely through them*. From the what I never experience anything about the sense and the manner of the that—at any rate, only that an entity of this what-content (*extensio*, for example) can have a certain manner of being. What this manner of being is, is not thereby made clear. Merely looking at the what-content means seeing the what as apprehended, given, constituted. The critical discussion of the reductions in terms of what they do to pose the question of being turns out to be negative, so much so that it shows that the determinations of being discussed in §11 cannot be genuine. But above all, this conception of ideation as disregard of real individuation lives in the belief that the what of any entity is to be defined by disregarding its existence. But if there were an entity *whose what is precisely to be and nothing but to be*, then this ideative regard of such an entity would be the most fundamental of misunderstandings. It will become apparent that this misunderstanding is prevalent in phenomenology, and dominates it in turn because of the dominance of the tradition.

If the intentional is to be interrogated regarding its manner of being, then the entity which is intentional must be originally given, that is, it must be originally experienced in its manner of being. The original relationship of being to the entity which is intentional must be attained. But does this original relationship of being to the intentional not lie in the starting position of the reductions? Does this start not take the psychic, the consciousness-of, just as it is given in the natural attitude, in the theoretical and still unmodified experience? In the end, this is at least where the sense of the intentional, even if it is not explicitly brought to the fore, must nevertheless be experienced.

Let us pose the first critical question: To what extent is the being of the intentional experienced and determined in the starting position—in the determination of the exemplary ground of the reductions? If the being, the 'reality' of the intentional, is experienced in the natural attitude itself, then we need only to supplement the considerations of the intentional and of the reduction as we have understood it up to now; we now need to pose the question not only of the what-content, the structure of the acts, but also of the essence of their being. The manner of being would then be grasped in the natural attitude and also determined ideatively in its essence. Presumably the mode of being (the reality) of the intentional understood as the psychic is also experienced here. In the natural attitude, the intentional at first ought to be given precisely as that which is then disregarded in ideation. Even if only to be immediately set aside, the intentional is here nonetheless experienced in its reality, although not thematically apprehended. What being is attributed to it?—that of real occurrences in the world, living beings which are objectively on hand, which in accord with their being are inserted into the 'fundamental layer' of all reality, into material thingness. The being of the intentional, the being of acts, the being of the psychic is thus fixed as a real worldly occurrence just like any natural process. And that is not all.

Since the formation of the region of pure consciousness is undertaken for the purposes of theoretical reason, the elaboration of the various ways in which the various realms of entities are constituted in consciousness seeks to determine each particular reality and objectivity. Anything real manifests itself in consciousness as a possible object of a directing-itself-toward-it. Reality is to be specified in each case in view of this self-manifesting aspect as such. Also subject to specification is thus the particular reality at issue for us: the animalia, the psychic in its factual actuality. In other words, the reduction and the development of the regions, these ways of being, have no other sense than to provide the scientific basis for specifying the reality of something real. The actuality of the intentional is likewise constituted as a reality in consciousness.

'Psychological consciousness,' that is, the consciousness of something, the intentional as it is an object of psychology understood as a science of the real, must itself still be understood as a correlate of pure consciousness. Standing over against " . . . empirical {psychic} lived experience, as a presupposition of its sense, is absolute lived experience."[1] *Persons*—"psychic personalities" are "empirical unities"[2]; just "like realities of any kind and level, they are mere unities of inten-

---

1. *Ideen I*, p. 106 (133). [Eng. tr., §54, p. 128.]
2. Ibid., p. 106 (134). [Eng. tr., §54, p. 128.]

tional 'constitution'—. . . ."[3] Thus they can be experienced as truly being and so are "scientifically determinable."[4] "*All* empirical unities {person, animal ego} . . . are *indicators of absolute experiential contexts* with a distinctive essential formation, in addition to which still other formations are conceivable; all empirical unities are transcendent in the same sense, merely relative, contingent."[5] "To take them as being in the absolute sense is therefore absurd."[6] Only pure consciousness is the "sphere of being of absolute origins."[7] "To ascribe reality as well"[8] to this pure consciousness is absurd.

By way of summary then:

> . . . the whole *spatio-temporal world*, which includes the human being and the human ego as subordinate individual realities, {is} *in accord with its own sense mere intentional being {being manifesting itself in acts}*, thus a being which has the mere secondary and relative sense of a being *for* a consciousness. . . . It is a being which consciousness posits in its experiences, a being which in principle can be intuited and defined merely as the identical element of harmoniously motivated experiential manifolds—*over and above this*, however, it is nothing.[9]

But it has thus become quite clear that the being of the psychic, the intentional, is first suspended in order to allow the pure region of consciousness to be reached. On the basis of this pure region it now first becomes possible to define the suspended being, reality. *The question of being is thus raised, it is even answered.* We have to do solely with the genuinely *scientific way of answering it*, which attempts to define the sense of the reality of something real insofar as it manifests itself in consciousness.

What then was the point of our critical question? Was it merely precipitous on our part that we discussed the question of being and even established a neglect, in view of the determinations of being which are attributed to pure consciousness? Still, this entire consideration stands under a 'but.' In fact, this difficulty does not concern the determination of the region as such, the characterization of pure consciousness. As we have already suggested, the basic difficulty with this determination of the reality of acts lies already in the starting position. What becomes fixed here as the datum of a natural attitude, namely, that man is given as a living being, as a zoological object, is this very atti-

---

3. Ibid.
4. Ibid.
5. Ibid., p. 105 (133). [Eng. tr., §54, p. 128.]
6. Ibid., p. 106 (134). [Eng. tr., §54, p. 128.]
7. Ibid., p. 107 (135). [Eng. tr., §55, p. 129.]
8. Ibid., p. 108 (136). [Eng. tr., §55, p. 130.]
9. Ibid., p. 93 (117). [Eng. tr., §49, p. 112.]

tude which is called natural. For man's way of experience vis-à-vis the other and himself, is it his natural mode of reflection to experience himself as ζῷον, as a living being, in this broadest sense as an object of nature which occurs in the world? In the natural way of experience, does man experience himself, to put it curtly, zoologically? Is this attitude a *natural attitude* or is it not?

It is an experience which is totally *un*natural. For it includes a well-defined theoretical position, in which every entity is taken a priori as a lawfully regulated flow of occurrences in the spatio-temporal exteriority of the world. Is this natural attitude perhaps only the semblance of one? This kind of comportment and experience is of course rightly called an *attitude* [*Einstellung*], inasmuch as it must first be derived from natural comportment, from the natural way of experience; one must so to speak "place oneself into" [*hineinstellen*] this way of considering things [and so assume an attitude toward them] in order to be able to experience in this manner. Man's natural manner of experience, by contrast, cannot be called an attitude. Another issue is whether the character of the reality of man and of the acts which appear in this way of experience is the primary and authentic character; whether I experience the specific being of acts there or whether the specific being of comportments as such is actually obliterated, and the being of acts is defined merely in terms of their having occurred. The situation thus remains the same: although here the reality of acts is in a certain sense examined, the specific act-being of the comportments as such is nevertheless not examined. On the contrary, the specific being of acts is just distorted by this so-called natural attitude. That this attitude passes itself off as natural just serves to support the prejudice that in this sort of attitude the being of acts is given originally and authentically, and that every question about the being of acts must refer back to it.

Even if the 'thing of nature called man' is experienced as the ζῷον occurring in the world and his mode of being and his reality are determined, this does not mean that his comportments, the intentional in its being, are examined and defined. What is thus examined and defined is merely his being on hand as a thing, *to which* comportments are perhaps added as 'appendages' but are not really relevant for determining the character of the being of this entity and do not constitute its way of being. But to the extent that this entity is characterized by comportments, its way of being must also be knowable in its comportments.

This then is the result of our deliberations: in elaborating intentionality as the thematic field of phenomenology, *the question of the being of the intentional is left undiscussed*. It is not raised in the field thus secured, pure consciousness; indeed, it is flatly rejected as nonsensical. In the course of securing this field, in the reduction, it is expressly deferred. And where the determinations of being are brought into play, as in the starting position of the reduction, it is likewise not originally raised. Instead, the being of acts is in advance theoretically and dogmatically defined by the sense of being which is taken from the reality of nature. *The question of being itself is left undiscussed.*

§13. Exposition of the neglect of the question of the sense of being itself and of the being of man in phenomenology

But what is the point of this questioning of being? What is it for? Is it not enough to specify the what and the variations of the what? To begin with, the 'what for' is not a primary criterion in knowledge! Quite generally, inquiring into the being of the intentional is nonetheless a possibility! And in the end a necessity?

The first thing to be said is that this exposition of the thematic field of phenomenology, of pure consciousness, itself aims precisely at drawing a distinction among entities, fixing the fundamental distinction among entities, and this basically involves an answer to the question of being. Husserl says:

> The system of categories most emphatically must start from this most radical of all distinctions of being—being *as consciousness* and being as 'transcendent' being *'manifesting'* itself in consciousness. It is clear that this distinction can be drawn in all of its purity and appreciated only through the method of phenomenological reduction.[1]

It is not merely that the basic distinction in entities is to be found with the securing of pure consciousness, but that the reduction itself has no other task than to fix and to demonstrate this fundamental distinction of being. But now we note something remarkable: here it is being claimed that the most radical distinction of being is drawn without actually inquiring into the being of the entities that enter into the distinction. This, moreover, involves a discussion of being, a distinguishing of extant regions; in other words, it is maintained that a distinction is made in regard to being. If we press further and ask what being means here, in regard to which absolute being is distinguished from reality,[2] we search in vain for an answer and still more for an explicit articulation of the very question. In drawing this fundamental

---

1. *Ideen I*, pp. 141f (174). [Eng. tr., §76, p. 171.]
2. In the fundamental separation between being as consciousness and being as reality "yawns a veritable abyss of meaning." Ibid., p. 93 (117). [Eng. tr., §49, p. 111.]

distinction of being, not once is a question raised regarding the kind of being which the distinguished members have, or the kind of being which consciousness has, and more basically, regarding what it is which directs the entire process of making this distinction of being, in short, what the sense of being is. From this it becomes clear that *the question of being is not an optional and merely possible question, but the most urgent question* inherent in the very sense of phenomenology itself—urgent in a still more radical sense in relation to the intentional than we have so far discussed.

So we see in fact that phenomenological research, in its formative period and even more so already in its breakthrough, operates in a *fundamental neglect*, and it does so in relation to the phenomenological investigation and determination of that which must be its theme: intentional comportment and all that is given with it.

Two fundamental neglects pertaining to the question of being can be identified. *On the one hand, the question of the being of this specific entity, of the acts, is neglected; on the other, we have the neglect of the question of the sense of being itself.*

But how is it possible that a form of research whose principle is 'to the matters themselves' leaves the fundamental consideration of its most proper matter unsettled? Is phenomenological research in fact so unphenomenological that it excludes its most proper domain from the phenomenological question? Before we conclude the critique and proceed to the positive reflection, we are obliged to bring out all the approaches we can find here which nevertheless do point in the direction of determining the being of the intentional out of itself. Does not phenomenology still expressly raise the question of the being of the intentional as such after all, and does it not do so over and above the 'naturalistic attitude' first discussed? Does not this question come up of necessity as soon as phenomenology sets itself off from psychology?

a) The necessary demarcation of phenomenology from naturalistic psychology, and its overcoming

We have seen the course of such a demarcation, which did not understand the question that we designated as essentially epistemological or drawn from the theory of reason, even though this road led directly to fundamental determinations of being. Such a demarcation of phenomenology from psychology was already necessary in its initial breakthrough, inasmuch as phenomenology was elaborated from a particular psychology, the Brentanean, if we can call it that. This demarcation must obviously deal with the being of acts. This demarcation, to the extent that it is clearly focused upon acts as such, will not drift in the direction of what we have called the naturalistic attitude, in which the acts are not defined as such, but instead are treated as appendages of a material thing. That phenomenology nonetheless overcomes *naturalism* in a certain sense becomes manifest when we take a closer look at its initial breakthrough.

In its initial stage, in its breakthrough, phenomenology understood itself immediately as a struggle against *naturalism*, but against naturalism in the particular form of *psychologism*, specifically psychologism in the particular field of logic.

There was a tendency in logic to take the laws of thought as laws of the psychic processes of thought, of the psychic occurrence of thought. In opposition to this misunderstanding, Husserl, like Brentano, showed that the laws of thought are not the laws of the psychic course of thinking but laws of what is thought; that one must distinguish between the psychic process of judgment, the act in the broadest sense, and what is judged in these acts. Distinction is made between the real intake of the acts, the judging as such, and the ideal, the content of the judgment. This *distinction between real performance and ideal content* provides the basis for the *fundamental rejection of psychologism*. To the extent that phenomenology works in this direction in logic against psychologism or naturalism, it was from the beginning safeguarded from the naturalistic misunderstanding. However, it must be noted that in this demarcation in the phenomenon of judgment—judged content as ideal being or valid being on the one hand and real being or the act of judgment on the other—the distinction between the real and the ideal being of judgment is indeed confronted, *but* that precisely *the reality of this real aspect of acts is left undetermined.* The being of the judgment, its being an act, that is, the being of the intentional, is left unquestioned, so that there is always the possibility of conceiving this reality in terms of psychic processes of nature. The discovery, or better the rediscovery of the ideal exerted a fascination, cast a spell, as it were, while on the other side, the acts and processes were relegated to psychology. The elaboration of the pure field here simply led once again to norms, as we saw, without raising the central question.

b) Dilthey's endeavor of a 'personalistic psychology'— his idea of man as a person

But this phenomenological critique of naturalism was open to the direction taken by Dilthey and in fact took over his initiatives. That is, Husserl went to work in carrying out, in a phenomenological way, the task which Dilthey set for himself, which was to launch a *personalistic* psychology against the reigning *naturalistic* psychology. The psychical was now to be understood not as an event of nature but as *spirit* and *person.*

It has already been pointed out[3] that Dilthey brought with him an original understanding of phenomenology, and that he himself influenced it in the direction of the question which concerns us. Dilthey's scientific work sought to secure that way of regarding man which, contrary to scientific psychology, does not take him for its object as a thing of nature, explaining and construing him by means of other universal laws of 'events,' but instead *understands* him as a *living person actively involved in history* and *describes* and *analyzes* him in this understanding. Here we find a recognizable trend toward a new psychology, a *personalistic* one. I have already pointed out that, after the appearance of *Logical Investigations* (1900–1901), as Husserl sought to develop his position further, Dilthey exerted a special influence upon him precisely in the direction of arriving at a new psychology. But in the horizon of our question there is also the attempt to determine the being of acts themselves strictly out of themselves, and to get away from the purely naturalistic objectifying regard of the acts and of the psychic. In view of the actual theme of phenomenology, this means that we need a reflection on the definition of the starting position in the further development of phenomenology, namely, the definition of the being of consciousness with regard to the way it is given in the natural attitude. This primary kind of experience, which provides the basis for every further characterization of consciousness, turns out to be a theoretical kind of experience and not a genuinely natural one, in which what is experienced could give itself in its original sense. Instead, the manner in which what is experienced gives itself here is defined by the feature of an objectivity for a theoretical consideration of nature, and nothing else. It thus follows that the starting point for the elaboration of pure consciousness is a *theoretical* one. At first, naturally, this in itself would not be an objection or a misfortune, but surely it is afterwards, when, on the basis of the pure consciousness derived from this theoretical basis, it is claimed that the entire field of comportments may also be determined, especially the practical. In the further course of development of phenomenology, of course, the influence of the new tendency we have mentioned comes into play, seeking to go beyond the specifically naturalistic attitude and to bring a personalistic attitude into its own.

It must be asked how human Dasein is given in specifically personal experience, and how this motivates the attempt to determine and found the being of acts and the being of man. To the extent that this attempt should succeed and provide the path upon which the being of the intentional, of acts, and of the concrete Dasein of man can be determined, the ground for our critique would be taken away. It re-

---

3. Cf. §4c above.

mains to be seen to what extent this new attitude attends to the question of the being of the Dasein of man, the being of acts and of the performer of the acts, and to what extent this being is determined. To see this, we once again turn briefly to Dilthey.

Dilthey was the first to understand the aims of phenomenology. Already in the eighteen-sixties, his work was directed toward an elaboration of a new psychology. Put very generally, this was to be a science of man which apprehends man primarily as he exists as a person, as a person acting in history. With this idea of man in mind, he sought to determine this same entity scientifically. In this aim he came into conflict with the reigning psychology, which was naturalistic in the extreme, patterned after natural science. In a narrower sense, it was even a psychology of the senses. Against this *explanatory psychology*, which explains by means of hypotheses, Dilthey wanted to establish a *descriptive psychology*. Against this constructive psychology he wanted an *analytical* one. The efforts toward such a psychology, which still exists in name only, come to an initial denouement in two treatises, "Ideas on a Descriptive and Analytic Psychology"[4] and "Contributions to the Study of Individuality."[5] After the appearance of *Logical Investigations* (1900–1901) Dilthey took up this problem of a genuine personal psychology anew. The first results after his acquaintance with phenomenology are recorded in a remarkable fragment, "Studies Toward the Founding of the Human Sciences,"[6] and once again in a work of grand design in his old age, "The Construction of the Historical World in the Human Sciences."[7] Of importance is what Dilthey set forth in his "Ideas" in Chapter 7, "On the Structure of Psychic Life," basic theses which are taken up by Husserl and Scheler and analyzed more pointedly in a phenomenological fashion: that the person in his particular selfness finds himself over against a world upon which he acts and which reacts upon him; that in every aspect of being the person, the total person, reacts, not simply in willing, feeling, and reflecting, but all together always at the same time; that the life-

4. Wilhelm Dilthey, "Ideen über eine beschreibende und zergliedernde Psychologie," *Sitzungsberichte der Berliner Akademie*, 1894, esp. Ch. 7. [Now more readily available in Dilthey's *Gesammelte Schriften*, Vol. V (Stuttgart: Teubner, 1924¹, 1974⁶), pp. 139–240.]

5. Wilhelm Dilthey, "Beiträge zum Studium der Individualität," [*Sitzungsberichte der Berliner Akademie*, 1896. Cf. Dilthey, *Gesammelte Schriften*, Vol. V, pp. 241–316, where this essay also bears the title "Über vergleichende Psychologie" and includes previously unpublished chapters.]

6. Wilhelm Dilthey, "Studien zur Grundlegung der Geisteswissenschaften," *Abhandlungen der Berliner Akademie*, 1905. [Cf. Dilthey's *Gesammelte Schriften*, Vol. VII (Stuttgart: Teubner, 1973⁶), pp. 3-75.]

7. Wilhelm Dilthey, "Der Aufbau der geschichtlichen Welt in den Geisteswissenschaften," *Abhandlungen der Berliner Akademie*, 1910. [*Gesammelte Schriften*, Vol. VII, pp. 79-188.]

context of the person is in every situation one of development. In the analysis and detailed elaboration, these theses are expounded with the crude and primitive means of the old traditional psychology. But the essential point here is not so much the conceptual penetration as the sheer disclosure of new horizons for the question of the being of acts and, in the broadest sense, the being of man.

c) Husserl's adoption of the personalistic tendency in the "Logos-Essay"

This preliminary work toward a personalistic psychology was taken up by Husserl and worked into the further development of phenomenology. The initial results of these reflections appear in his published work in the already mentioned "Logos-Essay" of 1910, entitled "Philosophy as Rigorous Science."

This essay is important in several respects: first as a transition stage from the *Logical Investigations* to the *Ideas*; then in regard to the concept of reduction: the relation between the eidetic and the transcendental reduction is still left unclarified; further, on account of the concept of phenomenon and the psychic, and the lack of clarity on the 'noematic' and 'noetic'; above all, however, in its second part it typifies Husserl's position toward the problem of history, a position which must be described as impossible, rightly evoking Dilthey's dismay. But this problem does not interest us now. Our sole problem is the extent to which this treatise exhibits tendencies toward a personalistic psychology, and whether it gets beyond its initial naturalistic approach.

The best way to make this clear is to ask: How is the sense of the phenomenological theme, of pure consciousness, defined here? In contrast to the transcendent, the physical in nature, the psychic is the immanently given. It is, as Husserl says here, "the counterthrust of nature."[7a] In view of this immanent psychic character we must now ask, what in it do we investigate as its being? This question, what do we investigate in consciousness as its being, is also formulated by Husserl in this way: what in it can we grasp and define, and fix as objective unities? *Being* for Husserl means nothing other than true being, *objectivity, true for a theoretical scientific knowing*. The question of the specific being of consciousness, of lived experiences, is *not* raised here. What is raised is the question of a *distinctive way of being an object for an objective science of consciousness*. How must I take the experiential context so that universally valid assertions can be made about it, in order to define the being of consciousness in them? The answer is: if the phenomena are psychic, and so not of nature, then they have an essence

---

7a. Editor's note: *Logos*, Vol. 1, No. 3, p. 314. [Eng. tr., p. 110.]

which can be grasped, and adequately grasped, in immediate beholding. By going from the individual description of the psychic to a contemplation of its essence, I arrive at a being of consciousness which is objectively definable. What is primary in the characterization of consciousness in its being is the sense of a possible scientific objectivity and not its specifically inherent being, which precedes any possible scientific treatment and has its own sense. It is in this horizon that we should understand what Husserl now says which points in the direction of a personal determination of consciousness:

> Not without misgivings, it is true, does one consider psychology, the science of the 'psychical,' merely as a science of 'psychical phenomena' and of their connections with the body. But in fact psychology is everywhere governed by those inborn and inevitable objectivations whose correlates are the empirical unities man and animal, and, on the other hand, soul, personality, or character, i.e., disposition of personality. Still, for our purposes it is not necessary to pursue the analysis of the essence of these unity formations nor the problem of how they by themselves determine the task of psychology. After all, it immediately becomes sufficiently clear that these unities are of a kind that is in principle different from the things of nature, realities which according to their essence are such as to be given through adumbrating appearances, whereas this in no way applies to the unities in question. Only the founding substrate 'human body,' and not man himself, is a unity of real thinglike appearance; and above all, personality, character, etc. are not such unities. With all such unities we are evidently referred back to the immanent vital unity of the respective 'consciousness flow' and to morphological peculiarities that distinguish the various immanent unities of this sort. Consequently, all psychological knowledge, too, even where it is related primarily to human individualities, characters, and dispositions, finds itself referred back to those unities of consciousness, and thereby to the study of *the phenomena themselves* and of their interconnections.[8]

Here it is clear that the "unity formations" understood as those formations of experiential interrelations which we take to be a person or a personality are in principle different in kind from the thinglike realities of nature, that in fact man is now to be approached for consideration as *not-nature*. Of course, if we ask what the positive sense of this personal being is, we are again referred back to the immanent structure of consciousness with which we are already familiar under the name of pure consciousness. At bottom, we are being led back to the same basis, to the immanent reflection of acts and lived experiences, without these acts on their part being actually defined.

---

8. Ibid., pp. 319f. [Eng. tr., pp. 117f.]

In the ensuing years (1914–1915) Husserl embarked upon the path toward personalistic psychology even more energetically and at the same time worked along the lines set by the first part of the just published *Ideas toward a Pure Phenomenology*. This initial elaboration of portions of a personalistic psychology has, to be sure, never been published, but has enjoyed a far-reaching literary life in the writings of Husserl's students. Since this initial elaboration of 1914 Husserl has, on more than one occasion, set to work on a new version of a personalistic psychology. In fact, since his tenure at Freiburg, since 1916, this took the form of a lecture course entitled "Nature and Spirit," which he repeated on several occasions. His lecture course for this semester demonstrates how important this approach to this problem has now become for him; concentrated solely upon a phenomenology of mind and spirit, it is entitled "Phenomenological Psychology."[9] It is characteristic of Husserl that his questioning is still fully in flux, so that we must in the final analysis be cautious in our critique. I am not sufficiently conversant with the contents of the present stance of his investigations. But let me say that Husserl is aware of my objections from my lecture courses in Freiburg as well as here in Marburg and from personal conversations, and is essentially making allowances for them, so that my critique today no longer applies in its full trenchancy. But it is not really a matter of criticism for the sake of criticizing but criticism for the sake of laying open the issues and bringing understanding. It almost goes without saying that even today I still regard myself as a learner in relation to Husserl.

In transmitting the manuscripts of the second part of the *Ideas*,[10] Husserl in the winter wrote to me: "Ever since I began in Freiburg, however, I have made such essential advances precisely in the questions of nature and spirit that I had to elaborate a completely new exposition with a content which was in part completely altered" (letter of February 7, 1925). Accordingly, the account which was first presented here is in some ways already antiquated. One characteristic of the approach to this personalistic psychology is the context in which it is placed. The first part of the *Ideas* makes the question of pure consciousness the basis for the constitution of every reality. The second part now brings us the constitutional studies themselves: 1. *The Constitution of Material Nature*. 2. *The Constitution of Animal Nature*. 3. *The Constitution of the Human Spiritual World*, with the title *The Personalistic Attitude in Contrast to the Naturalistic*.

9. Editor's note: Edmund Husserl, *Phänomenologische Psychologie*, Husserliana Vol. IX, ed. Walter Biemel (The Hague: Nijhoff, 1962).

10. Editor's note: Edmund Husserl, *Ideen zu einer reinen Phänomenologie und phänomenologischen Philosophie, Zweites Buch* Husserliana Vol. IV, edited by Marly Biemel (The Hague: Nijhoff, 1952). [Hereafter cited by the German editor as *Ideen II*.]

The main point now is not to view the context of lived experience as an appendage to physical things but to see that experiential context as such and the ego as a psychic ego-subject.

In order to depict the naturalistic attitude, Husserl analyzes it in an example, in terms of how a cat is first given as a thing found in the world, as a material thing characterized by a corporeality with physical and, above all, aesthesiological properties. This means that this physical thing entails certain structures and moments which we call irritability, sensitivity, and the like. The surplus of reality in a living thing beyond the merely physical is not separable of itself, standing alongside this physical dimension, as it were, but is real in and with the physical itself. Because of this peculiar interconnection we can say that the psychic, the soul in its broadest sense, even though it is without extension, without spatiality, is nonetheless located in space. I can say that the cat ran over there, and I thus localize something psychic. This has a legitimate basis, made possible on the basis of the intimate connection of the aesthesiological with the physical. In this way man also can be regarded purely objectively. On the other hand, we now have a new attitude in view which in a certain sense *is quite natural but not naturalistic*. What we experience in it is not nature but, so to speak, the *psychical counterpart of nature, the counterthrust*. We slip constantly and quite effortlessly from one attitude to another, from the naturalistic to the personalistic. In living with one another, in being related to one another in attitude and in action, we experience ourselves as *persons*. This natural experience is not an artificial one which must first be acquired by special means. In fact, the attitudes are not even on the same plane, for the naturalistic is *subordinated* to the personalistic.

The priority and the understanding of the personalistic attitude is in theory clearly articulated here. But when we look more closely at how the definition of the person given in personal experience is carried out, we are referred once again to what is already familiar to us. The personalistic attitude and experience is characterized as *inspectio sui*, as an inner inspection of itself as the ego of intentionality, that is, the ego taken as subject of *cogitationes*. The very expression here already reminds us quite clearly of Descartes. Every such ego at once has its nature side as the underground of subjectivity. Mind is not an abstract ego but the full personality. Ego, man, subject as persons cannot dissolve into nature, for then what gives sense to nature would be missing.[11] "For if we eliminate all minds from the world, there is no longer a nature. But if we eliminate nature, the 'true' objectively intersubjective existence, there is always still something left: mind as individual mind. It has merely lost the possibility of sociality, the possibil-

---

11. *Ideen II*, p. 297.

ity of a comprehension which presupposes a certain intersubjectivity of the body."[12] "In the mind's stream of consciousness, however, what manifests itself in each case is its unity, its individuality."[13] Unlike things, the mind has its individuality in itself.[14] *"Minds are not really unities of appearances* but unities of absolute contextures of consciousness,"[15]—the immanently given. "Nature is the X and in principle nothing but an X defined by universal determinations. Mind, however, is not an X, but that which is itself given in the experience of mind."[16]

This is the same reflection that relates to pure consciousness as the residue of the annihilation of the world. Husserl here merely returns again to his primal separation of being under another name. Everything remains ontologically the same. The considerations of the concluding sections of this third part are typical: [§61] The Spiritual Ego and its 'Substratum'; [§62] Interplay of the Personalistic and the Naturalistic Attitude (the relationship of mind, soul, body, physical nature); [§63] Psychophysical Parallelism and Interaction; [§64] Relativity of Nature—Absoluteness of Spirit. This affords a clear glimpse into how this analysis has recourse again to the person and how it is ultimately oriented toward Descartes. The determinations of the person and its constitution end in typical considerations, in the question of the interplay of the personalistic and the naturalistic attitude, then in the question of the relationship of soul and body, spiritual and physical nature. Also raised here is the old problem of psychophysical parallelism, much discussed in the 19th century. The section concludes with the determination of the relativity of nature and the absoluteness of spirit.

d) Fundamental critique of personalistic psychology on a phenomenological basis

The answer to the question of how far this consideration of the person in the personalistic attitude has led to an intrinsic determination of the being of acts and of life itself must again prove to be relative. The fact that Husserl makes allowances for the personalistic attitude does not force us to recant and revise our critique. On the contrary, we shall see that the personalistic attitude itself serves to obstruct the question of the actual being of the acts, of the being of the intentional

---

12. Ibid.
13. Ibid., pp. 297f.
14. Ibid., pp. 298ff.
15. Ibid., p. 301.
16. Ibid., p. 302. [In the following listing of the titles of the last sections of *Ideen II*, the section numbers of the manuscript in Heidegger's possession are translated into those of the 1952 edition.]

—a thesis which applies to Dilthey's position as well. Accordingly, once again we are fundamentally on the same basis as we were with the critique of the determinations of the being of pure consciousness.

The trend toward a personalistic psychology upon a phenomeno-logical foundation of course is to be regarded positively, but under-stood in terms of our guiding reflections it still remains fundamen-tally mired in the old form of inquiry. This is shown by the first version of such an attempt, planned as the second part of the *Ideas* and carried out right after the first part. We must critically elucidate this position of personalistic psychology in three respects. We must take into account 1) that this reflection stays in the wake of the ques-tion of the constitution of reality and objectivity; 2) that the mode of access to the person is nothing other than the already defined imma-nent reflection (*inspectio sui*) upon lived experiences, from which all the theses of absolute givenness and the like are derived; 3) that the predetermination of the unity of the experiential context as a spirit and person adheres to the traditional definition of man—*homo animal rationale*—as its guide. This knowledge is in this context the most important.

[1.] The context and order in which the question of the person sur-faces is indicative of how this reflection remains in the constitutive mode. The context is prescribed by the thematic of *Ideas I*. Here it is stated how an entity as real manifests itself in its reality and how the unity of the stream of lived experience is to be defined as a unity of a comprehended objective manifold. This question is ordered accord-ing to the sequence in which the matters of the real themselves stand. The *fundamental stratum* is still the *naturally real*, upon which the psy-chic is built, and upon the psychic the spiritual. Now comes the ques-tion of the constitution of the spiritual world. It is true that the genu-ine naturality of the personalistic attitude is thematically emphasized, but the actual account still gives precedence to the investigation of nature. *The being of the person is not as such experienced in a primary way.*

[2.] The matter instead remains in the reflection on acts, in the *in-spectio sui*. Only now the theme is not the pure consciousness and pure ego but instead the isolated individual consciousness and ego. But the isolation is always conditioned by the body. Of course, it is explicitly stated that the experiential context has its intrinsic individuation, it is always the context of a particular ego-subject, but the kind of being of acts is left undetermined. Acts are performed; the ego is the pole of the acts, the self-persisting subject. This is certainly not the last step taken by Husserl in the elucidation of the unity of the stream of lived experience. We shall discuss this more appropriately first in the analy-sis of time under the caption "Stream of Lived Experience and Abso-lute Time-Consciousness."

[3.] But even if the being of acts and the unity of the experiential stream were determined in their being, the question of the *being of the full concrete man* would still remain. Can this being be, so to speak, *assembled* from the being of the material substrate, of the body, and from the soul and the spirit? Is the being of the person the *product* of the kinds of being of these layers of being? Or is it just here where it becomes evident that this way of a prior division and a subsequent composition does not get at the phenomena? Is it not just so, with any approach to the personal, that the person is taken as a *multilayered thing of the world* whose being is never reached by way of a determination of the reality of its self-directedness, no matter how extensively it is pursued? What is retained then is always only the being of an already given objective datum, of a real object. This means that it always only comes down to being as objectivity, in the sense of being an object of a reflection.

Now, this division of man and the ordination of acts, of the intentional, into such a context: the physical, body, soul, spirit—that is, the personalistic attitude—merely introduces anew the kind of consideration by which the elaboration of pure consciousness was also guided: the traditional definition of man as *animal rationale*, in which *ratio* is understood in terms of the *rational person*. The position already characterized is maintained despite or even because of the personalistic attitude. It certainly does not take man as a reality of nature, but he is still a *reality of the world which constitutes itself as transcendence in absolute consciousness*.

As superior as his analyses in the particular certainly are, Husserl does not advance beyond Dilthey. However, at least as I see it, my guess is that even though Dilthey did not raise the question of being and did not even have the means to do so, the tendency to do so was alive in him. Since Dilthey's formulations are very indefinite precisely in the dimension of the fundamental phenomena, it is impossible to document the presence of this tendency objectively.

The consideration of the possibility of the personalistic attitude has led us to a correct insight: in the background of all questions about the intentional, the psychic, about consciousness, lived experience, life, man, reason, spirit, person, ego, subject, there stands the old definition of man as *animal rationale*. But is this definition drawn from experiences which aim at a primary experience of the being of man? Or does it not come from the experience of man as an extant thing of the world—*animal*—which has reason—*rationale*—as an intrinsic property? This experience does not necessarily have to be naturalistic in an extreme sense; as we shall see, it has a certain justification not merely for a zoological and physiological consideration of man. The latent or patent prevalence of this definition provides the clue for the question of reality insofar as it is directed toward acts, whether the question is posed naturalistically or personalistically.

e) Scheler's unsuccessful attempt in determining the mode of the being of acts and of the performer of acts

Even the route taken by Scheler to define the intentional and its acts, the person and the human being, basically does not take us any further, since he also takes his orientation from the traditional definition of man as *animal rationale*. But because as he is strongly influenced by Bergson and Dilthey within the traditional way of questioning, he comes closer to the question which concerns us, which is why we expressly consider him here. For he expressly emphasizes the special character of being a person. Also, in his determination of lived experiences, acts, and the ego, he wants nothing to do with the specifically rationalistic orientation of Husserl. But Scheler also tends to regard the acts as non-psychic and to demarcate them from the psychic. He also adheres to the definition: the person is the *performer of acts*. It is true that he at the same time emphasizes that the unity of the person is not the product of lived experiences, a unity which results in a unity of form in itself, but rather that the being of the person on its part actually first determines the being of the acts. Moreover, Scheler emphasizes, as a law of essence, that the being of the person is not a universal egoity but is in each case an *individual person*.

Only a few characteristic determinations might still be presented. I do not want to go much further into Scheler's theory of the person, since this would bring in nothing new for our critical question.

A person should "never be regarded as a *thing* or a *substance* . . . endowed with whatever capacities or powers," for example, "reason." "Person is rather the immediately co-experienced *unity* of living-through [*Er-lebens*] our lived experiences" and not a thing merely thought behind and outside what is immediately lived-through.[17] A person is not a "thinglike or substantial being. . . ."[18] Every person as such (every finite person) is as person an *individual*, and initially not because of the particular contents of living-through experience or a body which fills space;[19] ". . . the being of the person can never be re-

---

17. Max Scheler, *Der Formalismus in der Ethik und die materiale Wertethik (mit besonderer Berücksichtigung der Ethik Immanuel Kants)*, Part II, Ch. 6, "Formalism and Person," *Jahrbuch für Philosophie und phänomenologische Forschung*, Vol. 2 (1916) pp. 242-464, esp. p. 243. [English translation by Manfred S. Frings and Roger L. Funk, *Formalism in Ethics and Non-Formal Ethics of Values* (Evanston: Northwestern University Press, 1973), p. 371.]

18. Ibid., p. 244. [Eng. tr., p. 372.]

19. Ibid., pp. 243f. [Eng. tr., p. 372.]

duced to being a subject of rational acts governed by certain laws."[20] A person is thus not a thing, substance, or object. This states what Husserl in the "Logos-Essay" already suggests, that the unity of the person, personality, displays a constitution essentially different from any thingness understood as nature's thingness.

What Scheler says of the person, he says even more expressly of the acts themselves. "Never, however, is an act also an object; for it belongs to the essence of the being of acts {here the question of the being of acts is explicitly raised} to be experienced only in their very performance and given in reflection"[21]—not in perception. Acts are themselves something non-psychic, belonging to the essence of the person, and the person exists only in the performance of intentional acts, so that it essentially cannot be an object.[22] The being of the first act consists rather in its performance. Precisely in this it is absolutely— not relatively—distinct from the concept of object. This performance can occur in a straightforward way and with "reflection." This reflection is not an objectification, not a "perception." Reflection is nothing but the accompaniment of a totally non-qualified consciousness of "reflections" which 'floats' with the acts being performed.[23] Reflection does not bear upon the "inner," upon objects, but upon the being of the person; it seeks to comprehend the wholeness of the being of man.

"Any psychological objectification," hence any conception of acts as something psychic, "is identical with *depersonalization*."[24] The person is in every case given as a performer of intentional acts which are bound together by the unity of a sense. Psychic being thus has nothing to do with being a person.[25] "The sole and exclusive mode of its givenness {of the person} is rather its very performance of its acts (including the performance of its reflection upon its acts)—in living its performance it simultaneously vitally experiences itself."[26] All that is act transcends psychology understood as apprehending inner events.[27] Acts are non-psychic, functions are psychic. Acts are performed, facts are effected. "Acts spring from the person into time,"[28] they are psychophysically indifferent.

We have thus noted that the mode of being of acts is not identical with psychic reality; the specific unity of acts in their being, the person in its turn, is not a thing or a substance. But when we positively ask,

20. Ibid., p. 244. [Eng. tr., p. 372.]
21. Ibid., p. 246. [Eng. tr., p. 374. The parenthetical remark is by Heidegger.]
22. Ibid., pp. 260f. [Eng. tr., pp. 387f.]
23. Ibid., p. 246. [Eng. tr., p. 374.]
24. Ibid., p. 355. [Eng. tr., p. 478.]
25. Ibid. [Correcting the German edition, which gives the wrong page number.]
26. Ibid., p. 260. [Eng. tr., p. 387; Heidegger's insertion.]
27. Ibid.
28. Ibid., p. 261. [Eng. tr., p. 388.]

how then does the being of acts get defined and what is the being of the person, the being of lived experience and the unity of such experiences, the only thing left to be said is: Acts get performed and the person is the performer. *On the mode of being of the act-performance and the mode of being of the performer of the act, silence reigns.* But it is nonetheless important for this determination of the person to try by all means to go further into the determination of acts and of their being. But when we ask fundamentally about the structure intended for being and about the conceptuality in terms of which this being is questioned, we find that the inquiry comes to a halt in these two vague determinations, "performance" and "performer." The more precise determination of acts, the connection of the act-totality understood as person with the psychic, the connection of the psychic with corporeality and of corporeality with the physical—all this is once again defined within generally traditional horizons, even though Scheler here once again makes some essential progress on the question of the relationship of the animate and psychic to corporeality. Surely in this question, Scheler, under the influence of Bergson, has made the furthest advances to date. We find these ideas discussed, admittedly in a very scattered way, in the *Ethics* of the second volume of the *Jahrbuch für Philosophie und phänomenologische Forschung* and in his text "Idols of Self-Knowledge." [29]

f) Result of the critical reflection: the neglect of the question of being as such and of the being of the intentional is grounded in the fallenness of Dasein itself

The critical reflection shows that *even phenomenological research stands under the contraints of an old tradition, especially when it comes to the most primordial determination of the theme most proper to it, intentionality. Contrary to* its most proper principle, therefore, phenomenology defines its most proper thematic matter not out of the matters themselves but instead out of a traditional prejudgment of it, albeit one which has become quite self-evident. The very sense of this prejudgment serves to deny the original leap to the entity which is thematically intended. In the basic task of determining its ownmost field, therefore, phenomenology is *unphenomenological!*—that is to say, *purportedly phenomenological!* But it is all this in a sense which is even more fundamental. *Not only is the being of the intentional,* hence the being of a particular entity, *left undetermined, but categorially primal separations in the entity* (consciousness and reality) *are presented without clarifying or even ques-*

---

29. [Cited in §10 above, note 8.]

tioning the guiding regard, that according to which they are distinguished, which is precisely *being in its sense*.

But this still *more fundamental neglect* [which leaves the sense of being as such undiscussed] is hardly a matter of mere negligence, merely overlooking a question that should have been raised, any more than the orientation to the traditional definition of man is a chance mistake. What shows itself in the neglect of the primary question of being as such is rather the force and weight of the tradition to a degree which cannot be easily overestimated. Whenever the being of entities is treated without the explicit question of it—this is the case not merely in the explicit ontologies, in particular those labelled as such [by the tradition]—then those determinations of being and categories whose basic traits were discovered by Plato and Aristotle come into play. But the results of these [traditional] reflections are in command to some extent *without* maintaining the ground from which they were drawn in the expressly interrogative experience or without first of all bringing them to such an experience. These results prevail without the initial vitality of the articulating question, that is, without the full force of the interrogative experience and its explication from which these categories originated.

The question posed by Plato in the *Sophist*,—τί ποτε βούλεσθε ση-μαίνειν ὁπόταν ὂν φθέγγησθε; "What then do you mean when you use (the word) 'being'?" In short, what does 'being' mean?—this question is so vigorously posed, so full of life. But ever since Aristotle it has grown mute, so mute in fact that we are no longer aware that it is muted, because from then on we have continually dealt with being in the determinations and perspectives handed down by the Greeks. So muted is this question that we think we are raising it without actually coming within its reach at all, without seeing that the mere application of old concepts, whether these be the expressly conscious and most traditional concepts or the even more abundant unconscious and self-evident concepts, does not yet and does not really include the question of being. So we are not really conducting our inquiry in this area.

The two neglects, 1) *the neglect of the question of being as such* and 2) *the neglect of the question of the being of the intentional* are not accidental oversights of philosophers. Rather, these omissions serve to manifest the *history of our very Dasein*—history understood not as the totality of public events but as the *mode of happening of this Dasein*. That this neglect is possible and reigns in this manner for thousands of years manifests a particular mode of the being of Dasein, a specific tendency toward decadence [*Verfall*].* This means that Dasein in this

---

*This sentence is interpolated from the Moser transcript as an indispensable transition in this context of meaning.

mode of being of *falling* [*Verfallen*], from which it does not escape, first really comes to its being when it rebels against this tendency. The dominance of the *ontological and anthropo*logical and thus also of the *logical tradition* will maintain itself in philosophy all the more readily and self-evidently, the more philosophy itself, in the projection of its tasks and questions, in the ways and means of its response to them, again inserts itself into the tradition. It does not insert itself into just any tradition but into one which is prefigured by the urgency of the matters themselves and by their treatment. In Husserl it is the assumption of the tradition of Descartes and of the *problematic of reason* stemming from him. More precisely regarded, it is the antipsychologistic impulse which in opposition to naturalism exhibits essential being, the priority of the theory of reason and especially of the epistemological—the idea of a pure constitution of reality in the nonreal—and *its idea of absolute and rigorous scientificity.*

In Scheler we can, at least at times, note the assumption of Augustinian-Neoplatonic and Pascalian motives of thought. In both cases the tradition of classical Greek philosophy* is operative latently. Insofar as it is a matter of the specific question of spirit, reason, ego, life, the tradition is governed by the definition of man already mentioned—*animal rationale*. Husserl is oriented more toward the secular definition, while Scheler expressly takes the specifically Christian definition of man into his formulation of the idea of person, and so makes his position several degrees more dogmatic. At this point I cannot go into the detailed history of this definition and its essential import for inquiry within philosophy, especially in theology during the Christian period. I shall characterize only very briefly the connection of the definition of person given by Scheler with the specifically Christian definition of man.

Inasmuch as Scheler sees the person in the unity of acts, which means in their intentionality, he says: the essence of man is the intention toward something or, as he puts it, the very gesture of transcendence. Man is an eternal out-towards, in the way that Pascal calls man a god-seeker. The only meaningful idea of man (Scheler) is a theomorphism through and through, the idea of an X which is a finite and living image of God, his likeness, one of his infinite shadows on the wall of being. This is of course more a literary formulation than a scientific explanation, but it still shows Scheler's definition of the being of man.

This conception of man can be found quite early, for example, in

---

*Reading *Philosophie* here instead of *Tradition*.

Tatian's Λόγος πρὸς Ἕλληνας:[30] "Here I do not mean man as ζῷον and in his conduct as a living being but as he is, in a certain sense, underway towards God." This is the definition that Calvin later formulated along the same lines when he says: "Man's first condition was excellent because of these outstanding endowments: that reason, intelligence, prudence, judgment should suffice not only for the government of this earthly life, but that by them he might ascend beyond, even unto God and to eternal felicity."[31] Here, clearly, the determination of the being of man is based on his transcendence, on this being-directed-out toward something. Similarly, Zwingli says: "Man thus also . . . *looks up* to God and his Word, he indicates clearly that in his very nature he is born somewhat closer to God, is something *more after his stamp*, that he has something that *draws him to* God—all this comes beyond a doubt from his having been created in God's image."[32] The emphasis here is not only on the characteristic determination of man as underway towards God but also on the constant orientation toward the statement in *Genesis*, "Let us make man in our own image and likeness,"[33] which even in the middle ages directed all anthropology and anthropological inquiry. Later Kant, in defining the rational person of man in his own fashion, adopted the old Christian definition of man, detheologized only to some extent.

This very rough account is presented only in order to come to understand the neglects uncovered by our critique, not as 'mistakes' which can be easily corrected, but as the power of the historical Dasein which we ourselves are condemned or called to be. To this last alternative we can surely respond only out of personal conviction. No scientific judgment is possible here. Perhaps even the alternative is no longer a genuine one.

---

30. Tatian, *Rede an die Griechen*, translated and provided with introductions by Dr. V. Gröne (Kempten, 1872), Ch. 15, p. 49.
31. Calvin, *Institutio* I, 15, §8.
32. Zwingli, "Von klarheit und gewüsse des worts Gottes" (*Deutsche Schriften* I, 56). [Page correction follows *Sein und Zeit*, p. 49, note 2.]
33. Genesis 1:26.

MAIN PART

Analysis of the Phenomenon of Time and Derivation of the Concept of Time

FIRST DIVISION

Preparatory Description of the Field in Which the Phenomenon of Time Becomes Manifest

Chapter One

The Phenomenology That Is Grounded in the Question of Being

§14. Exposition of the question of being from the radically understood sense of the phenomenological principle

Our critical reflection on phenomenology has clarified in what horizon of being intentionality, its theme, has been placed. It has shown that this determination of the thematic field does not draw that field from a prior and original explication of the being of the intentional; and that the task of drawing the fundamental distinctions of being does not take up the basic task which precedes it, that of raising the question of the sense of being as such. Together with these insights, it became evident that these two questions, that of being as such and that of the character of the being of the intentional, must be raised in the light of the principle most proper to phenomenology. At the very least, it became evident that the development of the phenomenological theme can proceed in a counter-phenomenological direction. This insight does not serve to drive phenomenology outside of itself but really first brings phenomenology right back to itself, to its ownmost and purest possibility.

The greatness of the discovery of phenomenology lies not in factually obtained results, which can be evaluated and criticized and in these days have certainly evoked a veritable transformation in questioning and working, but rather in this: it is the *discovery of the very possibility of doing research in philosophy.* But a possibility is rightly understood in its most proper sense only when it continues to be taken as a possibility and preserved as a possibility. Preserving it as a possibility does not mean, however, to fix a chance state of research and inquiry as ultimately real and to allow it to harden; it rather means to keep open the tendency toward the matters themselves and to liberate this tendency from the persistently pressing, latently operative and spurious bonds [of the tradition]. This is just what is meant by the motto "Back to the matters themselves": to let them revert to themselves.

Phenomenological questioning in its innermost tendency itself leads to the question of the being of the intentional and before anything else to the question of the sense of being as such. Phenomenology radicalized in its ownmost possibility is nothing but the questioning of Plato and Aristotle brought back to life: *the repetition, the retaking of the beginning of our scientific philosophy.*

But does this not once again relinquish all the critical caution necessary when one is dealing with the tradition? Is the question of being, just because of its venerable antiquity going all the way back to Parmenides, in the end not also a prejudice of the tradition? Why do we make an exception here? Should we ask about being only because the Greeks asked? Is the question of being to be put so that phenomenology may be more radically defined, thus only so that there may be a phenomenology? Neither of these reasons can be the basis for our inquiry. Are there still presuppositions, specifically presuppositions which allow us to recover the ground for the question of being simply from the question itself? The sole ground of possibility for the question of being as such is *Dasein itself insofar as it is possible, in its discoveredness in possibilities.*

Four presuppositions can be named: 1) the principle itself; 2) the question of being is somehow already emphatically there in understanding; 3) entities are experienced; 4) the distortion of the question of being and its deflection from its course can be found in the history of Dasein and grounded in Dasein only if something like the propensity toward the question of being belongs to its being and its historicity. There is a neglect only because Dasein is defined as *care.*

All of this would in fact be dogmatic and contrary to the phenomenological principle of working and questioning out of the matters themselves, if phenomenology itself included one or more theses which already contained a statement about particular domains of subject matter or about the priority of certain concepts. But we have noted that phenomenology is first of all a *pure methodological concept* which only specifies the *how* of the research. The aspiration to carry it through to completion is nothing other than setting out to do the most radical research in philosophy. But inasmuch as phenomenology is also defined by its theme (intentionality), it still includes a prior decision on just what, among the manifold of entities, its theme really is. Why this should be precisely intentionality is not definitively demonstrated. We have only an account of the fact that the basic theme in the breakthrough and development of phenomenology is intentionality. Our critical investigation has specifically led us beyond this theme.

The neglect of the question of the being of the intentional revealed in itself a more original question, that of being as such. To be sure, this question is also already a specific question, but we shall have to consider whether it, when taken as a scientific question, might not be a prejudgment, something dogmatic and prejudiced.

A question is a prejudgment when it at the same time already contains a definite answer to the issue under question, or when it is a blind question aimed at something which cannot be so questioned. But now, entities are familiar to us and being is in a certain sense understood. The question of being as such, however, when it is put in a sufficiently formal manner, is the *most universal* and *emptiest*, but perhaps also the *most concrete* question, which a scientific inquiry can ever raise. *This question can be attained in any entity*; it need not be intentionality. It does not even have to be an entity taken as a theme of a science. But we come to the question of being as such only if our inquiry is guided by the drive to *question to the very end* or *to inquire into the beginning*, that is, if it is determined by the sense of the phenomenological principle radically understood—which means by the matter itself—*to allow entities to be seen as entities in their being.*

To put this question phenomenologically means, if we follow its sense, to put it as an exploratory question which questions from the matters themselves. But this at the same time implies what was already said about "setting out to do the most radical research in philosophy." It is "in philosophy" and not in an already given theory laden with definite problem-horizons, disciplines and conceptual schemata that philosophy, under the guidance of the phenomenological principle, is to be restored to itself.

If the phenomenologically attained *fundamental question* of being is presented as the question which came to life with the classical scientific philosophy of the Greeks, this historical fact should not be taken as an authority which establishes the correctness of the question. Rather, it can only be taken as an indication that this question is itself apparently in line with our research inquiry. Why should philosophy raise precisely this most universal question of being? What is philosophy, when it must raise this question? Whence is the being of philosophy itself to be understood? More later on what all this implies.

a) Assumption of the tradition as a genuine repetition

The assumption of the tradition is *not* necessarily traditionalism and the adoption of prejudices. The *genuine repetition* of a traditional question lets its external character as a tradition fade away and pulls back from the prejudices.

This process of having recourse and seeking a connection to traditional philosophies has also been the way the conception of phenomenology is defined for the broader scientific public. The two main directions of phenomenology, established by Husserl and by Scheler, were regarded directly in terms of the degree to which they established a connection with already extant philosophies, while the truly positive tendencies and the positive work itself were far less appreciated and understood. The matters discovered were not understood phenomenologically but were taken for granted. The new horizons for researching such matters were explained instead from what was traditionally known and so assimilated by modification. But this process of having recourse and seeking a connection to the tradition includes the assumption of particular interrogative contexts and particular concepts which certainly in turn are then clarified relatively along phenomenological lines and conceived more or less rigorously. However, we not only want to understand that such a contact with the tradition brings prejudices with it. We also want to establish a genuine contact with the tradition. For the opposite way would be just as fantastic, represented in the opinion that a philosophy can be built in mid-air, just as there have often been philosophers who believed that one can begin with nothing. Thus, the contact with the tradition, the return to history, can have a double sense. On the one hand, it can be purely a matter of traditionalism, in which what is assumed is itself not subjected to criticism. On the other hand, however, the return can also be performed so that it goes back *prior* to the questions which were posed in history, and the questions raised by the past are once again originally appropriated. This possibility of assuming history can then also show that the assumption of the question of the sense of being is not merely an external repetition of the question which the Greeks already raised. If this formulation of the question of being is a genuine one, then the repetition must rather bring us to understand that the Greek formulation of the question was conditioned and provisional and, what is more, had to be so.

b) Modification of the thematic field,
the scientific way of treating it
and the previous self-understanding of
phenomenology by critical reflection on the
fundamental question of being as such

The critical reflection revealed the phenomenologically fundamental question of being as such without also bringing out the ground of this question. But this ground, and with it the presupposition of the question, can be made clear only after the question is first raised. Pronouncing and uttering the interrogative sentence does not yet raise the question itself. After the manner of the statements of idle chatter, there are also questions which are merely asserted. The critical reflection at this point showed us that phenomenological questioning can begin in the most obvious of matters. But this "matter of course" means that the phenomena are not really exposed to the light of day, that the ways to the matters are not without further ado ready-made, and that there is the constant danger of being misled and forced off the trail. This in general is precisely what constitutes the sense of phenomenology as expository research.

We already noted that inherent in the phenomenon is the possibility of pretending-to-be: *semblance*. Put positively, this at the same time means: so much seeming, so much being. This means that wherever something passes itself off as this or that, what passes itself off retains the possibility of becoming manifest in itself and thus receiving definition. Accordingly, wherever semblance is identified, wherever semblance is apprehended and understood, there one already finds the allusion to something positive of which the seeming is the semblance. This 'of which' is not something 'behind' the experience but shines forth in the semblance itself. This precisely is the essence of seeming.

Just as the phenomena cannot be given without effort—it is rather incumbent upon research to arrive at the phenomena—so likewise is the concept of phenomenology not something which can be definitively determined in a single stroke. Our critical reflection has led us to question whether the thematic field of phenomenology is adequately determined. But this at the same time suggests that the scientific way of handling the theme is modified in its sense in accordance with the more radical conception of the thematic field. The critical reflection likewise gives us reason to doubt the previously given definition of phenomenology as 'analytic description of intentionality in its apriori.' Perhaps the phenomenologically original definition of intentionality and in particular the fundamental conception of its being entail a modification of the method of 'analytic description in the apriori.' In the end, there is also a modification of the customary division in phenomenology of the different groups of investigations into the phenomenologies of act, subject matter, and relation. Intentionality is indeed the doublet of *intentio* and *intentum*. In these two directions, one distinguished the elaboration of the *intentio*, the act, of the *intentum*, that to which the act is directed, and finally the elaboration of the relation between these two. A more refined conception of the entity having the character of the intentional will permit us to see and so supersede the threefold basis of this distinction. The closer determination of being will further lead to a more refined conception of the sense of the apriori. Heretofore, the apriori was specified as that which is always already there, that is, it was characterized on the basis of a particular concept of being, the Greek concept.

The more radical conception of being as such will bring a modification of the concept of the apriori, but this will be accompanied by a modification of our way of apprehending the apriori as well, of ideation. As before in phenomenology corresponding to its apriori, which was not truly understood but conceived in conjunction with the Greek concept of being, so likewise is ideation, in its corresponding logic, conceived as a logic of the experience of this sort of being, a logic which is then apprehension of the general, generalization. The more precise determination of the thematic field will later pave the way for a more suitable conception of the mode of apprehension, which up to now was seen only as description, a descriptive account of the simply apprehended subject matter itself. This tells us nothing about the *sense* of its apprehension. Something can be made of that sense only when the matter itself is clearly specified in the sense of its being. It will thus become apparent that description has the character of *interpretation*, since that which is the theme of the description becomes accessible in a specific kind of interpretation, *expository interpretation*.

But for the time being, we are faced with the sole task of elaborating the fundamental question *What is meant by being?* according to the phenomenological principle, in a phenomenologically radical manner. Results of the phenomenological research and the definition of this science may for the moment be left undecided.

c) Unfolding the question of being with time as our guiding clue

The introductory considerations operating as immanent criticism have led to the fundamental question: What is meant by being? What is the being of the intentional? Our preliminary remarks clarifying the theme of the lecture course have already suggested that *time* has a distinctive function to play in distinguishing the kinds of being, and that the traditional realms of being are distinguished according to temporal, supratemporal, and extratemporal being. It was even stated there that the *history of the concept of time, that is, the history of the discovery of time, is the history of the question of the being of entities.* It was also suggested there that the history of the attempts to determine entities in their being is perhaps the *history of the decline and the distortion of this basic question of scientific research.*[1]

When we now take up the question of being, we shall in the course of these considerations come across the phenomenon 'time' and in accord with our question be led to an explication of time. The first portion of our actual considerations is accordingly *the exposition of the question of being.* Let us recall the outline given earlier:

The First Part {that is, the Main Part} has as its theme *The Analysis of the Phenomenon of Time:*

1) The preparatory description of the field in which the phenomenon of time becomes manifest. This is nothing other than what the critical deliberations have now revealed as necessary—*the exposition of the question of being.*

2) The exposition of time itself.

3) The conceptual interpretation.[2]

If we proceed in this way, it might seem that what we have thus far considered and gone through is unrelated to what follows, so that we could have spared ourselves this passage through phenomenology in the form of an immanent critique, especially since it was expressly emphasized that the question of the being of entities can in principle be put to any entity. We do not need the specific entity of intentionality in order to awaken the question of the being of entities. Why this circumstantial and complicated consideration, and possibly a consideration of that which in a way is antiquated? What was the point of the consideration if we are assuming no propositions from phenomenology but, in the spirit of phenomenology, once again have to demonstrate any proposition which may possibly be taken up?

But the connections of the following considerations with the presuppositions are not so simple. Also, to begin with, we do not wish to speak any further about this. We only emphasize that we certainly do not presuppose any phenomenological results in the sense that we made deductions from them; we inquire always and only in a phenomenological way without going along with particular theses and results. There is an *intrinsic material connection between* what we treated in the Introduction [i.e., Preliminary Part] and what we now take as our

---

1. Cf. §2 above, p. 6.
2. Editor's note: Cf. §3 above, p. 8. These titles match our division headings. The third was not carried out.

theme. And we shall soon see that the very next steps that we take will lead us back to what we have already discussed from a particular perspective.

We now proceed to the First Division of the Main Part: *Preparatory Description of the Field in Which the Phenomenon of Time Becomes Manifest.* We shall confront this task more accurately under the heading which points to its material connection to the previous considerations: *The Elaboration of the Question of Being in Terms of an Initial Explication of Dasein.*

Chapter Two

Elaboration of the Question of Being in Terms of an Initial Explication of Dasein

§15. Emergence of the question of being
from an indeterminate preunderstanding of Dasein—
question of being and understanding of being

The question of being must be *articulated*. In other words, this question, What is being?, must not be raised blindly and arbitrarily. And the answer to this question must not be guessed at aimlessly and arbitrarily. The question must be *articulated*, that is, *it must be raised as a question for research*. It is asked with the intention of doing investigative work. To articulate the question of being means to elaborate it as a question in such a way that this elaboration will arrive at the secure horizon of inquiry into the being of entities (the horizon of the question) along with the outline of the way and the steps of the investigation which seeks to find the answer. This outline is the prefiguration of that from which the answer is drawn and in which it is confirmed.

The question asks about being. What does being mean? Formally, the answer is: Being means this and that. The question seeks an answer which determines something which is somehow already given in the very questioning. The question is what is called a *question of definition*. It does not ask whether there is anything like being at all, but rather what is meant by it, what is understood under it, under 'being.' When we thus ask about the sense of being, then being, which is to be determined, is in a certain way already understood. In a certain way: here this means according to a *wholly indeterminate preunderstanding*, an indeterminacy whose character can however be phenomenologically grasped. We ('Anyone') do not know what 'being' means, and yet the expression is in some sense understandable to each of us. Whatever the sources of the influx of such understanding into the individual, whether they are transmitted theories and opinions, whether they are obtained in explicit appropriation or are merely taken over, whether there is a knowledge of this influx and its resources, all this at first makes no difference. There is an understanding of the expression 'being,' even if it borders on a mere understanding of the word.

The question is asked on the basis of this indeterminate preunderstanding of the expression 'being.' What is meant by 'being'? Even this unoriented and vague preunderstanding is *still an understanding*. It bears as it were the possibility of the question within itself. It is the source of the questioning in the sense of seeking for the grounded demonstration of what is not yet understood. More precisely, the explicit questioning is in its sense immediately understood from this understanding. The questioning is itself as it were still indefinite. We constantly make use of this indefinite meaning and concept 'being,' so extensively, in fact, that we are not even aware that we are using 'being' in an indefinite meaning. This is so even as we elaborate the question: What '*is*' being? What '*is*' pertinent to its '*being*'? We *always already live in an understanding of the '*is*'* without being able to say more precisely what it actually means. This indicates that the understanding of 'being' and a certain concept of 'being' is always already there. Why this is so, and how this fact is to be understood more precisely, shall be discussed later.

§16. Interrogative structure of the question of being

The question asks about what being means. *The sense of being is what is asked for* [*das Erfragte*] in the question, what is to be arrived at in the question. This means that what the question as such has to attain, what is to be brought out in the answer, is the sense of being. Examined more carefully, what is *asked about* in what is thus asked for? When being is thus asked for, it involves inquiring into the basic character of the entity, what defines an entity as entity. What defines the entity as entity is *its being*. The sense of being implies *what is asked about* [*das Gefragte*]—*the being of the entity*. In other words, what is asked for implies what is asked about. If the entity is to be defined in its being, it must be interrogated on its being. What is asked about—the being of the entity—and so the demonstrative definition of the sense of being is demonstrable only if the entity itself as entity is *interrogated* on its being. This means that the entity must in itself be accessible in its being. *What is interrogated* [*das Befragte*] is the entity itself. What is asked about implies what is interrogated, the sense of being of an entity implies the entity itself. Thus, to begin with, we have elicited a threefold distinction in the structure of the question and the inquiry. Very formally, these are: 1. What is *asked for*: the sense of being.

2. What is *asked about*: the being of entities. 3. What is *interrogated*: the entity itself.

The question is properly articulated when the inquiry is worked out in the right way in these three essential parts. The question must therefore be expounded more clearly in terms of these three parts.

Let us begin with the third part. In order to seek the being of the entity through questioning, the entity itself must be interrogated on its being. For this, *what is interrogated* must necessarily be experienced in itself. We call many a thing an entity or what is, and many of them in a different sense. What-is is in a certain sense everything of which we speak, which we intend, toward which we act, and, even if only as to something inaccessible, everything to which we are related and all of that which we ourselves are and how we are. Now *which* entity is to be experienced in itself? Which entity is it then in which the potential sense of being can be obtained and read off? And in the event it can be determined, what is the mode of experience and of access to this entity, so that it can become manifest in itself? In regard to the determinations of what is interrogated, the unfolding of the question of being contains a double determination: first, that of *the* entity which is to give the sense of being originally and authentically; and the other is the determination of the *right sort of access* to the entity in order to bring out the sense of being.

Second, the question contains *what it asks about*. This implies that what is interrogated, the entity, is *interrogated on something*. In the inquiry the entity is not accepted purely and simply in itself; it is undertaken 'as' and taken up *as this and that*; it is *taken* in *regard to* its being. In the question the interrogated is addressed: one as it were *inquires of it* about its being. What is interrogated is an entity insofar as something is sought in it. The inquiry includes this interrogation on something. This interrogation needs the indication of a direction which it has to take in order to bring out in the entity its being. Not only must the right kind of experience of the entity itself be fixed, but also the *regard* in which I have to take the interrogated entity must be determined, so that I may catch a glimpse of the likes of 'being' in it at all. We shall provisionally determine the regard from these two points of view: first from the direction of the inquisitive looking upon, and second from the on-which in the entity, in regard to which what is interrogated is to be quizzed.

Finally, there is in what is asked about, thirdly, *what is itself asked for*, the being whose sense is sought. In other words, the inquiry is in search of what being *means*, how it is to be conceived. What is asked for includes the search for its *concept*. The articulation of the question, if it is to be a lucid research question in which distinctions can be drawn, must contain a determination of the possibility and kind of conceptuality pertinent to what is asked for, the sort of sense it has, whether it is a category or the like. More accurately, this means that we shall now have to stipulate, quite apart from the characterization of its content, just what 'being' actually is with a view to its determinability, whether it is something like a category or in that vein. *The inquiry thus includes this threefold aspect*: 1) the originary prior experience of what primarily is to be interrogated and the specification of the kind of experience; 2) the preparatory outlook in the interrogating regard itself upon what is sought in it, being; 3) the characterization of the sense of what is asked about as such, its conceptuality.

The formal framework of the question of being is thus relatively easy to characterize. By contrast, the necessity of a concrete elaboration of the articulation of the question brings us before special tasks. This elaboration is concerned especially with the development of clues. What must the elaboration of the articulation do?

Starting from what is interrogated, we have to determine the original mode of experience and of access regarding what is asked about, the way of looking at it and the content of the regard. In relation to what is sought by asking, what needs clarifying is the specific manner of conceiving and of understanding the concepts in which the answer to the question of being is to be given, the specific conceptuality. But what is it which must be determined here: the access to, the experience of, the looking upon, the considering as, the conceiving and understanding as? Are not such modes of access and of experience themselves already entities? In order to properly articulate the question of the being of entities, do we not in advance and to this end itself have to define and delimit an entity? The question of being and its articulation will become all the more lucid, the more truly we have made this entity manifest, namely, the being of the questioning of the questioner himself. In order to answer the question of the being of entities, therefore, what is demanded is the *prior elaboration of an entity on its being*, that entity which we call questioning.

Is this not an obvious circle? We shall let this objection stand in order to settle it later. Let us only stress this for the time being: The objection that there is a circle here only has sense where it is a matter of deducing and proving propositions from other propositions. Thus there is a circle when propositions C and D, which are to be deduced from propositions A and B, are themselves brought into play to prove A and B, to prove that by which they themselves are to be proved. In our case, however, it is not a matter of deducing propositions and propositional sequences from one another, but of working out the access to the matters from which propositions are to be drawn to begin with. But above all, it should be noted that formal objections, like this alleged circle, at first and right in the beginning of such fundamental considerations are always sterile. They decide nothing at all for the understanding of the matter but only retard these investigations. And the beginning of these investigations is itself unmistakable: either we articulate the question of the being of the entity, or we leave it un-articulated and let the answer remain in the dark. But when one dispenses with the articulation of this question, then one deprives oneself of the right ever to say anything at all conceptually and scien-tifically about being and about an entity as entity. But if the question is to be articulated, then we have here at the very least agreed that it must itself be worked out as a lucid question. In that case, the entity whose character is access, experience, etc., must itself be illuminated in its being, to the point where the danger of a circle exists. But this would be a circle of searching, of going and of being, a 'circle of being,' a circularity of an entity which it is pertinent to understand. It is from this circularity that the popular and traditional objection of a circle in the proof first arises. In any case, there is no circle of proof involved here.

§17. Correlation of the question of being and the questioning entity (Dasein)

The more authentically and purely this entity of questioning, expe-riencing, and conceiving is worked out in its being, the more radically will the answer to the question of being be given. This entity will be more purely elaborated, the more originally it is experienced, the more adequately it is conceptually determined, the more authentically the relationship of being to it is secured and conceived. Such a rela-tionship will be secured more genuinely, when prejudices and opin-ions about it play a less decisive role, be these ever so obvious and gen-erally recognized; and the more it can show itself from out of itself, the more it becomes definable as a phenomenon.

When it comes to the task of working out this very questioning of being, then it must be remembered that this questioning in its turn is already an entity. The questioning is itself an entity which is given with the question of the being of an entity in the act of carrying out the questioning, whether it is expressly noted or not. For now this en-tity must be secured more precisely. The more authentically this oc-curs, the more assurance we have that the question of being will be articulated with lucidity. We thus have a very distinctive questioning inasmuch as in the content of the question, in what is asked for, what is asked for is itself what the questioning itself is. What is asked for in it, the sense of being, is thereby given in all indeterminacy, as indeter-minate as only what is sought can be.

If the questioning is genuine, then it has to be adequate to what it asks for, to the degree that this is possible. The questioning must therefore rightly understand what it asks when it asks about being. What it asks for here as such refers back to the very questioning, inasmuch as this questioning is an entity. In asking about being, however, we do not raise the question of the being of the entity which the questioning itself is; but we do satisfy the sense of the question of being when we first uncover the questioning as an entity simply in what it is. We cannot yet explicitly ask about the sense of this questioning, since it is itself seeking to specify more precisely this questioning and this raising of the question as an entity in terms of its 'what,' as an already given what. As what is this entity, of which we say that it questions, looks upon, considers as, relates, etc.—already given? It is *the* entity which we ourselves are; this entity, which I myself am in each particular instance, we call the *Dasein*.

To work out the articulation of the question of the sense of being thus means to exhibit the questioning, that is, the Dasein itself, as an entity; for only in this way does what is sought become something sought in its most proper sense. The questioning is here itself co-affected by what it asks for, because the questioning is after being and questioning is itself an entity. This affectedness of the questioning entity by what is asked for belongs to the ownmost sense of the question of being itself. In accordance with this, the phenomenological principle ["Back to the matters themselves!"] must be taken into account if the question is to be lucidly articulated. The questioning is the entity which is expressly given with the question, but at the same time it is also given in such a way that at first and before all it is overlooked in the course of the questioning. Here the attempt will be made precisely not to overlook this entity from the very start, not to overlook it precisely in view of the questioning of being itself.

The actual elaboration of the articulation of the question is accordingly a *phenomenology of Dasein*; but it already finds the answer and finds it purely as a research answer, because the elaboration of this articulation concerns the entity which has within itself a *distinctive relationship of being*. Dasein is here not only *ontically* decisive but also *ontologically* so for us as phenomenologists.

If we turn back to history, back to the time when the question of being appeared for the first time, in Parmenides, here we already see this peculiar bond. The union is here taken to be so close that in a sense what is asked about and is determined in its being is identified with the interrogative and experiential comportment: τὸ γὰρ αὐτὸ νοεῖν ἐστίν τε καὶ εἶναι, "Being is the same as the apprehending of the entity in its being." Here the question about what being is already expressly includes the act of experiencing what is interrogated, even

though the question itself is still not even explicitly present in its structure. Later, when the question of being is worked out at a higher level,
in Plato and Aristotle, the question of οὐσία includes a corresponding
consideration of the act of interrogative determination, of the λόγος,
the question of being includes the διαλέγεσθαι, the dialectic; the apprehension of εἶδος includes the ἰδεῖν. But the characteristic feature
is that the λόγος and the ἰδεῖν, the addressing and the viewing, are
treated as accessory, as concurrent, because a concurrent treatment of
λόγος and ἰδεῖν is necessary in order to be able to treat the question at
all meaningfully. That Plato came to the question of *logos* in the sense
of dialectic lies simply in the sense of the very question which he
posed and as he posed it, in the sense of the question of being, which
itself calls for the determination of questioning as an entity.

The very matter which is asked for, which here is being, demands
the exhibition of the entity *Dasein*. Only the phenomenological tendency—to clarify and to understand being as such—bears within itself the task of an explication of the entity which is the questioning
itself—the *Dasein* which we, the very questioners, are. The explication
of Dasein does not stem from some sort of special interest in the psychology of man, nor from a question of world view asking about the
sense and purpose of our life. Nor is it an outstanding problem which
is still left over, like the elaboration of a philosophical anthropology
within the framework of the remaining philosophical disciplines,
which leads to this primal task of an analysis of Dasein, but solely the
fully understood and phenomenologically secured sense of the question—what is asked for, what is asked about, what is interrogated, and
the questioning.

Working out the articulation of the question is the preliminary experience and explication of the questioning entity itself, of the Dasein
which we ourselves are. It is a matter of an entity to which we have this
distinctive, at any rate noteworthy, relationship of being: we are it itself—an entity which is only insofar as I am it. It is a matter of an
entity which to us is the nearest. But is it also what is first given to us,
that is, the immediately given? In this respect it is perhaps the farthest. Thus it happens that when we ask about it as such, when this
entity is defined, it tends not to be defined at all from an originary
apprehension of itself. This entity which we ourselves are and which
in respect to its givenness is the farthest from us is to be defined phenomenologically, brought to the level of phenomenon, that is, experienced in such a way that it shows itself in itself, so that we draw out of
this phenomenal givenness of Dasein certain basic structures which
are sufficient to make the concrete question of being into a transparent question. That we with good reason or almost of necessity first
ask about this entity, the Dasein, in such a way that we exhibit it provi-

sionally, that we necessarily begin with it, will be established from our growing knowledge of the structure of the being of this very entity. It will be shown that the necessity in the question of being to start from the clarification of questioning as an entity is demanded by this entity itself, by the questioning. This entity, the questioner, itself makes use of a particular sense of being, just the sense which, as we already noted, maintains itself in a certain lack of understanding, a lack which must be defined. Our next task is now the explication of Dasein as the entity whose way of being is questioning itself.

Chapter Three

The Most Immediate Explication of Dasein Starting from its Everydayness. The Basic Constitution of Dasein as Being-in-the-World.

In this explication of Dasein we shall come upon a series of formulations which at first will seem strange and above all will perhaps seem quite involved. But this clumsiness in formulation and definition lies in the theme and in the very nature of the investigation. For to give a narrative account of an entity is one thing, and to comprehend that entity in its being is another. For the latter task, often not only the words are lacking but the very grammar as well. For our language, for reasons which we shall have to consider, in following its natural bent, first addresses and expresses the entity as a world and not the entity which is speech itself, so that our stock of words and expressions is first oriented in its sense to entities which we in our case here really do not have as our theme. But even when we try to explicate the being of the entity whose expression is first intended in language, namely the entity of the world as it is there for us, even here there are enough difficulties in finding a suitable formulation for the structures of being in the entity; for here too the propensity is first toward the entity and not toward being. If we are forced here to introduce ponderous and perhaps inelegant expressions, it is not a matter of personal whim or a special fancy for my own terminology, but the compulsion of the phenomena themselves. Those who have explored these matters and can claim to be far greater than we have not escaped the difficulty of adequate expression in this field. One might compare the passages which analyze being in Plato's *Parmenides* or Aristotle's *Metaphysics* Z 4 with a narrative chapter in Thucydides. Then one would see the difference in linguistic style and, if one has some feel for the language, note the outrageous formulations which made presumptuous demands upon the Greeks of their time. But for us what is at issue is the analysis of an entity which is even more difficult than what Plato took for his theme, while on the other hand our powers are much more modest for this task of securing this entity in a first approximation. If such formulations come up often, no offence should be taken. There is no such thing as the beautiful in the sciences, least of all perhaps in philosophy.

§18. Acquisition of the fundamental structures of the basic constitution of Dasein

It must basically be stressed that the following considerations will not try to present the thematic analysis of Dasein as such; but several essential basic structures are first located in what we have in advance in order to permit us to ask even more basic questions from them. Dasein is to be laid out in its *basic constitution*, in its *average* understanding, so that we may articulate the question of being lucidly. In the initial explication only a few phenomena are to be made manifest. But these are the very phenomena which we are to understand as *fundamental structures* of Dasein. The first aim of this analysis is therefore not so much a fully realized apprehension of all specific structures. Its first aim is rather to lay out the basic constitution of this entity as a whole. This does not require the unbroken fullness of the structures included in this totality along with the adequate and full research horizon which accompanies these structures in their entirety. This is why it is so important first of all to gain the security of the line of sight and to have the theme of the investigation clearly before us. This theme is not a strange and unfamiliar matter but on the contrary the nearest, which is perhaps precisely why it leads us astray into mistakes. What constantly conceals the phenomenal context to be laid open in this entity is the mistaking and misinterpreting indigenous to our intimate familiarity with the entity. But just to the extent that this entity is in one respect especially close to the investigator, it is that much easier to pass over. The obvious is not even a possible theme at the outset. Since the securing of the direction of vision and the setting aside of misleading lines of questioning remains the immediate requirement, it is urgent at the outset to bring an immediately phenomenal and basically coherent set of structures into view.

a) The Dasein is in the 'to be it at its time'

We have already alluded to the fundamental determination of the entity under consideration: Dasein is the entity which *I myself am in each instance*, in whose being I as an entity 'have an interest' or share, an entity which *is* in each instance *to be** it in my own way. This determination indicates the distinctive relationship of being which we 'have' to this entity: *to be it itself*, not in the manner of an entity of nature, solely to apprehend it, to have it available in some way. This is the phenomenal motive for calling this entity which we ourselves are *Dasein* [literally "to be there"]. This peculiar fundamental character which we can now render manifest only in a very formal way is to be regarded more closely as our considerations continue.

This designation 'Dasein' for the distinctive entity so named does not signify a *what*. This entity is not distinguished by its what, like a chair in contrast to a house. Rather, this designation in its own way expresses *the way to be*. It is a very specific expression of being which is here chosen for an entity, whereas at first we [normally] always name an entity in terms of its what-content and leave its specific being undetermined, because we hold it to be self-evident.

This relationship of being to the entity which I myself am characterizes this '*to-be*' as the '*in each instance mine*.' The mode of being—*to be it*—is essentially *to be it in each instance mine*, whether I expressly know about it or not, whether I have lost myself in my being (cf. the Anyone) or not. The fundamental character of the being of Dasein is therefore first adequately grasped in the determination, *an entity which is in the to-be-it-at-its-time*. This 'in each particular instance' [*je*], 'at the (its) time' [*jeweilig*], or the structure of the 'particular while' [*Jeweiligkeit*] is constitutive for every character of being of this entity. That is, there is simply no Dasein which would be as Dasein that would not in its very sense be '*at its time*,' *temporally particular* [*jeweiliges*].** This character belongs ineradicably to Dasein insofar as it is. But this implies that Dasein, if it as 'being-here' is a *being-possible*, can modify itself in accordance with this being-possible back and forth with regard to the Anyone. The mode of being of this modification as *historicity* and *temporality* is itself no restless exchange! This insight becomes impor-

---

*This is the first reference to Dasein's basic character of *Zu-sein* and one of the rare places where Heidegger uses it in the grammatical construction in which the *zu* suggests the modals of obligation and possibility. This character tends to be replaced by *Existenz* in *Being and Time* (cf. "On the Way to *Being and Time*.") The existentials are here called *Weisen zu sein*, 'ways to be,' but sometimes these characters of Dasein are also called *Seinsweisen*, 'ways of being.'

**The basic components of this family of words referring to temporal individuation is perhaps captured most simply in a German phrase like *jede Weile*, "each while"; perhaps its most common usage would be something like *der jeweilige Präsident*, "the president at the time"; *je* brings in the note of distributive universality: *je zwei und zwei*, "two at a time," "by twos." Our typical translations: *je*, "in each (particular) instance"; *jeweils*, "at any given (particular) time"; *jeweilig* (adverb), "at the (that, its) time"; *jeweiliges* (adjective), "(temporally) particular"; *Jeweiligkeit*, "the particular while" or "temporal particularity." Cf. "On the Way to *Being and Time*" on the importance of this most central of the characters of Dasein.

tant in regard to the '*Anyone*' and to the concept of *authenticity* and *inauthenticity*.

The *particular while* as such belongs to the structure of the being of this Dasein. With this fundamental character of Dasein, that I am it in the 'to be it in each particular instance,' the initial determination for Dasein is secured. But it is likewise the final determination, that determination to which every analysis of being again returns. This means that every character of the being of Dasein is governed by this fundamental determination. Thus, when a multiplicity of such structures of being is exhibited in what follows, they are all to be regarded from the outset in the light of this fundamental character.

But the provisional indication of this character at the same time contains specific directions for us relating to the subsequent analysis. The specification 'to be' the being directs us to understand all phenomena of Dasein primarily as ways of its 'to-be.' This prohibits us from experiencing and interrogating this entity, Dasein, on its 'outward appearance,' on what it is composed of, on parts and layers which a particular kind of consideration can find in it. Outward appearance, be it ever so broadly defined, in principle never gives the answer to the question of the way 'to be.' Body, soul, spirit may in a certain respect designate what this entity is composed of, but with this composite and its composition the way of being of this entity is from the beginning left undetermined; the least of all the possibilities is to extract it afterwards from this composite, since this determination of the entity which characterizes it as body, soul, and spirit has placed me in a completely different dimension of being really extraneous to Dasein. Whether this entity 'is composed of' the physical, psychic, and spiritual and how these realities are to be determined is here left completely unquestioned. We place ourselves in principle outside of this experiential and interrogative horizon outlined by the definition of the most customary name for this entity, man: *homo animal rationale*. What is to be determined is not an outward appearance of this entity but from the outset and throughout solely *its way to be*, not the what of that of which it is composed but *the how of its being and the characters of this how*.

b) The Dasein in the 'to-be' of everydayness for its particular while

Moreover, the Dasein is to be understood in its way to be, to begin with, not in a kind of being which is somehow emphatic and exceptional. The Dasein is not to be taken by setting some sort of aim and purpose for it, neither as '*homo*' nor even in the light of some idea of 'humanity.' Instead, its way to be must be brought out in its *nearest everydayness*, the factic Dasein in the how of its factic 'to-be-it.' But this does not mean that we now give a kind of biographical account of a particular Dasein as this individual Dasein in its everyday life. We are reporting no particular everyday life but we are seeking the *every-dayness of everyday life*, the fact in its facticity, not the everyday of the temporally particular Dasein but *to be the everydayness for its particular while as Dasein* is what matters to us.

This task of conceiving Dasein in its everydayness does not mean describing the Dasein at a primitive stage of its being. *Everydayness is in no way identical with primitiveness.* Everydayness is rather a distinctive how of the being of Dasein, even when and precisely when this Dasein has an inherently highly developed and differentiated culture at its disposal. On the other hand, even primitive Dasein in its way has possibilities of exceptional, non-everyday, and unusual being, which means that it also has in its turn a specific way of everydayness. But often the consideration of primitive forms of Dasein can more readily provide directions in seeing and verifying certain phenomena of Dasein, inasmuch as here the danger of concealment through theory, which Dasein itself characteristically supplies rather than something else outside of Dasein, is not yet so powerful. But it is just here that an especially critical attitude is needed, for what we know from primitive stages of Dasein is at first purely historically, geographically, and in world view furthest from us and alien to our culture. What is thus imparted to us about 'primitive life' is already pervaded by a particular interpretation. Indeed, it is an interpretation which cannot be based on an actual fundamental analysis of Dasein itself but which works with categories of man and human relationships taken from some sort of psychology. The fundamental analysis of Dasein is just the right presupposition for an understanding of the primitive, and not the reverse: there is no reason to believe that the sense of this entity can in some way be assembled by putting together bits of information about primitive Dasein. This point is being made because of the fact that we shall on occasion, but only sparingly, resort to primitive Dasein to exemplify certain phenomena. The exemplification must of course remain subject to this critical consideration, it is no more than an exemplification. The contents and the structures being evoked here are drawn from the matters and from envisaging the entity itself which we are.

The fundamental character of this entity, that it is in my 'to be it in each particular instance,' must be maintained. In what follows, an abbreviated form of expression will be used for it. The theme is the Dasein in its way *to be*—the being of Dasein—the constitution of the being of Dasein. By way of abbreviation, we shall speak of the *constitution of Dasein* and always mean by it *"in its way to be."*

Dasein in its everydayness, a highly complicated phenomenon, regards and defines it more authentically when a life is more differentiated. When we analyze Dasein in its everydayness and its being in everydayness, this should not be construed as saying also that we want to derive the remaining possibilities of the being of Dasein from everydayness, that we want to carry out a genetic consideration on the assumption that every other possibility of the being of Dasein could be derived from everydayness. Everydayness persists everywhere and always every day; each is a witness as to how Dasein has to be and how it is in everydayness, even though in a different way. It is easy to foresee that everydayness is a specific concept of *time*.

In these preliminary considerations it is becoming clear to us that even if we are not falsely educated by philosophical prejudices and theories about the subject and consciousness, even if we approach these phenomena to some extent without encumbrances, there are still difficulties in actually seeing what must be seen. The natural approach, even though it is not philosophically reflected and conceptually defined, does not really move in the direction of seeing the Dasein as such. Instead, inasmuch as it is a mode of being of this very Dasein, it tends to live *away from itself*. Even the way in which it knows itself is determined by this peculiarity of Dasein to live away from itself. In order to have a preliminary orientation at all on the sense in which all the characters of this being are to be taken, we offer the pointer that this entity is the very entity which we ourselves are.

If we orient ourselves historiologically, we can say (although even here the comparison is already quite dangerous) that the *cogito sum* of Descartes, to the extent that it is explicated, is directed precisely toward the determination of the *cogito* and the *cogitare* and leaves out the *sum*. In our consideration, however, we at first are leaving the *cogitare* and its determination alone and are bent on obtaining the *sum* and its determination. To be sure, the comparison is dangerous because it could be taken to imply that we could here intend the Dasein in the way in which Descartes approaches the ego and the subject, in isolation. But we shall see that this approach by Descartes is an absurdity.

§19. The basic constitution of Dasein as being-in-the-world. The in-being of Dasein and the being-in of things on hand

Maintaining a constant orientation to the indicated fundamental character of Dasein, we shall now try to lay open a basic constitutive state of being: Dasein is to show itself as *being-in-the-world*. This primary datum must be brought to light. The main structures of this constitutive state of the being of Dasein must be exhibited. Such an exhibition will lead us to understand that all the structures are governed by the indicated fundamental character [that of the 'to be it in each instance']. The basic constitutive state of being-in-the-world is a necessary structure of Dasein. But the being of Dasein is far from being sufficiently determined by it.

The determination of Dasein as being-in-the-world is a *unified* and *original* one. Three elements can be brought out in this basic constitutive state and traced more closely back to its phenomenal composition: 1) being-in-the-world in the particular sense of the *world*, 'world' as the how of the being—*ontologically*, the *worldhood of the world*; 2) the *entity* as it is determined from the *'who'* of this being-in-the-world and from the *how* of this being, how the entity itself is in its being; 3) *in-being as such*.

Though this basic constitution becomes the theme of the analysis according to three aspects, it is still always *wholly* there as itself in each particular consideration. What the aspects bring out in each case are not pieces, detachable moments out of which the whole may first be assembled. Bringing out the individual structural moments is a purely thematic accentuation and as such always only an *actual apprehension of the whole structure in itself*. In order to indicate at the outset that this highlighting is a thematic accentuation, that in regarding the first, the in-the-world, we also always already co-intend the second and the third, we shall anticipate the comprehensive analysis of the first phenomenon, in-the-world, by an account orienting us to the last phenomenal constituent to be mentioned, in-being as such.

We begin by asking what *in-being* means. What is seen and intended by it in the being of Dasein itself? At first, we complete in-being [*In-Sein*] by adding 'in-the-world' and are inclined to understand this in-being as 'being-in . . .' [*Sein-in*]. In this latter formulation, it designates the kind of being of an entity which is 'in' another, the relationship of being of something 'in' something. When we then try to give intuitive demonstration to this 'in,' more accurately to the 'something-in-something,' we give examples like the water 'in' the glass, the clothes 'in' the closet, the desks 'in' the classroom. By this we mean that one is spatially contained in another and refer to the relationship of being with regard to place and space of two entities which are themselves extended in space. Thus both the first (water) and the second (glass), wherein the first is, are 'in' space; both have their place. Both are only 'in' space and have no in-being.

Both entities which are here subject to an 'in-relationship' have the same kind of being, that of *being on hand*. If we broaden this relationship of being to suit the purpose, we can simply go on and say: the desk in the classroom, the classroom in the university building, the building in the city of Marburg, Marburg in Hessen, in Germany, in Europe, on Earth, in a solar system, in world-space, in the world—a uniform relation of being which is in principle no different in all of these connections. This 'in' defines the place of the one entity in relation to the other such that in fact both of them are defined as places themselves in space. This being-'in' pertains to their outward appearance. The entities whose being-in-one-another is at issue here in each case have the same kind of being, that of being on hand, as things which happen to be found and occur in the world, which as such can be discovered.

But 'in-being' as a structure of the being of Dasein, of the entity which I am in each instance, does not refer to this being-in-one-another, 'being-in' as a spatial containment of entities which takes place in the form of an occurrence. It does not refer to a corporeal thing called 'human body' being on hand in a spatial container (room, building) called 'world.' This cannot be the intention from the start, if we keep to what the fundamental character of Dasein itself implies. Dasein is not to be taken as an entity with a view to its outward appearance, as it looks to others in one or another state. Instead, it is to be taken only in its way to be. 'In-being' does not refer to such a spatial in-one-another any more than 'in' originally means just that kind of spatial relation.

'In' comes from *innan*, which means to dwell, *habitare*; '*ann*' means: I am accustomed, I am familiar with, I take care of something—the Latin *colo* in the sense of *habito* and *diligo*. Dwelling is also taken here as taking care of something in intimate familiarity, being-involved-with [*Sein-bei*].[1]*

This same entity which we characterize as in-being we also define, as I have already said, as the entity that I *am* [*bin*]; and '*bin*' is connected with '*bei*.' 'I am' thus amounts to saying, I dwell, I abide in the world as with something familiar. Being as in-being and 'I am' means dwelling with . . . , and 'in' primarily does not signify anything spatial at all but means primarily *being familiar with*. Why and how it, along with this primary sense, also has a genuine sense of place, which however is still essentially distinct from the spatial being-in-one-another of the things mentioned earlier, shall be examined later. But it should already be stated that the local sense of place, which this correctly understood in-being can also have, that I as an entity in the world am

---

*This context in particular explains why we have usually translated 'bei' with phrases such as 'involved with' or 'intimately involved in' to distinguish it from our translation of the prepositions *mit* and *in*. The German *bei* here has the same connotations of intimacy and habitual familiarity which the French *chez* possesses.

1. Cf. Jakob Grimm, *Kleinere Schriften*, Vol. VII, p. 247.

always somewhere, has nothing to do with the spatial in-one-another we first named; even my local experience of standing here in this place, insofar as it characterizes being as being-in-the-world, is essentially distinct from the being on hand of the chair in this space. This in-being, which we now should never understand in a primarily local and spatial sense, is rather, as being-involved-with, defined by temporal particularity, it is in each instance mine and each instance this.

Such possible modes of in-being belonging to everydayness include: working on something with something, producing something, cultivating and caring for something, putting something to use, employing something for something, holding something in trust, giving up, letting something get lost, interrogating, discussing, accomplishing, exploring, considering, determining something. In a way still to be clarified, these modes of in-being have the character of *concern*, in the sense of taking something into one's care, having it in one's care. Even the pertinent modifications of not being concerned, neglecting, relaxing, refraining belong in principle to the same kind of being. Even when I do nothing and merely doze and so tarry in the world, I have this specific being of concerned being-in-the-world—it includes every lingering with and letting oneself be affected.

The declaration of the genuine meaning of in-being does not also already guarantee seeing the phenomenon which it expresses. But at the same time it is also more than a mere verbal definition; it fixes our line of sight above all prohibitively, it indicates where we do not have to look. But from our account of the fundamental character we already know that, to demonstrate all the determinations of being under discussion, we should look to the entity which in each instance we are, to the extent that and as we are it. Dasein, insofar as it is at all, is in the way of being of in-being. This means that in-being in the sense already defined is not a 'property' of the entity called Dasein, not a property which it has or does not have, which devolves upon it or which it might add to itself, *without* which it could *be* just as well as with it, so that at first one could conceive the being of Dasein otherwise, to some extent without in-being. In-being is rather *the* constitution of the being of Dasein, in which every way of being of this entity is grounded. In-being is not merely something thrown into the bargain for an entity which even without this constitutive state would be Dasein, as if the world, in which every Dasein as Dasein always already is, were at times first added to this entity (or conversely this entity to it) so that this entity then could at its leisure enter into a 'relation' with the world. Such entering into relations with the world is altogether possible only insofar as Dasein already is being-in-the-world on the basis of its being-involved-with . . . .

This characteristic phenomenon of in-being and its characteristic of defining Dasein in its very being must be made perfectly clear from the outset and kept in view as an apriori of every particular relationship to the world. I shall therefore try to make this clear in a roundabout way, inasmuch as this structure of in-being was in a certain way always already seen wherever Dasein was examined. It would even be incomprehensible if such a basic phenomenon of Dasein had been totally overlooked. It is another question whether it is experienced and apprehended so that its authentic structure shows itself and thereby presents the possibility of determining the being of the entity so structured in a phenomenally suitable way.

§20. Knowing as a derivative mode of the in-being of Dasein

From early on the relation of Dasein to the world was defined primarily in terms of the mode of being of *knowing*. Or as it is said, in a formula which in fact does not coincide with the one above, the 'relation of the subject to the object' was first conceived primarily as a 'cognitive relation,' and a so-called 'practical relation' was incorporated later. Even if it were a matter of taking this kind of being as the primary one in the sense of cognitive being in the world, which is not the case, everything depends on first seeing it in a phenomenally genuine way.

When this relationship of being between subject and object is reflected upon, for ordinary observation there is an entity called nature already given in the widest sense, which becomes known; this entity is also always found first, cultivated and cared for by Dasein precisely because it is being-in-the-world. In this entity, the knowing which knows it is not to be found. This knowing must therefore be somewhere else, if it is at all. Likewise, however, in the entitative thing which knows, in the human thing, knowing is not on hand and so not perceivable, ascertainable like the color and extension of this human thing. But the knowing must still be in this thing, if not 'outside' then 'inside'; this knowing is 'inside,' 'in' this subject-thing, *in mente*.

The more unequivocally we now maintain that knowing is actually and from the start 'inside,' the more we believe we are proceeding without presuppositions in the question of the essence of knowledge and of the determination of the relationship of being in which the subject stands to the object. For now the question arises, how does knowing, which according to its being is inside, in the subject, come out of its 'inner sphere' into an 'other, outer sphere,' into the world?

In such an approach to the question of knowing, a relation between two entities which are on hand is assumed beforehand, explicitly or otherwise. This relationship of two things on hand is now applied more specifically to the determination of a relation between inner and outer when one asks: How is this relation of being between the two entities, subject and object, possible? This is asked, presumably in compliance with the facts of the case of knowing, without having even in the least determined the sense of being of this knowing, the sense of being of this relationship between subject and object, without having clarified the sense of being of the subject and delimited it from that of the object. To be sure, we are assured that the inside and this 'inner sphere' of the subject is not actually spatial; it is certainly not a 'box' or anything like a receptacle. But we do not learn what its positive meaning is, what this immanence after all is in which knowing finds itself enclosed, and how the being of the subject is to be understood if, as primarily immanent, it is only with itself. No matter how such an 'inside' and the sense of this inner sphere may be defined, as soon as the question is raised as to how knowing gets 'out of' it to . . . , then the way of dealing with the phenomenon of knowing has turned out to be one founded upon a semblance. But in the whole approach to this question, even when it is embedded in an epistemological problematic, one is blind to what is thus asserted about Dasein when knowing taken as a mode of being is attributed to it. This says nothing more and nothing less than: *knowing the world is a mode of being of Dasein such that this mode is ontically founded in its basic constitution, in being-in-the-world.*

When we reproduce the phenomenal findings in this form: *Knowing is a mode of being of in-being,* someone oriented to the traditional horizon of epistemological questions is inclined to reply that such an interpretation of knowing actually nullifies the problem of knowledge. But what authority decides *whether* and *in what sense* there is supposed to be a problem of knowledge, outside of the subject matter itself? When we ask about the mode of being of knowing itself, then it must be kept in mind from the outset that every act of knowing always already takes place on the basis of the mode of being of Dasein which we call in-being, that is, being-always-already-involved-with-a-world. Knowing is now not a comportment that would be added to an entity which does not yet 'have' a world, which is free from any relation to its world. Rather, knowing is always a mode of being of Dasein on the basis of its already being involved with the world.

The basic defect of epistemology is just that it fails to regard what it means by knowing in its original phenomenal datum as a way of being of Dasein, as a way of its in-being, and to take from this basic consideration all the questions which now begin to arise on this ground.

The contention that there is no longer a problem of knowledge, if it is maintained from the outset that Dasein is involved with its world, is really not a contention but only the restoration of a datum which any unbiased seeing sees as obvious. Moreover, it is nowhere prescribed that there must be a problem of knowledge. Perhaps it is precisely the task of a philosophical investigation ultimately to deprive many problems of their sham existence, to reduce the number of problems and to promote investigation which opens the way to the matters themselves. Not only does a correct interpretation of knowing as a mode of in-being not deny a problematic of knowledge; it actually first makes such a problematic possible, especially when knowing, as its sense of being requires, is understood as a mode of in-being, of being-in-the-world, but *not as a basic kind of being-in-the-world*. Then comes the question which actually can be explored: How does the Dasein, which at any given time is in a particular but primarily non-cognitive and not merely cognitive mode of being, *disclose* its world in which it already is? Correlatively, which modes of concealment are essentially co-given as temporally particular ways for Dasein to be in its world? What is *the temporally particular scope of discoverability* corresponding to a particular mode of being of Dasein in its world? What are the apriori conditions of being for this Dasein (in-being) itself and accordingly for the original, all-surpassing, transcendental-ontological, that is, *ontological-existential understanding of being* as such and the ontological possibilities of being toward the world? What is meant by *truth* in each case for the knowing of entities of the most diverse types? What is the sense and the justification and the kind of binding force, a force which a kind of truth and level of truth has at any given time? What is the demonstrability and conceptuality belonging to such truth? The basic problem is precisely to see this fundamental structure and to define it in its genuine apriori in an ontologically suitable manner. The problem of knowledge is not disposed of by an arbitrary act but first becomes a problem when it is placed upon its possible ground. The problem and the pseudo-problems must be brought to light.

All of these genuine phenomena can be investigated and correctly understood from the outset only if it is made clear that knowing, according to its sense, is already a mode of the in-being of Dasein; that knowing is not something by which Dasein, not yet in the world at first, upon knowing would produce a relation to the world. How should this initially worldless being of the subject even be understood? There can never be a problem, for example, on how the opposition of the two entities, subject and object, is possible. Knowing understood as apprehending has sense only on the basis of an *already-being-involved-with*. This already-being-involved-with, in which knowing as such can first 'live,' is not first 'produced' directly by a cognitive performance; Dasein, whether it ever knows it or not, is as Dasein already involved with a world. The priority which has always been granted to cognitive comportment from ancient times is at the same time associated with the peculiar tendency to define the being of the world in which Dasein is primarily in terms of how it shows itself for a cognitive comportment. In other words, the manner of being of the world was characterized by referring to its specific objectivity for world cognition. Regarded in this way, there is accordingly an inner connection between the manner of being defining the world and the basic characterization of Dasein itself with respect to its primary relation to the world as knowing.

More accurately, knowing now shows—I can indicate this only very briefly here—a *phased structure*, a specific interconnection in which it is *temporalized* as a mode of being of Dasein. The first phase in the temporalization of knowing is the *directing-itself-toward* something, the specific comportment of taking up a direction toward something; but this already on the basis of in-being in the world. The second phase is *dwelling-with* that toward which Dasein is now directing itself. This dwelling with an entity toward which it is directing itself is itself grounded in this directing-itself-toward. That is to say, the directing-itself-toward an object *holds out to the end*, and dwelling with an entity takes place within it. The directing-itself-toward is not put out of play at the phase of dwelling with an entity but persists throughout, anticipating all other modes of comportment and determining them. Here, directing-itself-toward means *taking a view*, conceiving as, the "from which" of viewing.

On the basis of the second phase, that of dwelling with an already given entity, now comes [third] the actual *apprehending, laying apart, laying out* or *interpreting* in a specific sense. Such a perceiving as a *having apprehended* is itself cultivated, fourth, to the level of *preservation* of what is apprehended. In its entirety, the process of knowledge would then look like this: *the knowing directing-itself-toward as dwelling-with and apprehending* tends toward the *apprehended* so as to *preserve* it, so that knowing in having apprehended, that is, in acquired knowledge, has the known even when it does not actually stand in relation to it; it *preserves* knowledge as a possession. This is understandable only by referring to the primary character of Dasein as 'to-be,' but not when the subject is something psychic which has representations which are stored up and of which it must be stated how they 'correspond.'

Fifth, the preserving retention of what is known is itself nothing but a new mode of in-being, that is, of the relationship of being to the entity which is known; the in-being characterized under the first point is now modified by knowledge.

The entire sequence of the phases of knowing, from the primary directing-itself-toward to the retaining, simply exhibits the *cultivation of a new stance of the being of Dasein* toward that which is known. It exhibits a possibility of being which was already also announced as science and research. Finally, this is a matter of *modes of temporalization*, such that the first mode anticipates all the others, sustaining itself in the others; and it is itself anticipatory only as in-being.

In directing-itself-toward and apprehending, Dasein does not first get out of itself, out of its inner sphere in which it is encapsulated. Rather, its very sense is to be *always already 'outside'* in the world, in the rightly understood sense of 'outside' as in-being and dwelling with the world, which in each instance is already uncovered in some way. Dwelling with the matter to be known does not involve abandonment of the inner sphere, as if Dasein leaps out of its sphere and is no longer in it but still is found only at the object. Dasein in this 'being outside' with the object is also 'inside,' rightly understood; for it is as being-in-the-world that Dasein itself knows the entity. [And in turn,] the apprehending of what is known is not like returning from an expedition of plunder with its acquired booty back into the 'housing' of consciousness, of immanence; for in the very apprehending as well and in having, preserving, and retaining what is apprehended, the knowing Dasein remains 'outside.' In knowing about a context of being of the world, even in merely thinking of it, in merely representing it without originally experiencing it, I am no less with the entities outside in the world, and I am not in the least with myself on the inside. If I merely represent the Freiburg Cathedral to myself, this does not mean that it is only immanently present in the representing; rather, this mere representing is in the genuine and best sense precisely with the entities themselves. Even the forgetting of something, in which the relationship of being to what is known is apparently obliterated, is nothing *but a particular modification of being-involved-with.* Only on this basis is forgetting possible. All delusion and all error, in which in a way no relationship of being to the entity is secured but is instead falsified, are once again only modes of being-involved-with.

In the entire edifice of knowing based on in-being, it is not the case that with apprehension the subject would somehow first introduce, first produce, its relation of being to the world. Rather, *apprehension is grounded in a prior letting-something-be-seen.* Such a letting-something-be-seen is possible on the basis of a letting-something-be-encountered, and this is possible only on the basis of always already being-involved-with. Only an entity which in its being has the aptitude to let another entity (world) be encountered stands in the possibility of apprehending something, of knowledge. Knowing is nothing but a mode of being-in-the-world; specifically, it is *not even a primary* but *a founded way of being-in-the-world,* a way which is always possible only on the basis of a non-cognitive comportment.

What we have set forth here as the in-being of Dasein and characterized in greater detail is the ontological fundament for what Augustine and above all Pascal already noted. They called that which actually knows not knowing but *love and hate*. All knowing is only an appropriation and a form of realization of something which is already discovered by other primary comportments. Knowing is rather more likely to cover up something which was originally uncovered in noncognitive comportment.

What Augustine identifies as love and hate and only in certain contexts specifies as Dasein's truly cognitive mode of being we shall later have to take as an original phenomenon of Dasein, though not in this one-sided restriction to just this comportment. Rather, we shall first learn to understand, from the more refined apprehension of the modes of being of Dasein within which knowledge is possible at all, that knowledge as such cannot even be grasped if we do not from the outset see the specific context of being in which knowing as such is possible. When this is truly understood, it will always appear grotesque to explain knowledge in terms of itself by way of an epistemology. And it remains absurd to approach this entity, which as Dasein is constituted in its being as being-in-the-world, without regard to its world. This involves approaching it in such a way that its basic constitution is after a fashion taken away from it; this denatured Dasein is then approached as a subject, which amounts to a complete inversion of its being. It now becomes the source of a problem of explaining how a relation of being between this fantastically conceived entity and another entity called world might be possible. To explain knowing on this basis which is no longer a basis, that is, to make sense of manifest nonsense, naturally calls for a theory and metaphysical hypotheses.

The in-being of Dasein remains a puzzle for every attempt to explain it as an entity which it a priori is not. For every explanation conducts what is to be explained back to its contextures of being. This must always be guided by the prior question of whether the entity to be explained is experienced beforehand in its being and whether it is adequately specified in its being. The in-being of Dasein is not to be explained but before all else has to be seen as an inherent kind of being and accepted as such; in short, it has to be deciphered ontologically. Hardly an arbitrary act, but just the opposite! Of course, this is easier said than done, especially in a truly expository analysis.

Before proceeding to this analysis, the phenomenon may be clarified by an analogy which itself is not too far removed from the matter at issue, inasmuch as this analogy is concerned with an entity to which we must likewise attribute, in a formal way, the kind of being which belongs to Dasein—'life.'

We may compare the subject and its inner sphere to a snail in its shell. Let it be expressly noted that we do not presume that the theories which speak of the immanence of consciousness and of the subject conceive of consciousness precisely in this sense of a snail-shell. But as long as the sense of the 'within' and immanence is left undefined, so that we never learn what sense this 'in' has and what relation of being this 'in' of the subject has to the world, it is at any rate in a negative way equivalent to our analogy.

We can say that the snail at times crawls out of its shell and at the same time keeps it on hand; it stretches itself out to something, to food, to some things which it finds on the ground. Does the snail thereby first enter into a relationship of being with the world? Not at all! Its act of crawling out is but a local modification of its already-being-in-the-world. Even when it is in its shell, its being is a being-outside, rightly understood. It is not in its shell like water in the glass, for it has the inside of its shell as a world which it pushes against and touches, in which it warms itself, and the like. None of this applies to the relationship of being of the water in the glass or, if it did, we would have to say even of water that it has the mode of being of Dasein, it is such that it has a world. The snail is not at the outset only in its shell and not yet in the world, a world described as standing over against it, an opposition which it broaches by first crawling out. It crawls out only insofar as its being is already to be in a world. It does not first add a world to itself by touching. Rather, it touches because its being means nothing other than to be in a world.

This applies similarly to a subject to which knowing is ascribed. If it is posited as an entity which is supposed to have this possibility of being, it is thereby understood as an entity which is in the mode of being in a world. But this positing is performed blindly, without an understanding of what in principle is already implied in knowing.

We have oriented the question of in-being in particular toward the relation of knowing because this mode of being of Dasein traditionally has priority in the philosophical determination of the relation of the ego (the subject) to the world; and yet this mode of being is still not originally conceived but instead remains the source of all sorts of confusion as a result of this indeterminacy in regard to its being. The so-called epistemological positions of *idealism* and *realism* and their varieties and mixtures are all possible only on the basis of a lack of clarity of the phenomenon of in-being, about which they formulate theories without having exposed it in advance. Idealism and realism both let the relationship of being between subject and object first *emerge*. Indeed, in idealism this leads to the assertion (in quite distinct ways, depending on whether it is logical or psychological idealism) that it is the subject which first of all *creates* the relation of being to the object. Realism, which goes along with the same absurdity, in contrary fashion says that it is the object which through causal relations first *effects* the relations of being to the subject. In opposition to these basically equivalent positions, there is a third position which presupposes the relationship of being between subject and object from the start, for example, that of Avenarius: between subject and object there is what is called a 'principal coordination,' and subject and object must from the start be regarded as standing in a relationship of being.[1] But this relationship is in its mode of being left undefined, as is the mode of being implied in subject and object. A position which wants to stand on this side of idealism and realism because it does not let the relationship first emerge, but which at the same time stands on the far side of idealism and realism because it tries to preserve and yet sublate both positions in their own rights, which they really do not have, is a position whose sense is always oriented to this theory. What has been said in our present consideration about knowing as a mode of being of in-being and suggested as a task of a phenomenology of knowing stands neither on this side nor on the far side of idealism and realism, nor is it either one of the two positions. Instead it stands *wholly outside of an orientation to them and their ways of formulating questions*.

Our further considerations will not only explicate the genuine sense of knowing more clearly. Above all, their aim is to show that knowing in its being is grounded upon more original structures of Dasein, that, for example, knowing can be true—can have *truth* as a distinctive predicate—only because truth is not so much a property of knowing but is rather a *character of the being of Dasein itself*. This may suffice as a provisional account of the phenomenon of in-being.

§21. Worldhood of the world

We now proceed to the task of disengaging the first structure, which we have identified and designated as 'world.' We ask what is meant by '*world*' (*worldhood* and the expectant present—state of making present and of expectancy)*? What phenomenal constituents are expressed by it?

a) Worldhood as the wherein for Dasein's leeway of encounter

From what has been said about the being of Dasein as in-being, namely, that this in-being does not refer to anything like a spatial in-

---

1. Richard Avenarius, *Der menschliche Weltbegriff* (Leipzig: Reisland, 1891), third edition in 1912.

*This parenthetical remark is a later insertion. *Gewärtigkeit* (expectancy, awaiting) plays no role whatsoever in this lecture course. In *Being and Time* (H. 337) it is identified with the "inauthentic future."

one-another, we can at least formally gather that *world is the wherein of Dasein's being*. Accordingly, the 'wherein' does not refer to a spatial container. At any rate, such a spatial container cannot constitute the primary character of world, if world is indeed taken as the wherein of the in-being indicated above. But spatiality or more accurately locality plays an especially distinctive constitutive role for the being of the world. In its ontic sense, 'world' is the entity which is obviously not the Dasein that is in it, but rather the entity *with which* [*wobei*] the Dasein has its being, the entity *toward* which the Dasein is. This *being-toward*, this being toward the world, has—as we have already suggested—the character of *concern*. We define this concern for the world, this being in it in various modes and possibilities, more precisely as *preoccupation** with it. In its preoccupation with the world the temporally particular being-in-the-world which the Dasein is temporalizes itself.

When we designate the world as the wherein correlative to in-being, it is so regarded now with a view to the mode of being of in-being understood as preoccupation, in the with-which of concerned preoccupation. In thus being preoccupied with the world, Dasein always already finds its world, and this finding is not theoretical apprehension. *The 'already-being-involved-with' is care in being concerned.* As concerned preoccupation with the world Dasein lets itself *encounter* its world. Concern as the basic mode of Dasein permits encounter. In thus letting the world be encountered, Dasein *discloses* the world. All knowing, which as a mode of being of concern is built upon concern, merely *lays out, interprets* the disclosed world and happens on the basis of concern. Indeed, a particular correlation appears here. The more the initially experienced world is *deprived of its worldhood* ("unworlded," as we shall later put it), that is, the more the initially experienced world becomes mere nature; the more we discover in it its mere naturality, for example, in terms of the objectivity of physics; the more cognitive comportment discovers in this way, then all the more does knowing itself become as such the proper way to disclose and to discover. It is in mathematics that knowing as such celebrates the triumph of the discoveries of entities. It is here that we in fact find knowing as such, which discovers, although even here not in a radical and definitive sense, rightly regarded.

Concerned being-in-the-world is what as such lets the world be encountered. We are of course still far too much encumbered by theories and opinions as well as by a certain natural conception, which has its justification, to see that it is precisely non-theoretical comportment

---

**Umgang.* This translation is intended to suggest both involved absorption in the world—*Umgehen* is at once an *Aufgehen*—and actively dealing with it. Accordingly, *Umgang* is sometimes translated simply as 'occupation.'

which *uncovers* not only the world but also Dasein itself. *Care* as the constitution of the being of Dasein uncovers the world.

When we ask about the phenomenal structure of the world, we are asking about the *how* of the being in which the entity we call the world *shows itself of itself as the encountered,* we are asking about the being of the entity which is encountered in the leeway for encounter granted by concern. The structure of encounter of this entity world is not a conglomerate of modes of conception with which a subject clothes an object, of forms with which a world-stuff is adorned. The structures of encounter of that entity are rather those of the being of the world itself, insofar as the world can show itself in everyday Dasein, upon which basis it is and can be discovered. This character of the being of the entity which we call world and which we shall now draw out shall be terminologically conceived as *worldhood*, in order to circumvent the obscurity of knowing 'worldhood' understood not as a character of the being of the entity but rather as the *character of the being of Dasein,* and only through it and along with it that of the entity!

To determine the worldhood of world is to lay open in its structure the *how* of the encounter, drawn from that encounter, of the entity in which Dasein is as in-being in accord with its basic constitution, in short to lay open the structure of the being of this entity. Phenomeno-logical interpretation of the worldhood of the world does not mean a narrative description reporting on the outward appearance of things in the world, that there really are mountains, streams, houses, stairs, tables, and the like, and how all of this stands. We shall also never come to grasp the sense of the world if we could run through the sum-total of all the things in the world. In such an inventory and in every characterization of the outward appearance of a world-thing and of the particular relations among several of them we always think of the world-thing in advance already as a *world*-thing. But the issue is not really all that can be found in the world but rather the how of the being of such an entity and of every entity of this sort: *the wherein as the possibility of being of the leeway of encounter of in-being. It is a matter of a transcendental exposition of worldhood from the being of Dasein qua in-being,* not a narrative report of world-occurrences but an *interpretation* of *worldhood*, which characterizes everything that does occur as *worldly.*

I am intentionally emphasizing the actual sense of the inquiry so forcefully because the question of the structure of the being of the world, of the *worldhood of the world*, is not at all so obvious. To put it more precisely, it is not at all obvious that the endeavor to grasp the being of the world originally now also automatically gives us the right approach to it. Furthermore, we shall see that the prevailing philo-sophical consideration of the being of the world already allowed itself to be guided completely by very definite presuppositions about the possibility of an original kind of apprehension of the world as well as about the sense of being which the world must have. We shall try to disregard all the wrong-headed presuppositions and to explicate the worldhood of the world as it shows itself in the everyday preoccupation of Dasein with its world. On this basis we shall then try to understand how this immediately given world, by virtue of particular motives which it in part entails, can in some of its directions be uncovered as *nature*. Such a discovery or interpretation is realized especially by the natural sciences.

b) Worldhood of the environing world: aroundness, the primary character of the space of the "around" as constitutive of worldhood

In what follows, we shall be concerned with the world as *environing world* [*Umwelt*] with respect to its worldhood, that is, with regard to the structure which characterizes every thing as a *thing of the environing world*. The worldhood of the world, that is, the specific being of this entity 'world,' is a specific concept of being. In opposition to the traditional question of the reality of the external world, we shall ask about the worldhood of the world as it is there in *immediate everyday concern*. We are asking about the world as it is encountered in the daily round of preoccupation; we are asking about the world around us, the environing world; more precisely, we are asking about the *worldhood of the environing world*. By asking in particular for an account of worldhood and specifying the *aroundness* in it, we thereby establish in its own right the genuine sense of *place* and *space* within the structural framework of the worldhood of the world. This gives us the division of the analysis of the worldhood of the environing world. 1. The *worldhood of the environing world as such*; 2. The *aroundness of the world as a constitutive feature of worldhood*.

Even *environing worldhood*, the being of the entity with which the caring, concerned preoccupation of Dasein first dwells, should not be understood in a primarily spatial sense. The '*around*' and the '*round about*' are not to be taken primarily spatially, and not spatially at all if spatiality is defined in terms of the dimensionality of metric space, the space of geometry. On the other hand, however, the continual resistance to spatiality which we are forced to adopt in the determination of in-being, in the characterization of world and still more in the account of the environing world, the constant necessity here to suspend a specific sense of spatiality, suggest that in all of these phenomena a certain sense of something like spatiality is still in play. This is in fact the case. For just this reason it is important from the start *not* to miss the question of the structure of *this* spatiality, that is, not to start from the spatiality which is specifically geometrical, a spatiality which is discovered in and extracted from the primary and original space of the world. Since it is a question of understanding the primary sense of world, a particular idea of space understood in terms of metric space must first be put out of play. On the contrary, we shall learn to comprehend the sense of metric space and the particular modification which motivates metrics in spatiality by reference to a more original spatiality. But first and foremost, we must come to understand the sense of worldhood. The outline of our reflection on the structure of the worldhood of the world is therefore marked off in the following two points: 1. The worldhood of the environing world as such, the encountered *'in order to'* [*Umzu*], the *deployment*;* 2. The aroundness, the primary spatial character of the 'around' [*Um*] as a constitutive feature of worldhood.

This division already gives us an indication of the primary direction in which this analysis will look: even when we analyze space and spatiality, we must have already understood the sense of worldhood from the start. Consequently, the outline at the same time already contains a *fundamental critique* of the traditional way of explicating the reality of the world, that is, its worldhood, insofar as such an explication has ever been done at all and carried out as an explicit task.

§22. *How the tradition passed over the question of the worldhood of the world. Descartes as an example.*

We now wish to proceed just as we did earlier by first trying to limit the phenomenal horizon prohibitively, defensively, which means to suspend the direction of vision which does not lead us to the authentic phenomenon. It is especially important in this analysis of the world in its worldhood, since the question of the structure of the being of the world was always formulated as the question of the structure of the being of *nature*, not only today and since modern science but in a certain sense already with the Greeks. Thus the entire constellation of concepts which we have at our disposal in characterizing the being of the world in a primary way comes from this way of considering *the world as nature*. In an *original* analysis of the world, which does *not* re-

---

*Bewandtnis, which we are translating generically as 'standing' (cf. p. 259 below and "On the Way to *Being and Time*"), when applied specifically to the world 'around us' could be translated as the 'circum-standing' or (less aptly and perhaps more misleadingly) circumstances. But to bring out the connotations of the employment and disposition of a tool, we are translating it here as deployment.

gard nature as primary, we are therefore at a total loss for concepts and even more for expression.

The most extreme counterinstance of the determination of the being of the entity as a world, both in method and in result, is represented by Descartes. In his analysis and determination of the being of the world he stands at a characteristic place in the development of this question. On the one hand, he assumes the determinations of the being of the world as they were drawn by the middle ages and so by Greek philosophy. And yet, on the other hand, because of the extreme way in which he raises the question of the being of the world, he prefigures all the problems which then emerge in Kant's *Critique of Pure Reason* and elsewhere.

Whenever Descartes asks about the being of an entity, he is asking, in the spirit of the tradition, about *substance*. When he speaks of substance, he is speaking mostly in the strict sense of *substantiality*. And substantiality is a particular mode of being, more accurately, the most distinctive and primary kind of being which can pertain to an entity at all. Now entities, entitative things in the broadest sense, which have the mode of being of substantiality, are substances. Descartes here follows, not only in expression and concept but also in subject matter, the Scholastic and so basically the Greek formulation of the question of entities. The word 'substantia' has a double meaning: first, the entity itself which is in the mode of being of substance, and at the same time substantiality. This corresponds to our distinction between world as the things which are in the world and worldhood as the mode of being of the world, where we must however emphasize that the sense of worldhood and the structure of substantiality are radically distinct. *Per substantiam nihil aliud intelligere possumus, quam rem quae ita existit, ut nulla alia re indigeat ad existendum.*[1] "By substance we can understand nothing other than something which '*is*' in such a way that it needs no other entity in order to be." Substantiality means *extantness*, being on hand, which as such is in need of no other entity. The reality of a *res*, the substantiality of a substance, the being of an entity, taken in a strict sense means extantness in the sense of non-indigence, not needing any producer or any entity which retains or bears this quality of having been produced. . . . *Substantia quae nulla plane re indigeat, unica tantum potest intelligi, nempe Deus*[2] [. . . only one substance which is in

1. René Descartes, *Principia Philosophiae* I, Principle 51, pp. 24ff. [Page numbers refer to the edition of Charles Adam and Paul Tannery, *Oeuvres de Descartes*, Vol. VIII (Paris: Leopold Cerf, 1905).]

2. Ibid. [English translations are provided in brackets in the body of the text when Heidegger's German translation is a variant or free rendering of the original. There is an English translation of portions of "The Principles of Philosophy" in *The Philosophical Works of Descartes*, translated by E. S. Haldane and G. R. T. Ross (New York: Dover, 1955), Vol. I, pp. 203-302.]

need of nothing whatsoever can be understood, and this indeed is God]. God is the only entity which satisfies this sense of substantiality. In other words, 'God' is the name for that entity in which the idea of being as such is realized in its genuine sense. Here 'God' is but a purely ontological concept and is therefore also called the *ens perfectissimum* [most perfect entity]. This determination of the being of God implies nothing whatsoever of a religious nature. God is simply the name for the entity in which we actually encounter an entity in accord with the concept of being as extantness. God is accordingly the only substance, the only entity which *is* in the supposedly 'authentic' sense of being. In the background of this talk of 'ens perfectissimum' there is of course a very specific concept of 'ens' and 'being' of which Descartes was no more clearly conscious than were the Greeks, who discovered it.

Alias vero omnes, non nisi ope concursus Dei existere posse percipimus.[3] "We clearly perceive from the very sense of substantiality that every other entity *is* only with help from, which means in need of, the co-presence [concurrence] of God." By its very sense, every entity other than God needs to be produced and sustained, while the presence of Something qua God is characterized by the absence of such need, non-indigence. An entity in need of production and sustenance in its existence and presence is therefore '*ens creatum*' when we regard its presence from the standpoint of authentic being.

In a certain sense, the term 'substance' taken strictly can be attributed only to God. But inasmuch as we also speak of the created entity as *being*, in characterizing the being of the uncreated and the being of the created, we use the *single* concept of being. This means that in a certain manner we can also designate created being as substance. *Atque ideo nomen substantiae non convenit Deo et illis univoce. Ut dici solet in Scholis, hoc est, nulla ejus nominis significatio potest distincte intelligi, quae Deo et creaturis sit communis*[4] [The word 'substance' does not apply *univocally* to God and to other things, as they say in the Schools; that is, no signification of this name which would be common to God and creatures can be distinctly understood]. This sense of being in the sense of substantiality, being in the manner of being on hand with no need of another, does not apply to God and to creatures in the same sense, as it was said in the Schools, that is, the middle ages. A concept is univocal (ὁμώνυμον) if its meaning content, that is, what it intends, what is addressed by it, is intended in the same sense. When I say, for example, 'God is' and 'the world is,' I certainly assert being in both cases but I intend something different thereby and cannot intend the

---

3. Ibid.
4. Ibid.

term 'is' in the same sense, univocally; for if that were the case, then I would thereby either intend the creature itself as uncreated or reduce the uncreated being God to a creature. Since according to Descartes there is an *infinite* difference between the kind of being of these two entities, the term 'being,' which is still used for both, cannot be used in the same meaning, not univocally but (which Descartes here does not particularly say, but as the Scholastics put it) *analogously*. I can only speak of both God and the world as entities analogously. In other words, the concept of being, insofar as it is generally applied to the entire manifold of all possible entities, as such has the character of an analogous concept. This analogy in the sense of being was first discovered by Aristotle, and this discovery is likewise his real advance in the face of the Platonic version of the concept of being.

This question, whether the concept of being is analogous or univocal in regard to the being of God and of the world, and in what sense it is univocal, played a great role in the middle ages, especially in the later middle ages. And this whole problem of the determination of the being of God and of the world along these lines also had a negative influence on the entire theological development of Luther. 'Being' in the two assertions 'God is' and 'the world is' is not meant in the way Descartes meant it when he says that . . . *nullus ejus nominis significatio potest distincte intelligi, quae Deo et creaturis sit communis*[5] [. . . no signification of this name which would be common to God and creatures can be distinctly understood]. When these two assertions of being are made, we cannot see distinctly that something common is thereby intended by both. Indeed Descartes in this formulation is essentially left behind by the insights of the middle ages, which were much more astute in this direction.

Now, the two sorts of entities of which it can still in a certain sense be said that they are substances are in any case *substantiae creatae*, created substances, entities which in a certain sense are in no need of the being of God, provided that we disregard the principal indigence of being produced and being sustained in their existence and presence as such. If I disregard this indigence of the created being as created, there are still some things in the realm of the created which in a certain way can be designated as having no need of another, *substantia corporea* and *substantia cogitans creata sive mens*, on the one hand the corporeal world, in short the world, and on the other hand *mens*, mind, spirit, 'consciousness.' These two entities are such *quae solo Dei concursu egent ad existendum*[6] [that they need only the concurrence of God in order to exist]. If they are at all in need of being, in one re-

---

5. Ibid.
6. Ibid., Pr. 52, p. 25.

spect they need only the copresence of God, otherwise they are in no need of any other entity, which means that they are substances in a certain way, that is, they are finite substances, while God is the *substantia infinita*.

I am intentionally presenting this somewhat deductive organization of Descartes's doctrine of being because here it becomes apparent that he organizes his entire consideration of the being of the world against the horizon of a pregiven doctrine of being. The question is, through what and how is an entity apprehended? Descartes says it is through the attribute, through that which in itself in its own content refers to an actual entity. In this context there follows an important remark whose sense cannot be easily exhausted and one which we also cannot pursue further at the outset.

Descartes says: *Verumtamen non potest substantia primum animadverti ex hoc solo, quod sit res existens, quia hoc solum per se nos non afficit . . .*[7] [Yet substance cannot be first discovered merely from the fact that it is a thing that exists, for this alone does not by itself affect us]. But an entity which is authentically, *the* substance, God, cannot be apprehended first of all from this alone, that it is. We thus cannot directly apprehend an entity primarily by relating to its way to be. It is precisely the being of an entity which is not accessible to us in this way. *Quia hoc solum*, for the being of an entity taken purely for itself, *per se nos non afficit*, by itself does not 'affect' us. Consequently, says Descartes, we have no primary and original access to the being of the entity as such. What Descartes expresses here in this way, that the being of an entity taken purely for itself does not affect us, is later formulated by Kant in the simple sentence, "being is not a real predicate"; that is, being is not a datum which can be apprehended by way of any kind of receptivity and affection. Precisely because we are not capable of apprehending the being of entities primarily and in isolation, but always first apprehend *what* an entity is, in Greek the εἶδος, its outward appearance, we must therefore, even in the apprehension of the being of the authentic entity, start with the attributes, through which the nature of the entity and its being are then presented. This peculiar principle, that being for itself cannot be experienced by us in the entity because it does not affect us, is perhaps, without Descartes knowing it and also perhaps without Kant ultimately understanding it in his thesis, the most clear-cut formulation of the being of the entity which we call world. In a wholly formal sense, it establishes that we are not affected by the being of the world as such. This concept of affection would of course require an elucidation of its subject matter, and this elucidation in turn would have to lean on a prior adequate analy-

---

7. Ibid.

sis of the being of the entity which we ourselves are. There is indeed an entity which can be grasped directly and *only* primarily from its *being* and, if it is to be understood philosophically, must so be grasped.

According to Descartes's orientation within Greek ontology, put briefly, in order to grasp the being of the entity we need a prior orientation to an attribute, to a determination of that which the entity in each case is. In conformity with the context in which we take up this question, we shall restrict ourselves now to one of the two created entities, *res corporea*. For we in fact first want to understand how Descartes defines the *being of the world*.

We can grasp the being of *res corporea* through its primary attributes, the primary *proprietates* which always belong to the entity as this entity and persist through all change. *Et quidem ex quolibet attributo substantia cognoscitur; sed una tamen est cujusque substantiae praecipua proprietas, quae ipsius naturam essentiamque constituit, et ad quam aliae omnes referuntur*[8] [And substance is indeed known through any one attribute; yet for each substance there is one principal property which constitutes its nature and essence and to which all the rest are referred]. For each substance there is an outstanding attribute, a what-determination of an outstanding kind, that is, a determination of the what of the entity which constitutes the 'nature,' the being of the entity with regard to that being and to which all other what-determinations of the entity must be referred—a determination which is already necessarily implied in every other determination. For every substance there is an outstanding what-determination, a property. *Nempe extensio in longum, latum et profundum, substantiae corporeae naturam constituit.*[9] "For extension in length, breadth, and depth constitutes the authentic being of the substance which we are calling 'world'" (*natura substantiae*, which is substantiality—the extant presence of this entity, what constitutes its being-forever).

The substantiality of the world, the authentic being of the world is constituted by *extensio. Nam omne aliud quod corpori tribui potest, . . .*[10] "everything else which we can attribute to such an entity which is a worldly thing" *extensionem praesupponit*, "presupposes extension" and is therefore *estque tantum modus quidam rei extensae*, "only a mode, a manner of extendedness," for example *divisio, figura, motus*. For example, *figura*, the shape of a worldly thing *nonnisi in re extensa potest intelligi*, "cannot be 'understood' other than in the horizon of extendedness"; *nec motus*, "also movement" *nisi in spatio extenso*, "cannot be understood other than in extended space." *Sed e contra*, "by contrast,"

---

8. Ibid., Pr. 53, p. 25.
9. Ibid.
10. Ibid.

however, *potest intelligi extensio sine figura vel motu,* "extension can be conceived without figure or movement." In other words, *extensio* is that determination of being in the entity of the world which must already be there prior to all other determinations so that the others can be. In short, space is the apriori.

Here you see a very clear prefiguration of the Kantian problematic. The same determination which Descartes here in the first part of the *Principia* carries out for *substantia creata* as *substantia corporea,* he also does for the other substance, *res cogitans.*

Extension was identified as that which truly determines the being, that is, the substantiality of this entity. How does Descartes now, on the one hand, proceed to determine and justify the being of the world as *res extensa*; on the other hand, what is the basis from which Descartes arrives at this determination of the being of the world, and what is the primary kind of experience which is supposed to make the worldhood of the world accessible? Our replies will show how the question of the reality of the world, the worldhood of the world, was forced by Descartes himself in a very clear-cut direction. This direction enabled him to assume once again from the tradition, with some conceptual modifications, all the categories for the specification of the being of the world which the Greeks had already created. This process of resumption continued right into Hegel's *Logic.*

Putting it in a very extreme form, we can say that Descartes derives his basic determinations of the being of the world, here of nature, from God. This continues in the philosophers who follow, including even Kant. God here is to be understood as an ontological concept in its specific categorial function: His being represents the sense of being which is then applied in a derivative way throughout to the different regions of being. This nexus of relations is especially clear in Descartes in the orientation of the two substances, *res cogitans* and *res extensa,* in regard to authentic substance, *substantia infinita, Deus.* Descartes in fact says that the authentic basic determination of God is precisely *perfectio,* specifically the *perfectio entis,* which is the most authentic being as such. On the other hand, however, he also emphasizes that we are not really capable of experiencing this being in itself primarily, that therefore infinite substance, just like finite substance, is accessible to us through the attributes. *Quin et facilius intelligimus substantiam extensam, vel substantiam cogitantem, quam substantiam solam,* . . .[11] "Indeed we even recognize extended substance or thinking substance, the substance laden with consciousness, more easily than substance alone, . . ." *omisso eo quod cogitet vel sit extensa,* "without regard to whether it thinks or is extended." Here he emphasizes anew that we

---

11. Ibid., Pr. 63, p. 31.

recognize the substantiality of substance only with difficulty, since substantiality differs from substance *ratione tantum*, "only in the way it is regarded" ["by reason alone"], and that substantiality cannot in reality be separated from substance. The two substances are thus given through the attribute or *proprietas*. The paramount property of the world as *corpus* is *extensio*; in it are grounded all the other determinations of the world, *figura, motus*, shape and movement. By conceiving these attributes as modes [of extension], we can account for the fact that one and the same body can vary its dimensional proportions while its total quantity, its total extension, remains the same. *Atque unum et idem corpus, retinendo suam eandem quantitatem, pluribus diversis modis potest extendi: nunc scilicet magis secundum longitudinem, minusque secundum latitudinem vel profunditatem, ac paulo post e contra magis secundum latitudinem, et minus secundum longitudinem.*[12] "And a body, while retaining one and the same quantity, can be extended in various ways: it can now be greater in length and less in breadth and depth, and later greater in breadth and less in length." In these modifications of dimensions and dimensional quantities, the total quantity still remains the same. It is clear what Descartes means here: Even in modifications of the shape of the body, its sameness is maintained. And because, according to the ancient concept of being, that truly is which always is, and because *extensio* always remains in every total change, extension is therefore the true and authentic being in the body.

. . . *itemque diversos modos extensionis sive ad extensionem pertinentes, ut figuras omnes, et situs partium, et ipsarum motus, optime percipiemus, si tantum ut modos rerum quibus insunt spectemus; . . .*[13] [And we shall similarly best apprehend the diverse modes of extension or whatever pertains to extension, such as all figures, the situation of parts, and their movements, if we regard them simply as modes of the things in which they are; . . .]. We thus apprehend body most authentically when we apprehend and determine everything in it in relation to extension. This includes movement, and movement certainly only then, *et quantum ad motum, si de nullo nisi locali cogitemus . . .*[14] "when we regard movement solely as change of place," *ac de vi a qua excitatur . . . non inquiramus,*[15] "but do not ask further about the force by which it is set in motion."

Descartes is aware that his definition of body really excludes force or, in today's terms, energy. And this is the phenomenon which later provided Leibniz with the opening, in the context of introducing *vis* into his system, to subject Descartes' determination of the being of nature to a fundamental critique.

---

12. Ibid., Pr. 64, p. 31.
13. Ibid., Pr. 65, p. 32.
14. Ibid.
15. Ibid.

Satis erit, si advertamus sensuum perceptiones non referri, nisi ad istam corporis humani cum mente conjunctionem, et nobis quidem ordinarie exhibere, quid ad illam externa corpora prodesse possint aut nocere; . . .[16] [It is sufficient for us to observe that the perceptions of the senses are related simply to the union of the human body with the mind, and that they indeed ordinarily show us what in external bodies can profit or hurt this union . . .]. It is, says Descartes, sufficient for the apprehension of nature in its authentic being if we observe that the *perceptiones* of the senses, that is, the kind of experience which the senses vouchsafe for us, are related to man only insofar as he is a *conjunctio corporis cum mente*, insofar as he is a conjunction of consciousness with corporeality; and if we observe that the senses *ordinarie*, according to their most proper sense, 'according to the usual order,' tell us nothing about what the world is but solely what use or harm the *externa corpora*, the world, the corporeal things out there, have for us, *prodesse possint aut nocere*. He says that the senses basically do not even have the function of knowledge or the communication of information, but that they are oriented specifically toward the preservation of corporeality or of the whole man as an organic being. We cannot really say "organic" here since, as everyone knows, Descartes regards the human body as a machine, and carries his extreme concept of nature over into the organic, to biological being. . . . ; *non autem . . . nos docere, qualia in seipsis existant;*[17] "the senses do not teach us how the bodies are in themselves." *Ita enim sensuum praejudicia facile deponemus, et solo intellectu, ad ideas sibi a natura inditas diligenter attendente, hic utemur*[18] [Therefore, we shall readily set aside the prejudices of the senses and rely here solely upon the intellect, attending carefully to the ideas implanted therein by nature]. Once we have recognized that the senses basically have no cognitive function at all, we can easily dismiss them and their prejudices and rely solely on the *intellectio*, on pure intellectual knowledge. Here it is clearly articulated that the only possible kind of access to the true being of the world lies in the *intellectio* (in the λόγος).

Intellectio has an essential priority over *sensatio. Quod agentes, percipiemus naturam materiae, sive corporis in universum spectati, non consistere in eo quod sit res dura, vel ponderosa, vel colorata, vel alio aliquo modo sensus afficiens: sed tantum in eo quod sit res extensa in longum, latum et profundum.*[19] "When we observe this, then we see that the authentic nature, the authentic being of matter, of the body, does not consist in the body being something hard, heavy, colored, or the like but that its being, its nature, consists solely in being extended in length, breadth, and depth."

16. Ibid. II, Pr. 3, p. 41.
17. Ibid.
18. Ibid.
19. Ibid. II, Pr. 4, p. 42.

Descartes maintains this not only in view of his attempt to carry out a critique of sensation with regard to its suitability for an objective apprehension of the world. At the same time, he shows that determinations such as *durities* (hardness), *pondus* (weight), and *color* (color) can to some extent be thought of as absent from bodily being without thereby modifying this being in any sense whatsoever.

> Nam, quantum ad duritiem, nihil aliud de illa sensus nobis indiciat, quam partes durorum corporum resistere motui manuum nostrarum, cum in illas incurrunt. Si enim, quotiescunque manus nostrae versus aliquam partem moventur, corpora omnia ibi existentia recederent eadem celeritate qua illae accedunt, nullam unquam duritiem sentiremus. Nec ullo modo potest intelligi, corpora quae sic recederent, idcirco naturam corporis esse amissura; nec proinde ipsa in duritie consistit. Eademque ratione ostendi potest, et pondus, et colorem, et alias omnes ejusmodi qualitates, quae in materia corporea sentiuntur, ex ea tolli posse, ipsa integra remanente: unde sequitur, a nulla ex illis ejus naturam dependere.[20]

> [For as far as hardness is concerned, sense shows us nothing about it other than that parts of hard bodies resist the motion of our hands when they touch these parts. But if, whenever our hands are moved toward some part, all the bodies there should recede with the same velocity as our approaching hands, we would never feel any hardness. Nor is it in any way intelligible that bodies which so recede would therefore lose their corporeal nature; hence this nature does not consist in hardness. And by the same reasoning it can be shown that weight and color and all the other qualities of this sort which are sensed in corporeal matter can be taken away from it while it remains entire: it thus follows that this nature depends on none of these.]

Weight, mass, color, hardness can be taken from the body while it remains intact in its authentic nature. But this means that the nature of body is not dependent on mass, color, weight, and hardness.

Descartes makes this clear by means of an example concerning hardness. Hardness is given to us, he says, in the resistance of a body to the touch, for example, of the hand. We can now assume, he says, that natural things, as extended, have a velocity which is equal to that with which I extend my hand toward the bodies to be touched. Since the velocities of the body to be touched and of the moving hand are equal, I never make contact. So it is not contradictory, says Descartes, for me to assume that the velocity of the world takes such a course. And if this assumption is not absurd, it serves to show that touch or resistance and thus hardness do not belong to the being of body. Here

---

20. Ibid.

it is clearly seen how a mode of access to the world like touch, which represents a very primary form of access, is from the start reinterpreted by Descartes into a natural process. In other words, he does not adhere to the phenomenal composition of touch as an experience of something; from the start, he interprets touch mechanically as nature in the sense of some sort of movement of a thing called a hand toward some other thing which recedes from it. He does not retain the phenomenal composition from the start, or rather he suppresses it. He sees it, of course, since he must after all reinterpret it into this mechanical relation of movement between touching and touched.

Leibniz tried in another way (which will not be explored any further here) to show that it will not do to define the being of body in terms of *extensio* and it alone. At the end of the second part of the *Principles*, where he in essence develops these structures of *extensio, spatium, locus, vacuum,* and the like, Descartes summarizes his interpretation by saying: *Nam plane profiteor me nullam aliam rerum corporearum materiam agnoscere, quam illam omnimode divisibilem, figurabilem et mobilem, quam Geometrae quantitatem vocant, et pro objecto suarum demonstrationum assumunt; . . .*[21] "I openly admit that I acknowledge no objectivity of corporeal things other than that which is in all ways divisible, shapeable, and mobile with respect to place. I mean that determination which the geometers and mathematicians call quantity and which the mathematicians take as the sole object, 'pro objecto,' of their proofs." . . . *ac nihil plane in ipsa considerare, praeter istas divisiones, figuras et motus; nihilque de ipsis ut verum admittere, quod non ex communibus illis notionibus, de quarum veritate non possumus dubitare, tam evidenter deducatur, ut pro Mathematica demonstratione sit habendum.*[22] "We are to consider and to regard as true nothing about the world other than what can be proven mathematically on the basis of these universal concepts of *extensio, figura, motus* [whose truth we cannot doubt]." *Et quia sic omnia Naturae Phaenomena possunt explicari, ut in sequentibus apparebit, nulla alia Physicae principa puto esse admittenda, nec alia etiam optanda.*[23] "And because all appearances of nature can be adequately explained by way of such measurement and determination of relations of extension, I believe that no principles are to be admitted in physics other than mathematical ones."

In what way is the being of the world defined here?—from a very precise kind of knowledge of objects, the mathematical. The being of the world is nothing other than the *objectivity of the apprehension of nature through calculative measurement.* Contrary to all ancient and me-

---

21. Ibid. II, Pr. 64, pp. 78f.
22. Ibid.
23. Ibid.

dieval knowledge of nature, physics is now *mathematical physics*. Only what can be mathematically defined in the world can be truly known in it, and only what is thus mathematically known is *true* being. Since for Descartes *verum ens* is equal to *certum ens*, this known true being is the authentic being of the world. The authentic being of the world is defined a priori by way of a particular and in fact possible kind of knowledge of the world as nature.

The being of the world is that which in it can be apprehended by means of a particular kind of apprehension, the mathematical, which Descartes takes as the very highest kind of knowledge. Underlying it is a very specific correlation of being and being-true and accordingly knowing. The world is not interrogated in regard to its worldhood as it first shows itself and thence determines spatiality, but rather the reverse: a particular idea of space, or a particular idea of *extensio* as the being-like condition for a particular knowability, is taken as the basis for an apriori evaluation of what can belong to the being of nature and what cannot. A particular *ideal of knowledge* with the criterion of *certainty* decides on what in the world is taken as authentic being.

But even if one does not adhere to this extreme standpoint of Descartes, extreme because the being of body is regarded solely in its *extensio*, even if one defines the corporeal more concretely, as Leibniz brought in energy as the basic determination of body, even then the world is still defined primarily as nature.

Even Kant conceived nature in this sense and so world in this sense. We can now say that in the end it is easy to see that this kind of apprehension of the being of the world in terms of mathematical-physical knowledge is one-sided. But because we see this, this kind of apprehension is just as easy to reverse, and Descartes in fact gives the best instructions for this in his famous *wax example* in the *Second Meditation*.

We need only to regard this particular piece of wax solely in regard to what is first given in it and not, in the terms of mathematical-physical knowledge, pay attention to what stays the same in every change of the initially sensed qualities. When we take the piece of wax as it is given with respect to *sapor, odor, color* . . . , this particular colored, flavored, sonorous, hard, cold thing of wax, we have the immediately given entity, the worldly thing, and the mode of access to it is sense perception. However, even sense perception is a theoretical apprehension of the thing, even here the entitative thing of wax is determined just as it is encountered in a *perceptual regard*. But ultimately, we can go one step further back and in the end also concede that this kind of apprehension still only shows the thing of wax as a thing of nature, even if it is now characterized by properties which are given in the most immediate kind of experience, even if it is now characterized not by quantities alone but by sense qualities. What it still lacks in order to characterize it as a worldly thing in the full sense are certain predicates of value: good, bad, plain, beautiful, suitable, unsuitable, and the like, which tend to adhere to the material thing of nature. These are predicates which all utensils, all objects of use, also intrinsically have. If we go so far as to grant some of the value-predicates of the sensory thing also to the sense qualities, then the *practical* thing, that is, the thing as it is first found in the world, would be completely defined by us. It is a thing of nature with the fundamental stratum of materiality, but at the same time laden with predicates of value.

It is in this way that one first tries even today in phenomenology to define the environmental thing in its being. Yet this definition is in its approach not essentially different from that of Descartes. Here too, a thing is approached as an object of observation and perception, and perception is then, as it is typically put, complemented by value judgment. As we shall see, the authentic environmental being of the thing is passed over here just as it is in Descartes's extreme formulation of *res corporea* as *res extensa*. This characterization of the worldly thing as a value-laden thing of nature is all the more fateful as it gives the impression that it is in fact a genuine and original characterization, where there is in fact in the background the full structure and the constitution of a thing of nature, a thing with properties, qualities, some of which are qualities of value, predicates of value. The thing remains naturalized; we do not come across the entity as an environing world, nor is the worldhood of this world brought into focus or for that matter explicated. Such concrete questions are not even asked because this determination arises from a characteristic exemplary approach to the world which prompts us to assume in the first instance that a thing is as it is present in an isolated perception of it. But when we make some fundamental inquiries into this kind of determination of the world, we see clearly, especially from Descartes, that the being of the world is always characterized relative to particular kinds of experience and capacities of apprehension—sensation, imagination, intellect—which have themselves arisen in the context of a particular characterization of man, namely, in the context of the familiar anthropological definition *homo animal rationale*. A particular biological and anthropological interpretation favors certain potential kinds of apprehension of the world and these decide on what is accessible in the world in its being and thus on how the being of the world is itself determined.

This division of the particular capacities of man is still dominant in philosophy and decides in advance on the possibility of determining the being of the world. Conversely, *spirit* and *person* are now characterized in reaction to the world thus determined, which means as it is correlated to these particularly conceived anthropological capacities.

Inasmuch as it is said that spirit and person, that is, the entity constituting the being of these capacities, are not nature, this means conversely (so that we are continually moving in a circle) that the being of spirit is now derived from the being of nature defined in this way. The *antinomies* in Kant, for example, arise from this nexus of relations.

The *antinomy of freedom* develops not so much from an analysis of the problem of freedom and an analysis of the specific existence of man, but from the fact that Kant sees the being of man also integrated into the being of nature. He conceives the being of nature in the manner of Descartes as the nature of the natural sciences and regards it as being defined by *causality* in the broadest sense. Two particular entities, both of which are characterized basically by way of their natural being, are juxtaposed in such a way that certain impossibilities, called *antinomies*, result from this opposition. The possibility of the antinomy is based merely on an inadequate analysis of the being of that which is posed in the antinomy itself.

It is thus in Descartes that we see most clearly and simply that a whole chain of presuppositions deviates from the true phenomenon of the world. We saw how Descartes tries to reduce all the determinations of corporeal being, what British empiricism, precisely in conjunction with him, later called the *secondary qualities of sensation* as opposed to the primary qualities, to the basic determination of *res extensa*, to *extensio*, in order to enable a knowledge of the world which in its degree of certainty is no different from the knowledge of *res cogitans*. But it is also already evident that the being of the world, which on the basis of certain judgments is first conceived as nature, cannot even be obtained by a theoretical reconstruction which goes from the *res extensa* back to the sensory thing and then to the value-laden thing, but that by doing so the specific theoretical objectification is retained and the analysis is led astray even further. The world would remain *deprived of its worldhood*, since the primary exhibition of the authentic reality of the world should be referred to the original task of an analysis of reality itself, which would first have to disregard every specifically theoretical objectification. The course of the scientific inquiry into reality shows, however, that the original mode of encounter of the environing world is always already given up in favor of the established view of the world as the reality of nature, so that we may interpret the specific phenomena of the world in terms of its theoretical knowledge of the objectivity of nature.

If we consider this work of Descartes in relation to the constitution of the mathematical sciences of nature and to the elaboration of mathematical physics in particular, these considerations then naturally assume a fundamentally positive significance. But if they are regarded in the context of a general theory of the reality of the world, it then becomes apparent that from this point on the fateful constriction of the inquiry into reality sets in, which to the present day has not yet been overcome. This constriction dominates the entire past tradition of philosophy. It was in a way prepared by Greek philosophy, not in the extreme sense of mathematization but in accord with a natural tendency of knowing. The world was experienced as πράγματα, as the "with which of having to do with it"; and yet it was not understood ontologically in this sense, but instead in the broadest sense as a thing of nature. That the question of the reality of the world continues to be oriented primarily to the world as nature also serves to show, however, that the original way of encountering the environing world evidently cannot even be directly grasped, that this phenomenon is instead typically passed over. This is no accident, inasmuch as Dasein as being-in-the-world in the sense of concern *is absorbed* in its world in which it is preoccupied, is so to speak exhausted by that world, so that precisely in the most natural and the most immediate being-in-the-world the world in its worldhood is not experienced thematically at all. The world is experienced expressly only when it is apprehended in some sort of theoretical intention. The world thus encountered in theoretical intention becomes thematic when we inquire into its being theoretically.

This peculiar fact, that the primary phenomenon of the world is passed over, along with the stubbornness and the constant pressure and intrusion of the kind of apprehension involved in the theoretical apprehension and determination of a thing, can itself be explained only by reference to Dasein's essential kind of being. When this happens, when the kind of being involved in this specific theoretical apprehension and its precedence are themselves understood, only then is this persistent prejudice rendered harmless for the primary analysis of the world.

§23. Positive exposition of the basic structure of the worldhood of the world

But how shall the worldhood of the world now be positively determined? How can something be said about the structure of worldhood so that we first of all disregard all theory and particularly this extreme objectification? We shall organize our considerations by following the plan already announced and exploring 1) the characters of the worldhood of the world as such and 2) the structure of aroundness as a distinctive constitutive feature of worldhood. The first task, the analysis of the worldhood of the environing world, in accord with the subject matter divides into three steps: a) the *exposition* of the characters of encounter of the world, b) the *interpretation* of the structure of encounter, that is, the exposition of the phenomenal correlation founding these characters of encounter, and c) the *determination* of the basic structure of worldhood as *deployment totality*.*

These steps serve to clarify *four questions about the tradition*: 1) why the authentic structure of the being of the world, [what we have called] primary worldhood, was from the start and has ever since been passed over in philosophy; 2) why this structure of being, even when a replacement phenomenon equipped with value predicates is brought in for it, is still held to be in need of explanation and derivation; 3) why it is explained by being clarified and founded in a fundamental stratum of reality; 4) why this founding reality is conceived as the being of nature and that in terms of the objectivity of mathematical physics.

In taking these three steps, we shall try to get close to the peculiar *presence* [*Präsenz*] of the world around us. We must keep to it from the beginning, since the understanding of the analysis is possible only by placing ourselves in the specific natural kind of preoccupation with the world in which we constantly move. We do not actually have to make this displacement but need only to make explicit the kind of comportment in which we constantly move everyday, and which, for the reasons stated, is at first the least visible of all.

a) Analysis of the characters of encounter of the world (reference, referential totality, familiarity, 'one')

The question is how the world shows itself in everyday concern. This entity, world, presents itself [*präsentiert sich*] in the character of 'serving to,' 'conducive to' or 'detrimental to,' 'relevant to,' and the like. The worldly is encountered as itself always *in and as a reference to another*. 'Reference' henceforth is used as a technical term.

The other element which as it were gets forced into *co-presence* in such reference (serviceability, conduciveness, and the like) is *that to which—for which* the conducive is what it is. These referential relations are such that in them a manifold of environmental things shows itself, for example, a public square with its surroundings, a room with its furnishings. The manifold of things encountered here is not an arbitrary manifold of incidental things; it is first and only present [*gegenwärtig*] in a particular *correlation of references*. This referential con-

---

Bewandtnisganzheit, which replaces *Bedeutsamkeit*, a change postdating the lecture course, as is indicated by the original title of this subsection §23c as it stands on page 200 below. Cf. "On the Way to *Being and Time*" on the late introduction of *Bewandtnis* into this lecture course.

texture is itself a *closed totality*. It is precisely out of this totality that, for example, the individual piece of furniture in a room appears. My encounter with the room is not such that I first take in one thing after another and put together a manifold of things in order then to see a room. Rather, I primarily see a referential totality as closed, from which the individual piece of furniture and what is in the room stand out. Such an environment of the nature of a closed referential totality is at the same time distinguished by a specific *familiarity*. The closed character of the referential whole is grounded precisely in familiarity, and this familiarity implies that the referential relations are *well-known* [*bekannt*]. Everyday concern as making use of, working with, constantly attends to these relations; everyone dwells in them.

It thus becomes clear that the references are precisely the *involvements* [*Wobei*] in which the concernful occupation dwells; it does not dwell among isolated things of the environing world and certainly not among thematically or theoretically perceived objects. Rather things constantly step back into the referential totality or, more properly stated, in the immediacy of everyday occupation they never even first step out of it. That they do not step out of the referential totality, which itself is encountered primarily in the form of familiarity: this phenomenon characterizes the *obviousness* and *unobtrusiveness* of the reality of the environing world. Things recede into relations, they do not obtrude themselves, in order thus to be there for concern. These primary phenomena of encounter: *reference, referential totality, the closed character of the referential context, familiarity of the referential whole, things not stepping out of referential relations*, are of course seen only if the original phenomenological direction of vision is assumed and above all seen to its conclusion, which means letting the world be encountered in concern. This phenomenon is really passed over when the world is from the start approached as given for observation or, as is by and large the case even in phenomenology, when the world is approached just as it shows itself in an isolated, so-called sense perception of a thing, and this isolated free-floating perception of a thing is now interrogated on the specific kind of givenness belonging to its object. There is here a basic deception for phenomenology which is peculiarly frequent and persistent. It consists in having the theme determined by the way it is phenomenologically investigated. For inasmuch as phenomenological investigation is itself theoretical, the investigator is easily motivated to make a specifically theoretical comportment to the world his theme. Thus a specifically theoretical apprehension of the thing is put forward as an exemplary mode of being-in-the-world, instead of phenomenologically placing oneself directly in the current and the continuity of access of the everyday preoccupation with things, which is inconspicuous enough, and phenomenally recording what is encountered in it. It is precisely this inconspicuousness of comportment and of its corresponding way of having the world which must be secured in order to see in it the specific presence of the world.

We speak of a priority of the presence [*Präsenz*] of the referential totality and of the references *over* the things which show themselves in these references. This peculiar priority of the referential totality over the things themselves becomes immediately apparent when we point out how things within the environing world become present [*gegenwärtig*] in an emphatic sense. This occurs when an entity of the character of 'serving to' *breaks down* in its serviceability, becomes unusable, is damaged.

When a thing in the world around us becomes unusable, it becomes *conspicuous*. The natural course of concern is brought to a halt by this unusability. The continuity of reference and thus the referential totality undergoes a distinctive disturbance which forces us to pause. When a tool is damaged and useless, its defect actually causes it to be present, conspicuous, so that it now forces itself into the foreground of the environing world in an emphatic sense. This dwelling on such a conspicuous thing of the environing world is however not that of a staring and scrutinizing but has and retains the mode of being of concern. Being held up in the mode of concern has the sense of restoring order, repairing, and the like. The disturbance is not present as a pure alteration of a thing but as a *break in the familiar totality of references*. Every alteration in the world, up to reversal and the simple turnover from something to something, is first experienced through this kind of encounter.

In order to give a more accurate portrayal of the phenomenal structure of the world as it shows itself in everyday preoccupation, it must be noted that what matters in this preoccupation with the world is not so much anyone's own particular world, but that right in our natural preoccupation with the world we are moving in a *common* totality of surroundings. 'One' moves in a world with which 'one' is familiar without thereby being conversant with the particular environing world of the individual and being able to move in his world.

Even the workshop of a craftsman whose craft is totally unfamiliar to us is in no way first encountered as a mere conglomerate of things scattered in disarray. Manifest in the immediate orientation of preoccupation are hand tools, material, manufactured finished pieces, unfinished items in process. What we primarily experience is the world in which the man lives. Even though it is strange, it is still experienced as a world, as a closed totality of references.

When something within the world is encountered in the character of being 'obstructive,' 'in the way,' that is, lying in the way of concern, this '*it doesn't belong here*' is possible only on the basis of the specific presence of the world as a fixed, familiar totality of references. There can be something like a not-belonging-here only against the background of a primary familiarity, which itself is not conscious and intended but is rather present in this unprominent way. The broken familiarity as *broken familiarity* constitutes the very contrasting and bringing into relief of the *pale and inconspicuous presence [Anwesenheit] of the world*. Because something like the 'obstructive' and 'disturbing' occurs in the familiar world, the obviousness of the world and its peculiar kind of reality undergo a hardening.

This is manifest even more clearly in the phenomenon in which some surroundings, especially the most familiar ones, become a compelling presence when something is *missing* in them. Because the specific presence of the environing world lies precisely in the familiar totality of references, missing something can allow us to encounter the inconspicuous extant thing. And *to be missing always implies an absence of a something belonging-here within the closed context of references*. The *absence* of something within the world of concern, absence as a breach of reference, as a disturbance of familiarity, thus has a distinctive function in encountering the environing world. We could put this in a very extreme form by asserting that *the specific handiness of the environing world of equipment as the world of concern is constituted in the absence of handiness, in not being handy*. But we do not wish to stop at such a perhaps somewhat paradoxical formulation. We want to understand its positive sense, namely, that this specific absence points to what underlies it as its possibility, that is, the *always-already-there* of a familiar continuity of references which is disturbed because something is missing, and which stands out through this specific absence.

We first see only very roughly that these characters of reference, referential totality, and familiarity together make up the specific presence of the world as environing world, but this does not give us a truly phenomenological understanding of this structure of worldhood. We can gain such an understanding only by an *interpretation* of the founding correlation among these phenomenal characters, that is, by laying open the way in which these phenomena (referential totality, references, familiarity) now constitute the specific manner of encounter of the environing world. We therefore proceed to the second point of our preliminary outline.

b) Interpretation of the structure of encounter of the environing world: the phenomenal correlation founding the characters of encounter themselves

Two things stand out from what has already been shown. First, the things of the environing world are encountered in and from references. The proper phenomenal way of envisaging worldhood allows us to encounter the world first rather than an isolated thing. This points to a priority of the reference over the thing which shows itself in the reference. The mode of access is concerned preoccupation and not a free-floating and isolated perception of the thing. The view that reality can be found in bodily presence and this in turn in the isolated thing of nature will even more strikingly prove to be a phenomenal and so a phenomenological deception.

On the other hand, however, it turned out that, second, it is really an *absence* in a distinctive sense which is constitutive for encountering an otherwise inconspicuous world, specifically absence understood here not in an arbitrary formal sense but the specific absence within the world of concern. But this means that *absence has this function of encounter on the basis of the world always already being present.* The breach in reference (when something is missing) is what it is only as a breach of a totality of references. This however implies that encountering the things of the environing world in their references comes about from a totality of references. This already indicates a certain structural correlation among the characters mentioned, namely, that it is the references which let things be *present* and that the references in turn become present or *appresented* through the referential totality. The apprehensibility and the objectivity of a thing is grounded in the encounter of the world, but objectivity is not a presupposition for the encounter. The very nearest thing which is on hand is there in its 'there' only from an 'already there' which accompanies and precedes it. This does not mean that in fact there are always some things on hand and we can proceed from the nearest one to another one. It means rather that it is a *world which appresents a thing of the world.* It is not world-things taken as real things which put together reality.

It is now a matter of discerning this peculiar structural correlation in which the world in its worldhood appresents the specific thing of the world, references are encountered in a totality of references and individual things are encountered in the references. It is to be shown that the environing world of concern has a distinctive function in the constitution of worldhood in general, and that it lets us encounter the world precisely in a *double* direction, first relating to the *presence of the nearest available things* and then relating to *the presence of extant things always already on hand.* The analysis of the structure of encounter of worldhood is accordingly divided into three parts: α) a more detailed phenomenological interpretation of the environing world of concern, which up to now has been drawn out only in very rough outline. We shall call this specific environing world of concern the *work-world*; β) the characterization of the specific function of encounter of this work-world for encountering the nearest things in the world around us, thus the sense of this specific character of reality, the character re-

ferred to when we say that something is *handy*; γ) the specific function of encounter of the work-world for letting us encounter that
which is always already there, which means the peculiar connection
whereby, out of the environing world of concern and in it, the world
as a whole, the public world and the world understood as nature are
appresented.

From this outline we already see the central position which the
work-world of the specific environing world of concern occupies overall in structuring the reality of the real.

α)The work-world: more detailed phenomenological interpretation of the environing world of concern

The worldly aspect of the environing world is encountered in references and, like these, first in concerned preoccupation. By way of example, we shall begin with an environing world and occupation of the
simplest sort, a handicraft and craftsman.

The tool has the character of being of '*in-order-to*.' The range of
usability of a tool is narrower or wider. A hammer has a wider range
of usability than a watchmaker's instrument, which is tailored precisely to his particular kind of concern. The narrower the sphere of
use, the more unequivocal the reference. Within its sphere a tool can
be applied now to particular parts and pieces of that which is to be
produced and then to particular stages in the course of production.
Encountered in concern as it is, the tool is not regarded in its outward
appearance. The genuine relation to it is to be occupied with it in
using it; the tool thus becomes absorbed in the reference. But this implies something essential: concern in a certain sense looks away from
the tool as thing; it is primarily not even there as such a thing, but
rather as a tool, as '*equipment for*,' which is *used*. And insofar as it is
encountered in use, this means that, in relation to sight, its genuine
reality appears in looking away from it as a mere thing on hand. Its
specific kind of being is encountered in use, and it is characteristic of
practical usage that *no scrutinizing objectification occurs*, not even the objectification of reference, that is, of the usability in which concern
dwells. Dwelling in it, that is, having the tool in use, means precisely
not having the reference itself objectively. But the attention of concern, that is, its attending to the references as its specific type of performance, has placed in its care the work to be produced, that to
which the tool in its specific usability refers. Occupation with the tool
[its very use] is performed as absorption in the reference on the basis
of already having present that to which the reference is directed,
namely, the *work* to be produced. This work to be produced is what
concerns us as such. It supports the referential totality of the craft re-

garded as concern. This work to be taken care of is thus itself, more accurately seen, a *work-world*. In order to grasp the specific constitutive function of work-worldhood for the 'reality' of the environing world, it is necessary for us to make the relations of this work-world to the environing world stand out more sharply.

The work-world is defined in the work. But the work, in accord with the kind of being it has, is itself in the character of 'conducive to.' The shoe is for wearing, the table for use, the clock for telling time. Once again, the *what-for* of its usability is discovered along with the work itself. Indeed, it is what it is only on the basis of this *its* usability, and this specific usability is what then in turn prescribes and modifies the manner of production, such that we distinguish alarm clock, stopwatch, and the like.

In simple craft conditions, every single work even has within it a reference to the particular prospective wearer and user. The work is as it were tailored to his body. Some goods are still custom-made and not mass-produced for the average "cross-section." Mass-produced articles themselves do not lack reference, but it is quite generic; they have an indeterminacy, an arbitrariness, but they nevertheless have a reference to indeterminate others. What is of primary importance here is not the variety of modifications in content which arise, but the already given context of being from which they arise and which characterizes the presence of the work to be produced in concern.

Along with the usability of the work, the work-world at the same time appresents the world in which users and consumers live, and in this way it appresents them too. In this relation, my *own environing world* is appresented as at the same time entering into a *public world*. More accurately, this public world is always already there with the work to be provided; because of it we encounter the work-world in a salient way. The boundary between my own environing world and a public one can be defined by modes of a varied disposability and by locality. The room in which I attend to my concern as a room in a house can belong to another; my environing world can be such that another disposes of it to some extent. To begin with, however, we ought not to bring these distinctions into our analysis. But what does matter now is to see the peculiarly unaccentuated manner of these relations between my own environing world and the public environment and first of all only this one relation, that my own and nearest work-world appresents a wider and public world not only occasionally, when I think of it, but essentially. The public world is included in the very sense of the work and its usability, even though it is not itself known.

But the work-world essentially shows still other relations which belong to its worldhood. A craftsman's work, the shoe, is in its sense usable for something. Concerned preoccupation with the work in its very production is however a matter of using something for the shoe to be produced. Not only is the work as finished itself usable for . . . , but as produced it already bears in itself the reference of usability: in the work as produced, materials are also used. The work itself has a way of *being-dependent-on*, the shoe on leather, thread, nails, leather from hides taken from animals which are raised by others and so become available. Here we should make note of something peculiar, namely, that these world-things, animals, actually produce themselves in reproduction and growth. Here we finally have the reference to something worldly, which of itself is always already there for the concerned preoccupation of production. The worldly as already extant is put to use not only in the work itself but also in tools like hammers, tongs, nails: steel, iron, ore, minerals, wood. Here too, the reference is to entities which in a certain sense ultimately do not need to be produced for concern, and for that very reason are in an emphatic sense usable, are always already present. Thus, along with the reference to the public environment, the work refers to the world of *nature*, but nature here understood as the world of the disposable, nature taken as the particular world of products of nature.

But even the public environment, as it is appresented by the work itself apart from what it consists of, in turn lets us encounter nature in a certain sense. Nature here is not taken as an object of natural observation, at any rate not so that observation itself would thereby be the specific form of preoccupation. These referential relations and the peculiar copresence of nature in our everyday environment are for the most part concealed from us. When we in our everyday concern orient ourselves to time by looking at the clock, we are not aware that by doing so what we are putting to use is the indicated time. Every day is oriented to the position of the sun according to the official astronomical ordering of time. Every time we look at a clock, we are simply making use of the copresence of the world-system.

β) Characterization of the specific function of encounter of this work-world for encountering the nearest things in the environing world— the specific character of reality of the handy

The world of concern always has first-order presence within the environing world. That in which concern is absorbed, the work-world, has a primary function in the encounter of the entire environment. But the world into which concern has *fallen* at any given time is not thematically perceived, not thought, not known, and it is just this which grounds the possibility of an *original reality*. The presence of the specific world of concern means precisely *non-objectivity* as some-

thing apprehended. For the time being, the following question is left
open: To what extent is there actually a world present in concern and
why does reality mean non-objectivity?

Before settling these important questions we must make the phenomenal ground even more secure, in order to possess the structure
of encounter of the world transparently; we have to see how the specific world of concern, the work-world, now appresents the nearest
environment and the wider world, the public world as well as the
world of nature. The question is: Where does the peculiar priority of
the work-world manifest itself within the environmental whole?

We maintain that the specific world of concern is the one by which
the world as a whole is encountered. Correlatively, we maintain that
the world in its worldhood is built neither from immediately given
things, not to speak of sense data, nor for that matter from extant
things always already on hand belonging to—as everyone puts it—a
nature existing in itself. The worldhood of the world is grounded
rather in the specific work-world. This proposition must now be demonstrated in the phenomena of the environing world.

When we follow this function of encounter of the work-world,
namely, that it appresents the nearest and the wider environment, we
find in it two aspects of reality which are characteristic for the entire
structure of the environing world: *being-handy*, or better, *handiness*—
the *handy* as the immediately available—and the *extant and on hand*,
the always-already-there.

It should be emphasized from the start that what we are here distinguishing in the environing world as a whole—*my own environment, public environment* and *world as nature*—are not regions juxtaposed in
themselves. Rather, they are themselves environmentally present on
the basis of a peculiar *exchange of presence*, as we have yet to see.

What is of concern [*Besorgtheit*]—that for the sake of which concern
is concerned—that which is primarily placed under care, lets us encounter everything *around it* toward which it is oriented, the referential connections of serviceability, usability, conduciveness, and these
references in turn then let us encounter what stands *in* them. What all
this means: '*to place under care,*' '*to stand in a reference,*' and to be encountered from it, can only be clarified later, specifically only by the
phenomenon of *time*.

If we refrain from the opposite direction of interpretation, if we do
not explain our encounter of the world from our apprehension of it
but instead understand the latter as based on the former, then it becomes clear that it is the *presence of what is of concern* which first and
foremost brings to light what we in the context of theoretical apprehension designate as the immediately given. The genuine immediate datum is thus once again not the perceived but what is present in

concerned preoccupation, the *handy* within reach and grasp. Such a presence of the environmental, which we call handiness, is a *founded presence*. It is not something original but grounded in the presence of that which is placed under care. If this handily nearest, the handy in concern, is already a founded presence, then this applies even more so to the character of reality which we learned about earlier and which Husserl claims to be the authentic presence of the world, what he calls *bodily presence* [*Leibhaftigkeit*].

In our analysis of perception, envisaging, perception of a picture, and empty intention, we explicated the kind of presence belonging to a chair as thing and already there pointed to a distinction between the environmental thing and the natural thing. This distinction was then only applied quite roughly. We can now clarify it and thus see that bodily presence is in no way a primary character but rather is grounded in handiness and what is immediately available within concern. Bodily presence is a character of encounter of world-things, insofar as the world is still encountered solely in a pure apprehension, a pure perception. It is a character of encounter of reality to the degree that preoccupation denies the world its full possibility of encounter; it is a specific environmental character which shows itself only when concern, concerned being-in-the-world, is a particularly conditioned mere looking at the world, only when the primarily given and experienced world is in a certain way excluded.

But handiness is the presence of an immediately available environmental thing such that preoccupation dwells precisely in the references of serviceability and the like as a concerned reaching for something, getting it ready for use. We can now expressly keep an eye on what is thus encountered, for example, in making an instrument present by looking after it and looking around to see whether in the end it should not be arranged differently in view of that for which it is an instrument. When we look at the tool in this way, the now handy environmental thing is thematic in its handiness. But this thematization still remains wholly and simply in the kind of sight which guides the genuinely concerned use of the thing, in *circumspection*. But at the same time this thematization of handiness is the transitional step to a potentially independent mode of concerned preoccupation—*in the care of merely looking at . . .* ; the handy entity placed under care is now merely *viewed*. For this to be possible, the environmental thing of utility must be concealed precisely in its specific referential relations as a utensil so that it may be encountered solely as a thing occurring in nature. This covering up or masking is performed by concern insofar as being-in-the-world is now modified to a state of solely *looking*, a mere looking which *interprets*. This modification of in-being means, so to speak, the attempt on the part of Dasein not to be in its most immediate environment any longer. It is only when we absent ourselves from the environing world by stepping out of it, as it were, that we gain access to the presumably authentic reality of the primary thing of nature. The mode of encounter of the natural thing in the character of bodily presence, a characteristic obtrusiveness which things of the world show insofar as they are merely perceived, this character of bodily presence has its basis in a specific *"unworlding" of the environing world*, a *deprivation of its worldhood*. Nature as object of natural science is in general *discovered* only in such an "unworlding." But the reality of the environing world is not a diminished bodily presence, a degraded nature.

Against this analysis of the founded sense of bodily presence, which is founded in handiness, which in turn is founded in the non-emergence of referential relations, and in turn again in the intimate presence of what is of concern, it can be objected that one can nonetheless let a pure thing be encountered at any time and directly in its naked bodily presence. One does not first need the performance of an initially unreflective concern. In other words, the founding connection is not at all necessary. This objection, that bodily presence is not a founded phenomenon since one does not have to run through the individual steps of founding it, is no objection at all, but perhaps only the unbiased confirmation of the phenomenal state of affairs which grounded our assertion that bodily presence is founded. In order to see this, it should be noted that the explicitness and the awareness of the modes of being and their ontological foundation in the course of being do not decide on what belongs to the phenomenal composition of a structure of being. The fact that I know nothing about a particular founding connection in the enactment of a way of being cannot be taken as justification for the conclusion that this founding connection is not constitutive for that way of being. Explicitness and awareness do not decide on these matters. Rather, the very lack of explicitness in traversing this course, the very lack of an awareness of going along with the founding steps is characteristic of all concerned being-in-the-world, inasmuch as we define it as *absorption* in the world, being drawn in by it. For why can I let a pure thing of the world be encountered at all in bodily presence? Only because the world is already there in thus letting it be encountered, because letting-it-be-encountered is but a particular mode of my being-in-the-world and because world means nothing other than what is always already present for the entity in it. I can see a natural thing in its bodily presence only on the basis of this being-in-the-world. I *can* means that I have this *possibility* at my disposal, and this possibility is of course nothing other than the basic constitution of my Dasein, of my I of which I am capable, to wit, that I am in the world. It is utterly unthinkable how something, a natural thing, could be encountered in its pure bodily presence, if not on the basis of the *prior presence of world*. Otherwise, in encountering this thing, not only would it have to show itself in its presence but all in all something like presence as such first of all would have had to arise. But why presence arises not for the Dasein but is itself with the Dasein which is in its world, this we understand only by reference to *time*, to this namely, that *Dasein itself*—as we shall later see—is *time*.

I can at any time perceive natural things in their bodily presence directly, that is, without running through the founding steps beforehand, because it belongs to the sense of being-in-the-world to be in these founding steps constantly and primarily. I have no need to go through them because the Dasein, which founds perceiving, is nothing but the way of being of these very founding steps, as concerned absorption in the world. Because bodily presence itself is founded in the immediate environmental data, this means that the world (or more accurately the worldhood of the world) is grounded in the primary presence of what is placed under care, in the specific handiness of the work-world. That environmental things do not come forward for perception into this particularly emphatic bodily presence is closely related to their particular kind of presence, handiness, which is founded in the references, which in turn are founded in the primary presence of what is of concern. This *founding character* permits us to understand a basic phenomenal trait of the worldhood of the environing world: *presence in the manner of inconspicuousness*, its presence precisely on the basis of not yet being apprehended and nevertheless having discovered primarily, permitting encounter.

It is on this basis that we understand the sense of a favorite expression, that of the '*in-itself*' *of the being* of the world. It is customary to point out that the world is first there not on account of a subject, the world is rather '*in itself.*' The frequent use of this expression '*in-itself*' of course never tells us anything about its sense. The opinion seems to be that the self-evidence in which this character of the environing world is experienced is tantamount to a categorial self-evidence. But what is clearly experienced as *ontically* self-evident need not be *ontologically* clear at all. The opposite holds true here and in all similar cases. Nothing at all has been said ontologically when the expression 'in-itself' is used without further clarification. It is because the specific presence of what is of concern is always centered in the specific work-world that every worldly entity, and precisely the very nearest real entity of this primary presence, and in its primacy a non-objective presence, is taken 'in itself.' '*In-itself*' thus means, *with respect to encounter, the founding of the handiness of a referential context in the presence of what is of concern.* The true phenomenal sense of the 'in-itself' is however fully visible in its structure only when we have clarified this very presence of what is of concern and understood it in its primacy. This will also show the extent to which non-objectivity is and can be constitutive of reality. The non-objectivity of the immediately given world is not nothing; it is a positive phenomenal character belonging to the presence of the environing world.

γ)The specific function of encounter of the work-world for letting us encounter that which is always already there— the extant on hand

Heretofore, however, the environing world was left unclarified precisely in regard to *non-objectivity*, inasmuch as its specific constitutive character manifests itself precisely in the second direction in which the work-world appresents. It is only with the exposition of this second function of appresentation of the work-world that we arrive at the full structural composition of the environing world.

What we have called the public environment and the *world of nature* in the broadest sense is in a particular sense *non-objective* within the environing world. We have already seen that the work-world bears within itself references to the public environment and the world of nature, insofar as the work in itself, in its composition, employs certain correlations of being. In the public environment, nature is constantly present to us, but this is nature in the sense of the world which concerns us. In the roads, bridges, rails, road signs, and similar installations, the world as nature and earth is constantly being made a concern. A covered railway platform takes the weather, stormy weather, into account. Public lighting, a simple street-lamp, takes darkness, the specific change over to the absence of daylight and the sun, into account. As I have already indicated, public clocks constantly take into account a particular constellation in the world-system, the 'position of the sun' in relation to the earth. In all of this something is present, something is taken into account specifically with regard to its detrimental character, insofar as it is threatening, obstructive, unserviceable, resistant. But we not only take 'nature' into account in terms of self-protection but also in terms of utility, as that which is put to use, as ways and means of business and commerce (water and wind transport), as earth which provides support and position, serves as ground and foundation for a house. The ground can serve as farmland or field, the forest as a preserve for animals, which we keep as hunting, draught, riding, and house animals. This is not taken in terms of some sense of objectivity of nature but always as something encountered in environmental concern. Especially in the public environment references are accordingly constitutive, referring to something *always already extant and on hand*, bringing it forward and uncovering it as extant. They refer to what is constantly available but is not expressly in the grip of concern, and what in its peculiar presence is not tailored to an individual, to a particular Dasein, but what each uses in the same way as the other (what '*everyone*' has at his disposal in the same sense), what is already there for '*everyone*.' This *already-present-something* is the entity within the environing world which we call the *extant and on hand*, in contrast to the handy.

It will perhaps be said that just this extant on hand, *environmental nature*, is the most real, the authentic reality of the world, without which earth, ground, everything earthy, earthen, and earthly cannot be, perhaps not even Dasein itself. The work-world bears within itself references to an entity which in the end makes it clear that it—the work-world, what is of concern—is not the primary entity after all. Precisely when we are led from an analysis of the work-world, in following its references to the world of nature, finally to recognize and to define the world of nature as the fundamental stratum of the real, we see that it is not the authentic being in every concern that is placed under care which is the primary worldly presence, but rather the reality of nature. This conclusion, it seems, cannot be avoided. But what does it mean to say that the world of nature is the most real? Literally, it still only refers to that entity in the world which satisfies the sense of reality, that is, worldhood in a superlative sense. But this does not mean that this sense of worldhood, which the world of nature as the always already on hand satisfies, is to be drawn from the world of nature understood as objectivity. Just because nature is of concern among the environmental things themselves in the environing world and is encountered in this concern, the sense of worldhood can *not* be read off from mere nature. The environmental references, in which nature is present primarily in a worldly way, tell us rather the reverse: *nature as reality can only be understood on the basis of worldhood.* The entitative relationships of dependence of worldly entities among themselves do not coincide with the founding relationships in being.

Here again, we have the same confusion as above in the characterization of the 'in-itself' and of the founding relationships in their explicitness. What stand among themselves in an entitative relation and these relations themselves are not identical with the founding relations in being. For the time being, it can only be said that even the extantness of nature as environing world, that is, as it is experienced quite implicitly and naturally, that just this presence is first discovered in its sense and is there upon and in the world of concern. The work-world appresents both what is always already on hand and what is immediately handy for the particular concern. It is thus becoming clear that the analysis of the worldhood of the world is centered more and more on this *distinctive presence of what is of concern.* Consequently, to the extent that we succeed in clarifying this presence, it will become possible to arrive at a phenomenological understanding of the structure of worldhood as a whole.

c) Determination of the basic structure of worldhood as meaningfulness

The founding of the proximally present handy entity in the always already present extant-on-hand, primarily the founding of these characters of being of handiness and extantness in the presence of what is of concern, has provided us with an initial phenomenological insight into the structure of encounter in worldhood. The function of encounter belonging to this presence of what is of concern has thus shown itself to us in a remarkable priority. If fundamental characters are exhibited in this way, further phenomenological interpretation of this presence must bring about a more transparent categorial understanding of worldhood. It is thus that the constitutive function of *familiarity*, which was expressly specified as a factor of worldhood, will then become clear. We shall later specify this moment in greater detail in conjunction with a closer determination of the presence of what is of concern, in particular, of the work-world. But now, this analysis of the structure of encounter belonging to the environing world is still in need of a fundamental clarification in the direction of the phenomenon which we simply introduced without further specification at the beginning of our analysis. There we said that environmental things are encountered in references in the character of 'serving to,' 'useful for,' 'conducive to,' and the like; worldhood is constituted in references, and these references themselves stand in referential correlations, referential totalities, which ultimately refer back to the presence of the work-world. It is *not things but references* which have the primary function in the structure of encounter belonging to the world, *not substances but functions*, to express this state of affairs by a formula of the '*Marburg School.*'

α) Misinterpretation of the phenomenon of reference as substance and function

In fact, the analysis we have given of the structure of the environing world could be explained in terms of this particular epistemology of the Marburg School, but this would also spoil our understanding of the phenomenon. To be sure, the contrast between the *concepts of substance and function*, to which the epistemology of the Marburg School attaches particular importance, has without question permitted us to see something significant, but in the first place only in the investigation of the objectivity of nature as object of the mathematical sciences of nature. This contrast was found right in this context, precisely in the orientation in which the specific determination of the objectivity of the world as nature proceeds by specification of spatio-temporal relations expressed in mathematical functional relationships. Accordingly, the authentic reality of nature is constituted in these functional relations expressed, for example, by a set of differential equations of mathematical physics. This is where the objectivity of nature and so the being of nature is given as valid knowledge. Therefore, the concept of function, the mathematical in the broadest sense, has a primary prerogative in the constitution of the world when compared to the concept of substance. In this context, this distinction is obtained solely by orientation to the scientific knowledge of nature.

Second, however, along with this restriction to a derivative level of reality, the contrast of substance and function is itself not made clear. Substance is not understood in its structure and genesis nor is function in its phenomenal genesis itself derived from a more original phenomenon. Function is simply posited as given with thinking itself and the thought process.

β) Sense of the structure of encounter belonging to world as meaningfulness

If we now wish to get a clearer sense of the structure of the worldhood of the environing world in the direction of referential correlations, to the extent that this is possible at the present stage of our considerations, then obviously the phenomenon of reference must be characterized in more detail. The term '*reference*' refers to a formal concept; deformalized, there are different senses of reference. The reference which we have in mind as a part of the structure of encounter belonging to world, we shall now more accurately designate as '*to mean*' [*bedeuten*]. The structure of encounter thus specified in references as *meaning* we shall call 'meaningfulness' [*Bedeutsamkeit*].

Inasmuch as we are introducing *meaningfulness* formally through *reference*, a misunderstanding is thereby averted to which this expression is again and again readily prone, namely, that the term '*meaningfulness*' says something along these lines: The environmental things, whose being is said to reside in meaningfulness, are not only natural things but also have a meaning, they have a certain rank and value. In ordinary language, 'to mean' and 'meaningfulness' are in fact so understood, and perhaps something of this sense also recurs in the terminological sense of the expression. The only question is, does this interpretation of a natural thing laden with predicates of value fit the phenomenon we have identified, or does it just distort it? The question is whether what is called value is an original phenomenon at all; or is it perhaps not something which again developed under the presupposition of that ontology which we identified as a specific ontology of nature, under the assumption that the things are first of all things of nature and then have something like a value, where value is taken ontologically in a specific reference back to the thingness of nature. Perhaps it is unavoidable to regard values as values, when being is in fact from the outset approached as nature.

Meaningfulness, as we use the term, understood negatively to begin with says nothing about meaning in the sense of value and rank. In another sense, meaning also signifies the *meaning of a word*, meaning as something which word-combinations can have. Even this sense of meaning is in a certain way connected with what we call meaningfulness, in fact much more properly than the first sense of meaning and meaningfulness in terms of value. That such delimitations, which we are making here quite formally in regard to the bare words, already become necessary itself points to a certain embarrassment in the choice of the right expression for the complex phenomenon which we want to call meaningfulness. And I frankly admit that this expression is not the best, but for years I have found nothing better, in particular nothing which gives voice to an essential connection of the phenomenon with what we designate as meaning in the sense of the meaning of words, inasmuch as the phenomenon possesses just such an intrinsic connection with verbal meaning, discourse. This connection between *discourse and world* will now perhaps still be totally obscure.

The term reference points formally to a structure which finds its expression in various phenomena. A sign is a kind of reference, and so is a symbol, symptom, trace, document, testimony, expression, relic. These phenomena of reference cannot be pursued in detail here, not only because they require comprehensive analyses but because we still do not have the basis for such an analysis, if it is to maintain a unified orientation. We want to arrive at this basis precisely with the interpretation of world and Dasein's in-being.

If we want to understand the reality of the real and not just recount something about the real, we must always look to the structure of being and not, say, to the founding relationships of entities among themselves. If the question is so oriented, then there is justification for saying that Dasein itself, ultimately the entitative things which we call men, are possible in their being only because there is a world. Of course, even here there is still, rightly understood, a difficult correlation, which we can deal with only at the conclusion of our considerations, namely, that in fact here Dasein exhibits itself as an entity *which is in its world but at the same time is by virtue of the world in which it is*. Here we find a peculiar *union of the being of the world with the being of Dasein* which itself can be made comprehensible only insofar as that which here stands in this union, Dasein itself with its world, has been made clear in its basic structures.

When we say that the basic structure of worldhood, the being of the entity which we call world, lies in meaningfulness, this amounts to saying that the structure as we have characterized it thus far, the references and the referential contexts, are basically *correlations of meaning, meaningful contexts*. In what follows, we shall treat only what is most necessary for the characterization of these phenomena, specifically to the extent that it contributes to the elucidation of meaningfulness. Phenomenology in particular has time and again sensed the urgency of bringing that complex of phenomena which is usually summarized under the heading of '*signs*' once and for all definitively out into the open. But these have remained only approaches. Husserl does some things in the second volume of the *Logical Investigations*, where the first investigation deals with signs in connection with demarcation of the phenomenon of verbal meaning from the universal phenomenon (as he says) of signs. Moreover, the universal scope of phenomena such as signs and symbols readily gives rise to using them as a clue for interpreting the totality of entities, the world as a whole. No less a figure than Leibniz sought in his *characteristica universalis* systematization of the totality of entities by way of an orientation to the phenomenon of the sign. Recently, Spengler, following Lamprecht's procedure, has applied the idea of symbol to the history of philosophy and metaphysics in general, without providing a properly scientific clarification of the group of phenomena named by it. Most recently, in his work *Philosophy of Symbolic Forms*,[1] Cassirer has tried to explain the various domains of life (language, knowledge, religion, myth) by viewing them basically as phenomena of the expression of spirit. He has likewise sought to broaden the *critique of reason* presented by Kant into a *critique of culture*. Here too the phenomenon of expression, of symbol in the broadest sense, is taken as a clue for explaining all the phenomena of spirit and of entities in general. The universal applicability of formal clues such as 'Gestalt,' 'sign,' 'symbol' thus easily obscures the originality or non-originality of the interpretation thus achieved. What can be a suitable approach for aesthetic phenomena can have exactly the opposite effect in elucidating and interpreting other phenomena. What comes to light here is in fact a peculiar context which generally determines the human [i.e., spiritual] sciences in their development. In relation to such attempts, which are basically always violent, the object, the spiritual, which is at issue here, offers less resistance than in the field of natural science, where nature immediately takes its revenge on a wrongheaded approach. Because of our specific non-relationship to the spiritual, such objects and phenomena are more readily subject to misinterpretation, since the misinterpretation real-

---

1. Ernst Cassirer, *Philosophie der symbolischen Formen* (Berlin: Bruno Cassirer, 1923).

izes itself as a spiritual product. It is understandable and applicable as a spiritual product and so can itself take the place of the subject matter to be understood, so that for a long time certain sciences of the spiritual could stand in a presumed relationship to it. This peculiar non-relationship is connected with the fact that this world of objects then seems to be easily understood and defined by anyone and by arbitrary means, and that in the field of these objects there is a peculiar lack of need for a suitable conceptuality, without which the natural sciences, for example, simply could not advance. Obviously, just such attempts at interpretation under the guidance of such universal phenomena from which all and sundry can be made—for ultimately each and every thing can be interpreted as a sign—pose a great danger for the development of the human sciences.

γ) Interconnection of the phenomena of meaningfulness, sign, reference, and relation

If we now try to provide an initial clarification of the basic structure of worldhood by an interpretation of the phenomenon of meaningfulness, we must remember that a full understanding of this phenomenon can be obtained only from an adequate interpretation of the basic phenomenon from which it is now drawn for thematic investigation, from *being-in-the-world* as the basic constitution of Dasein. Only the progressive explication of this structure of being-in-the-world can insure an understanding of meaningfulness. At the present stage of the analysis, therefore, we must try to grasp this phenomenon of meaningfulness less by tracing its own structures than by distinguishing it from kindred structures. These kindred phenomena, *reference, sign, relation*, point back to meaningfulness as the root of their phenomenal genesis.

The interconnection of the phenomena of meaningfulness, sign, reference, relation may first be formally indicated in the following propositions, which say something only if they have themselves arisen from the clarification of the *phenomena* themselves, and are understood in this way rather than as mere formulas. Thereupon it can be said: every reference is a relation but not every relation is a reference. Every sign, or better, 'indication,' is an ontic reference, but not every reference is a sign. This at the same time implies that every sign is a relation, but not every relation is a sign. Moreover, every sign *means*, which here signifies that it has the mode of being of meaningfulness. Meaning, however, is never a sign. *Relation is the most universal formal character* of these phenomena. Sign, reference, meaning are all relations. But just because the phenomenon of relation is the most universal, it is *not* the origin of these phenomena, that out of which the relationships which organize their particular structures can in turn be understood.

In order to clarify the sense of meaningfulness we shall proceed by way of a brief characterization of *sign* and *indication*. For this purpose we have chosen an example which we shall meet again with some modifications in the discussion of another phenomenon, that of place and direction.

Signs are encountered environmentally; signs are environmental things. The latest automobiles have a rotating red arrow. At an intersection, the particular position of the arrow indicates the direction which the car will take. Its concern is to direct the other party to get out of the way in time. The arrow is a sign indicating the direction by its position. The position of the arrow is controlled by the driver and is thus a constantly handy environmental thing used in driving. Earlier, the driver's hand had the same function, whenever he stretched it out of the car in one or the other direction.

The arrow is now encountered in the character of reference like any environmental thing; it is present in this specific environmental '*in order to*,' in a particular serviceability—for indicating. This referential structure 'for indicating,' this particular serviceability in the mode of handiness as a structure of the presence of the sign as utensil, that is, as 'indicator,' this structure of 'in order to indicate' is not the indicating itself. This reference of 'in order to' as mode of handiness, presence, cannot be identified with the indicating; rather, *this ontic indicating is grounded in the structure of reference.* The specific reference of serviceability 'in order to indicate' is constitutive for the potential environmental handiness of the arrow. The reference is not the indicating itself, the latter is rather that to which the reference refers, *in* which reference the arrow is encountered as sign and indicating. Just as a hammer is *for* hammering, so a sign is *for* indicating. But this reference of serviceability in the structure of the environmental thing hammer does not make the hammer into a sign. In the use of a hammer, concern is absorbed in this 'in order to,' 'for hammering,' just as sign usage is absorbed in its corresponding serviceability, in indicating with it.

But what is of concern in using a sign is now just the indicating, more accurately put, being a signal, that the direction be indicated. The sign gives the direction. Strictly conceived, the perception of the sign, taking something encountered for a sign is not an identification (in our case of this arrow, it is not an identification of the direction); rather, in perceiving this sign, insofar as I encounter it environmentally, I draw from its indication *my* particular comportment at the time. I draw from the sign the manner in which I go and indeed have to go my own way. Primarily, the sign conveys no information but gives an *instruction*. The environmental sign-thing, the arrow, stands in an environmental correlation of references, and it *appresents, makes present, the environing world*, in this case the local constellation of the next moment. This sign at the same time *points forward* toward something which will be environmentally on hand, the way and the places which the way will traverse, a particular constellation which determines and modifies my own and every other being in the world insofar as it is oriented locally. The arrow thus appresents the environing world for concerned commerce, going about one's rounds, here for going in a narrow sense.

With the use of the sign, the employment of the arrow, and the corresponding taking of the sign from the vantage of the one who understands it, *a particular appresentation of the environing world* is accordingly *explicitly placed under care*. This explicit concern in encountering the environing world is not focused on information but on the being-in-the-world which at first does not know thematically. It is this concerned being-in-the-world and not, say, the propensity of an isolated knowing, which *institutes signs*, simply because world is inexplicitly encountered in references. It is because world is present, uncovered as the wherein of Dasein, and worldhood has this referential structure as a comprehensible structure, it is on this basis that the environmental sign-things are on hand and handy. As environmentally handy things, signs are always *instituted*. But we must pay heed to the correct sense of the institution of signs; that is, a twofold distinction must be noted: 1) merely *taking something as a sign* and 2) *producing a sign-thing*.

Thus the south wind can be a sign of rain. It is more accurately an omen, and first and strictly an omen which is addressed to everyday concern, where it is encountered and as such discovered by everyday concern in the course of directing itself toward the weather (cultivation, harvest, or a military venture). Neither the south wind nor the rain, nor their conjunction and being on hand in the world as natural processes, none of these entities is instituted in the sense of being produced; in each instance, it is a matter of something always already on hand of itself. The south wind's being a sign is instituted by taking it as a sign. This sign-taking institution comes about by taking the weather into account, which in turn is grounded in a particular concernedness, in everyday affairs, the everyday work of the farmer himself; more accurately, this is the primary discovery as an entity before any explicit elaboration. The sign-taking is grounded in this concernedness. The sense of this sign-taking would be mistaken if one were to say that the south wind 'in itself,' 'objectively,' is not a sign, it is so construed merely 'subjectively.' It is thus overlooked that this sign-taking, taking the south wind as a sign, is not a subjective construal, any more than this apparent mere construal has the sole sense of divulging the objective, which means the environing world, equipment in its character of handiness and in its nature, of letting us encounter this world and making it accessible. The interpretation of the sign as a subjective construction parts with the authentic sense of sign-taking, which consists precisely in appresenting the world more authentically in a certain direction, in bringing it out more emphatically and not in subjectively construing it in some way. This favored interpretation of the sign stems once again directly from the latent naturalization of objectivity. Once again, we have the tenacious prejudice that nature first of all is always objective, whatever goes beyond that is brought in by the subject, and so the matter rests.

The second kind of institution of signs is the *explicit production of sign-things*. Now, not only is something already on hand taken as a sign, but that which is to be a sign and put to use as a sign is itself produced. Examples of such signs are arrows, flags, the storm ball in the marine weather-bureau, signal arms, road signs, and the like. In the *first* kind of institution of signs, the sign is to some extent found in advance; more accurately, *the indicating sign is grounded in a particular circumstance in which the sign and what it indicates are already handy together*. Both from the outset stand in a correlation of being. For the most part, however, this is not the case for the sign-things which are produced. Taken in itself, the storm ball, this thing of a ball, has nothing at all to do with the storm. Since signs are environmental things and their indication is instituted and this institution is concerned with indicating something explicitly, it belongs to its condition of possibility that a sign be serviceable, which means that it actually indicates. Here we have a specific kind of being with which we are already familiar, namely, being handy. The sign itself must in any case have a *superior handiness, familiarity, and accessibility*.

On these is based the *conspicuous* status of signs. That signs must be conspicuous betrays their kind of serviceability. Consider the familiar 'knot tied in a handkerchief.' Its conspicuousness is based precisely on the inconspicuousness of what is handy and used everyday. This inconspicuousness of a thing constantly encountered in use, the handkerchief, makes the knot suited to serve as a sign. This sign is thus a pure mark, and not an omen like the south wind. The indication of this mark is defined anew with every new institution, which here is a production in a certain sense. To the breadth of what this mark can indicate corresponds the narrowness of comprehensibility of this sign. Not only is it for the most part comprehensible only for the one who institutes it, but often even for him what it is supposed to indicate and its indication becomes inaccessible; it does not thereby lose its sign-character; on the contrary, it is encountered in a disquieting sense precisely as a sign, but as a sign for something which is no longer comprehended.

The sign-relation is not, say, the specific reference which constituted the serviceability of a sign; rather, the serviceability is itself determined by the indicating. Sign and indication have a particular meaning in virtue of the formal character of relation as such in the theoretical reflection on entities, but also typically in the primitive and elementary interpretation of life, even though caution must be exercised in the interpretation of this primitive thinking on signs.

The characteristic feature in the primitive relationship to the sign, in all fetishism, magic, and the like, is this: For primitive man, the sign coincides with what is indicated. The sign can itself stand for what is indicated, not only in the sense of replacing it but such that the sign-tool itself always is what is indicated. This remarkable coincidence of the being of the sign and of what is indicated does not imply, as it has been interpreted, that the sign-thing has already undergone a certain 'objectification,' so that the sign is taken as a thing and is thus displaced into the same region of being as the thing signified. But this 'coincidence' is basically not a coinciding of two previously isolated things. It is just that the sign-thing has not yet become free from what it signifies; and this is because such a preoccupation and such an elementary life with signs and in signs is still totally absorbed in what is indicated, so that the sign-tool itself to some extent cannot be taken separately. The coincidence is not tied to an initial stage of objectification of sign-thing and what is indicated, but rather to the fact that it is not yet objectified, that the concern still lives totally in the indicating tool and draws what is indicated into the sign, because it is the nearest, the present. But this phenomenally means that the sign-tool is not discovered at all, that the handy environmental thing does not yet even have the character of a tool at all.

So that the sign can now fulfill its function as purely as possible, that is, so that it may acquire the character of the handy and the element of conspicuousness, the sign is produced from what is always already on hand. This 'materialization' of the sign, if we may put it that way, has however nothing to do with any sort of materialism or materialistic point of view, as if the indicating and the sense of the sign were tied to 'matter.' Instead, 'matter' here really does not have a material function but a specifically 'spiritual' one, which is to guarantee the universally constant accessibility. From an extended use of signs in primitive thinking, it still cannot be concluded that this thinking has in a way not yet actually apprehended the 'spiritual,' the 'meaningful'; on the contrary, the presence of the sign and what is indicated is itself the most elementary proof. To some extent in philosophical interpretation, however, one should not hold to the things as things, following the old tradition that nature or wood or stone really comes first. It is not the case that wood and stone are there first and then are furnished with a sign-character.

Thus all taking, using, and instituting of signs are only a particular development of the specific concern in the environing world, insofar as it is to be made available. At this point, I cannot enter into a more detailed classification of the phenomena of signs like omen, vestige, symptom, mark, and distinguishing mark. I can at least say that they retain the two-fold distinction in the kind of institution, while at the same time providing insight into the character of a superior presence which is constitutive for being a sign.

δ) Being-in-the-world, as concerned and understanding, discloses the world as meaningfulness

It was said that because world is present, that is, because it is *disclosed* and in some sense encountered for the Dasein which is in it, there is in general something like sign-things, they are handy. It belongs to the being of Dasein, inasmuch as it is being-in-the-world, to let its world be encountered. The kind of being belonging to letting the world be encountered in the primary mode of concern is itself one of *understanding*. The correlate of this understanding which guides all concern is that with which care dwells and which always shows itself in understanding, even though in an ever so indefinite familiarity. This primary state of knowing one's way about belongs essentially to in-being; it belongs to its sense of being and is not just something that is thrown into the bargain. But this implies that understanding primarily does not mean a mode of knowing at all, unless knowing itself has been seen as a constitutive state of being for being-in-the-world. But even then it must be said that the sense of understanding is not merged with having knowledge of something, but involves a *being toward something*, that is, the being of Dasein. In-being as self-understanding in understanding its world discloses the understanding of its world. Formulated in another way, it is only because understanding is the primary being-relationship of Dasein to the world and to itself that there can be something like an independent understanding and an independent cultivation and appropriation of understanding as in historical knowledge and exegesis. We shall now have to interpret the previous account of the structure of the world in correlation with the basic constitution of Dasein as the understanding concernful being-in-the-world.

Worldhood is the specific presence and encounter for an understanding concern. Understanding absorption in the world *discovers* the world, the referential connections in what they uniquely are, in their *meaning*. An understanding concern thus encounters what is understood—*meaning*.

The references and referential connections are primarily meaning. The meanings are, according to our earlier considerations, the structure of being of the world. The referential whole of the world is a whole of meaningful connections, meaningfulness. If we define mean-ingfulness as the specific structure of the whole of understandability, this should not be coupled with the assertion that here again the world and worldhood are still conceived only as objectivity; here we do not have the very being of the world but the world as objective, to be sure now not objective for observation and research but for con-cerned understanding; here again as well meaningfulness only refers to the way of being apprehended. We shall return later to this poten-tial objection.

Meaningfulness is first of all a mode of presence in virtue of which every entity of the world is discovered. Concern as constantly oriented, de-fined by insight and understanding, already lives in primary contexts of meaning disclosed by its concern in interpretive circumspection. Since Dasein is moreover essentially determined by the fact that it *speaks, expresses itself, discourses, and as speaker discloses, discovers, and lets things be seen*, it is thereby understandable that there are such things as words which have meanings. It is not as if there were first verbal sounds which in time were furnished with meanings. On the contrary, what is primary is being in the world, that is, concerned understand-ing and being in the context of meanings. Only then do sounds, pro-nunciation, and phonetic communication accrue to such meanings from Dasein itself. Sounds do not acquire meaning; rather, it is the other way around: meanings are expressed in sounds.

Typically, two extreme theories are specially distinguished among the various theories on the 'origin of language.' First, there is the opinion that language originated from simple emotive sounds and that those of fear, anxiety, and surprise are the primary forms of ut-terance for the origin of language. The other extreme theory is that the origin of language lies in the imitative sounds, in the phonetic copying of what is found in the world, in speaking. First of all, it is in itself absurd to make the origin of language understandable by start-ing from sounds. This applies also to the attempt to regard one of these phonetic groups as the original one. Inasmuch as all talking and speaking is a matter of *expressing oneself about something*, there is in the unity of all talking both emotive and imitative sound. In other words, both become comprehensible only in such a way that in them the spe-cific Dasein, which is also determined by corporeality, makes itself un-derstood through sounds. Here it is only a matter of seeing the con-nection between the levels of verbal sound and meaning; meanings are to be understood on the basis of meaningfulness, and this in turn means only on the basis of being-in-the-world.

If we have truly seen this, then we have gained an insight which is methodologically of great significance for the theory of meaning as such. It means that we are in a position to put an end to the usual wrongheaded approaches to the analysis of meanings, which are in part still common even in phenomenology. We would thus no longer pose the question, in starting from a verbal sound: How can a word have meaning, and how can a word mean something? This question is contrived, totally uprooted from the phenomenal composition of speaking and language. On the other hand, it is clear that linguistic meanings and generally meaning-contextures, structures, conceptuality, the entire context of problems with which *logic* in the strict sense would have to deal, can be understood only in reference to an actual fundamental analysis of Dasein itself, which has meanings in the primary sense.

In order to make meaningfulness as such understandable in a provisional way, we must return to a more original phenomenon of being-in-the-world, which we call understanding and understanding concern. It is only because being-in-the-world as understanding and concerned absorption appresents the world that this being-in-the-world can also be concerned with this appresentation of the world explicitly, and does in fact attend to it by means of environmental things produced expressly for that purpose, namely, by means of signs. Sign-things have their origin and sense in Dasein itself; there is nothing accidental about them. Being a sign is rooted in environmentality. This is why an environmental thing which at first is not a sign at all but simply an environmental thing, *as* an environmental thing can at any time become a sign (for example, a hammer or a stone-ax). They can become signs in the sense that a stone-ax, for example, in its extantness can point to an environment as *having been*. It is that type of sign which we call a vestige.

The fact that there are such signs, which is founded in environmentality, provides the basis for the environmental thing to be able to function as a source for historiological discovery and determination. Such odd things as historical sources are not self-evident and simple to see in their specific structure of being. In this case, the stone-ax is discovered as something still on hand, whereas before its discovery it was to a farmer perhaps only a chance stone which lies in the way of his wagon and foot, on which his plow gets nicked. The stone is inaccessible to him, not because the thing is not bodily there, not because he does not have the historical source so to speak as an extant thing, but precisely because he still only appresents this thing in its extantness, as it is disclosed for him through his specific concern. By virtue of his being-in-the-world as a farmer doing his plowing, he is not capable of discovering the stone as it actually was and still is. For him it is merely a thing, not a thing in the theoretical sense, but once again a thing encountered in his environing world as obstructive, unserviceable. It is not only inaccessible to him but access is expressly put off by him, perhaps even finally blocked, in that he positively takes it for what it is to him, an obstacle, and shatters it against the nearest rock.

In the same way, a roll of parchment covered with writing, for example, can still be merely on hand as a thing which someone is preserving somewhere. But its character as a sign and source forms a much more complicated situation. Here in this context, I can only briefly allude to these problems, which belong in a hermeneutics of the historiological disciplines. To begin with, the roll itself, like the ax, is a relic from an earlier time, from the time in which it was written. But at the same time, it can through what is written on it refer back to a still earlier time. Now this reference is altogether peculiar: it communicates. Inasmuch as the communication here is founded in a discourse set down in writing, in what is written, it itself has its own kind of comprehensibility; access to it presupposes its own kind of understanding. In turn, the written discourse can now be a narration and report taken from a communication on what is being narrated. Or what is communicated can be taken from the original witnesses. The character of the testimony of the communication itself varies according to the variety of ways of being witness; being-witness-to varies according to that to which the source claims to have been witness, that to which it claims to testify. Accessibility or inaccessibility to such a source is decided in principle in the same dimension as accessibility to the stone-ax as an environmental thing of a past world; it is decided on the basis of the extent to which understanding is understanding, that is, the extent to which it is the relationship of being to what is encountered as a source and witnessed in the source. The possibility of being a source is grounded primarily not in the fact that there is a parchment and that one can write but in the fact that there *was* something like what is communicated and witnessed. What is decisive for the fact that this thing is taken as a source at all is the understanding relationship of being to the witnessed past. Everything that transpires with the source afterwards in some sort of interpretation or other scientific pursuit is governed by this primary understanding. This primary understanding decides how and whether the manifold of, for example, what is witnessed in the source may be evaluated quantitatively and formally; and whether it makes any sense to say, in view of what is witnessed in the source, that it contains much that is insignificant and only very little of significance; or whether, commensurate with the very sense of the subject matter being witnessed in the source, there is but little of significance, but this small amount determines all that is insignificant primarily and uniquely even in its insignificance, so that such a source cannot be partitioned in the way a botanist sorts out the appropriate and the less appropriate plants on his table.

These relations invested in a source can be disengaged in their structure with conceptual rigor only against the background of the entity which understands and discovers in understanding. I cannot pursue these structures any further here; they only aim to demonstrate that being a sign, the being of a source, of testimony, and the like is grounded in this, that there is something like a world, a world whose mode of encounter and of being is meaningfulness; and that the access to what is indicated and going along with its indication is an environmental understanding, and this always also means an understanding of the in-being in this world, which is grounded in the understanding of Dasein itself.

With regard to the phenomenon of relation and its relationship of being to reference, sign and meaningfulness, it must be said that, as the formal structural element, relation is accessible at all times in references and signs. It is accessible specifically by way of a disregard, not only of the concretion and material content of these phenomena, but also that it is itself an indicating and referring of the relational kind, in order to let us see only the empty in-order-to. The apprehension of pure relations as such is a supreme way, but at the same time also the emptiest way of objectifying entities. It is a making present which does not go along with references and sign-taking in a primary way; rather, it only looks at and thus takes in the whole as a whole of relations.

Some things should be said about meaningfulness by way of summary. Being-in-the-world as concerned understanding lets us encounter something self-signifying in self-meaning. This self-signifying meaning [*sich deutendes Bedeuten*] constitutes meaningfulness and is the presence of the world, insofar as it is discovered in understanding concern. *Presence of the world is the worldhood of the world as meaningfulness.* The correlations of meaning which we now take as references are not a subjective view of the world, which in addition and to begin with would still be something else, for instance, an initially immediate world, which then would refer to something else for the preoccupation with it. Rather, concern itself is the being of the entity, which is only in this way and has no other being.

If the worldhood of the world is defined as a totality of references, this should not be misunderstood as saying that the environmental things, the 'substances,' are now dissolved into lawlike correlations of functions. Instead, the specification of reference as meaning points to the appresentational sense of references. This sense is what it is only in its grounding in the presence of what is of concern, of the work-world. As I have already emphasized, all further understanding will go back to the phenomenon of the presence of what is of concern in the authentic sense, to the analysis of being-in-the-world in its particular sense as concern, which has the mode of being of pure *letting-*

become-present—a remarkable kind of being which is understood only when it is seen that this *making present and appresenting is nothing other than time itself.*

§24. Internal structuring of the question of the reality of the external world

Our task now is to see the structure of meaningfulness, which we are trying to bring out as the authentic constitution of worldhood, in the context of the question of an interpretation of Dasein with regard to the question of being as such. In order to reach this goal, it is necessary, by means of a summary consideration, to extricate the question of the world understood as meaningfulness from a perverse horizon oriented to some theory or other of the reality of the external world or even to an ontology of actuality. The provisional clarification of meaningfulness and the prior stage of the interpretation of the reality of the world antecedes such an epistemology or ontology of the world with the exposition of the question of being as such, that is, with the interpretation of Dasein. The complex of questions involving epistemology (subject-object) or ontology (of nature) thus does not touch the interpretation of Dasein in its being at all. In order to attain this end and to bring this provisional analysis of meaningfulness to a conclusion, we shall consider five points: a) The reality of the external world is exempt from any proof of it or belief in it. b) The reality of the real (the worldhood of the world) cannot be defined on the basis of its being an object and being apprehended. c) Reality is not interpreted by way of the character of 'in itself'; rather, this character is itself in need of interpretation. d) Reality is not to be understood primarily in terms of the bodily presence of the perceived. e) Reality is not adequately clarified by the phenomenon of resistance as the object of drive and effort.

I list the discussion of the phenomenon of resistance last because this interpretation of reality comes closest to the one I advocate and of late has been advanced by Scheler. This rapprochement in our interpretation probably stems from a common source, from presentiments (more they cannot be called) which Dilthey had in this direction.

a) The reality of the external world is exempt from any proof of it or belief in it

The initial question of the worldhood of the world, which was set forth as meaningfulness, is not at all the question of whether there is something like an external world, whether the external world is after all real. This line of questioning implies the view that the reality of the world *must* and *can* be proved or that at least, as Dilthey thought,[1] our claim in believing in the reality of the external world should be justified. Both views are absurd. To wish to prove that the world exists is a misunderstanding of the very questioning. For such a questioning makes sense only on the basis of a being whose constitution is being-in-the-world. It is absurd to wish to subject to a proof of existence that which founds in their very being all questioning of a world and all attempts to prove and demonstrate that the world exists. World in its most proper sense is just that which is already on hand for any questioning. The question persists only on the basis of a constant misunderstanding of the mode of being of the one who raises this question. For this mode of being and this being, that is, for this questioning, it is constitutive that something like the world is always already discovered, can be encountered as an entity, can show itself as an entity.

The question of the reality of the external world is in part defined on the basis of an extrinsic understanding of Kantian philosophy, or better put, under the influence of considerations which Descartes initiated. It is a question which has continuously occupied the epistemology of the modern era more or less explicitly. But this was always under the assurance that naturally no one doubted the reality of the external world. It is nonetheless always presupposed here that this reality, worldhood of the world, basically is still something which perhaps could be proved, or more accurately, if we were in an ideal state, we would in the end have proved it. That the world is real is however not only *not in need of proof*, it is *also not something which for lack of rigorous proofs must then be merely believed*, in view of which one has to dispense with knowledge and be content with faith. This talk of *faith* in the reality of the "world" presupposes that it can actually be proved. The view goes back to the first one, which aspires to some sort of proof. But here it should be noted that the recourse to a belief in reality does not correspond to any phenomenal finding. Dilthey's treatise also took this line of inquiry. This treatise is not important because it so formulates* the problem, which just shows that Dilthey did not understand the actual problem. It is important in relation to another phenomenon, that of *resistance*, which he touched on here and which we have to discuss later in greater detail.

But if we for once refrain from all discussion of this theory, it becomes clear that nothing exists in our relationship to the world which provides a basis for the phenomenon of belief in the world. I have not yet been able to find this phenomenon of belief. Rather, the peculiar

---

1. Wilhelm Dilthey, "Beiträge zur Lösung der Frage vom Ursprung unseres Glaubens an die Realität der Aussenwelt und seinem Recht (1890)." *Gesammelte Schriften*, Vol. V, pp. 90-138.
*Reading *formuliert* here instead of *fundiert*.

thing is just that the world is 'there' *before* all belief. The world is never experienced as something which is believed any more than it is guaranteed by knowledge. Inherent in the being of the world is that its existence *needs no guarantee in regard to a subject*. What is needed, if this question comes up at all, is that the Dasein should experience itself in its most elementary constitution of being, as being-in-the-world itself. This experience of itself—unspoiled by any sort of epistemology— eliminates the ground for any question of the reality of the world. That it is real stands in opposition to any move to prove it. And even any purported belief in it is a theoretically motivated misunderstanding. This is not a convenient evasion of a problem. The question rather is whether this so-called problem which is ostensibly being evaded is really a problem at all. I 'know' that the world is real only insofar as I am. It is not *cogito sum* which formulates a primary finding but rather *sum cogito*. And this *sum* is not taken in the ontological indifference in which Descartes and his successors took it, as the extantness of a thinking thing. *Sum* here is the assertion of the basic constitution of my being: I-am-in-a-world and therefore I am capable of thinking it. But this Cartesian proposition has been taken in the opposite way, and rightly so, since Descartes himself wanted it thus understood, such that the *sum* was not questioned at all. Instead consciousness as the inner was thought to be given absolutely as an absolute starting point, from which all the puzzles of 'inner' and 'outer' then arise.

The reality of the world is not a problem in the sense of whether it actually exists or not, but the question of the reality of the world persists in the question of how worldhood is to be understood. But even if it is said that the initial question of the existence of the world is naturally and obviously contrary to sense, which is often heard, this will not do phenomenologically. This countersense must be allowed to assault the phenomenon, so to speak, by way of the positive vision of the phenomenon of in-being and the world. In other words, the basic constitution of Dasein as being-in-the-world must be seen in order to be able to make the statement that it contravenes sense, it infringes the basic constitution of that of which we speak. The 'self-evidence' of the existence of the world must become transparent in a Dasein by way of the positive vision of the phenomenon of in-being. *Ontic-existentiell self-evidence is given with the being of Dasein, but ontologically it is puzzling.*

b) The reality of the real (worldhood of the world) cannot be defined on the basis of its being an object and being apprehended

The second question of the reality of the real, the question of the being of the worldhood of the world, cannot mean an investigation into how the world now actually manages to be. To begin with, such a question, if it is to be scientifically useful, presupposes that we understand what is meant by 'being' if we wish to explain how the entity brings it about, *that* it is. But this understanding of 'being,' to be acquired in advance, then no longer even lets us get to the point of asking in this way. For this question involves taking *being as its own entity*, it *tries to explain being in terms of an entity*. When it becomes clear how absurd it is to expect, so to speak, a trick from being which it uses in order to be, and when a question of being thus understood is then referred back to the entity, this in no way means that nothing can be made of 'being-in-itself' but always only of the entity insofar as it is *something apprehended*, something objective in a consciousness. This would bring us to the familiar proposition that an entity always is only *for* a consciousness. This proposition is known as the '*principle of immanence*,' which keeps all epistemologies busy over its pros and cons. It has led directly to the problem of knowledge, without benefit of asking what might be meant by 'immanence,' what findings from the phenomena themselves are taken up in it, if it says anything at all, and what is basically meant by the proposition "An entity always is only for a consciousness."

What the proposition basically means, what is seen in it, is not that an entity is dependent on consciousness in its being nor that something transcendent is actually at the same time something immanent. The phenomenal finding in this proposition is rather that *a world is encountered*. The phenomenon itself thus directs us to interpret the structure of encounter, the activity of encountering. And the more we go about this without prejudice, the more authentically is the entity encountered ascertainable in its being.

The being of entities does not lie in the activity of encountering, but the encounter of entities is the phenomenal basis, and the sole basis, upon which the being of entities can be grasped. *Only the interpretation of the encounter with entities can secure the being of entities, if at all*. It must be stated that the entity as an entity is 'in itself' and independent of any apprehension of it; accordingly, the being of the entity is found only in encounter and can be explained, made understandable, only from the phenomenal exhibition and interpretation of the structure of encounter. In this case *explanation* is inadequate, inasmuch as it is a derivative, inferior mode of expository interpretation and uncovering of the entity. Every explanation, when we speak of an explanation of nature, is distinguished by its involvement in the *incomprehensible*. It can be flatly stated that *explanation is the expository interpretation of the incomprehensible*, not so that this exposition would let us comprehend the incomprehensible, for it remains incomprehensible in principle. *Nature is what is in principle explainable and to be explained* because it is in principle incomprehensible. It is *the incomprehensible pure and simple*. And it is the incomprehensible because it is the "*unworlded*" world, in-

sofar as we take nature in this extreme sense of the entity as it is discovered in physics. This is connected with the fact that in this kind of
explanation and discovery of the world as nature, nature is still investigated and interrogated only with regard to the presence of the entity in it; and this entity is admitted only insofar as it is determined by
laws of motion which remain invariant, unaltered, always the same for
every possible approach and regard under which the consideration of
nature is placed. It should be observed here that all propositions and
proofs given in physics or mathematics are certainly comprehensible
as propositions, as discourse about something, but that about which
they speak is itself the incomprehensible. As the incomprehensible, it
is likewise the entity which simply does not have the character of Dasein at all, while Dasein is the entity which is comprehensible in principle. Since understanding belongs to its being as being-in-the-world,
world is comprehensible to Dasein insofar as it is encountered in the
character of meaningfulness.

c) Reality is not interpreted by way of the in-itself; rather, this character is itself in need of interpretation

When we consider the determination of the 'in-itself' as a character
of worldhood, we can here very briefly recall what we said earlier, that
the 'in-itself' is not an original character; it still has a phenomenal
genesis, it is still in need of expository interpretation, even though it is
generally taken to be in no need of interpretation. Why is the reality
of the world so readily characterized by the 'in-itself'? Why do we find
comfort in the mere stipulation of this character without any clarification of it? It has to do with the fact that this 'in-itself' of the world is
introduced *reactively*, so to speak, *against* an interpretation of the
being of the world as apprehended, against the determination of the
actuality of the actual as objectivity for a scientifically objective knowledge. It is reactive in the counterclaim that the entity is 'in itself.' Appeal is made to the fact that all 'natural' and scientific knowing aims at
the determination of an entity which is in itself in its being. But then
the matter is allowed to rest with this appeal, without asking what it
now really means.

If the being of the world were definable only in terms of being apprehended, then the one chance of nevertheless still clarifying the 'in-
itself' would be by an ever greater disregard of the subject. But how
would that be possible without the basic constitutive state of in-being?
But since the being of the world becomes comprehensible in the encounter, the understanding of the entity in itself is as such revealed
only in a radical interpretation of Dasein. The more originally and the

more authentically this entity is explicated in its being, the more radically can knowing and entities as potentially knowable then be explicated. Because objects are independent of the subject, their being can be
explicated only in subjectivity properly understood, but it cannot consist in being a subject.

d) Reality is not to be understood primarily in terms of the bodily presence of the perceived

But reality is just as little to be understood primarily in terms of
bodily presence. It must of course be admitted that bodily presence is a
genuine phenomenal character to the extent that I keep to the particular kind of access to entities which perceives, merely looks at them.
But precisely in this kind of access to worldhood, especially if I take
perception to be the simple perception of a thing, the world is no
longer accessible in its full worldhood, in its full meaningfulness as it
encounters concern. In the pure perception of a thing, the world shows
itself instead in a *deficient meaningfulness*. I am using the word 'deficient,' *deficiens*, in accordance with the old traditional term. Meaningfulness as it is encountered in perception is deficient, it lacks something which it actually has and would have to have as a world. It
detracts from the originality of the world when we merely look at it as
a manifold of things.

The traditional categories of thingness, which for definite reasons
are also identified as *the* categories of being—thingness, substance, accident, property, causality—have their phenomenal genesis in this deficient meaningfulness. These categories are already drawn from a
kind of access (a prepossession of presence and its fundamental determinations) which occurs in the process of a characteristic "*unworlding*." Now why are these categories really the first to be discovered?
This is equivalent to the question which we already asked earlier and
have not yet answered: Why does natural Dasein, in the elucidation of
the world in which it is, simply *pass over* the environing world? Why, in
the categorial characterization of the being of the world, does it always already apply developed categories like thingness as *the* basic
determinations?

The Aristotelian categories: οὐσία, ποιόν, ποσόν, ποῦ, ποτέ, πρὸς
τί (ὑποκείμενον—συμβεβηκότα—that which must always be together
with extantness—the apriori possibilities of something as something),
traditionally substance, quality, quantity, place, time, relation: these
are all already obtained in this special dimension of *merely apprehending a thing* and a particular kind of discourse about it, that of the *theoretical assertion*. But already for Aristotle, these categories became the
categories of being pure and simple. They were at the same time the

basis for the determination of the categories of objects in general, determinations which belong to every something, to the extent that it is something at all, whether it is in the world or is something thought. So bodily presence is also not a primary character of the environing world.

e) Reality is not adequately clarified by the phenomenon of resistance as the object of drive and effort

But reality is not adequately clarified even by the phenomenon of resistance. The Greeks obviously had this phenomenon already in mind when they proposed the σώματα, the corporeal things, as the authentic οὐσίαι with respect to pressure and impact.[2] In more recent times, Dilthey in particular, in the context of the inquiry mentioned above, has pointed to the phenomenon of resistance, specifically *resistance as a correlate of impulse*. For every impulse which comes from the subject and is operative in the subject there is a correlative resistance. To be sure, Dilthey did not come to a more rigorous formulation of the phenomenon, but, and this is what is most important, he already saw quite early that reality is experienced not only in knowledge and awareness but in the whole "living subject," as he puts it, in this "thinking, willing, feeling being." He wants to get to the totality of the subject which experiences the world and not to a bloodless thinking thing which merely intends and theoretically thinks the world. But he seeks the whole within the framework of a traditional anthropological psychology, as you can see from the very formulation, this "thinking, willing, feeling being." He just does not see that the adoption of this old psychology necessarily forces him away from the authentic phenomenon. This old psychology is not overcome by his new analytical psychology but only reaffirmed, thereby preventing a genuine apprehension of what is anticipated.

Most recently, Scheler has advocated a similar theory of the being of the real, but on the basis of an essentially clearer theory of the structure of the psychic, which is that of the phenomenological analysis of acts. He himself designates his theory of the 'existence' ('Dasein' in the sense of being-on-hand, extantness) of the world as "a voluntative theory of existence," which asserts that the extantness of the world is primarily correlative to will, thus to impulse, striving.

Scheler observes

> . . . that knowing itself, however, is a relationship *of being*; that the being-so of an entity can at the same time be *in mente* and *extra mentem*,

---

2. Cf. Plato, *Sophist* 246a and Aristotle, *Metaphysics*, Book Lambda (XII), Ch. 1-6.

but existence [*Dasein*] is always *extra mentem*; that moreover the having of existence as something that is there is *not* based at all upon intellectual functions (whether it be intuition or thinking) but alone upon the *resistance* of the entity originally experienced solely in the act of striving and the dynamic factors of attention: this I have proposed in lectures for seven years as the *first* fundament of my epistemology.[3]

The being of objects is given immediately only in their relation to the instincts and will, and not in some form of knowing.[4]

Scheler here has a special need to note the time when he first presented this theory. In this regard I want to stress that I also have proposed this theory already for seven years. As I have already said, however, this agreement obviously comes from the common root of Dilthey's initiative and the phenomenological way of putting questions. I want to emphasize expressly that Scheler's theory, especially insofar as it takes into account the specific function of corporeality in the structure of the reality of the world, will lead us to discover some essential phenomena. This is because Scheler has worked out these phenomena of the biological in an essential way and has probably gone the farthest of all today in the exploration of these phenomena and their structure. We can therefore expect his anthropology to be an essential advance in the exploration of these phenomena.

All the same, it must be said that the phenomenon of resistance is not the original phenomenon. Rather, resistance in its turn again can only be understood in terms of meaningfulness. The authentic correlation of world and Dasein (if we can speak here of correlation at all, which is not my opinion) is not that of impulse and resistance or, as in Scheler, will and resistance, but rather *care and meaningfulness*. This correlation is the basic structure of life, a structure which I also call *facticity*. For something can be encountered in its resistivity as a resistance only as something which I do not succeed in getting through when I live in a wanting-to-get-through, which means in being out toward something, which means that something is already primarily present for caring and concern, which presence is the basis upon which there can first be a presence of the resistant at all. No resistance, however great, is capable of giving something objective. If resistance

---

3. Max Scheler, *Die Formen des Wissens und die Bildung*, lecture delivered in 1925 (Bonn: Friedrich Cohen, 1925), p. 47, note 24. Editor's note: Cited according to Max Scheler, *Späte Schriften*, edited by Manifred S. Frings (Bern/Munich: Francke, 1976), p. 112, note 1. [This later edition introduces a variant version of this note which makes it untranslatable. We have accordingly reverted to the original version cited in Heidegger's manuscripts and found in all editions prior to this one. The problematic phrase should read: ". . . sondern allein auf dem *im* Akte des Strebens und *der* dynamischen Faktoren der Aufmerksamkeit allein ursprünglich erlebten *Widerstand* des Seienden. . . ."]
4. Ibid., note 25.

were the authentic being of entities, then the relationship of being of two entities with the greatest resistance between them, and so the intense pressure of one entity against another, would involve bringing something like a world into presence. But this is not directly given between two entities in a relationship of resistance. The pressure and counterpressure, thrust and counterthrust, of material things never allow something like a world in the sense of worldhood to come into being. Instead, *resistance is a phenomenal character which already presupposes a world.*

In addition, this phenomenon of resistance is inadequate because it is basically oriented only to the correlation of acts, just as it was in Dilthey. Scheler is thus also forced, as a basis for this old proposal of a subject which has acts, to draw again upon the distinction of *in mente* and *extra mentem*. Notwithstanding, here, quite independently from another quarter within phenomenology comes the insistence that reality can never be understood in terms of the mere knowledge of something, that above all an epistemology cannot be oriented toward judgments or the like. All this is worth noting, and Scheler emphasized particularly the latter quite forcefully when he said that today still three-fourths of all epistemologies are of the wrongheaded opinion that the primary aspect from which the object of knowledge, the entity in itself, can be apprehended is the judgment.

Resistance as well as bodily presence find their ground in this, that worldhood already is. They are particular phenomena of an isolated encounter, isolated to a particular kind of access involved in sheer striving. The conception of the entities of the world as resistance is then associated in Scheler with his biological orientation, with the question of how a world in general is given for primitive life forms. In my view, this method of clarifying by analogy from primitive life forms down to single-celled animals is wrong in principle. It is only when we have apprehended the objectivity of the world which is accessible to us, that is to say, our relationship of being toward the world, that we can perhaps also determine the worldhood of the animal by certain modified ways of considering it. The reverse procedure does not work, inasmuch as we are always compelled to speak on the basis of the analogy in analyzing the environing world of the animals. This environing world therefore cannot be the simplest one for us.

When we have seen that the elucidation of the reality of the real is based upon seeing Dasein itself in its basic constitution, then we also have the basic requirement for all attempts to decide between *realism* and *idealism*. In elucidating these positions it is not so much a matter of clearing them up or of finding one or the other to be the solution, but of seeing that both can exist only on the basis of a neglect: they presuppose a concept of 'subject' and 'object' without clarifying these basic concepts with respect to the basic composition of Dasein itself. But every serious idealism is in the right to the extent that it sees that being, reality, actuality can be clarified only when being, the real, is present and encountered. Whereas every realism is right to the extent that it attempts to retain Dasein's natural consciousness of the extantness of the world. But it immediately falls short in attempting to explain this reality by means of the real itself, in believing that it can clarify reality by means of a causal process. Regarded strictly in terms of scientific method, therefore, realism is always at a lower level than every idealism, even when that idealism goes to the extreme of solipsism.

With this I want to bring to a provisional conclusion our analysis of the world with respect to its structure of meaningfulness. I stress that we shall come upon this consideration again at an essentially higher stage, after we have clarified the being of being-in-the-world, the kind of being involved in letting something be encountered, and the mode of being of understanding itself. On this basis we can then first make clear why the encounter of the world must be conceived *as presence* [*Anwesenheit*] and *the present* [*Gegenwart*].

§25. *Spatiality of the world*

The theme under consideration is Dasein in its basic constitution, being-in-the-world. This unitary phenomenon was first brought into view by regarding one of three directions, that of the structural moment of the world, understood as the world of everyday Dasein. We first worked out this worldhood in its general structure as meaningfulness.

We thus did not begin with *extensio*, with the definition of reality which can be obtained in an extreme epistemological orientation. This possibility nevertheless remains of such a correct definition of the world primarily on the basis of extension and spatiality and with a view to a certain objectivity of natural knowledge. And this indicates that in some sense *spatiality* still belongs to the world, *that spatiality is a constitutive element of the world*. But this certainly does not mean that the being of the world could be defined primarily and solely in terms of spatiality, as Descartes sought to do, that all other possible characters of the reality of the world are founded upon spatiality. Instead, the question arises whether it is not just the other way around, whether spatiality is to be explicated from worldhood, whether the specific spatiality of the environing world as well as the type and structure of space itself and its discovery, the manner of its possible encounter, pure metric space for example, can be made understandable only upon the worldhood of the world. And this is in fact the case.

Space and spatiality as a basic constitution of the world are to be explicated only upon the world itself in compliance with the task of phenomenological analysis. This means that spatiality is to be exhibited phenomenally in the world of everyday Dasein and made manifest in the world as environing world. *That world is environing world is due to the specific worldhood of space.* It is incumbent on us to see this worldhood of space, to see primary spatiality, and to understand the space of the environing world and its structural correlation with Dasein. Only then are we in the position to avoid a course which is always and above all adopted, even by Kant, for the definition of spirit and spiritual being. This course always involves defining spirit negatively against the spatial, defining *res cogitans* negatively against *res extensa*, conceiving spirit always as non-space. By contrast, the original analysis of worldhood and its spatial character leads us to see rather that Dasein itself is spatial. There is absolutely no reason to oppose this and to think, on the basis of whatever metaphysical presuppositions, that spirit, person, the authentic being of man, is some sort of an aura which is not in space and can have nothing to do with space, because we associate space primarily with corporeality and so move in constant fear of materializing the spirit.

We shall designate the phenomenal structure of the worldhood of space as the *aroundness* of the world as environment [*Umwelt*, the world *around* us]. We have accordingly already ordered our analysis of worldhood so that we first dealt with worldhood and in the second place put the aroundness of worldhood as the constitutive aspect of our closest world.[1]

The explication of aroundness can be divided into three steps: [a], the highlighting of the phenomenal structure of aroundness as such; [b], aroundness, the environmental as a primary character of world and of spatiality, that is, as a primary character of the encounter of world and so of Dasein itself as in-being; [c] the specific spatializing of the world, that is, the discovery and elaboration of pure space as an unworlding of the world.

In order to make headway in what follows, I will deal only very sketchily with the last two points. Of primary importance for me is the elaboration of the structure of aroundness. The structure of the aroundness of the world, this specific environmentality, is defined by three interconnected phenomena: *remotion, region, orientation* (directionality, directedness).

---

1. Cf. §21a) and b) above.

a) Highlighting of the phenomenal structure of aroundness as such is constituted by: remotion, region, orientation (directionality)

The first two phenomena, remotion and region, refer back to orientation. If spatiality belongs primarily to worldhood, then it is not surprising if we now show phenomenally that in the analysis of the worldhood of aroundness we have already made use of its characters, albeit implicitly. Among the characters of the world relative to its worldhood we have cited that of being handy, which we defined as the presence of what is immediately available in concern. This determination of the 'immediately' includes the phenomenon of *nearness*.

Furthermore, the analysis of the sign and of indicating made it clear that concern in an independent mode, as a special task, can undertake the discovery and release, the advance presentation of what can be pursued in the local constellation of the environing world at a definite moment. The arrow on the car indicates where the car is going, the way to this and that direction. Thus, the phenomenon of aroundness includes the distinctive characters of *nearness* and *direction* (way to . . .).

Nearness implies distance [Ferne] or, as we shall later put it more precisely, *nearness is only a mode of remotion [Entfernung]*. Nearness and distance, which characterize the things of the world under concern as they are encountered in concern, already give us the phenomenon of remotion. Let us note at once that 'remotion' does not refer to the spacing between two points, even when we do not take them as pure points but as worldly things (say, the distance of the chair from the window). It refers rather to the temporally particular nearness or remotion of the chair or window to *me*. Only on the basis of this primary remotion, that the chair, insofar as it is there in a worldly way, as such is removed from me, as such has a possible nearness and distance to me, only on this account is it possible for the chair to be remote from the window, and that we can designate this referential connection of the two as remotion, although this usage of remotion is already secondary. The relation of the two points here can now no longer be designated as remotion. For these two points as geometric points are not remote but have a spacing [*Abstand*]. Spacing and remotion do not coincide. Instead, spacing is ontologically founded in remotion and can only be discovered and defined when there is remotion.

The character of the indicated constellation into which a particular environmental thing can move, for example, a car in taking the way to . . . , includes the original form of '*where to*,' that is, 'to' a location, more precisely put, to a *place*, and this implies a particular *region*. Region is nothing but the '*where of a whereto*.' Region is essentially oriented to the 'to' of a whereto, to *direction*. These phenomena—nearness, distance, direction—give the first basic structure of the aroundness. If we take these phenomena in their unity and uniformity, we can say that *the aroundness in the world is the regional nearness and distance of the intimate with-which of concern*. That with which I dwell in everyday concern is defined by the near and far, specifically by regional, oriented, directed nearness and distance. But both structural moments—region, near and far—imply being oriented to the concerned Dasein itself. Near and far as well as region have this characteristic reference back to concerned preoccupation. Only with this back reference seen from the vantage of environmental things, with this orientation of the near and far and of what is defined in the character of the region, is the full structure of the '*around*' of aroundness secured.

Already in natural language we understand 'around' as the 'round-about-us.' The 'round-about-us' as environing world is not a manifold which has been arbitrarily thrown together; rather, ordered by nearness and distance, the actual is articulated as that which always "plays its part" [*hat ein Bewenden*] in something. More accurately, the environmental things are all *placed*. Something is near and far insofar as it has a regional place, a place oriented to Dasein, in particular its place on hand with it or its handy place allocated in concern. Everything worldly, with which concern is preoccupied, always has its place in a double sense. First, it has its place already on hand with it according to the manner of its worldly being as being-on-hand. In the natural experience and seeing of the sky the sun has its particular places. Second, however, immediately handy environmental things always have their allocated place. Concern has the possibility of allocating its particular place to a thing, which is not at all obvious.

What is actually meant by 'place' now? '*Place*' *is the where of the belonging* of what is handy or on hand in concern. "It belongs there"—such a belonging is a *region* and the determination of this belonging as placing is prescribed by concern and by what is primarily present in a concern. The placing of environmental things right down to the arrangement of a room is governed by what I already have in my everyday concern and how my Dasein is itself determined as being in the world. The placing of environmental things, the determination of where they belong in a region, is in turn founded in the primary presence of concern. It is the source of the determination of the 'thither' and 'hither' of what must be immediately handy, usable in concern, what is immediately unusable and stands in the way, and must be 'cleared' out of the way. This characteristic 'clearing' is a particular concern for the aroundness of the world. Belonging to a where, to an oriented where, is given with the meaningfulness of the world. It is concern which, starting each time from this presence of what we are to be concerned with, primarily discovers the places of the worldly taken as the immediately handy. For only these places of the handy can be assigned, in a way analogous to the signs which must be instituted, while the places of the extant on hand are simply found—found as places by reference to the orientedness of the nearest world and toward this world.

Nearness can now be negatively defined as the 'not far removed,' spoken with regard to the horizon of everyday concern: 'not far' means the 'immediate' in the sense of what is instantly available in every now, which can be appresented in every now instantly and constantly (without loss of time)—the worldly, the near which in referentially being handy is always at the same time co-handy with others.

What is near today for the owner of a radio is a concert in London. In the radio Dasein today realizes an appresentation of its 'roundabout' which is not yet fully comprehensible in its meaning for Dasein, a peculiar extension of the process of bringing the world nearer. More accurately regarded, nearness is nothing but a distinctive remotion which is available in that particular temporality. All the increases in velocity, which we go along with today more or less freely and compulsively, involve the overcoming of distances. This peculiar overcoming of distances is in its structure of being (I ask you to understand this without any value judgment!) a frenzy for nearness, which in its being is based in Dasein itself. This frenzy for nearness is nothing but reduction in the loss of time. But reduction in the loss of time is the flight of time from itself, a kind of being which can have something like time only in this way. Flight from itself does not flee somewhere else, but is one of its own possibilities, which is the present. In the flight from itself, time remains time.

b) The primary spatiality of Dasein itself: remotion, region, orientation are determinations of the being of Dasein as being-in-the-world

The nearness and distance of environmental things among themselves are always grounded in primary remotion, which is a character of the world itself. It is because world in its very sense is 'remote' that there is something like nearness as a mode of distance. In other words, Dasein itself as being-in-the-world, as a being which makes present, a presentifying being intimately involved with something which is the world, is itself in its very sense of being a being which 'remotes' and so at the same time nears. I thus use the word 'remotion' to a certain extent in a transitive, active sense: re-moting [Ent-fernen, etymologically "removing distance"], making distance disappear (nearing as bringing forward or bringing itself away, bringing forward such that the bringing-itself-away becomes available on an average at any time and with ease. Here we do violence to natural linguistic usage, but it is demanded by the phenomenon itself.

Dasein itself is re-motive: the constant overcoming of distance in making what is on hand present. The re-moting itself is given with Dasein as being-in-the-world. World itself is discovered as removed or near. Re-motion as well as resistance, for example, are *hermeneutic concepts*; they express something which in its sense is understandable as a structure of Dasein, a structure of being in which I myself dwell as an entity who is there, an entity of the character of Dasein. Re-motion therefore expresses a mode of being which I myself can be and constantly am.

All environmental things have a remotion only insofar as they as worldly things are generally remote. If their specific environmental character is dimmed and the things are "unworlded" down to two geometric points, they finally lose the character of remotion. They are left only with *spacing*. The spacing itself is a quantum, a how-much. Spacing is what remotion in its sense first of all is not, a definite so-much which is solely defined by the manifold of that which stands in the spacing [*Abstand*, etymologically a "standing apart"]. In other words, the spacing between these two units, this definite so-much, is defined by the manifold of points which are themselves spaced here. *Spacing is a deficient remotion*. This peculiar transformation of environmental remotion—*re-moting as an existential of Dasein* and *remoteness as a category*—results precisely from the process of "*unworlding*" which has already been mentioned frequently. We cannot follow the structure of this process more closely at this stage, because for that we need the phenomenon of time.

Nearness and distance as characters of the worldly likewise had the determination of the *regional*, of that which lies in a region. The region is the where of the whither of a belonging to, going to, bringing away, looking at, and the like. This 'out-to' is the *directedness* that belongs to all concern as being-in-the-world. This means that, since in-being is always re-motive, every re-motion as a basic determination of being-in-the-world is a directedness-towards. The orientation can thereby be fixed and determined successively and variously. The very fixation of orientedness can in turn be possible by various means, purely environmentally through signs or purely mathematically through a graphical calculation. But the condition of possibility of this fixation is the determination of the region on the basis of meaningfulness.

The celestial regions are discovered primarily by way of the rising and setting of the sun. Here the sun is not understood as an astronomical thing but as something environmentally on hand constantly used in everyday concern, namely as that which gives light and warmth in the cycle of day and night. This its kind of being, its usability, itself changes with its position; mornings it is still cold and dim. The various places of the sun in the sky, specifically the distinctive positions of sunrise, midday, and sunset, are particular regions which are constantly on hand. As environmental, they enable an orientation such that every environmental region is in turn defined by east, south, west, north in relation to the sky. Every movement in the environing world, every location of a field or the like is oriented to the *world region*. It should be noted that in the primary discovery of the world regions these have for ages not been geographical concepts. This is shown clearly in the fact that earlier and even today churches and graves are oriented in very definite directions. These regions under question here, for example, east, west, have no relation at all to geographical contexts but to sunrise and sunset, life and death, hence to Dasein itself. If we recall Caesar's *De bello gallico* [*On the Gallic Campaign*], the military camp there was always laid out in a very definite orientation. On the basis of these orientations, which at first are not geographically measured at all and are not any other kind of theoretically fixed determinations and regions, every single region in the environmental world is articulated. The where of environmental belonging, this whole of aroundness in which I move, is at any particular time brought into relief in this or that way, according to what predominantly stands under care. The spatialities which are thus articulated, the spatiality of a house or the spatial whole, the environmental whole of a city, are not anything like a three-dimensional manifold which would be filled up with things. A region of the world can be discovered as such only because disclosive being-in-the-world is itself oriented. This is a fundamental proposition which in its converse formulation gives an essential insight into the primary character of Dasein: Since a region can be discovered only by way of an oriented Dasein, this Dasein itself is already originally being-in-the-world.

Thus we see that again and again the articulation of region and thus the fixing of near and far is determined on the basis of the meaningfulness of encountered things. The nearest world, the things encountered in it are not placed along the lines of a geometric-mathematical system of points but within environmental contexts of reference: on the table, by the door, behind the table, on the street, around the corner, by the bridge. These are very definite orientations which bear the character of meaningfulness purely environmentally, which means the where of the whereabouts of everyday concern. In this structure of aroundness, which is concentrated on concern by means of nearness, distance, region, and orientation, and in all of these founded by meaningfulness, there is still absolutely nothing of any sort of structure of a *homogeneous space*.

What is homogeneous is the pure space of metrics, of geometry. For these have destroyed the peculiar structure of aroundness only in order to arrive at the possibility of the discoverability of homogeneous space and with this to be able to calculate nature in its processes of motion as pure local motion, mere changes of location in time. This means that all calculating is itself only a particular kind of appresentation.

I have intentionally only pointed to that which we shall consider more closely in due time, namely, to the basic function which remoting or nearing have in Dasein: *there is in Dasein itself a characteristic inclination to nearness*—to nearness, which in its sense stands in a correlation of being with the *present*. But the present is *one* possibility of time itself.

The region and its concretion in place are always environmentally determined by already extant regions, which in their turn are again determined by a presence of what is to be of concern. The determination of remotion follows along the lines of everyday interpretation. It is not a measurement of spaced intervals but an estimate of remoted distances. And this estimate in turn is not relative to a fixed measure but to remotions which are familiar on the everyday level and always belong to Dasein's understanding of being. Gauged by the measure, seen for example on the meter stick, these estimates are very inaccurate. But as everyday interpretations they have their *own definiteness* and original justification.

We thus say that it is but a short walk or a stone's throw to there, to a particular place. Such measurements are not reduced to quantitative determinations. A short walk is different for different persons, but still is familiar enough in the community of being with one another. Even when we use a measure for determining distances by numbers that measure time, for example, when we say it is a half-hour or an hour to there, this measurement is again estimated in very different ways. A road which is travelled daily, and for which an objective measure of time is perhaps familiar, can be unequally long each day. This merely reflects that I myself am the one who covers the distance each time as *my* way of removing the distance. I travel the road upon which I remove myself from something or bring something nearer, which I myself have placed in my concern and which is not an arbitrary point in space, but where I already am to some extent from the start in my Dasein. These re-motions [which I cover daily in my rounds] belong to my temporally particular "*being-intimately-involved-with*." Such relationships are not stretches that I pace off, like an applied measure which is, so to speak, pushed along the stretch to be measured. Rather I myself am the one who at any given time overcomes his re-motion.

The duration of such a remotion is determined here according to how I have time—more accurately, *how I am time at any given time.* An 'objectively' longer way can be shorter than one which is 'objectively' quite short but which, as we say, seems infinitely long. The diversity of this duration is grounded in concern itself and in what has been placed under care for the time being. *The time which I myself am each time yields a different duration according to how I am that time.*

The objectively spaced intervals of the world do not coincide with the experienced as well as interpreted remotions. In a primary orientation to 'objective world nature' and the spacing of its distances, which seem absolutely determinable, we are inclined to call the above interpretations and estimates of distance 'subjective.' But it should be noted that this 'subjectivity,' in which we determine all remotions from ourselves, constitutes the authentic vitality of being-in-the-world. Viewed on the basis of Dasein itself, it is perhaps the 'most objective' that there is, because it belongs to the mode of being of Dasein itself and has absolutely nothing to do with 'subjective' caprice.

Strictly regarded, there is also no coincidence, and this is important, between the environmental distances fixed at any given time and the spaced intervals. The 'nearest' is really not that from which I am separated by the slightest interval, it is rather that which is removed from me in a certain average range of reach and vision. Because Dasein as being-in-the-world is re-motive, it moves in an 'environment' which is always removed from it by a certain "elbow-room," with a measure of free play and leeway. I always look and listen beyond what is nearest of all, from the perspective of intervals. Seeing and hearing are distance senses because Dasein as re-motive dwells especially in them. For the person who wears glasses, which in the objective terms of intervals are nearest to him, these glasses are nonetheless always further removed from him than the table at which he is seated. The 'nearest' in interval is not at all what is encountered immediately in everydayness. On the other hand, the sense of touch and its extensive function cannot be cited as a counterinstance precisely because the explicit function of grasping and touching is predominantly not that of bringing near. This is clearest in a very elementary action of preoccupation, of "going-about," that of walking.

In walking on the street we touch and come in contact with the ground with every step, but we do not really live in what is touched and brought near in such touching. The ground that I walk on is not at all the 'nearest.' What is nearest is rather an acquaintance who is approaching me perhaps some twenty steps removed. It is thus clear that in-being as bringing something near and making it remote is always defined by the presence of concern, of the primary being-intimately-involved-with-something. And insofar as this involvement stands in the closest connection with time and in a certain sense is time itself, the interpretation of remotion is determined on this basis. Such an interpretation is at first always distinct from the computation of intervals. Computation of intervals is always a modification of the interpretation of remotion, of in-being. That making remote and being remote belong to Dasein as to its basic constitution of in-being is moreover manifest in this, that I can *never cross* such a remotion in which I constantly live. I can surely cross the interval between the door and the chair but never the remotion in which I am at this place toward the door. This remotion, which I myself am as a 'being-toward,' can never be crossed by me. If I try to do so, something peculiar comes to light: I take the remotion with me; *I take it with me because I am it.* This is also related to a broader and certainly complicated constitutional consequence, that I can never jump over my own shadow, because with the jump the shadow jumps ahead of me. I can never wander about in this primary spatiality of the environing world in which I constantly am. For it is the spatiality which belongs to my very being-in-the-world, which I constantly take with me and, as it were, cut out from 'objective world-space' everywhere that I am, at every place.

The possibility of indicating is grounded in the constitution of orientation. Indicating lets a 'there' be seen and experienced. This 'there' brings with it the discovery of the corresponding 'here' of indicating and of the indicator. The fact that environmental signs are encountered, understood, and used means that being-in-the-world, concerned preoccupation in the world, is as such oriented. It is because Dasein in its being is oriented in-being that there is *right* and *left*. More accurately put, because oriented Dasein is corporeal Dasein, corporeality is necessarily oriented. The orientation of apprehension and looking articulates the 'straight ahead' and the 'to the right and left.' Dasein is oriented as corporeal, as corporeal it is in each instance its right and left, and that is why the parts of the body are also right and left parts. Accordingly, it belongs to the being of bodily things that they are co-constituted by orientation. There is no such thing as a hand in general. Every hand, or every glove, is a right or a left one, since the glove in use is in its sense designed to go along with bodily movements. Every bodily movement is always an '*I move*' and not 'it moves itself,' if we disregard certain well-defined organic movements. Thus things like gloves are intrinsically oriented to the right and left but not, say, a thing like the hammer, which I hold in my hand but which does not go along with my self-movement in the strict sense; rather, it is moved by me such that it moves itself. Accordingly, there are also no right and left hammers.

Orientedness is a structural moment of being-in-the-world itself and not the property of a subject which has a feeling for right and left. It is only from the basic constitution of Dasein as being-in-the-world that we can understand why concern can constantly orient itself, that is, can in each instance comport itself in its orientation in such and such a way, determining itself on the basis of that with which it intimately dwells and concerns itself. An isolated subject with the 'feeling for right and left' could never find its way in its world. This phenomenon can be clarified only when the subject is taken for what it actually is, as always already in its world. The appropriation and determination of a 'there' is indeed impossible without a right and left, but it is just as impossible without a world, without the always prior presence of an environmental thing upon which Dasein orients itself. In short, it would be impossible if Dasein were not in-being, already intimately involved with something at the time; for only then does it orient itself in certain directions according to a region.

Kant is therefore in error when he says that I orient myself by the mere feeling of a distinction between my two sides.[2] The subjective basis for the differentiation, if right and left can be called that, falls short of apprehending the full phenomenon of orientation. Since orientation is a structure of being-in-the-world, there is always a 'world' already from the outset inherent in the appropriation of an orientation, that is, in operating within an ever particular being-in-the-world. A subject with the 'mere feeling' for right and left is a construction which does not get at the being of the Dasein which I myself am. This becomes evident also from the example that Kant cites and the way in which he accounts for the phenomenon of orientation.

Suppose I step into a familiar but darkened room which in my absence has been rearranged so that everything which was on my right is now on my left (everything switched from right to left and left to right). The feeling for right and left is now of no help to me at all for orientation, as long as I do not latch on to a definite object "whose position I have in mind," as Kant incidentally remarks. But what does "have in mind" mean other than my orienting myself necessarily from and in my already being in my world. When I latch on to an object "whose position I have in mind," this is no less constitutive for finding my way than the feeling for right and left. An inadequate concept of Dasein, that of the isolated subject, leads Kant astray into an inappropriate interpretation of the condition of possibility of the right-left orientation. Conversely, we see from Kant's analysis that he must tacitly make use of the phenomenon which belongs to orientation, namely, the object I latch on to, "whose position I have in mind." But

---

2. Immanuel Kant, "Was heisst: Sich im Denken orientieren?" (1786) *Werke (Akad. Ausgabe)*, Vol. VIII, p. 135.

this is only a psychological interpretation of the ontological state of affairs whereby Dasein in each instance is always already as such in its world in order to be able to orient itself at all. Only for a Dasein oriented in this way is there right and left at all along with the possibility of appropriating and interpreting the orientation.

Kant sees neither the authentic founding context of orientation nor the right phenomenal composition. His intention from the beginning was of course not so much to clarify the phenomenon of orientation as to show that all orientation contains a 'subjective principle,' by which he meant the feeling for right and left. Since we are here suspending the concept of subject in the Kantian sense, which goes back to Descartes, and are taking the phenomena from Dasein itself in its full constitution of being, it would be premature and inappropriate to call right and left 'subjective principles.' If we wanted to call right and left 'subjective principles' in this context, then the basic constitutive state, whereby a world is always already present for Dasein, would also have to be called a 'subjective principle.' But surely it is not admissible to characterize the presence of a world as a 'subjective principle.' To do so shows just how little the traditional concept of the subject really does justice to what constitutes the authentic structure of Dasein, which is the structure of what the concept of the subject naturally always means *de facto*. But the way in which we appropriate orientation, the condition that makes it possible for us to orient ourselves, already shows that orientation belongs to Dasein itself.

These specifications of remotion, region, and orientation may suffice in relation to what we need for *time* and the *analysis of time*.

c) Spatializing the environing world and its space— space and extension in mathematical determination using Leibniz as an example

At this point, we shall only outline a brief guide to the process of spatializing the environing world by way of the fundamental concepts to which such a spatialization of this world and its space is oriented. We shall accordingly approach this by way of the concepts of space and extension, which are then taken as a basis for mathematical determination. Here we shall not go by Descartes's definition but by the essentially more advanced definition of Leibniz.

He says: *Spatium est ordo coexistendi seu ordo existendi inter ea quae sunt simul.*[3] "Space is the order of being present together, the order of

---

3. Gottfried Wilhelm Leibniz, *Mathematische Schriften*. Initia mathematica. Mathesis universalis. Vol. VII: *Die mathematischen Abhandlungen*, edited by C. I. Gerhardt (Halle, 1863). Photographic Reprint of the edition, p. 18.

being on hand for those things which are simultaneous." This definition, in *coexistendi* and in *inter ea quae sunt simul*, already shows how
time is here constitutive of space. He then defines extensio: *Extensio est
spatii magnitudo.*[4] "Extension is the magnitude of space, the quantity of
space." Leibniz then adds, typically: *Male Extensionem vulgo ipsi extenso
confundunt, et instar substantiae considerant.*[5] "Those who confound Extension with the extended and regard it as a substance are making a
superficial and false move." Here he is naturally referring to Descartes. *Si spatii magnitudo aequabiliter continue minuatur, abit in punctum
cujus magnitudo nulla est.*[6] "If the magnitude of space, *extensio*, is reduced in a uniform and constant fashion, it disappears in the point,
whose quantity is nil" and which therefore has no extension. *Quantitas
seu Magnitudo* (the determination of quantity, which we then need
later in the measurement of time) *est, quod in rebus sola compraesentia
(seu perceptione simultanea) cognosci potest.*[7] "Quantity or Magnitude is
that which can be known in things solely through a compresence of
something, through a *perceptio simultanea*" of two objects, namely, of
the handy span of distance and the ruler, the standard of measure.
The compresence of the measuring standard is thus constitutive for
the apprehension of quantity and for every measurement, whereas
for the apprehension of quality *nec opus est compraesentia*, "no such
compresence is needed." Rather, anything qualitative *singulatim obser-
vatur*,[8] "is in itself regarded individually for itself."

   I have presented these determinations of the basic structures of homogeneous world-space, which is regarded as the basis for nature, because they are simpler than those which would have to be given relative to contemporary physics and mathematics. But it should be noted
that the simplicity of these determinations does not mean that they
are already categorially transparent. For those who are somewhat
more thoroughly conversant with mathematical things, I refer to an
investigation carried out within the purview of phenomenology by
Oskar Becker.[9] Here, to be sure, the essential question of the genesis
of the specifically mathematical space of nature from environmental
space is not developed, although it stands in the background for the
author. He begins immediately with the problem of space as it is approached in mathematics, specifically in modern geometry, but still

---

4. Ibid.
5. Ibid.
6. Ibid.
7. Ibid.
8. Ibid., p. 19.
9. Oskar Becker, "Beiträge zur phänomenologischen Begründung der Geometrie
und ihrer physikalischen Anwendungen," *Jahrbuch für Philosophie und phänomenologische
Forschung*, Vol. VI (1923), pp. 385ff.

provides detailed perspectives for the individual stages within geometry itself. To begin with, there is the pure morphological description of geometric shapes, which involves no measurement whatsoever. It is the kind of description which is also employed in botany when it describes the different shapes of leaves. This sort of work fixes well-defined morphological concepts which have their own exactness and cannot be mathematized. The second stage is that of *analysis situs* [topology], the analysis (geometry) of position, and the third stage is the truly metrical stage, the only one to which the term geometry in the strict sense applies.

This concludes our analysis of the world with regard to its worldhood. The structure of this analysis of the worldhood of the world is important for the understanding of the subject matter, since it seeks to show that spatiality can be interpreted only on the basis of worldhood. This applies in particular when it is a matter of rendering intelligible the structure of homogeneous space, which is regarded as a basis in natural science.

§26. The 'who' of being-in-the-world

We shall now try to grasp the basic phenomenon of Dasein as being-in-the-world in a second direction. We are saying that this entity which has the mode of being of being-in-the-world must now be more accurately defined. But with this formulation we in a certain sense move away from a rigorous consideration of the phenomenon of Dasein. This becomes evident when we recall that this entity which we call Dasein has its what-determination in its '*to-be*.' It is not any specific "what" which in addition would have its mode of being; rather, what the Dasein is is precisely its being. This indicates that we cannot undercut this expression 'the entity which has the mode of being of Dasein' with something that reverses the entire line of questioning. When we say, actually wrongly, 'the entity which has the mode of being of Dasein,' we cannot mean that this entity is something like a thing on hand in the world, which is first specifiable of itself purely in its "what" and which on the basis of this what-content now also has a specific mode of being just like a thing, chair, table, or the like. Because the expression 'the entity of the character of Dasein' always suggests something in the order of the substantiality of a thing, it is basically inappropriate.

Let us further recall that this entity which we call Dasein, thus designating it more appropriately by a pure expression of being, is the entity which I myself am in any given time. Belonging to this being, called Dasein, is the *temporal particularity of an I* which is this being.

When we ask about this entity, the Dasein, we must at least ask, *Who* is this entity?, and not, What is this entity? It is therefore a matter of defining the who of this being. With this formulation, we have first of all at least terminologically avoided the danger of understanding it as a thing which is on hand. The word 'I,' in the meaning in which we first immediately understand it in an average way, is thereby left un-defined. The more open we leave this word, not relating it directly to a 'subject' and the like, the less burdened the term remains and the more opportunity we then have to fix it more rigorously by way of the phenomena themselves. The answer to the question of the *who of this entity*, which we ourselves in each instance are, is *Dasein*.

a) Dasein as being-with—the being of others as co-Dasein (critique of the thematic of empathy)

In the preceding analysis of the basic constitution of Dasein as being-in-the-world, we have thematized the world as the wherein of Dasein in its specific sense of in-being. But also in this analysis of the world we have not brought into relief all the phenomena which showed themselves there. In explicating the environing world of the craftsman, the phenomenon of the public world appeared. In the work under concern as well as in the material being employed and the hand tool being used, there are *others*, for whom the work is, by whom the tool in its turn is produced, *there with* [the craftsman]. In the world of concern, others are encountered; and the encountering is a *being-there-with*, not a being-on-hand. We did not consider these others any further with respect to their mode of being. And so far, we have not considered the manner of their encounter at all.

In addition, we have spoken of the public environment in contrast to one's own, and of the fluid boundary between the public and one's own being-in-the-world. The environing world, we said, is not only mine, but also that of others. Once again, the phenomenon of the others comes to light, without our having brought it into relief more sharply—the others, of whom we say that they encounter us. When it comes to this phenomenon of 'the others' who are there with me in the environing world, we have actually not overlooked it in the phenomenal contexts already treated, but have intentionally focused the analysis of the world only on the environmental things encountered. This is a violent constriction of the analysis of the world, which however is mandated by the theme itself, a point which will become apparent later.

We have indeed not considered the others and their being before, but neither have we, let it be noted, assumed a starting point for our analysis such that we said: first I am alone in the world, or first only the 'I' is given without the world. With the rejection of this approach and the uncovering of being-in-the-world, there can be no question of an isolation of the I, and therefore no talk of 'I am alone in a world.' Already the last formulation of the primary phenomenal finding in Dasein, 'I am in a world,' would be essentially more appropriate than this: 'first a bare subject exists without a world.' But even this formulation of the starting point, 'first an I is given with my being-in-the-world,' is false. Therefore, when we dealt with being-in-the-world, we always spoke of concern as a proximally everyday concerned absorption in the world, in which the other is there with me. But there was no talk of a 'subject' and 'I' which stands over against an 'object' or 'not-I.' This indeterminacy in which we left the 'who' that the Dasein is, along with the lack of prominence given to the others who are also encountered in the world, was methodologically deliberate, because this was mandated by the basic phenomenal composition of everyday Dasein.

What is now meant by this indeterminacy of the 'who' and the non-prominent status of the others in the environing world for the being of Dasein? Nothing but this: *As being-in-the-world, Dasein is at the same time being with one another*—more rigorously, *'being-with.'* The phenomenological statement, 'Dasein as being-in-the-world is a being-with with others,' has an existential-ontological sense and does not intend to establish that I in fact do not turn out to be alone and that still other entities of my kind are on hand. If this were the intention of the stipulation, then I would be speaking of my Dasein as if it were an environmental thing on hand. And being would not be a determination which would belong to Dasein of itself by way of its kind of being. Being-with would rather be something which Dasein would have at the time just because others happen to be on hand. Dasein would be being-with only because others do in fact turn up.

Being-with signifies a character of being of Dasein as such which is *co-original* with being-in-the-world. And it is the formal condition of possibility of the *co-disclosure* of the Dasein of others for the Dasein which is in each instance one's own. This character of being-with defines the Dasein even when another Dasein is in fact not being addressed and cannot be perceived as on hand. Even Dasein's being-alone is a being-with in the world. Being-alone is only a deficiency of being-with—the other is absent—which points directly to the positive character of being-with. The other is absent: this means that the constitution of the being of Dasein as being-with does not come to its factual fulfillment. The other can be absent only insofar as my Dasein is itself being-with. The absence of the other is a modification of the being of my very Dasein and as such is a positive mode of my being; only as being-with can Dasein be alone. On the other hand, Dasein's being-alone is not eliminated by having a second specimen of the species man stand next to him, or perhaps ten others. Even when ten or more are on hand, Dasein can be alone, inasmuch as being-with-one-another is not based upon having similar specimens of subject-things on hand together. Just as Dasein is far from being first only a world-less subject and an 'interior' to which the world is added, so is it far from becoming being-with because an other turns up in fact.

This *co-Dasein of others* right in everydayness is characteristic of in-being as absorption in the world under concern. The others are there with me in the world under concern, in which everyone dwells, even when they are not bodily perceived as on hand. If others were encountered merely as things, perhaps they would not really be there. All the same, their being-there-with in the environing world is wholly immediate, inconspicuous, obvious, similar to the character of the presence of world-things.

The tool I am using is bought by someone, the book is a gift from . . . , the umbrella is forgotten by someone. The dining-table at home is not a round top on a stand but a piece of furniture in a particular place, which itself has its particular places at which particular others are seated everyday. The empty place directly appresents co-Dasein to me in terms of the absence of others.

Furthermore, what is procured in everyday concern can be present in care such that it appears as something which is intended to be of use to others, excite them, get the better of them, which stands in some sort of relation to the others, mostly without explicit awareness of it. The others are there with us everywhere in what we are preoccupied with and directly in the world-things themselves, specifically those others whom one is with everyday. Even in absorption in the world, Dasein does not disavow itself as being-with, as which my being-with with others and the co-Dasein of others with me can be grasped. This being-with-one-another is not an additive result of the occurrence of several such others, not an epiphenomenon of a multiplicity of Daseins, something supplementary which might come about only on the strength of a certain number. On the contrary, it is because Dasein as being-in-the-world is of itself being-with that there is something like a being-with-one-another. This being of others, who are encountered along with environmental things, is for all that not a being handy and on hand, which belongs to the environmental things, but a *co-Dasein*. This demonstrates that even in a worldly encounter, the Dasein encountered does not become a thing but retains its Dasein-character and is still encountered by way of the world. In comparison to what was said earlier, a discordant note is heard here. We have here a worldly encounter of something whose mode of being can be taken neither as being handy nor as being on hand. This indicates that the structure of worldhood is more than what the previous analysis yielded. This structure involves not only the appresentation of environmental things. A world can also appresent Dasein, that of others as well as my own.

The others can be encountered environmentally. The poorly cultivated field along which I am walking appresents its owner or tenant. The sailboat at anchor appresents someone in particular, the one who takes his trips in it. But this encounter has a different structure of appresentation here. These others do not stand in the referential context of the environing world but are encountered in that with which they have to do, in the 'with which' of their preoccupation (field, boat) as the ones who are preoccupied with it. They are encountered as they are in their being-in-the-world, not as chance occurrences but as the ones who till the field or sail the boat. They are there in their being-in-the-world, and insofar as they are there for me in this way, they are there with me, I myself who have this being of being-in-the-world. They are there with me in the one world.

The referential contexts which we brought out earlier always appresent something environmental. But the environing world can now in turn, as a particular world, at the same time appresent a being intimately involved with it—Dasein. For such an appresentation it is not necessary for others to be 'personally' near, so to speak. But even when the others are encountered personally or, as we can most appropriately put it here, "in the flesh," in their bodily presence, this being of the others is not that of the 'subject' or the 'person' in the sense in which this is taken conceptually in philosophy. Rather, I meet the other in the field, at work, on the street while on the way to work or strolling along with nothing to do—always in a concern or nonconcern according to his in-being. He is appresented in his co-Dasein by his world or by our common environment. The distinction between a personal meeting and the other's being gone takes effect on the basis of this environmental encounter of one another, this environmentally appresented being-with-one-another. This with-one-another is an environmental and worldly concern with one another, having to do with one another in the one world, *being dependent on one another*. The most everyday of activities, passing by and avoiding one another on the street, already involves this environmental encounter, based on this street common to us. Avoiding makes sense only for an entity who is with one another, for an oriented and concerned being-in-the-world. Avoiding is merely a phenomenon of being preoccupied with one another, an everyday phenomenon pushed to the extreme, which is for the most part a caring for and with one another in having nothing to do with one another.

The strangest man whom we encounter is with me in my world and is experienced as such in avoiding and passing each other by. A stone or a brick which falls from the roof strictly speaking does not move past a window. The latter way of being-with-one-another, an everyday way which is far-reaching, that of having nothing to do with one another, is not nothing, but rather a specific modification, a privation of being-with as being-dependent-upon-one-another. It is only insofar as Dasein as being-in-the-world has the basic constitution of being-with that there is a *being-for* and *-against* and *-without-one-another* right to the indifferent walking-alongside-one-another.

It is important for this basic phenomenal composition of being-with-one-another to be made perfectly clear. In spite of all the former prejudices of philosophy and all the usual attempts to explain and deduce such phenomena, this phenomenon must be brought to an unadulterated givenness. And this is possible, since from the start the basic constitution of Dasein as being-in-the-world already stands before us. In order to understand not only this character of being-with but also the following characters, it must be kept in mind from the start that all these phenomena, which we naturally can discuss here only in a sequential treatment, are not derived from one another in accordance, say, with their structure of being, but are *co-original* with each other. It is true that all other characters can be made understandable only in terms of the basic constitution of in-being, but they do not first turn up in the course of being Dasein or in any other development of Dasein.

Being-with-one-another, which combines the structure of being of my own temporally particular Dasein as being-with and the mode of being of others as co-Dasein, must be understood in terms of this basic constitution of being-in-the-world. Here it should be noted that the closest kind of encounter with another lies in the direction of the very world in which concern is absorbed. Our procedure is therefore not to lay down some concept of man and then maintain, since man presumably has to be a 'social being,' that the structure of being-with belongs to Dasein. Instead, from the phenomenal state of the everydayness of Dasein itself it becomes evident that not only the others but remarkably 'one oneself' is there in what one attends to everyday.

This being-with-one-another is now determined by all the characters which we pointed to earlier in relation to in-being. That is, even the most indifferent being-with-one-another along the lines of directedness toward one another (for example, in spatial orientation), even this is understandable only if being-with-one-another means *being-with-one-another in a world*. This is the basis upon which this being-with-one-another, which can be indifferent and unconscious to the individual, can develop the various possibilities of community as well as of society. Naturally these higher structures and the ways they are founded cannot be pursued in greater detail here.

We must therefore keep in mind that the worldhood of the world appresents not only world-things—the environing world in the narrower sense—but also, although not as worldly being, *the co-Dasein of others and my own self*. But this means that a worldly encounter of something does not yet decide for itself about the kind of being of what is encountered. This can be appresented as being handy and being on hand, co-Dasein or self-Dasein. Not to be denied phenomenally is the finding that co-Dasein—the Dasein of others—and my own Dasein are encountered by way of the world. On the strength of this worldly encountering of others, they can be distinguished from the world-things in their being on hand and being handy in the environing world and demarcated as a '*with-world*,' while my own Dasein, insofar as it is encountered environmentally, can be taken as the '*self-world*.' This is the way I saw things in my earlier courses and coined the terms accordingly. But the matter is basically false. The terminology shows that the phenomena are not adequately grasped in this way, that the others, though they are encountered in the world, really do not have and never have the world's kind of being. The others therefore cannot be designated as a 'with-world.' The possibility of the worldly encounter of Dasein and co-Dasein is indeed constitutive of the being-in-the-world of Dasein and so of every other, but it never becomes something worldly as a result. Whenever the qualification 'with' is added to the phenomenon 'world' and we speak of a 'with-world,' things are turned the wrong way. This is why I now have used the term '*being-with*' from the start. By contrast, the world itself is never there with us, it is never Dasein-with, co-Dasein; it is that in which Dasein is at any given time as concern. Of course, that still does not adequately clarify this remarkable possibility of the world, namely, that it lets us encounter Dasein, the alien Dasein as well as my own. We shall be able to make this clarification only in later contexts.

Being-with as a basic constitution of Dasein first has to be understood wholly within its mode of being of everydayness. We have thus characterized the world as defined by the structure of meaningfulness. This means that the world can always be understood by the Dasein which is in it in very different degrees of expressness and definiteness. For since being-in-the-world is itself *understanding*, and understanding is not a kind of knowledge but a primary kind of being of being-in-the-world itself, and being-with-one-another is conceived as an original constitution of Dasein, it follows that the latter is *eo ipso* an *understanding of one another*. Such an understanding operates in a milieu of changing familiarity and understandability. Even a savage transplanted among us exercises his understanding in this world, even though it can be utterly strange to him in its detail.

The apparently presuppositionless approach which says, 'First there is only a subject, and then a world is brought to it,' is far from being critical and phenomenally adequate. So is the assumption which holds that first a subject is given only for itself and the question is, how does it come to another subject? Since only the lived experiences of my own interior are first given, how is it possible for me to apprehend the lived experiences of others as well, how can I "*feel my way into*" them, *empathize* with them? It is assumed that a subject is encapsulated within itself and now has the task of empathizing with another subject. This way of formulating the question is absurd, since there never is such a subject in the sense it is assumed here. If the constitution of what is Dasein is instead regarded without presuppositions as in-being and being-with in the presuppositionless immediacy of everydayness, it then becomes clear that the problem of *empathy* is just as absurd as the question of the reality of the external world.

It also becomes clear, already from the way in which everyone encounters himself by way of the world, that the experience of alien 'psychic life' as well as my own does not first need a reflection on lived experience, taken in the traditional sense, in order to apprehend my own Dasein. Likewise, I do not understand the other in this artificial way, such that I would have to feel my way into another subject. I understand him from the world in which he is with me, a world which is discovered and understandable through the regard in being-with-one-another. It is because understanding is drawn from the world that there is the possibility of understanding an alien world or a world mediated by sources, monuments, and ruins. For then I no longer have the persons with whom I am supposed to empathize, but only the remnants of their world. It is in this comprehensibility of a world that incomprehensibility and distance is first of all possible.

The rejection of this pseudo-problem of empathy—how does an initially isolated subject reach another?—by no means implies that being-with-one-another and its comprehensibility does not stand in need of phenomenal clarification. It only claims that the question of co-Dasein must be understood as a question of Dasein itself. This "ontically existentiell" originality is not ontologically obvious. It does not eliminate the ontological problem of empathy.

b) The Anyone as the who of the being of with-one-another in everydayness

The structure of Dasein must now be displayed in terms of how such a being-with-one-another determined by the world and the common understanding given with it are constituted in Dasein. The question is, who is it really who first of all understands himself in such a being-with-one-another? How is such an understanding itself to be interpreted as a kind of being-with-one-another in terms of the constitution of the being of Dasein? Upon this basis we can then ask a further question. But this question is not how understanding in general comes about but how the mutual understanding, which is always already included with Dasein by virtue of its possibilities of being, can be obstructed and misled; how is it that Dasein does not come to a genuine understanding precisely because there is always already an understanding of one another? Instead, this latter understanding is always held down to a distinctive average mode of being of Dasein itself.

Thus the exposition of this new character of in-being—being-with—specifically in its mode of being drawn from the world, also presses toward the question from which we started: *Who is this Dasein in its everydayness?* We must not succumb to the deception that when we say, "Dasein is in each instance mine"—the being which I myself am—, the answer to the question of the who of Dasein in its everydayness is also already given. Precisely because the Who asks about the who of its being, it codetermines itself with regard to the being of the Dasein which in its manner of being is in each instance *what* it is. This phenomenological explication takes the Dasein in its mode of being of everydayness, in concerned absorption with one another in the world. Dasein as being-with is this being-with-one-another. The who of the being of being-with-one-another therefore receives its answer from this being-with-one-another. The who of everydayness is the '*Anyone*' [*das 'Man'*].

It was already suggested that in the "first of all and most of all" of everyday concern, the temporally particular Dasein is always what it pursues. *One* is what *one* does. The everyday interpretation of Dasein takes its horizon of interpretation and naming from what is of concern in each particular instance. *One* is a shoemaker, tailor, teacher, banker. Here Dasein is something which others also can be and are. The others are environmentally there with us, their co-Dasein is taken into account, not only because what is of concern has the character of being useful and helpful for others, but also because others provide the same things of concern. In both respects to the others, the being-with with them stands in a relationship to them: with regard to the others and to what the others pursue, one's own concern is more or less effective or useful; in relation to those who provide the exact same things, one's own concern is regarded as more or less outstanding, backward, appreciated, or the like. The others are not only simply on hand in the concern for what one provides with, for, and against them; rather, concern as concern constantly lives in the *concern* [*Sorge*] *over being different from them*, even if only to equalize that difference; it may be that one's own Dasein is falling behind the others and wants to catch up, as it were, or that it has an advantage over them and is intent on keeping them down. This peculiar structure of being, which governs our being with others in the everyday manner of concern, shall be called the phenomenon of *apartness*—Dasein's concern over being apart—regardless of how conscious we are of it. On the contrary, it is just when everyday concern is not aware of it that this kind of being with the others is perhaps much more stubbornly and primordially there. There are human beings, for example, who do what they do purely out of ambition, without any bearing on what they are pursuing. All of these particulars here of course involve no moral judgments or the like. They only characterize movements in the raw sense, so to speak, which Dasein makes in its everydayness.

One's own concern—Dasein as being-with—has placed the others in its care in this way [in its concern over being apart]. To put it more adequately, Dasein as being-with *is lived* by the co-Dasein of others and the world which concerns it in this or that way. Right in its own-most everyday pursuits, Dasein as being with the others is not itself. Instead, it is the others who live one's own Dasein. These others more-over do not have to be definite others. Any other can represent them. It really does not matter who it is at the time. What matters is only the others to whom one's own Dasein itself belongs. These others, to whom one oneself belongs and who one is in being-with-one-another, constitute the 'subject,' so to speak, which in its constant presence pursues and manages every everyday concern.

Now insofar as Dasein in its concern for its world is being-with and as such is absorbed with the others in the world, this common world is at the same time the world which each one of us has placed in his care as a public environment which one puts to use and takes into account and moves about in. Here we move with others in modes of being which every other is just as I am, where every distinction in occupation and profession collapses. The being-with-one-another dissolves one's own Dasein totally into the mode of being of the others. The Dasein allows itself to be carried along by others in such a way that the others in their distinctiveness vanish even more. In the sphere of its possibilities of being, each is totally the other. It is here that the peculiar 'subject' of everydayness—the *Anyone*—first has its total domination. The public being-with-one-another is lived totally from this Anyone. We take pleasure and enjoy ourselves as *one* takes pleasure and we read and judge about literature as *one* judges, we hear music as *one* hears music, we speak about something as *one* speaks.

This Anyone, who is no one in particular and 'all' are, though not as a sum, dictates the mode of being of everyday Dasein. The Anyone itself has its own ways to be. We have already characterized one of them with the phenomenon of *apartness*. The tendency of being-with to be on the basis of being different from others has in turn its ground, inasmuch as this being-with-one-another and concern have the character of *averageness*. This averageness is an existential determination of the Anyone; it is that around which everything turns for the Anyone, what is essentially at issue for it. That is why the Anyone holds itself factically in the averageness of what belongs to it and what it takes as valid. This polished averageness of the everyday interpretation of Dasein, of the assessment of the world and the similar averageness of customs and manners watches over every exception which thrusts itself to the fore. Every exception is short-lived and quietly suppressed. Anything original is smoothed out overnight into something which is available to Everyman and no longer barred to anyone. This essential averageness of the Anyone is in turn grounded in an original mode of being of the Anyone. This mode is given in its absorption in the world, in what can be called the *levelling* of being-with-one-another, the levelling of all differences.

There is an existential interrelation among the phenomena of *apartness*, *averageness*, and *levelling*. The Anyone as that which forms everyday being-with-one-another in these ways of its being constitutes what we call *the public* in the strict sense of the word. It implies that the world is always already primarily given as the common world. It is not the case that on the one hand there are first individual subjects which at any given time have their own world; and that the task would then arise of putting together, by virtue of some sort of an arrangement, the various particular worlds of the individuals and of agreeing how one would have a common world. This is how philosophers imagine these things when they ask about the constitution of the intersubjective world. We say instead that the first thing that is given is the common world—the Anyone—, the world in which Dasein is absorbed such that it has not yet come to itself, just as it can constantly be this way without having to come to itself.

We noted that Dasein *first of all* does *not* live in its own and nearest. First of all and everyday, one's own world and own Dasein are precisely the farthest. What is first is precisely the world in which one is with one another. It is out of this world that one can first more or less genuinely grow into his own world. This common world, which is there primarily and into which every maturing Dasein first grows, as the public world governs every interpretation of the world and of Dasein. This public world advances its claims and demands, it is right in everything, not by virtue of an original relationship to the world and to Dasein itself, not because it might have a special and genuine knowledge of the world and of Dasein, but precisely by talking over everything while not going 'into the matters' and by virtue of an insensitivity to all distinctions in level and genuineness. The public is involved in everything but in such a way that it has already always absolved itself of it all. But because it is involved in everything and determines the interpretation of Dasein, it has already decided for all choosing and deciding. The public deprives Dasein of its choice, its formation of judgments, and its estimation of values; it relieves Dasein of the task, insofar as it lives in the Anyone, to be itself by way of itself. The Anyone takes Dasein's 'to-be' away and allows all responsibility to be foisted onto itself, all the more as the public and the Anyone have to answer for nothing, because no one is there who has to answer. For the Anyone is precisely *the who which all and none are*, the being of which it can always be said, "It was really no one." And yet most things in our Dasein happen through the being of that of which we must say, "It was no one."

Thus, this further constitutive state of the being of the Anyone shows itself in the public, namely, that it always *unburdens* a person's own Dasein. Insofar as there is in Dasein the tendency to take and do things lightly, this unburdening of being which Dasein cultivates as being-with obligingly accommodates it. In thus accommodating Dasein with this unburdening of its being, the public maintains a stubborn dominion. Everyone is the other and no one is himself. The Anyone, which answers the question of the *who* of everyday Dasein, is the *Nobody*, to whom every Dasein has of itself already surrendered itself in the public being-with-one-another.

But now it must be noted phenomenologically that this 'nobody,' which I have just exhibited in bold outlines from various sides, is in fact not nothing. The Anyone is an undeniable, demonstrable phenomenon of Dasein itself as being-with in the world. It cannot be said that, because there are no categories for it and because one is of the opinion that only something like a chair really is, this Anyone is actually nothing. Instead, the concept of being must itself be directed toward this undeniable phenomenon. The Anyone is not nothing, but it is also not a worldly thing which I can see, grasp, and weigh. The more public this Anyone is, the less comprehensible it is and the less it is nothing, so little that it really constitutes the who of one's own Dasein in each instance in everydayness.

This Anyone must be comprehended as in a way the 'realest subject' that there is for Dasein. Its phenomenal structure shows that the authentic entity of Dasein, the who, is not a thing and nothing worldly, but is itself only a way to be. If we follow the component elements phenomenally, we do not come upon an entity but upon the Dasein, insofar as it is in this specific way. This again justifies our designation of the entity which we ourselves are by the expression of being, 'Dasein.' This element of the Anyone prohibits us phenomenally from seeking an entity which could be Dasein. Even the return to an 'ego,' to an 'ego-pole' freed of all thingness, is still a concession to a dog-

matic and (in the bad sense) naive interpretation of Dasein, which attributes a subject-thing to the Dasein and then must still keep it as an
'ego-thing' and 'person-thing.' On the other hand, however, the 'ego'
and the 'self' are also not epiphenomena, not, say, the fallout resulting
from a specific constellation of the being of Dasein. The 'ego,' the
'self,' is nothing other than the who of this being, the very being which
as the Anyone has the possibility of being of the 'ego' itself. That the
Dasein can be so, that it first and foremost is not itself but is absorbed
in the Anyone, is a phenomenal finding which at the same time indicates that the being of Dasein is to be sought in its possible ways to be
itself.

Even when we ask about the who, the drift of ordinary language
already brings with it the ready implication that we are asking about
an entity on hand as a setting, so to speak, in which Dasein takes place.
This makes it all the more urgent to revert to phenomenological research: Before words, before expressions, always the phenomena
first, and then the concepts! On the basis of the phenomenological
finding of the Anyone, we must now maintain our orientation toward
the *authenticity of Dasein*, toward the *self* which Dasein can be, such that
it does not really extricate itself from this being-with-one-another but,
while this remains constitutive in it as being-with, it is still itself.

This peculiar mode of being, which characterizes everydayness in
the Anyone as concerned absorption with one another in the world,
now also brings with it an everyday kind of self-interpretation of Dasein. Since Dasein encounters itself primarily in the world, and the
public itself defines the goals and views of Dasein in terms of the world
of common concern, all the fundamental concepts and expressions
which Dasein first forms for itself will also probably be obtained with
an eye to the world in which it is absorbed. This state of affairs, which
can be very clearly shown in the *history of language*, nonetheless does
not mean, as has been thought, that languages are first oriented only
toward material things and that the so-called 'primitive' languages
hardly get beyond the view of material thinghood. This is a total confusion of the interpretation of speaking and self-interpretation. As we
have yet to see, language and speech themselves belong to Dasein as
being-in-the-world and being-with-one-another. And we shall see how
on this basis certain self-interpretations of Dasein, certain concepts
which Dasein forms of itself, are necessarily prefigured, without being
able to say that these concepts are primitive. When these phenomenal
structures of being-with-one-another in the Anyone and of absorption in the world are kept in mind, then there is no longer anything
puzzling in the fact that Dasein, insofar as it explicitly refers to itself
and articulates itself, employs characteristic meanings and interpretive senses.

Wilhelm von Humboldt was the first to point out that certain languages, when they want to say 'I,' formulate this 'I' which is to be expressed—the Dasein itself—by the word 'here,' so that 'I' means as much as 'here.' The 'thou'—the other—is the 'there,' and the 'he'—the one who first of all is not directly and expressly present—is the 'yonder.' In grammatical terms, the personal pronouns—I, thou, he—are expressed by locative adverbs. But perhaps this formulation is already inverted. There is a long-standing dispute over what the original meaning of these expressions 'here,' 'there,' 'yonder' really is, whether it is adverbial or pronominal. But in the end, the dispute is without foundation, once it is seen that these locative adverbs in their sense relate to the 'I' qua Dasein itself. They have within themselves what we earlier designated as the *orientation* to Dasein itself. 'Here,' 'there,' 'yonder' are not real determinations of place as characters of world-things, but are rather *determinations of Dasein*. In other words, these determinations of Dasein 'here,' 'there,' 'yonder' as 'I,' 'thou,' 'he' are not locative adverbs at all. They are also not expressions for 'I,' 'Thou,' 'He' in a pointed sense such that they would refer to certain special things that are. They are rather *adverbs of Dasein* and as such *pronouns* at the same time. This shows that grammar simply fails in the face of such phenomena. Grammatical categories are not tailored to such phenomena and are not at all derived by regarding the phenomena themselves but rather with regard to a particular form of assertion, the theoretical proposition. All grammatical categories are derived from a particular theory of language, from the theory of *logos* as proposition, that is, from 'logic.' There are thus difficulties from the start if one tries to clarify such linguistic phenomena as we have discussed by means of these grammatical categories. The proper approach is to get behind the grammatical categories and forms and to try to determine the sense from the phenomena themselves. The source of this phenomenon, which Humboldt exhibited without understanding it in its ultimate ontological consequences, lies in this, that Dasein, to which we have attributed an original *spatiality*, when it speaks of itself, speaks in terms of that in which it finds itself. In everyday self-articulation, Dasein considers itself in terms of spatiality, to be taken in the sense described earlier of the remotive orientation of in-being. It must be noted that the sense of 'here,' 'there,' and 'yonder' are just as problematic and difficult as that of 'I,' 'thou,' and 'he.' We shall succeed in exhibiting the actual phenomenon only when Dasein itself is defined by in-being, so that we see how the average way of being-with-one-another, and at the same time the way which defines being-in-the-world, expresses itself in this manner in terms of spatiality. It would be basically wrong to think that such modes of expression are signs of a backward language, still oriented to space and matrix instead of to the spiritual 'I.' But are 'here,' 'there,' and 'yonder' less 'spiritual' and puzzling than the 'I'? Is it not rather a more appropriate expression of Dasein itself if one does not cut oneself off from understanding it only because spatiality is oriented toward the distinctive space of natural science?

Chapter Four

A More Original Explication of In-Being: The Being of Dasein as Care

§27. In-being and care—an outline

So far, we have considered the question of the structure of the world as worldhood (meaningfulness) and the question of the who of this being-in-the-world. Here the theme was always being-in-the-world, which we identified as the basic constitution of Dasein. The special explication of the world and of the Anyone were always only specific emphases of this structural whole of being-in-the-world itself. Finally, it was shown that the Dasein in the Anyone itself represents only a specific way of being-in-the-world. The who of Dasein is in each instance a way to be, whether *authentically* or *inauthentically*. Thus the question of the who of this entity also referred back to a kind of being, to a kind of being-in-the-world. But this implies that the being of Dasein is to be defined ultimately from *in-being as such*, and that only the correct explication of this basic phenomenon, of in-being, provides the warrant for founding the remaining co-original structures of Dasein. This is also why, already at the beginning of the analysis, we interjected a provisional characterization of this constitutive state of being, in which we first clarified in very rough fashion the sense of this 'in' in contrast to a merely spatial 'in.' It can now be asserted more clearly that the being of Dasein is not of the mode of being of the world, it is neither the being-handy nor the being-on-hand of something. It is just as little the being of a 'subject,' whose being would repeatedly, in a formally unexpressed way, have to be taken as being on hand. Should we be permitted to maintain the orientation to a world and a 'subject,' however, we could then say that the being of Dasein is precisely the being of the '*between*' subject and world. This 'between,' which of course does not first arise by having a subject meet with a world, is the Dasein itself, but once again not as a property of a subject. This is the very reason why, strictly speaking, Dasein cannot be taken as a 'between,' since the talk of a 'between' subject and world always already presupposes that two entities are given between which there is supposed to be a relation. In-being is not a 'between' of real entities but the being of Dasein itself, to which a world belongs at any given time and which for the time being is mine, and first and foremost is the Anyone. That is why it is always wrong, at least if we want to speak in a conceptually rigorous way, to designate human Dasein as a microcosm over against the world as a macrocosm, since the mode of being of Dasein is essentially different from any kind of cosmos.

The analysis of the world and of the Anyone time and again encroaches upon this phenomenon of in-being. We must now follow this direction; we must try to find out how far the specific phenomenon of in-being itself can be uncovered and specified. On this path of an even more original explication of in-being, we shall try to advance to *the* structure of the being of Dasein, from which we shall then draw and formulate the comprehensive terminology for the determinations of the constitution of Dasein. We call this structure of being *care*.

With this explication of in-being as such, we come to the third stage of the analysis of the basic phenomenon of being-in-the-world as a whole. Through the analysis of in-being, we must now also be in a position to clarify the phenomena which already necessarily had to be drawn into the earlier analyses: *concern*, of which we constantly spoke in its function of primary appresenting, and which we also defined as understanding; then *knowing*, which we characterized as a specific way of cultivating understanding. The investigation of this basic character of Dasein [in-being] is therefore divided into four parts. It will highlight 1) the phenomenon of *discoveredness*, 2) *falling* as a basic movement of Dasein, 3) the structure of *uncanniness* (away from home—familiarity), and 4) *care*.

The course of the explication thus leads through the phenomenal structures to the phenomenon which allows us to come upon the being of Dasein, even though not explicitly and in sufficient scope. These phenomena are connected among themselves; and the order in which they are advanced here at the same time serves to manifest a certain founding correlation among them.

§28. *The phenomenon of discoveredness*

a) Structure of the discoveredness of Dasein in its world: disposition

The analysis of Dasein as being-with relating to its mode of being as the Anyone served to show that Dasein itself, more accurately *one* oneself, is *co-discovered* in the world of concern precisely in the public world. The world is at any given time not only *disclosed*, in letting something be encountered in concern, in its meaningfulness as the oriented wherein of the being of Dasein, but Dasein is itself there relative to its in-being, *itself there for itself*. Dasein in its being-there-with, intimately involved in what is of concern, is itself discovered in a certain sense.

These two phenomena, the disclosedness of the world itself along with the fact that being-in-the-world is in turn co-discovered, define the unified phenomenon which we call *discoveredness*.[1] This expression seeks to note above all that here it is still not and for the most part never a matter of a special thematic knowledge of the world or even a definite knowledge of itself; what alone is at stake here is the structure of the being of Dasein itself which first and foremost founds such a knowledge and so makes it possible, so that the world as disclosed can be encountered in a '*there*.' '*There*' is the very being which we call Dasein [there-being]. In thus being co-discovered, this Dasein is not expressly thematically had or known. This structure of discoveredness is to be taken rather as a structure of being, as a way to be. The adverbs of Dasein with their pronominal sense of 'I' and 'thou' make my own in-being as Dasein and the other as co-Dasein evident only as a 'here' and a 'yonder.' 'Here' and 'yonder' are possible only insofar as there is something like a 'there' at all. This 'there' is our being toward being-with-one-another insofar as the possibility of a stanced totality [*Bewandtnisganzheit*] for orientation subsists at all. A material thing occurring in the world is itself never a 'there' but is instead encountered in such a 'there.' We accordingly designate the entity which we also call man as the entity which *is itself its 'there.'* With this, we first come to the strict formulation of the meaning of the term '*Dasein*.'

In our terminological usage in accord with the phenomena, 'Dasein' means not so much occurring like a 'there' and 'yonder' but *being the 'there' itself*. The 'there' character resides in the mode of being of an entity which has the structure of the discoveredness of world and with this the discoveredness of being-in-the-world itself. The being of Dasein as being-in-the-world, as a remoting being which brings forward, is the there itself. An entity such as Dasein *brings its there with it from the very beginning*, so that a world can first be discovered. Dasein brings its there with it from the very beginning not in the sense of a dead property but as that to be which, namely, to be its there, is just the authentic sense of the being of Dasein. According to what was said about the

---

1. Editor's note: The terms 'discoveredness' and 'disclosedness' are here not so firmly circumscribed in their meanings as they later will be in *Being and Time*. At this stage, rather, the opposite tendency is noticeable: 'discoveredness' is attributed to Dasein as an existential and 'disclosedness' is a specification of the being of the world. Cf. the Editor's Epilogue.

Anyone, this 'there' is first of all always being-there-with others, which is the publicly oriented there in which every Dasein constantly remains, even when it withdraws completely into itself.

The specific discoveredness of the world, which we have called *disclosedness* to distinguish it from that of in-being, is provisionally defined sufficiently by the analysis of meaningfulness and worldhood as that disclosedness which is given because the entity having the character of Dasein discloses or has disclosed a world. The co-discoveredness of in-being itself, that I am to my Dasein itself first in a worldly way, that is, I have myself in a worldly way with and in concerned absorption in the world, is not a consequence of the disclosedness of the world, but is co-original with it. The structure of this co-discoveredness of Dasein with its world must now be defined in more detail.

We said that concern is absorbed in meaningfulness. It is a dwelling intimately with the world by way of concern, with the world in its conduciveness, usefulness, and the like. Insofar as the world is encountered in these characters of meaningfulness, it encounters concern, it addresses itself as it were constantly to a being which is *dependent* upon the world, a being which has *the sense of caring*, of being involved in caring about something. This concerned dependence upon the world, which defines the mode of being of Dasein, is constantly being *solicited* by the world itself in this or that way. The world solicits concern: This means that, as it is discovered in concern, the world does not meet with a mere looking and staring at something on hand; rather, it primarily and constantly meets with—even in looking at the world—a *caring* being-in-it. In other words, being-in-the-world is so to speak constantly being summoned by the *threatening* and *non-threatening* character of the world. In all preoccupation with the world, Dasein as in-being is in some way solicited and summoned (way of *being disposed*); this may only be in the form of an undisturbed performance, the soothing uniformity of an unthreatened employment, the indifference of the everyday handling of what is placed under care.

These characters of indifference: undisturbed preoccupation, the soothing uniformity of everyday action, the indifference in handling matters can (and even will) at any time be replaced by restlessness and uneasiness, or in turn by the sense of being unencumbered and letting oneself go to the point of soaring frenzy. The phenomena of indifference and its interruptions by solicitation are in general possible only because concerned being-in-the-world can be addressed originally by the *threatening* and the *non-threatening*, in short, by the world as meaningfulness. It is only because Dasein itself is in itself care that the world is experienced in its threatening character, in its meaningfulness. This does not mean that the caring Dasein thus construes the world 'subjectively.' That would be a complete inversion of the elements involved. Rather, the caring in-being discovers the world in its meaningfulness.

In thus being elevated, or in its contrary of being depressed, the same phenomenon appears again and again as a constitutive state of Dasein, namely, that in all of its preoccupation with the world Dasein is always *found* in this or that way. It finds itself in this or that way, it is disposed in this or that *mood*. When we say, it *finds itself*, this 'itself' first does not really refer expressly to a developed and thematically conscious 'I.' In the very everyday absorption in the Anyone, it can be this Anyone itself in its indeterminacy, and this is just what it is. This co-discoveredness of being-in-the-world in being solicited by the world is possible only because Dasein originally always *finds itself* in each of its modes of being, because Dasein itself is discovered for itself. We call this basic form of primary co-discoveredness of Dasein *disposition*.*

A stone never finds itself but is simply on hand. A very primitive unicellular form of life, on the contrary, will already find itself, where this disposition can be the greatest and darkest dullness, but for all that it is in its structure of being essentially distinct from merely being on hand like a thing.

Finding itself in being-in-the-world, in short, disposedness, belongs with being-in-the-world as such. We choose this term in order to avoid from the start regarding the finding-itself as some sort of a reflexion upon itself. We shall learn to see this phenomenon more rigorously with the analysis of care itself. Dasein 'has' its world, has it as a disclosed world, and Dasein finds itself. These are two phenomenological statements which refer to one and the same state of affairs, to the basic structure of being-in-the-world, to discoveredness. *Disposition expresses a way of finding that Dasein is in its being as being in each instance its own there, and how it is this there.* We must therefore totally give up any attempt to interpret disposition as a finding of inner lived experiences or any sort of apprehension of an inner something. Disposition is rather a basic mode of the being of Dasein, of its in-being. This character of discoveredness in disposition is related to being-in-the-world as such, specifically in the everyday way where one always finds oneself where one dwells, such that in all of what we do and where we

---

*Befindlichkeit. Disposition is intended to suggest the affective state of being disposed, in Heidegger's later words, 'thrust' into being, and so further suggests being on the receiving (passive, passional, e-motive) end of existence, in Heidegger's words 'solicited,' 'summoned,' and so disposed by and toward the world. The emphasis is therefore on the results of the revelations of 'finding itself' (*Sich-befinden*), i.e., *how* one finds oneself, its state-of-being, its 'standing' in being, its situation. The common question, *wie befinden Sie sich?*, "how are you?" (literally "how do you find yourself?") is here an inquiry into your state-of-being rather than your state of health or "state-of-mind."

Befindlichkeit will occasionally be translated as 'disposedness' to accentuate its proximity to discoveredness and disclosedness.

dwell, we are in some sense—as we say—'affected.' This being affected does not need to be conscious and can be a matter of complete
indifference—the sense of sameness, dreariness, emptiness, and stale-
ness of Dasein—characters which in the most fleeting moment of Dasein are always constitutive of absorption in the world.

The phenomenon of *mood*, of *being attuned*, which up to now has
been left totally in the dark in our elucidation of the structure of Dasein, is an exponent of disposition. All these essential phenomena of
mood and attunement can be explicated only on the basis of those
structures of Dasein which we have already exposed. What are otherwise called 'feelings' and 'emotions' and treated as a special class of
lived experiences remain unclarified in their primary structure of
being as long as one does not take up the task of exposing the basic
constitution of Dasein and here in particular its discoveredness, so as
to draw these phenomena back into this constitutive structure. These
phenomena of feeling and emotion can of course always be described
up to a certain point, but this always gives us a 'popular concept,' to
speak with Kant, especially if we also demand that these phenomena
must be defined in their phenomenal structure before we begin to describe them in detail. Even the most extensive psychology will never
unravel the authentic structure of these phenomena, because psychology in principle does not enter into the dimension of the structure of
Dasein as such, since this problematic is in principle closed to it. To
put it very generally without regard to the analysis of Dasein, the neglect of these phenomena of feelings and emotions is connected with
the fact that *anthropology* generally is primarily oriented to *knowing*
and *willing*, in short, to *reason*. Feelings are then just what *accompanies*
knowing and willing, as hail accompanies a storm. Kant puts forward
the idea that the feelings are something which hamper or impair ra-
tionality and so must be classed with sensibility, with the μὴ ὄν in man.
One has thus cut oneself off in advance from understanding the sense
which these phenomena have for the structure of being itself. In analyzing these structures in greater detail, we shall have to avoid classify-
ing them in some sort of table of emotions or feelings. They are to be
understood only in conjunction with the basic movement of Dasein
itself.

Also, in coordinating the phenomena of feelings and emotions to
the structure of disposition, nothing is said about the cognitive character of these structures. But it has been pointed out that such emotions and ways of feeling in fact have the possibility of uncovering Dasein itself in its being. But at the same time these same phenomena, by
virtue of a peculiar correlation of being in Dasein which we shall soon
come to know, can also have the tendency and possibility of *covering
up* Dasein itself and the world. Thus, together with discoveredness,
there arises the possibility of covering up, deception. Deception does

not arise from a mistaken inference but always from a primary not-understanding, that is, from a covering up, which again must be understood from Dasein's kind of being.

Disposedness is the apriori for discoveredness and disclosedness. It is a co-original character along with disclosedness and constitutes with it what we call discoveredness. Discoveredness itself is not a property but, like every structure of Dasein, a way of its very being and consequently a way of its being which it as care in turn constantly places under care. In other words, Dasein constantly takes care of its there, its discoveredness.

Disposition itself is now the genuine way to be Dasein, the way to have itself as discovered, the mode in which Dasein itself is its there. The there is thereby certainly not understood as an object, as a possible theme of apprehension. In-being as finding-itself rather means that this "there" is unthematically, but for this very reason, authentically discovered, so that this discoveredness constitutes nothing other than the way to be. Discoveredness as a constitutive state of an entity whose essence it is to be, can therefore only be understood as a *kind of being* and *possibility of being of Dasein itself.* This is only the application of a general ontological principle which is valid for all characters of the being of Dasein, that they are not properties but are all *Dasein's possibilities to be*, modes of its very being.

Discoveredness belongs to being-in-the-world constitutively. This means that Dasein as concern is essentially a situated [*befindliches*] being, a being disposed toward the disclosed world. Disclosing a world is always already a self-finding. The original belonging-together of disposedness and disclosedness of world must be brought home phenomenally: Dasein does not first find itself by itself in order then from there to look around itself for a world. Rather, disposition is itself a character of in-being, which means always already being in a world. The most immediate phenomenal concretion of this structure of in-being in discoveredness must, as always, be sought in the everydayness of being with one another.

b) Understanding: the enactment of the being of discoveredness

Discoveredness as a way to be is always of concern along with the concern for the world. Dasein is its there and lets us encounter the world in the there. With disclosedness and disposition, possibilities are given for Dasein to be its there, to be its discoveredness in one way or another. *The enactment on the level of being [Seinsvollzug] of those possibilities of being which we call discoveredness we shall designate as understanding.* We obtain here the strict definition of understanding in terms of the structure of the being of Dasein itself. We have already suggested earlier that understanding cannot be conceived as knowing, certainly not primarily, even when knowing is taken as a mode of being of Dasein.

Understanding is a kind of being of the entity of the character of in-being. It is the *being-involved-with* of disclosed concernability, specifically a disposed involvement such that it always co-discovers itself. *Understanding as disposed disclosure and having disclosed the world is as such a disclosive self-finding.* As discoveredness makes up the structure of being of the full constitution of Dasein, since it applies to the world, in-being, and every way to be, so also the enactment of being belonging to it, understanding, always extends to the *full* understandability, which means to world, co-Dasein, and one's own Dasein. It can thus be the case that the enactment of understanding at the time thematically refers in particular to the world, for example, or to the co-Dasein of others or to my own Dasein. But in each case the phenomena which belong to the scope of discoveredness, that is, to the full understandability of Dasein itself, are always co-understood. This is an apriori principle for understanding, without which we would constantly go astray in defining this phenomenon. It is a deception, which is connected with ignorance of the genuine structure of Dasein, to think that there is a separate understanding of a bare world or of an alien Dasein. This structure of understanding, which is grounded in Dasein itself and which defines understanding as the enactment of the being of discoveredness, provides crucial orientation points for all problems of *hermeneutics*. Such a hermeneutics is possible only on the basis of the explication of Dasein itself, the kind of being to which understanding belongs. The possibility that there is something which cannot be understood is first given with the orbit of understandability marked out by discoveredness, an orbit which encompasses the world, in-being, and the co-Dasein of others. Every 'not-there' and everything understood in the there is but a modification of the there. It is only on the basis of understandability that there is a possible access to something which is in principle incomprehensible, that is, to nature. Something like nature can be discovered only because there is history, because *Dasein is itself the primarily historical being*. And only because of this are there natural sciences.

The understandability of Dasein and of co-Dasein as well as non-understanding themselves always vary in direct relation to the understanding of the world, and conversely. The discoveredness of Dasein and of being-with-one-another at a particular time modifies the understanding of the world. In other words, understanding as a *whole* always is what it is in terms of the being of the discoveredness of Dasein. This is the basis of what, viewed from the outside, is called the *circle in understanding*. We find a circle in understanding only if we do not see that an understanding of world, Dasein, and co-Dasein belongs to every understanding as such. It is therefore neither an accident nor a mere inconvenience when it is said, in reference to certain tasks of understanding in the historical disciplines, "It unfortunately depends upon the personal standpoint of the historian. We have to put up with it, but the ideal would be to be free of this subjectivity." Such a view is absurd. The ideal is precisely that the understanding Dasein does belong to the understanding of itself. And the consequence is not to feel sorry about it but to see a task there. The task is to bring Dasein itself into the kind of understanding which pertains to its being at the time so that it can have access as understanding to the matter to be understood.

The primary sense of the term 'understanding' as we use it here becomes clear in certain idioms which we often find in language. When I say to another, 'you have understood me,' I mean thereby, 'You know where you're at with me as well as with yourself.' Understanding in this sense gives the authentic original sense, that is, *understanding is the discoveredness of the whereat-being with something*, how matters stand with it, the discoveredness of the standing [*Bewandtnis*]* which it has with the environing world, my own Dasein, and the being of others. Discoveredness of the standing, such that one has become it in his in-being, means *having understood*. Having understood means nothing other than being this temporally particular standing. It is only a matter of a variation of this authentic understanding when this becomes but an investigative understanding engaged in taking cognizance, which however involves specific modifications in the being of what is understood.

In the detailed factual steps of its enactment, understanding may seem to disregard itself understanding, but only so long as it is a matter of determining an already discovered region of matters of fact in greater detail. The more detailed determination follows the course of an interpretive determination within an already given horizon. But Dasein cannot disregard itself and its own understanding when it is a matter of the decisive enactment of understanding, that of first discovering the subject matter as such. From the various possibilities of understanding, (which we naturally cannot consider here and) which are always possibilities of the being of Dasein, also arise the various levels and forms of theoretical understanding, particular forms of possible "understanding sciences." But it must always be kept in mind that understanding can never be gained by amassing a large quantity

---

*Cf. "On the Way to *Being and Time*" for an extended discussion of this translation of *Bewandtnis*. But here note the added bonus of this translation in correlating 'standing' with under-standing.

of information and proofs. On the contrary, all knowing, cognitive proving, and the producing of arguments, sources, and the like always already presuppose understanding.

By the odd fact that we must distinguish between *authentic* and *inauthentic understanding*, it is already apparent that understanding as enactment of the being of discoveredness is itself subject to specific modifications which are given with Dasein itself. There is in Dasein itself the possibility of operating with an understanding which only looks like but is not understanding. This characteristic pseudo-understanding dominates Dasein to a large extent.[2] Since understanding as a structure of the being of Dasein is subject to this possibility of *semblance*,[3] any understanding requires *appropriation, consolidation*, and *preservation*. This implies that the process and state of understanding can *slip away*, and what is understood can in turn become *distorted* and inaccessible. Understanding becomes non-understanding. This does not mean that there is no longer anything at all here; for this is absurd, inasmuch as discoveredness and so understanding always belong to Dasein. Rather, there is something more fundamental here than nothing, namely pseudo-understanding, a semblance of understanding, a look-alike, as though this incomprehension were still a genuine comprehension. There is in Dasein itself the possibility of bringing itself into deception.

c) The cultivation of understanding in interpretation

The cultivation of understanding is accomplished in *expository interpretation*. We saw that understanding is the enactment of the being of discoveredness. *Interpretation is the mode of enactment of this enactment of the being of discoveredness. Interpretation is the basic form of all knowing.*

From what was said earlier, this means that interpretation as such does not actually disclose, for that is what understanding or Dasein itself takes care of. Interpretation always only takes care of *bringing out what is disclosed* as a cultivation of the possibilities inherent in an understanding. The most proximate everyday mode of interpretation has the functional form of appresentation, specifically the appresentation of meaningfulness in the sense of bringing out the referential correlations accessible at any given time.

The child's question, "What is this thing?", is thus answered by stating what it is used for, defining what one finds in terms of what one

---

2. Cf. §26b) above.
3. Cf. §9a, α) above.

does with it. This definition and interpretation at the same time make reference to in-being, to preoccupation with the thing under consideration. And with such an interpretation, this thing only now actually enters the environing world as something present and understandable, even though only provisionally, for it is truly understood only when one has entered into the standing [*Bewandtnis*] which the environmental thing has. The interpretation appresents the *what-for* of a thing and so *brings out* the reference of 'in-order-to.' It brings to prominence '*as what*' the encountered thing can be taken, how it is to be understood. The primary form of all interpretation as the cultivation of understanding is *the consideration [Ansprechen] of something in terms of its 'as what,' considering something as something*. This amounts to an appresenting in talking over what is thus appresented in the primary and guiding consideration. This functional form of interpretation, '*considering something as something*,' thereby does not need to be expressed in the linguistic form of a proposition. The grammatical form of the proposition is always but a form of expression of the primary and authentic proposition, namely, this consideration of something as something. In thus bringing out the *what-for* and the *forsake-of-which* of something, the incomprehensibility is removed, the meaning of meaningfulness is made *explicit, it is put into words.* As a meaning thus brought out, it can now itself get its word. And only now is there the possibility of distinguishing the highlighted meaning as a verbal meaning from the subject matter meant—a process complicated in its structure and varying in turn in various possibilities of interpretation, the account of which belongs to logic.

But there is something essential for us in what has just been said: There is *verbal expression—language*—only insofar as there is considering, and such a consideration of something as something is possible only insofar as there is interpreting; interpretation in turn is only insofar as there is understanding, and understanding is only insofar as Dasein has the structure-of-being of discoveredness, which means that Dasein itself is defined as being-in-the-world. This continuity which founds the several phenomena—considering, interpreting, understanding, being discovered, in-being, Dasein—at the same time serves to define *language*, or gives the horizon from which the essence of language can first and foremost be seen and defined. Language is nothing but a distinctive possibility of the very being of Dasein, where Dasein is to be taken in the previously explicated structure.

d) Discourse and language

In what follows, we shall first consider the *discourse* of everydayness. *Language* is the possibility of the being of Dasein such that language makes Dasein manifest in its discoveredness by way of interpretation and thus by way of meaning. Dasein is thus at least already exposed in the way we understand its constitution in regard to in-being and being-with. The structures already considered are necessary structures for the essential structure of language itself, but they are not yet sufficient.

Language makes manifest. First of all, it does not produce anything like discoveredness. Rather, discoveredness and its enactment of being, understanding as well as its continuation in interpretation, being grounded in the basic constitution of in-being, are conditions of possibility for something becoming manifest. As conditions of being, they enter into the definition of the essence of language, since they are conditions of possibility for such manifestation. If language is a possibility of the being of Dasein, then it must be made evident in its basic structures in terms of the constitution of Dasein. Henceforth, the apriori of the structures of Dasein must provide the basis for linguistics.

As *self-articulation* of in-being and being-with, speaking is being toward the world—discourse. It expresses itself first and foremost as a speaking concern for a world. This means that *discourse is discourse about something*, such that the *about-which* becomes manifest in the discourse. This becoming manifest of what is under discussion for all that does not need to become known expressly and thematically. Likewise, *discoursing about* . . . does not stand primarily in the service of an investigative knowledge. Rather, making manifest through discourse first and foremost has the sense of interpretive appresentation of the environment under concern; to begin with, it is not at all tailored to knowledge, research, theoretical propositions, and propositional contexts. It is therefore fundamentally wrong to begin the analysis of language by examining the theoretical proposition of logic or the like. But to understand this, the founded sense of the being of knowing and interpreting must first become evident.

As being-in-the-world, discoursing is first discoursing about something. Every discourse has its *about-which*. This about-which of discourse is purely and simply what is under consideration, which as such is therefore always already there from the start, having the character of world or of in-being. This about-which of discourse becomes manifest insofar as something is said about something in every discourse. From the about-which of discourse we must distinguish a second structural moment, the *said* as such. When I talk about a thing, for example, a chair, this thing is in itself, as it is on hand in the world, the about-which. When I say, 'it is upholstered,' this being-upholstered of the chair is the said as such; it does not coincide with the chair. In what is thus said, the about-which is talked *over*; in talking anything over what is considered is talked over as well.

All discourse, in saying something about something, which it does first of all wholly in the course of concerned preoccupation and being with one another, is, as a mode of the being of Dasein, essentially being-with. In other words, the very sense of any discourse is *discourse to others and with others*. It therefore makes no difference for the essential structure of discourse whether a fixed address directed to a specific other is of current interest or not. Discourse as a mode of being of Dasein qua being-with is essentially *communication*, so that in every discourse that about which it is, is *shared with* the other through what is said, through the said as such. Communication accordingly means the enabling of the appropriation of that about which the discourse is, that is, making it possible to come into a relationship of preoccupation and being to that of which the discourse is. Discourse as communication brings about an appropriation of the world in which one always already is in being with one another. The understanding of communication is the *participation in what is manifest*. All subsequent understanding and co-understanding is as being-with a *taking part*. Communication must be understood in terms of the structure of Dasein as being with the other. It is not a matter of transporting information and experiences from the interior of one subject to the interior of the other one. It is rather a matter of being-with-one-another becoming manifest in the world, specifically by way of the discovered world, which itself becomes manifest in speaking with one another. Speaking with one another about something is not an exchange of experiences back and forth between subjects, but a situation where the being-with-one-another is intimately involved in the subject matter under discussion. And it is only by way of this subject matter, in the particular context of always already being-with in the world, that mutual understanding develops.

We already know that the manifest world is a mode of disclosedness and belongs to the discoveredness of Dasein. Discoveredness itself is defined essentially by disposition. This means that in any discourse, if it is indeed a possibility of Dasein, Dasein itself and its disposition are co-discovered. Discoursing with others about something as a speaking-about is always a *self-articulating*. One oneself and the being-in-the-world at the time likewise become manifest, even if only in having the disposition 'manifested' through intonation, modulation, or tempo of discourse. We have thus found four structural moments which belong essentially to language itself: 1) the *about-which talked over*, 2) the *discursive what* [the said as such], 3) the *communication*, and 4) the *manifestation*.

These four moments are not merely an accidental conglomerate of properties which can be discovered in language now and then and from various angles. They are structures which themselves are given because language itself is a possibility of the being of Dasein.

With *manifestation* it is to be noted that communication has the sense of discoursing with one another about something such that, in a genuinely understood sense, those discoursing with one another are first of all and primarily involved in the same subject matter; the one who is pointing out is so in a more original sense than the one who is listening. But discoursing with one another is not to be regarded as if it involved a reciprocal relation to one's own inner experiences, which somehow become observable through sounds.

The four structural moments belong together in the very essence of language, and every discourse is essentially determined by these moments. The individual moments in it can recede, but they are never absent.

The various definitions of the 'essence of language' which have hitherto been devised: as 'symbol,' as 'expression of knowledge,' as 'manifestation of lived experiences,' as 'communication,' or as a 'shaping' of one's own life, all of these definitions in each case always allude to only *one* phenomenal character in language itself and one-sidedly take it as a basis for an essential definition. Of course, little would be gained if the various and now familiar definitions of language were now collected and uniformly merged in some way, as long as we do not lay out in advance the structural totality in which language itself must be founded in its being, and which makes it understandable as a possibility of Dasein's being. The sense of a *scientific logic* is the elaboration of this apriori structure of discourse in Dasein, the elaboration of the possibilities and kinds of interpretation, of the stages and forms of conceptuality developed in it. Such a scientific logic is nothing but a *phenomenology of discourse*, of λόγος. What otherwise circulates under the name 'logic' is a confused mixture of the analysis of thinking and knowing, theory of meaning, psychology of concept formation, theory of science or even ontology. It is only from the horizon of this idea of 'logic' that its history and with it the course taken by philosophical research itself become understandable.

Rhetoric is a first part of logic rightly understood. The phenomenal orientation of language to the exhibited structure of Dasein can give us an understanding of the remarkable definition which the Greeks gave for man: ζῷον λόγον ἔχον, a living being capable of discourse. It is noteworthy that the Greeks had no word nor even a concept for language. From the start, they took language as discourse, and discourse is immediately linked with the ζῷον, with life, without a more precise insight into the structures themselves, but rather from a primary experience of discoursing as a specific mode of Dasein's being.

Discoursing now has an emphatic function in being-with-one-another as the possibility of talking something through. As such a possibility, it easily takes the form of a dispute, a theoretical disputation.

Discourse and λόγος for the Greeks thus assume the function of theoretical discussion. The λόγος accordingly gets the sense of exhibiting what is talked over in its whence and what about. The exhibition of the entity in its reasons, what is said, what is exhibited in discourse, the λεγόμενον as λόγος, is then the ground or reason, what is apprehended in understanding comprehension, the *rational*. Only in this derivative way does λόγος get the sense of *reason*, just as *ratio*— the medieval term for λόγος—has the sense of *discourse, reason*, and *ground. Discoursing about . . . is exhibiting reasons, founding, letting something be seen referentially in its whence and how.*

We now have discourse as the phenomenon which thus underlies language: *There is language only because there is discourse*, and not conversely. Our task will be to make this state of affairs still more evident phenomenally by considering the following four points: 1) Discoursing and hearing, 2) discoursing and silence, 3) discoursing and idle talk, 4) discourse and language.

α) Discoursing and hearing

The enactment of the being of discoveredness, in the two directions of disclosedness of the world and discoveredness of the Dasein involved with itself in its disposition, is understanding as the enactment of the being of discoveredness. The mode of enactment of understanding is interpreting, specifically as the cultivation, appropriation, and preservation of what is discovered in understanding. *The meaningful expressness of this interpretation is now discourse.* Expressness is taken here in the sense of the appresentation of meaningfulness and of in-being in correlations and contexts of meaning. Discourse is a mode of being of understanding and so a mode of being of being-in-the-world, since discourse is understood only on the basis of discoveredness.

We typically employ 'understanding' in a double meaning, first in the sense of the understanding access to something, in the emphatic meaning of ground-breaking disclosure, of discovering—understanding in this productive sense—in the superlative sense of men to whose lot the special function of discovering falls, who understand something for the first time. But then we also use 'understanding' in the sense of apprehending, specifically of *hearing* and *having heard*. When we have not rightly heard, we also say 'I have not rightly understood.' Understanding in the first sense of disclosing is communicated in interpretation, and the appropriation of interpretation is itself co-understanding in the sense of participation in what is uncovered. In this co-understanding, understanding at the same time is taken as a listening to, a heeding. This capacity to listen to the other with whom one is, or to oneself who one is in the mode of discoursing, where it is not at all a matter of utterance in the sense of external speaking, is grounded in the structure of being of the original being-with-one-another.

Here is something essential to keep in mind: Phonetic speaking and acoustical hearing are in their being founded in discoursing and hearing as modes of being of being-in-the-world and being-with. There is phonetic speaking only because there is the possibility of discourse, just as there is acoustical hearing only because being-with-one-another is characterized originally as being-with in the sense of listening-to-one-another. Being-with is not being on hand also among other humans; as being-in-the-world it means at the same time being 'in bondage' [hörig] to the others, that is, 'heeding' and 'obeying' them, listening [hören] or not listening to them. Being-with has the structure of belonging [Zu(ge)hörigkeit] to the other. It is only by virtue of this primary belonging that there is something like separation, group formation, development of society, and the like. This listening to one another, in which being-with cultivates itself, is more accurately a compliance in being-with-one-another, a co-enactment in concern. The negative forms of enactment, non-compliance, not listening, opposition, and the like are really only privative modes of belonging itself. It is on the basis of such a capacity to listen constitutive of in-being that there is something like *hearkening*.

Even hearkening is phenomenally more original than the mere sensing of tones and perceiving of sounds. Even hearkening is an understanding hearing. In other words, 'originally and to begin with,' one does not really hear noises and sonorous complexes but the creaking wagon, the 'electric' [streetcar], the motorcycle, the column on the march, the north wind. To 'hear' something like a 'pure noise' already requires a very artificial and complicated attitude. But the fact that we first directly hear things like motorcycles and wagons, which basically still sounds remarkable, is the phenomenological evidence for what has already been underscored, that in our very being in the world we are first always already involved with the world itself, and not with 'sensations' first and then, on the basis of a kind of theater, finally involved with the things. We do not first need to process and shape a tumult and medley of feelings; we are right from the start involved with what is understood itself. Sensations and sensed are first of all outside the scope of natural experience.

Even in hearing discourse we first in fact hear what is said. Even when we do not understand the discourse, when it is unclear or perhaps the language is foreign, even then we first hear *incomprehensible* words and not mere phonetic data. We first hear what is said and not its being said, not the process of discourse as such but the about-which of the discourse. We can of course at the same time listen to the way it is being said—the diction—but even this is heard only in the prior co-understanding of the about-which, for only then do I have the possibility of grasping how something is being said. The reply to a discourse likewise follows first from understanding the about-which of the said, from its sense at the time. Hearing belongs to discoursing as being-with belongs to being-in-the-world. Hearing and discoursing are both phenomenally given co-originally with understanding. Hearing is the basic mode of being-with-one-another which understands. Only he who can discourse and hear can speak. That something like ear lobes and eardrums are given for this hearing is purely accidental. The possibility of hearkening exists only where there is the possibility of being able to discourse and to hear. Someone who genuinely cannot hear, as when we say of a man, 'he cannot hear' (where we do not mean that he is deaf), is still quite capable of hearkening, and precisely for this reason, because "not hearing but only hearkening" is a particular privative modification of hearing and understanding.

β) Discoursing and silence

Just as hearing is constitutive of discourse, so also is silence. Only an entity whose being is defined by the ability to discourse can also be silent. But this carries the phenomenal implication that *silence as a mode of being of discourse is a particular way of articulating oneself about something to others*. He who is silent in being with one another can more authentically manifest and 'give to understand,' that is, discourse in the original sense of its being, than the man of many words. Talking a lot does not in the least guarantee that the about-which of discourse becomes manifest sooner and more fully. On the contrary, talking a lot not only can uncover nothing but can actually cover things up and reduce everything to incomprehensibility, to babble. But silence still does not merely mean being mute. For the mute person has the propensity for discourse and expression. He would speak if he could. A mute person still has not proven without further ado that he can be silent. But the silent person could speak if he wanted to. No more than the mute person does the one who tends to say little need to prove that he is and can be silent. Rather, one can be silent precisely in speaking, and only in speaking can one be silent in a genuine way. If one never says anything, he can never be silent. Because the possibility of manifesting lies in silence, but silence as a mode of enactment of discourse cultivates understanding, brings the discoveredness of Dasein to fruition [*zeitigt*] with understanding, silence in being with one another can *summon and call Dasein back to its ownmost being*. And it can do this just when Dasein in the everydayness of its being has allowed itself to be taken in by the world being talked over and by the discourse about it. Because discursive talk in the beginning is always manifest in talking to one another in public—in communication—, the summoning of Dasein to itself and to its original and genuine disposition must in the end have the mode of discourse and interpretation that is silence. To be able to be silent, one must at the same time have something to say. In other words, it is precisely when discoveredness is a genuine and rich disclosedness of the world that it can then evoke a response in a disposition of Dasein which has the mode of discoveredness of *reticence*. Reticence is a way of being disposed which does not so much conceal and only conceal. Rather it gives precedence to being, prior to all talk about it and counseling over it, and this precisely in concerned preoccupation and being with one another. Genuine ability to hear comes from such reticence, and genuine being-with-one-another constitutes itself in this ability. Thus, discourse becomes visible as a mode of being of Dasein in the two phenomena of hearing and silence.

γ) Discoursing and idle talk

We shall now consider the third phenomenon which is given with discourse: *idle talk*. In cultivating the discoveredness of Dasein, discourse has a distinctive function: it lays out or interprets, that is, it brings the referential relations of meaningfulness into relief in communication. In communicating in this way, discourse articulates the meanings and meaningful correlations thus brought out. In being articulated, in the articulated word, the meaning highlighted in interpretation becomes available for being-with-one-another. The word is articulated in public. This articulated discourse preserves interpretation within itself. This is the sense of what we mean when we say that words have their meaning. This verbal meaning and the verbal whole as language is the interpretation of world and Dasein (in-being) communicated in being with one another. *The utterance of interpretation is a secularization of discoveredness, making it worldly.*

Genuinely enacted and heard, communication brings an understanding being-with to fruition in what is talked over. Since the communication is being said in words, what is said is 'verbal' for the other, which means that it is available in a worldly way. The articulated is accompanied by an understanding in public, in which what is talked over does not necessarily have to be appresented as something on hand and handy. In other words, articulated discourse can be understood without an original being-with involved in what the discourse is about. This means that in hearing and subsequent understanding, the understanding relation-of-being to that about which the discourse is can be left undetermined, uninvolved, even emptied to the point of a merely formal belief in what the original understanding had intended. The matter being spoken of thus slips away with the absence of the understanding relation of being. But while the matter being talked about slips away, what is said as such—the word, the sentence, the dictum—continues to be available in a worldly way, along with a certain understanding and interpretation of the matter. The discourse is of course uprooted in the absence of right understanding, but it still retains an understandability. And since such a discourse, which has become groundless, always remains discourse, it can be repeated and passed along without proper understanding. The hearing of discourse is now no longer participation in the being of being-with-one-another involved in the matter being talked over, for the matter itself now is no longer uncovered in an original way. Instead, hearing is being-with involved in what is said in terms of its being said as such. Hearing is now hearing *mere talk as talk* and understanding is understanding based on mere *hearsay*. Things so heard and in a certain way understood can be passed along, and this process of passing along and repeating now produces a growing groundlessness of what was originally articulated. Discourse undergoes an increase in groundlessness in repetitive talk to the extent that a hardening of a specific opinion being expressed in discourse corresponds to such groundlessness. Such discourse, which is cultivated in the uprooting engendered by repetitive talk, is *idle talk*. I am referring to a well-defined phenomenon with this term, which as such carries no disparaging connotation whatsoever.

Idle talk is itself posited with Dasein and its being. Like hearing and silence, it is a constitutive phenomenon given with discourse as a mode of the being of Dasein. Idle talk is not restricted to oral communication in speaking; much more idle talk today comes from what is written. Repetitive talk here is not talking from hearsay but hearing and talking from what is picked up by reading. Such reading takes place characteristically without understanding the subject matter, but in such a way that the reader—there are purported to be such readers in the sciences as well—acquires the possibility of dealing with the matters with great skill without ever having seen them. Something being said here to some extent acquires an intrinsic authoritative character. That it is said at all and that something definite is said is sufficient to assume that what is said is true and to proceed to repeat it and pass it along on the strength of its being said. What is talked about in idle talk is meant only in an indeterminate emptiness, which is why discourse about it is disoriented. Accordingly, when men who have to deal with a matter do so solely on the basis of the idle talk about it, they bring the various opinions, views, and perceptions together on an equal basis. In other words, they do so on the basis of what they have picked up from reading and hearing. They pass along what they have read and heard about the matter without any sensitivity for the

distinction of whether or not that opinion or their own is actually relevant to the matter. Their care in discovering does not apply to the
matter but to the discourse. And idle talk, which rules precisely on the
basis of a lack of basis, provides such discovery with the consolidation of its rule as a way of being in the interpretation of Dasein. The
groundlessness of idle talk does not bar its entry into the public arena
but directly promotes it. For idle talk is just the possibility of interpreting something without first making the matter one's own. Idle talk,
which anyone can pick up, dispenses us from the task of genuine understanding. One can talk along and be taken seriously in idle talk.
This *free-floating interpretation, which belongs to everyone and no one*,
dominates everydayness, and Dasein grows up in such a temporally
particular interpretation, and more and more into it. This interpretation of the world and of Dasein, which is prevalent and consolidated
as idle talk, we shall call the *everyday way in which Dasein has already been
interpreted.*

Every Dasein moves in such an interpretation, which for the most
part coincides with the way the generation of a particular time has
been interpreted and which is modified with the time. This way of
being interpreted includes what one says about the world and Dasein
in public being-with-one-another. What *one* says has taken the lead in
all interpretation and thus taken over the temporalization of understanding. This means that what *one* says is really what controls the
various possibilities of the being of Dasein.

Interpreting means an uncovering which considers something as
something. The 'as-what' in which something is taken is the crucial
feature for interpretation. Its originality lies in how the 'as-what' is
drawn out and made one's own. For example, nowadays one says, and
everyone hears it and has heard it, that Rembrandt is esteemed. *One*
says that. The manner of preoccupation and seeing is thereby prescribed, so that for that very reason one is excited by a Rembrandt
without experiencing why, perhaps even against the insight that one
oneself finds nothing in it. But *one* says it, and therefore it is so for
one. The smooth talk of the public way of interpretation presses toward an indifferent understandability and accessibility for Everyman.
Idle talk thus becomes the ineradicable mode of being, because it becomes *the mode rooted in Dasein itself, the mode of being of the Anyone*,
where idle talk especially exercises its rule. The Anyone has in idle
talk its true form of being.

δ) Discourse and language

But this way of being interpreted undergoes a further hardening inasmuch as communicated discourse is always spoken, and the
spoken character of the interpretation (language is nothing else) has
its rise and its fall. Language itself has Dasein's kind of being. There is

no language in general, understood as some sort of free-floating essence in which the various "individual existences" would partake.
Every language, like Dasein itself, is *historical* in its very being. The
seemingly uniform and free-floating being of a language, the being in
which Dasein always first operates, is only its lack of pertinence to a
definite, temporally particular Dasein, which is language in its most
proximate mode of being in the Anyone. Out of this comes the enabling possibility of an original appropriation of language, or an original and proper being in it. This being in language can in a certain
sense arise from a mastery of the manifold of words, but it can also
come from an original understanding of the matter. It is because language as a mode of the being of Dasein also has the full structure of
this being that there can be anything like a 'dead' language. The language no longer grows in a spoken way but can still be alive as discourse and as a way in which things have been interpreted. The
'death' of a language does not exclude the 'life' of the discourse and
the discoveredness which belong to it, just as a deceased Dasein can
historically still be alive in an eminent sense, perhaps more authentically than in the time in which the Dasein itself properly was. The
discoveredness invested in a language can survive its 'extinction,' or
can be renewed. In a genuine historiological understanding of the
Dasein of the Romans, for example, the Latin language is alive, although it is 'dead.' Its utilization as an ecclesiastical language no
longer represents it as a 'living' language. It is not by chance that ecclesiastical language is a 'dead' language; it is 'dead' not because Latin
in this case fosters the international understanding of dogmas, propositions, definitions, and canons, but because as 'dead' this language is
no longer subject to changes in meaning, because it is the suitable
form of expression for a stabilization of definite propositions and be-
liefs, whereas in any 'living' language contexts of meaning change
with changes in the interpretation of historical Dasein at the time. If
such propositions were translated, they would be translated into the
historical intelligibility of the time, and the univocal leveling of the
propositions would immediately disappear.

A language has its genuine being only as long as new correlations of
meaning and so—although not necessarily—new words and phrases
accrue to it from understanding, that is, from care for the discoveredness of Dasein. As a spoken language, it varies according to the level
of interpretation of the Dasein at the time, in changes which do not
always necessarily become evident in the coining of words. Within any
prevailing language in which Dasein itself is with its history, every age
and generation also has its own language and its specific possibility of
understanding. This appears clearly in the prevalence of certain words
and formulas. Before the war, for example, we had a tendency to interpret Dasein in terms of 'experiencing' and 'lived experience.' Every-

one, philosophers included, talked about 'experiencing' and 'lived experience.' The word has nowadays lost its pre-eminence; there is even a reluctance to use it at all. Nowadays we talk in its stead of the 'questionability of existence' and 'decision.' It is already the fashion for existence to become 'questionable.' Everything is 'decision' nowadays, but it remains open whether those who talk in this way have ever 'resolved' themselves or will ever 'decide,' just as it was an open question whether those who talked of 'lived experience' still in fact had the possibility to 'experience' anything, or whether this possibility was rather not exhausted precisely because idle talk about it had begun. Catchwords and catchphrases are indices of idle talk, which is a mode of being of Dasein in the Anyone.

But even relatively original and creative meanings and the words coined from them are, when articulated, relegated to idle talk. Once articulated, the word belongs to everyone, without a guarantee that its repetition will include original understanding. This possibility of genuinely entering into the discourse nevertheless exists and is documented especially in this, that the discoveredness which is given with a word can be rectified with certain sentences and developed further. Indeed, articulated discourse can help first by grasping possibilities of being for the first time which before were already always experienced implicitly. The discoveredness of Dasein, in particular the disposition of Dasein, can be made manifest by means of words in such a way that certain new possibilities of Dasein's being are set free. Thus discourse, especially *poetry*, can even bring about the release of new possibilities of the being of Dasein. In this way, discourse proves itself positively as a *mode of maturation*, a *mode of temporalization* of Dasein itself.

§29. *Falling as a basic movement of Dasein*

a) Idle Talk

As discourse, idle talk in its being tends to discover. It is in this sense that the everyday way in which things have been interpreted lives in idle talk. Now the forms of this idle talk are quite varied, but they are always forms of a specific being-in-the-world. Dasein conforms to the Anyone and the Anyone assumes command of what one regards as the real events in which Dasein makes its decisions. Nowadays it is especially easy to demonstrate this being in the Anyone.[1]

Nowadays, one decides about metaphysics or even higher matters at congresses. For everything which must be done nowadays, there is

---

1. Cf. §26b) above.

first a conference. One meets and meets, and everyone waits for some-one else to tell him, and it doesn't really matter if it isn't said, for one has now indeed spoken one's mind. Even if all the speakers who thus speak their minds have understood little of the matter, one is of the opinion that the cumulation of this lack of understanding will never-theless eventually generate an understanding. There are people now-adays who travel from one conference to another and are convinced in doing so that something is really happening and that they have ac-complished something; whereas in reality they have shirked the labor and now seek refuge in idle talk for their helplessness, which they of course do not understand. The characterization of these phenomena should not be interpreted as a moral sermon or the like, which has no place here. Our sole concern here is to draw attention to a phenome-non, to a possibility which is constitutive of the structure of Dasein. It is not as if we today have the prerogative of this phenomenon. An-cient sophistry was nothing but this in its essential structure, although it was perhaps shrewder in certain ways. This would-be attendance is particularly dangerous because one is in good faith, since one believes that it is all to the good and that one is obliged to attend the con-gresses. This peculiar kind of idle talk, which governs Dasein in being-with-one-another, is a function of uncovering, but now in the remarkable mode of *covering up*.

For discourse to cover up, to interpret in a deficient way, one does not need an explicit intention of deception, say, of a discourse which consciously passes something off as something. It is enough for some-thing to be said with groundless excess and repetition in order to transform the essential sense of the discourse, which is interpretation as the cultivation of discoveredness, into a covering up. Because of its inherent neglect to consider matters in an original understanding, idle talk is from the very beginning *in itself a covering up*. In commu-nicating, idle talk puts a view, an opinion, in front of the matter which is disclosed or to be disclosed. The deficient mode of disclosing the world is the *disguising* of it, and the corresponding mode of covering up disposition is *inversion*. With the emergence of certain ways of being attuned, of feeling, a disposition can develop which inverts a Dasein into an alien one. The state of being familiar with oneself is turned upside down, so that one is no longer who he actually is. *Dis-guise and inversion are the modes of falling, of the lapse* of interpretation and so of the discoveredness of Dasein.

Idle talk covers up more than it uncovers. It covers up especially by retarding uncovering, by way of its inherent presumption of already having uncovered. Because Dasein first dwells in the Anyone, which in turn is interpreted in idle talk, the tendency to cover up appears right in the tendency of Dasein's being toward the Anyone. Since this covering up installs itself in opposition to every express intention, manifest in it and in the tendency toward it is a structure of Dasein's being which is given with Dasein itself. The covering up which Dasein temporalizes from itself manifests the peculiar kind of being which we call the *deviation of Dasein from itself*—deviation from its authentic original disposition and disclosedness. Insofar as Dasein in its being as everydayness deviates from itself, this kind of being may be called *falling*.

The term 'falling' designates a *movement of the being of the happening of Dasein* and once again should not be taken as a value judgment, as if it indicated a base property of Dasein which crops up from time to time, which is to be deplored and perhaps eliminated in advanced stages of human culture. Like discoveredness, being-with and in-being, falling refers to a constitutive structure of the being of Dasein, in particular a specific phenomenon of in-being, in which Dasein first constantly has its being. If we orient ourselves once again in the 'between' of world and Dasein, then the dwelling in the Anyone and in the idle talk of this being is in an uprooted state of suspension. But this uprooting is just what constitutes the solid everydayness of Dasein, [and idle talk is] one way of falling in which Dasein loses itself.

b) Curiosity

A second way of uprooting and falling manifests itself in another mode of Dasein's being, which we call *curiosity*.

It was said that interpretation, as a cultivation of discoveredness, is the primary knowing. Discoveredness is constitutive of in-being. All concern is as such discovery and interpretation, inasmuch as it appresents its disclosed environing world, the work-world, in its references. Concern has its orientation and guidance. Concern, whose care has been fixed in a for-the-sake-of-which, and which as concern moves in an around-which and for-which, is guided by a *looking around*, by *circumspection*. Circumspection oriented to the presence of what is of concern provides each setting-to-work, procuring, and performing with the way to work it out, the means to carry it out, the right occasion, and the appropriate time. This sight of circumspection is the skilled possibility of concerned discovering, of concerned seeing. Seeing is here neither restricted to seeing with the eyes nor is the term in this usage related primarily to sense perception. Rather, seeing is here used in the wider sense of concerned and caring appresentation.

This remarkable priority of seeing over other ways of perceiving was already noticed by Augustine, but in the last analysis he was unable to illuminate this phenomenon. Thus, when he speaks in the *Con-*

fessions[2] of the *concupiscentia oculorum*, of the "lust of the eyes," he says: *Ad oculos enim videre proprie pertinet.* "Seeing belongs properly to the eyes." *Utimur autem hoc verbo etiam in ceteris sensibus cum eos ad cognoscendum intendimus.* "But we use this word 'seeing' also for the other senses when we take them in their cognitive performance." *Neque enim dicimus: audi quid rutilet; aut, olfac quam niteat; aut, gusta quam splendeat; aut, palpa quam fulgeat: videri enim dicuntur haec omnia.* "For we do not say 'Hear how it glimmers' or 'Smell how it sparkles' or 'Taste how it shines,' or 'Feel how it flashes'; but in all of these cases, 'See,' we say that all this is seen." *Dicimus autem non solum, vide quid luceat, quod soli oculi sentire possunt.* "But we not only say 'See how it shines,' when the eyes alone can perceive it;" *sed etiam, vide quid sonet; vide quid oleat; vide quid sapiat; vide quam durum sit.* "We also say, 'See how it sounds,' 'See how it is scented,' 'See how it tastes,' 'See how hard it is.'" *Ideoque generalis experientia sensuum concupiscentia sicut dictum est oculorum vocatur, quia videndi officium in quo primatum oculi tenent, etiam ceteri sensus sibi de similitudine usurpant, cum aliquid cognitionis explorant.* "Thus the experience of the senses in general is designated as a 'lust of the eyes,' for when it comes to knowing, the other senses by way of a similitude take over the work of seeing, which first belongs to the eyes." The other senses in a way take on this sort of perceptual performance insofar as it is a matter of a *cognitio*, an apprehension of something. It becomes clear here that seeing has a pre-eminence in apprehending and that the sense of seeing is therefore not restricted alone to perceiving with the eyes. Seeing rather, as was continually the case also already with the Greeks, is identified with apprehending something. Augustine did not address himself to the task of actually elucidating this pre-eminence of seeing and the meaning of its being in Dasein, although this text does furnish essential insights on the *concupiscentia oculorum*.

We find something similar already in ancient philosophy. The treatise which stands first in the collection of Aristotle's writings on ontology begins with the sentence: πάντες ἄνθρωποι τοῦ εἰδέναι ὀρέγονται φύσει.[3] "The care for seeing is essentially inherent in man's being." Aristotle puts this sentence at the beginning of his metaphysics, where this discourse is actually reversed. At any rate, this sentence stands at the beginning of an introductory consideration which has the function of explaining the origin of theoretical comportment as the Greeks then regarded this origin. For Aristotle, curiosity leads di-

---

2. Augustine, *Confessions*, Book X, Ch. 35.
3. Aristotle, *Metaphysics*, Book Alpha (I), Ch. 1, 980a21. ["All men by nature desire to know." English translation by W. D. Ross in McKeon, *The Basic Works of Aristotle*, p. 689.]

rectly to an original comportment, from which theoretical comportment, θεωρεῖν, but regarded in the Greek sense, receives its motivation. This is no doubt a one-sided interpretation, but one motivated
by the Greek way of considering such matters. The only point of
importance for us is that εἰδέναι (which should not be translated as
knowing) is in fact constitutive for the φύσις of man.

Concerned preoccupation in everydayness can take a rest, whether
it be relaxing in the form of a break or finishing up with what needs to
be taken care of. Taking a rest and relaxing is a mode of concern. For
care does not vanish in rest, only now in relaxing, the world is no
longer appresented for the achievement of concern. The world is
no longer encountered in circumspection but rather in the relaxed
tarrying-in. In such a tarrying, the seeing of circumspection becomes
free, no longer bound by specific relations of reference as these determine our encounter of the world of work. This liberated seeing,
which becomes free from circumspection, as a modification of concern is still care, where care now slackens to a liberated condition of
merely seeing and perceiving the world.

But seeing is a perceiving of distance. The care in such a liberated
seeing is a concern for distance. It involves a leaping over and a leaping away from the nearest world of our concern, the everyday world
of work. As a free-floating seeing, a perceiving of distance, relaxed
tarrying *eo ipso* tends not to tarry in what is nearest. This tendency is
the care for the discovery and the bringing-near of what is not yet experienced or of what is not an everyday experience, the care of being
'away from' the constantly and immediately handy things.

In relaxing, the care of *curiosity* becomes free, which means that it is
always already there, only it is bound, so to speak; and it only attends
to the encountered world in seeing and perceiving. The first characteristic structure of this freed seeing, which only attends to the
outward appearance, the "looks" of the world, is its *not tarrying*. This
means that it does not dwell on something definitely and thematically
grasped, but prefers characteristically to jump from one thing to another, a feature which is constitutive of curiosity.

Relaxed tarrying is not a staring at what is on hand. The cessation
of a particular form of work does not put a stop to handling, so that I
now remain as it were fixated on what it provides. Relaxing is *eo ipso* a
movement away from the immediate and familiar. But also the new
element which this perceiving of curiosity appresents does not become thematic. This can be made clear in the structure of appresentation in concern. This appresentation of the environing world comes
about from that upon which care primarily dwells, from that for the
sake of which something is undertaken. But how does bringing the
world near come about in the non-tarrying perception of curiosity?

As the care of merely perceiving which has been taken in by the en-countered world, the concern of curiosity does not pass over to a binding and thematic presence, to a definite worldly for-the-sake-of-which which is now to be seen purely and simply, or to definite events and things of the world. Rather, curiosity appresents something solely *in order to have seen it*, that is, in order to be able to proceed again and again from what is thus seen to the next. The for-the-sake-of-which of curiosity is not a definite presence but the possibility of a constant change of presence. In other words, the non-tarrying of curiosity is basically concerned with not having to get involved and with merely being entertained by the world. What comes into play here is a being-in-the-world to which a characteristic disposition corresponds, a par-ticular restlessness and excitement which in its sense is unharried by the urgency and the need of everyday Dasein, which is not dangerous and in its sense not binding and obligatory. This kind of disposition is appresented along with the temporally particular presence provided by curiosity. In short, the non-tarrying concern for seeing only in or-der to see provides *distraction*. *Not tarrying* and *distraction* belong to the structure of the being of curiosity thus characterized. Distraction dis-solves the uniqueness and the uniformity of an actively concerned preoccupation and its relation to the world, because the presence of that with which curosity is concerned, as something to be seen, in its essence constantly changes, because what curiosity is concerned with is just this change.

These two characters, not tarrying and distraction, now bring out in Dasein a peculiar *state of being unsettled*. The care over approaching ever new worlds and alien Daseins (someone constantly seeks, for ex-ample, to make new acquaintances), but only for the sake of con-stantly having something new present, now manifests itself as a possi-bility in which Dasein loses sight of familiar everyday things and gets lost in the unfamiliar. This distractive non-tarrying constitutive of Da-sein includes a mode of the uprooting of Dasein, a kind of being in which it is everywhere and nowhere and where it tends to be loosed from itself. In such a curiosity, Dasein organizes a *flight from itself*.

The mode of being of falling becomes apparent in the phenome-non of curiosity, just as it did in idle talk. Curiosity and idle talk are constitutive ways of the being of being-in-the-world. The Anyone, which in idle talk defines the public way of having been interpreted, at the same time controls and prescribes the ways of curiosity. It says what one must have seen and read. Conversely, what curiosity dis-covers enters into idle talk. Not that these two phenomena exist side by side; rather, one tendency to uproot drags the other along with it. Curiosity's way of being everywhere and nowhere is relegated to idle talk, which is for no one and everyone.

c) Ambiguity

As everyday being-with-one-another in the world, Dasein is of itself subject to idle talk and curiosity. As concern it is concerned also with covering up its discoveredness. In interpreting, for example, it sees itself in the way it has been interpreted by the Anyone and so is always concerned also with a flight from itself. When we say here that Dasein is simultaneously concerned with its own falling, it should be noted that in such a related concern falling does not become manifest directly and from the outset, as though there were in Dasein an explicit intention in this direction. On the contrary, since Dasein in curiosity knows everything within a certain sphere and talks over everything in idle talk, it arrives rather at the opinion that such a being in the Anyone is true and genuine being. The universal validity inherent in what one says and how one sees is for the public and the Anyone the greatest guarantee that it has for the infallibility of its being. This means that the self-interpretation of everyday being-with-one-another also adopts this presumption. But with this presumption an *ambiguity* enters into Dasein. This is the third phenomenon of falling. It has the function of aggravating in a special way the falling given in idle talk and curiosity.

There is a double ambiguity involved in this phenomenon. The first affects the world, which is what is encountered and what happens in being-with-one-another. In this regard, the aggravation of falling stemming from ambiguity has the functional sense of suppressing the Dasein in the Anyone. The second ambiguity affects not only the world but being-with itself, my own being and that of others. With regard to this being-toward-one-another, the aggravation of falling at the time is a prior neutralization cutting off the genuine rootedness of Dasein in itself, which means that the ambiguity does not let Dasein come to an original relationship of being in being with one another.

Insofar as what is encountered in everyday being-with-one-another by way of the world is such that everything is accessible to everyone and everyone can discourse about everything, to that extent it no longer can be decided who does and who does not actually live by a genuine understanding. The linguistic capacity for expression and the routine of a certain average understanding of all that there is can publicly be so extended that the way of interpretation in which the Anyone operates easily plays everything into everyone's hand. What thus plays itself out in the atmosphere of public interpretation becomes ambiguous. It looks as if the matter is genuinely seen and discussed, and yet basically it is not; it does not look that way, and yet perhaps it is.

But ambiguity not only affects the way we dispose of and deal with what is accessible for use and enjoyment, but extends much further. Not only does everyone know and discuss the current topics and events, what we call the "passing scene," but everyone also already knows how to talk about what must first happen, what is not yet current but must be made actual. Everyone has already guessed in advance what others also guess and sense. This being-on-the-scent, naturally on the basis of hearsay, is the most insidious way in which ambiguity holds Dasein down. Supposing that what is guessed and sensed in advance would one day in fact be realized, ambiguity has already taken care that interest in the matter realized would then die away. For this interest exists for curiosity and idle talk only as long as there is the possibility of a non-committal only-guessing-with. Idle talk is concerned only with being able to guess with someone, without having to follow through. In other words, being "in on it" with someone when one is on the scent forgoes followers once the guess gets carried out. Carrying it out in fact demands that Dasein be forced back on itself. Publicly regarded, such a being is boring; and besides, when confronted with the realization of what was once guessed, idle talk is always ready with a pat answer: "we could have done it too—for we had already guessed as much." In fact, in the end idle talk is even indignant that what it guessed and constantly demanded in idle talk now *actually* takes place. For with that, it has lost the opportunity to guess some more on this score.

The ambiguity of the public way of being interpreted, which is defined by curiosity and idle talk, holds being-in-the-world down by passing off its inquisitive sensing and its talking of things ahead of the game as what is really happening, while carrying out the matter and understanding it are labelled as unimportant. With this ambiguity, the public way of having things interpreted insures its constant pre-eminence, and this all the more, the more it lets curiosity have what it seeks, namely, what today is not yet on hand but tomorrow may come to pass.

But when Dasein places itself in the reticence of carrying things through, its time is different. Publicly regarded, its time is essentially slower than the time of idle talk, which "lives faster." This idle talk has long since gone on to something else, whatever happens to be "brand new" at the time, the "latest thing." In view of this "very newest thing," what was once the hunch is now "passé," "behind the times," "out of date." Idle talk and curiosity thus take care that the genuine and authentic new creation is *eo ipso* out of date for publicity. For the most part then, the new creation becomes free in its positive possibilities, prevails, when idle talk in its function of covering up and holding down has become ineffective, or when the concealment has been expressly cleared away. This happens in the process of genuinely free-

ing the past, that is, it happens as *history*. Genuine historiology is
nothing but the struggle against this movement of the being of Dasein
in the direction of covering up by way of its own public way of having
things interpreted.

Second, however, curiosity and idle talk in their ambiguity even
dominate being-with-one-another as such. If we first speak from the
nearest environment and what can be there with us in this initially
daily world, this says that the other is there with us from what one has
heard of him, from the talk about him, from where he comes from.
Idle talk first of all insinuates itself into the interstices of original
being-with-one-another from the matters of common concern and its
world. At first and above all, everyone keeps an eye on the other to see
how he will act and what he will say in reply. Being-with-one-another
in the Anyone is in no way a leveled and indifferent side-by-side state,
but far more one in which we intensely watch and furtively listen in on
one another. This kind of being-with-one-another can work its way
into the most intimate relations. Thus, for example, a friendship may
no longer and not primarily consist in a resolute and thus mutually
generous way of siding with one another in the world, but in a constant and prior watching out for how the other sets out to deal with
what is meant by friendship, in a constant check on whether he turns
out to be one or not. Inasmuch as such a being-with-one-another can
now come into play from both sides, it can lead to the most profound
conversations and discussions, and one thinks one has a friend. From
the very beginning, idle talk and curiosity thus deprive the superlative
possibilities of being-with-one-another of the ground from which they
could take root and grow. With-one-another is a secret against-one-
another under the mask of for-one-another, which gets its richness
and presumed genuineness only from the intensity of talking.

Ambiguity has been exhibited in idle talk and curiosity as the way of
being of the everyday discoveredness of Dasein. As such, ambiguity
can make manifest how Dasein slips away from itself in its tendency of
being toward the Anyone, and moreover, that it of itself foments and
aggravates this tendency in everyday concern. Being toward the world
as well as toward others and itself is disguised by the Anyone which
constantly insinuates itself into these structures.

Dasein in the Anyone moves as it were in a *whirlwind*, which whirls it
into the Anyone, and thus tears it away from what matters and from
itself and, as a whirlwind, draws it into the constancy of being de-
flected from its course. Thus, an enduring flight of Dasein from a
possible and original being-in-and-with is revealed in the absorption
in the Anyone.

d) The characters of the inherent movement
of falling

The phenomenon of falling exhibited as a way of being of Dasein now at the same time shows an *inherent movement* in its structure, whose characters can now be easily highlighted.

Concern is never present as an indifferent being-in-the-world, possibly in analogy with the pure occurrence of a thing. Rather, in-being as being-with-one-another is absorption in the world under concern. Since the Anyone is a way of being which temporalizes Dasein itself, idle talk, that is, the public way of interpreting things in ambiguity, brings with it the cultivation of a possibility of missing itself, of seeking itself only in the Anyone. Dasein itself cultivates this possibility of being, advancing it as its possibility of missing itself. It should be noted that this way of being peculiar to falling is not the result of any sort of circumstances and contingencies of the world. Dasein as falling is in its being itself *tempting*, inasmuch as it lays the possibility of falling before itself. Tempting itself in this way, it maintains itself in its fallenness by cultivating the supposition that the full realm of its own possibilities is guaranteed to it with its absorption in the Anyone and in idle talk. This means that *the falling that tempts is tranquilizing*. It thus increasingly sees no need ever to force this being in the Anyone before a question or even to modify it. This tranquilizing of fallenness is however not a matter of its standing still in its movement but rather involves a creeping intensification. In the tranquilized obviousness of such a being, Dasein drifts toward *alienation* from itself. In other words, seductive tranquilization in its very sense is alienating, so much so that Dasein leaves no possibility of being open for itself other than that of being in the Anyone.

The phenomenal characters of the movement of falling, the *tempting*, the *tranquilization*, the *alienation*, make it clear that the Dasein which is in its essence delivered to the world gets *entangled* in its own concern. It can yield to this tendency of falling to such a degree that it thereby cuts itself off from the possibility of returning to itself, where it no longer even understands such a possibility.

The important thing is to regard all of these phenomena always as characteristic and primary modes of the being of everyday Dasein. It is not my intention to use what I have just said for moral applications or anything of that sort. My intention is only and can only be to display these phenomena as structures of Dasein, in order then, by starting from them—this is in fact the drift of all of my considerations—to see Dasein not in terms of any sort of theory of man, but to see the basic determination of its being directly in terms of the everydayness

closest to it, and to proceed from there back to the fundamental structures themselves. Now none of these phenomena—this is characteristic precisely of the Anyone—is in any way conscious or intentional.
The obviousness, the matter-of-course way in which this movement of
Dasein comes to pass also belongs to the manner of being of the Anyone. Because the movements of being which Dasein so to speak makes
in the Anyone are a matter of course and are not conscious and intentional, this means simply that the Anyone does not discover them,
since the discoveredness which the Anyone cultivates is in fact a covering up.

e) The fundamental structures of Dasein
from the horizon of fallenness

The structure of falling can now be phenomenologically elucidated
in such a way that the fundamental structures of Dasein itself are seen
from it. We want to make a brief attempt at least to arrive at the horizon of these fundamental structures as they are prefigured in the phenomenon of falling.

Concern includes both circumspective performance in the broadest
sense, which does its work by looking around, and the tarrying which
only looks, and in turn includes both of these in the calm of careless-
ness as well as in the restlessness of anxious concern. The leveling and
the disappearance of Dasein in the Anyone is a *falling apart* of Dasein
which is covered up by the public and everyday character of the Anyone. This falling apart temporalizes itself as a *falling away of Dasein
from its authenticity* into the falling which we have already described.
Authenticity here must be understood in the literal sense of "having itself for its own in intimacy with itself." Falling away is a kind of falling
constitutive of Dasein itself insofar as it is an entity of the character of
being-in-the-world and Dasein is in each instance mine. This sort of
falling as a tendency of being is a priori possible only on the basis of a
propensity for it. This propensity [*Hang*], to which our analysis of falling keeps referring in a phenomenal way, constitutes a basic structure
of Dasein which we call *destiny* [*Verhängnis*]. We use the term 'destiny'
here not as a fact but as a meaning, like our usage of 'encounter'
[*Begegnis*] and 'knowledge' [*Erkenntnis*], so that 'destiny' here does not
refer to a particular state but to a structure, an *existential* structure.
This destiny is nothing but the *flight of Dasein from itself*, a flight from
itself into the world discovered by it. A propensity in its being is not
something original, but in itself refers back to a possible *urge*. There is
a propensity only where there is an entity which is determined by an
urge. Propensity and urge in their turn are to be defined more fundamentally in the phenomenon which we call *care*.

It should be noted here that the explication of these structures of Dasein has nothing to do with any doctrine of the corruption of human nature or any theory of original sin. What is involved here is a pure consideration of structures, which *precedes* all such considerations. Our consideration must be differentiated quite sharply from any theological consideration. It is possible, perhaps necessary, that all of these structures will recur in a theological anthropology. I am in no position to judge how, since I understand nothing of such things. I am of course familiar with theology, but it is still quite a way from that to an understanding. Since this analysis time and again incurs this misunderstanding, let me emphasize that it proposes no covert theology and in principle has nothing to do with theology. These structures can just as well determine the mode of being of a man or the idea of a humanity in the Kantian sense, whether one assumes with Luther that man is "sodden with sin," or that he is already in the *status gloriae*. Falling, falling apart and all of these structures first of all have nothing to do with morality and ethics or the like.

§30. The structure of uncanniness

a) The phenomenon of flight and fear

But before we analyze these primary structures of Dasein, it is necessary to bring into sharper focus the phenomenon which we have just now arrived at, namely, *the flight of Dasein from itself*. We shall therefore start with the exposition of that *from which* Dasein flees in its flight, in order to exhibit in this fleeing a basic disposition of Dasein which is constitutive of the being of Dasein *qua* care, and for this very reason is the most radically concealed.

We therefore ask: What is this fleeing of Dasein from itself? What is the *from which* of the flight of Dasein? It can be stated formally that it flees from a being-threatened. Now how is this being-threatened and this threatening thing experienced? Something threatening is not given primarily in a fleeing from it but in that in which the flight itself is founded, namely, in *fear*. All fleeing is grounded in fearing. But not every falling back before something is necessarily also already a fleeing and so a being afraid.

These two meanings are generally intermingled in the ancient concept of φυγή and in the medieval concept of *fuga*, both of which we simply translate as "flight." *Flight* is sometimes equated with falling back before something, which does not have to mean fleeing in the strict sense at all. But the term can also mean flight directly. Fleeing from something is grounded in being afraid of something. Accordingly, that from which flight flees must be made manifest in that of which fear is afraid. The mode of being of fleeing must be explicated by way of the mode of being of fear, or the structures of being which themselves lie in fear. So in order to phenomenologically grasp this phenomenon of the flight of Dasein from itself, it is first necessary to explicate the phenomenon of fear.

In doing so, we must bear in mind that the phenomenon of fear is a way of being toward the world, and that fearing is always a fearing related to world or to co-Dasein. To the extent that the phenomenon of fear has been investigated, it is in fact always taken in this way, and all the different modifications of fear are defined on the basis of this being afraid of something within the world. But we have already stated that the flight of Dasein in falling is a flight of Dasein from itself, and so not a flight from the world and from a particular thing of the world. If it is true that Dasein flees from itself, then the fear which founds this flight cannot, strictly speaking, actually be fear, inasmuch as fear is always a mode of being which is essentially related to something worldly. In other words, it will become apparent that the traditional analysis of the phenomenon of fear is in principle insufficient, that *fear is a derivative phenomenon* and is itself grounded in the phenomenon which we call *dread*.

Dread is not a mode of fear. Rather, it is the other way around: *All fear finds its ground in dread.* To facilitate our phenomenological apprehension, our consideration will start with fear and then go back to the phenomenon of dread. We shall consider five points: 1) fear as being afraid of something, 2) the modification of the being of fear, 3) fear in the sense of fearing about and fearing for another, 4) dread, and 5) uncanniness.

α) Fear as being afraid of something considered in its four essential moments

This phenomenon was first investigated by Aristotle in the context of an analysis of the passions, the πάθη, in his *Rhetoric*.[1] The analysis of fear which Aristotle presents here as well as his analysis of the emotions generally serve to define the interpretation of the Stoics and so that of Augustine and the middle ages. Then, in the revival of the Stoic doctrine of the emotions in the Renaissance, this entire complex of analyses of the emotional was introduced into modern philosophy, which is where things have remained. Kant, for example, operates almost without exception within these ancient definitions. Of course, we cannot go into these historical connections here, especially since they offer nothing essentially new when compared to Aristotle, except that

---

1. Aristotle, *Rhetoric* B5, 1382a20-1383b11.

the Stoics, to note at least this much, classified various modifications of fear.

Theologically, the problem of fear is of special significance in connection with the theory of repentance, penance, love toward God, love of God, which itself substantiates fear. For an orientation, I refer to the investigation by Hunzinger.[2] There is here a brief survey of the development of the concept, though in fact the interpretation of Augustine there is in need of essential revisions. Thomas Aquinas[3] has dealt with fear in a comprehensive way in the context of a general theory of the emotions.

Also, I cannot embark here on a more detailed interpretation of Aristotle's analysis in his *Rhetoric*. That would be possible only on the basis of an actual understanding of the main structures of Dasein itself. We only begin to see what Aristotle saw when we first bring the phenomena home to ourselves. Characteristic of the basic conception of fear in Aristotle is its consideration in connection with the task of rhetoric. Among other things, the orator, in order to put across his plan and his proposals or to get someone to consider them, can appeal to the instincts and passions of the crowd (public meeting). In order to make the assembly more tractable, he can, for example, work for the passage of war credits by instilling fear in his listeners. He strikes fear in them by theatening them with the destruction of the state. The fear thus aroused makes them ready to take counsel, and brings them to support and to accept his proposals much more readily. This being afraid of something as a constitutive moment of oratory is analyzed by Aristotle.

The following analysis is oriented toward the previously elaborated structure of the being of Dasein, but it also makes regular reference to the Aristotelian definition. In the phenomenon of being afraid we shall distinguish 1) the *of which* of being afraid, and 2) the way of being toward that of which one is afraid. (We have no proper term for the first, one would actually have to say the 'frightful,' 'frightening,' or 'fearful,' if one takes these terms in a purely formal structural sense without any sort of devaluation.) Then we have 3) the *about which* of fearing. Being afraid is not only being afraid of, but at the same time always afraid about. Finally, we must investigate 4) the ways of being toward that about which fear is in fear.

In regard to the first structural moment, the *of which* of fearing, we can say that the of-which of fear has the character of something we encounter and confront in a worldly way, and so has the character of

2. A. W. Hunzinger, "Das Furchtproblem in der katholischen Lehre von Augustin bis Luther," 1906, First Section of no. 2 of the Luther Studies.

3. Thomas Aquinas, *Summa theologiae* II[1], questions 41-44.

286 More Original Explication of Dasein [395–396]

meaningfulness. What confronts fear in the character of meaningfulness is something *detrimental*, as Aristotle says, a κακόν, *malum*, an evil.
In particular, this detrimental thing is always something definite. If
we already had the concept here, we would say something historical,
something definite breaking into the familiar world of concerned preoccupation. It is now crucial to see how this detrimental thing is encountered, namely, as something not yet on hand, but just coming.
What is not yet present but coming—a peculiar presence—is in this
way moreover essentially in the *neighborhood*. More accurately, it is not
yet on hand precisely as something which approaches and draws
nearer. What is still in the remote distance is, as Aristotle rightly says,
not really feared. Or else fearing it can be eliminated by making it
clear to oneself that there is in fact still time before it comes and, since
it is still so remote, it probably will not come at all. The peculiar nearness of something coming but not yet on hand constitutes the structure of the encounter and confrontation of this detrimental thing. As
the definite but not yet present detrimentality, it presses of itself toward becoming on hand. Anything which has such a structure of con-
fronting us is what we call *threatening*. Inherent in the threatening
character are the structural moments of not yet present but coming,
something detrimental, not yet on hand but drawing near. The of-
which of fear thus has a threatening character, it is a *malum futurum* or
a κακὸν μέλλον, not in the sense of an objectively established event
which is sure to come, but a *futurum* which in its imminent approach
can also fail to appear.

With that, the second moment of being afraid, the way of being toward the threatening, already becomes evident. This being toward
the threatening is a way of being approached by the encountered
world. It is not at first an awareness of an impending evil to which a
dose of dread would then be added. Rather, fearing is precisely the
mode of being in which something threatening is uniquely disclosed
and can be encountered in concern in being approached by the world.
As Aristotle rightly says (not literally but *de facto*), fear is not a φαντασία in the sense of letting something threatening be seen, but is ἐκ
φαντασίας, *from* letting the imminently detrimental (κακὸν μέλλον)
be seen. To be sure, the proper founding connection between this
φαντασία and actually being afraid is left undefined by him and later
by Scholasticism, and so at bottom it is still incomprehensible.

But from what was said earlier, we know that representing something that will come is always founded primarily in a prior concern
and care, where we are already approached by something and allow it
to encounter us. In a certain sense, at first I am not aware of what is
threatening in its full and proper being, but rather the reverse: I see
and can only see the threat in its genuine character and can only have

the threatening thing as such from the primary access to it in fearing. It is from this source that I first receive the possibility of now apprehending this threatening thing itself in a thematic consideration. If I view and consider something threatening solely in terms of its becoming an objective being for me, I never come to the fearing itself.

Now inasmuch as what is threatening in fear is in each case a specific worldly thing, it always meets with a specific concern, a specific being-involved-in and a specific being-in-the-world. The threatening thing comes upon a concern which, along with what it has at its direct disposal, is insufficient to cope with the threatening thing. This means that, in order to come to the third moment, that about which we are afraid in fear is being-in-the-world itself.

The threatening thing always endangers the concern at the time, or the project of that concern. This also determines the last moment, the way of being toward that about which fear fears. With concern endangered by the threatening thing (a situation which is appresented in being afraid), self-finding is thrown into confusion. In short, oriented concern is disturbed. This embattled sense of not being up to the situation is typified by the tumult of running around in panic, in which the stable relations of orientation within the referential contexts of the familiar environment are disturbed. This is the sense of the confusion which more or less accompanies fear, naturally in varying degrees according to the situation.

β) The modifications of fear

Proceeding from these moments of being afraid, we can now clarify 2) the modifications of the being of fear. Distinct modifications of the being of fear emerge in accord with variations in these constitutive moments of being afraid of something. It was already made plain that the threatening thing includes the element of impending onslaught. Nearness, which belongs to the structure of encounter of the threatening thing, is here the acute form of encounter of what is not yet present, more precisely, of the 'not yet' which however can strike at any moment. When such a threatening thing in its 'in fact not yet, but at any moment' now suddenly bursts into the presence of the party concerned, fear becomes *fright*.

Here, in what is threatening, we must distinguish the proximate approach of the menacing thing, which is constitutive of every form of being afraid. Over and above this, there is still the way in which this impending approach is encountered, here its suddenness. Take for example a grenade suddenly striking or piercing the ground nearby and with it the sudden appresentation of the imminent approach of the explosion, which can occur at any moment. Thus, the threatening is itself also an everyday familiar thing. At least it was so in this example [!]. That of which we are frightened can be (and most of the time is) something with which we are very well acquainted.

If, however, the threatening has the character of the utterly un-familiar, not merely the utterly unexpected but otherwise well-known, then fear becomes *horror*. When something threatening is encoun-tered in the character of the horrible and at the same time has the mode of encounter of fright, namely, its peculiar suddenness, then fear becomes *terror*.

Conversely, something worldly encountered as threatening can also be insignificant, but can nonetheless modify other moments constitu-tive of being afraid. For the way of being-in-the-world in concern can have the character of insecurity. A concern can be unsure of its own subject matter, and so can at bottom be unfamiliar with it. In this case, encountering an insignificant threat can arouse a fear which has the peculiar character of being suspicious, what we call *anxiousness*. We cannot go any further here into these other phenomena which belong in this context. They include the further modifications of *timidity*, *shyness, misgiving*, and *becoming startled*. We only want to maintain that these phenomena can themselves be understood only by starting from the primary analysis of being afraid of something, and perhaps not solely here, but first from that in which every form of being afraid of something is grounded, from dread.

γ) Fear in the sense of fearing about

A third moment to be distinguished from being afraid of some-thing is *fearing about and for another*. That about which we fear is first of all the others with whom we are. In other words, fearing about, which is primarily related to others and only indirectly to things in the world, is a way of being-with with the others, specifically in their being threatened. I fear for him, specifically because of what threatens him from the world. Fearing about another is or can be a genuine way of being-with the other by way of the world.

This fear for another as a being-with another is however not a fear-ing with another, since I can fear for the other without his being afraid. In fact, perhaps I am right in my fear about him precisely be-cause the menace as such does not confront him, because he is blind to it or foolhardy. Fearing for another also does not mean that I take his fear away from him, so that he does not necessarily have to be in fear at all, since I can fear for him. What is threatened here, about which I fear in fearing about the other, is the being-with with the other, his co-Dasein, and thus at the same time my own being-with with him. But my own being-with with him is not that about which I am directly afraid in my fearing about the other. In other words, in this fearing about and for the other I myself am not actually afraid.

Fearing for another thus proves to be a distinctive phenomenon of being-with. And it becomes clear that being with one another by way of the world is constitutive of it. The specific relations are as follows: the co-entity in the sense of the one who fears for the others, is with the other precisely when he is not in the other's mode of being; thus either he is not afraid with the other in the true sense of being afraid; or the other is not necessarily afraid when I am in fear about him. This fearing about is in a way an anticipation of fear for the others, without oneself necessarily having to be afraid. I cannot go any further here into the final correlations which are revealed here in regard to the structure of being with one another.

b) Dread and uncanniness

We shall now consider dread as a fourth phenomenon in connection with our analysis of fear. In addition to all of these modifications of fear there is a being afraid which at bottom can no longer be called that. For the of-which of fear can remain indefinite, no longer being this or that worldly thing on hand. Correspondingly, in-being as being-involved-with is no longer affected in a definite way. No real confusion ensues, since the possibility of confusion exists only when a definite orientation of concern gets all mixed up, that is, when the circumspectively disclosed in-being in its definite, factual, environmental possibilities falls into disarray. What threatens is nothing definite and worldly, and yet it is not without the impending approach which characterizes the threatening. Indeed, what threatens in this indefinite way is now quite near and can be so close that it is oppressive. It can be so near and yet not present as this or that, not something fearful, something to be feared by way of a definite reference of the environing world in its meaningfulness. Dread can 'befall' us right in the midst of the most familiar environment. Oftentimes it does not even have to involve the phenomenon of darkness or of being alone which frequently accompanies dread. We then say: one feels *uncanny* [or in more idiomatic English: "Things look so *weird* all of a sudden" or "I'm getting this *eerie* feeling"]. One no longer feels at home in his most familiar environment, the one closest to him; but this does not come about in such a way that a definite region in the hitherto known and familiar world breaks down in its orientation, nor such that one is not at home in the surroundings in which one now finds himself, but instead in other surroundings. On the contrary, in dread, being-in-the-world is totally transformed into a 'not at home' purely and simply.

Being-in-dread-of likewise has its specific of-which. More precisely put, our question is: As what must we define that of which dread is in dread?

When dread has run its course we say, 'It was really nothing.' This kind of talk strikes the very heart of the matter. It was nothing; *the of-which of dread is nothing*, that is to say, nothing that takes place in the world, nothing definite, nothing worldly. But since it can nevertheless be oppressively present in an obtrusiveness, it is much more than something threatening for fear, for it is the *world in its very worldhood*. The indefiniteness of the of-which, this nothing as nothing worldly, is phenomenally quite definite. It is the world in its worldhood, which of course does not give itself like a world-thing. As that which threatens, this nothing is very close, so that what thus threatens (the worldhood of the world or the world as such) in a way wraps itself around someone and takes his breath away, without being something of which one could say: this thing here.

For this peculiar and wholly original phenomenon there now are, as for all such phenomena, characteristic delusions, delusions of dread which, for example, can be induced purely physiologically. But this physiological possibility itself exists only because this entity, which is corporeally determined, can by virtue of its being be in dread at all, and not because some physiological occurrence could produce something like dread. It is for this reason that we speak of inducing a dread which is always possible and to some extent latent.

Because that of which dread is in dread is this nothing in the sense of "nothing definite and worldly," the nothing amplifies its proximity, that is, the possibility of the can-be [*Seinkönnen*] and of "being able to do nothing against it." This absolute helplessness in the face of the threatening, because it is indeed indefinite, because it is nothing, offers no ways and means of overcoming it. Every orientation draws a blank. This worldly indefiniteness of that of which dread is in dread is in its constitution now accompanied by the indefiniteness of that *about which* dread is in dread.

It is not this or that concern which is threatened, but *being-in-the-world as such*. Inherent in being-in-the-world, however, (and now we need to bring in what we have already discussed for the understanding of the entire analysis of dread) is the world in its worldhood. The of-which of dread, which is nothing worldly, is the in-which which is constitutive of Dasein, of in-being itself. That *of which* dread is in dread is the *in-which of being-in-the-world*, and that *about which* one is in dread is this *very same being-in-the-world*, specifically in its primary discoveredness of 'not at home.' In dread, therefore, the of-which of dread and the about-which of being in dread are not only indefinite in a worldly sense, but they coincide. More precisely stated, in dread they are not yet even separated; *Dasein is the of-which and the about-which*. In dread being-in-the-world as such discloses itself, and that not as this definite fact but in its *facticity*. Dread is nothing but *the disposition to uncanniness*.

The of-which and the about-which of dread are both Dasein itself, more accurately, the fact that I am, that is, "I am" in the sense of the naked being-in-the-world. This naked factuality is not that of being on hand like a thing, but the kind of being which is constitutive of finding oneself [in a situation].

Dasein is 'on hand' in a radical sense, in the sense of facticity. It does not find itself solely as something on hand in the sense of the ground and foundation, *that* it is. Rather, the ground is an *existential* ground, which means a disclosed ground—and a "bottomless ground," an *abyss* at that. This is the existential positivity of the nothing of dread. Facticity as a constituent of existence is not grafted onto something on hand, and man is not existence as the union of an extant soul and an extant body. In other words, existence rightly understood is not the union of the separated, but the original kind of being which defines this entity ontologically.

Dasein is such that it is this peculiar factic dimension; in short, Dasein *is its very facticity*. The 'fact' that Dasein 'is' at all and 'is not not' is not a mere property in it, but can be experienced by Dasein itself in an original experience; this is nothing but the disposition of dread. Facticity of Dasein means: It is in a manner of its being this being, *that it is*; more accurately: *It is its very 'there' and 'in.'*

In dread worldhood as such presents itself together with my being in it, without bringing any definite datum to the foreground. Earlier, in analyzing Descartes's concept of the subject, I referred to his statement that we actually have no affection of being as such. But there is such an affection (if one wants to use this mode of expression). Dread is nothing other than the pure and simple experience of being in the sense of being-in-the-world. This experience can, though it does not have to—just as all possibilities of being come under a 'can'—assume a distinctive sense in *death* or, more precisely, in *dying*. We then speak of the *dread of death*, which must be kept altogether distinct from the fear of death, for it is not fear in the face of death but dread as a disposition to the naked being-in-the-world, to pure Dasein. There is thus the possibility, in the very moment of departing from the world, so to speak, when the world has nothing more to say to us and every other has nothing more to say, that the world and our being-in-it show themselves purely and simply.

This analysis of dread depicts a phenomenon which in its nature simply cannot be forced and whose analysis here also has nothing whatsoever to do with any sort of sentimentality. The analysis has exhibited this phenomenon of dread as the foundation in being for Dasein's flight from itself. This phenomenon of dread is not something invented by me but has already been seen repeatedly, even though not in these concepts. Here I am only trying to provide the concepts for things which are usually treated in a nebulous way in the sciences, and at times also in theology.

Augustine did not regard the phenomenon of dread in a thematic way, but he in fact caught a glimpse of it in a short study "On Fear" within a collection of questions, "On Various Questions of the Eighty Tribes."[4] Luther then dealt with the phenomenon of dread in the traditional context of an interpretation of *contritio* and *poenitentia* in his commentary on Genesis.[5] In recent times, particularly in connection with the problem of original sin, Kierkegaard made the phenomenon of dread the theme of his separate work, *The Concept of Dread.*[6]

I cannot go into greater detail here into the various modifications whereby dread as implicit is directly concealed by the phenomenon of being afraid. We shall consider them in the persistent retrograde movement from discoveredness towards falling. From falling to dread we now come to the last fundament of being, which gives to dread in general, which means to being-in-the-world, its original constitution. This fundament is the phenomenon of care.

c) More original explication of falling and dread (uncanniness) as a preview of the basic constitution of Dasein as care

The explication of the movement of falling as a flight of Dasein from itself led to the phenomenon of dread as a basic disposition of Dasein to itself, namely, to itself in its pure being, where being must always be taken in the sense already exhibited as being-in-the-world. The foregoing reflections on dread which we have just cited suffer from the basic deficiency of not really seeing the conceptual, existential structure of Dasein, so that dread then becomes a psychological problem, even in Kierkegaard. *But dread is dread of this being itself, such that this being-in-dread-of-it is a being in dread about this being.* But this implies that Dasein is an entity for which in its being, in its being-in-the-world, "it goes *about* its very being" [*es geht um sein Sein selbst*], for which, that is, *its very being is at issue.* This is the sense of the selfsame-

---

4. Augustine, *De diversis quaestionibus octoginta tribus*, questions 33, 34, 35, Opera Omnia, Migne, *Patrologiae Latinae* XL, Vol. VI, pp. 22ff.

5. Martin Luther, *Enarrationes in genesin*, Ch. 3, *Werke* (Erlangen Edition), *Exegetica opera latina*, Vol. I, pp. 177ff.

6. Soren Kierkegaard, *Der Begriff der Angst*, 1844, *Gesammelte Werke* (Diederichs), Vol. 5.

ness of the of-which and the about-which of dread which has just been expounded.

This selfsameness must not be understood in such a way that the essential structural moments of the of-which and the about-which would become fused in dread. The selfsameness rather only serves to show that the essence of dread is Dasein itself. Dasein occurs twice, so to speak, in the disposition of dread. This formulation of the phenomenon is of course the very worst way of putting it, its only sense being to give us a preliminary indication of a peculiar state of affairs, namely, that Dasein is an entity in whose being its own being is at issue. But is this actually a phenomenal composition of the being of Dasein itself? For it seems to be directly contradicted by the phenomenon of falling, the flight of Dasein from itself. It became evident in falling that everydayness moves Dasein away from itself. It therefore cannot be said that Dasein is intimately involved with itself in its everydayness. This, however, is still a blind and unphenomenological way of arguing.

In falling, in the flight from itself, Dasein is still constantly there for itself. In the flight from itself it gets behind itself, so that it constantly sees itself implicitly in falling, even if this is in the deceitful way of not wanting to see. But where Dasein in its being flees to, namely, to the being of the Anyone, is indeed itself still only a way of being of Dasein itself, in the sense of a specific being-at-home. What is at stake in the flight from uncanniness [*Unheimlichkeit*, not-being-at-home] is precisely a cultivation of Dasein itself as being-in-the-world, so much so that it lets itself be determined primarily from the world. It is precisely in the Anyone that Dasein is its discoveredness as uncanniness in the manner we have described. Not only is it not the case that falling detracts from the composition of being we are discussing; falling itself first becomes comprehensible precisely from this composition.

§31. Care as the being of Dasein

a) Determination of the articulated structure of care

It is this peculiar structure of the being of the entity, that it is an entity for which, within its in-being, that very being is at issue, which we must now grasp in greater detail. But how? We shall define this structure terminologically as *care* and designate it as a primal structure, the structure of Dasein itself. But I would like to emphasize expressly that this structure does not uncover the ultimate context of the being of Dasein. It is the *penultimate* phenomenon, so to speak, on the way toward the authentic structure of the being of Dasein. *Care is the term for the being of Dasein pure and simple.* It has the formal structure, *an entity for which, intimately involved in its being-in-the-world, this very being is at issue.*

In view of this state of affairs in an analysis of Dasein with regard to its being, it is apparent that 'being' is not at all a simple concept, let alone the simplest concept. This is one error made by the tradition, and perhaps the most fateful. It is based on a determination of being which naturally starts from entities taken as a world, formalizes this being of the world or worldhood by disregarding every particular world-thing, in order to thus arrive at a formal concept.

The definition of the structure of care already shows that this phenomenon, which thus authentically comprehends being, exhibits a multiple structure. And if Dasein in its being is generally defined by care, then these phenomena must have already been in our sights in the foregoing analyses of Dasein. In fact we dealt with the phenomenon of care in a certain way right from the start, when we spoke of concern as the authentic mode of being-in-the-world. *Concern itself is but a mode of being of care,* specifically because care is the character of being of an entity which is essentially defined by being-in-the-world. To put it better, care *qua* structure of Dasein is in-being as concern. Caring as it is in the world is *eo ipso* concern. The expression which we use in the definition of the formal structure of care, 'being is at issue,' must now be more accurately defined.

'Its own being is the issue for Dasein': This first presupposes that in this Dasein there is something like a *being out for something.* Dasein is out for its own being; it is out for its very being in order 'to be' its being. *As such a being-about care is this being out for the being which this very being-out is.* This must be understood in such a way that Dasein as it were *anticipates* itself there. If the being of Dasein is what is at issue for care, then Dasein has always already held its own being ahead of itself, even if not in the sense of a thematic consciousness of it. The innermost structure of Dasein's caring about its being can be conceived formally as *Dasein's being-ahead-of-itself.* But we must understand this being-ahead-of-itself of Dasein in the context of the structures which have hitherto already been exhibited. This being-ahead is not a kind of psychological process or a property of a subject, but rather an element of the entity which, in accord with its sense is in the world, that is, in accord with its original character of being, insofar as it is at all, *is always already intimately involved in* something, namely, in the world. We thus arrive at the overall structure of care in the formal sense: *Dasein's being-ahead-of-itself in its always already being involved in something.* This formal structure of care applies to every comportment. There are only different modalities of the individual structural moments of care, such that they can assume the kinds of being which *urge* and *propensity* have. We shall have to envisage these two phenomena in still greater detail in order to come to understand how the specific *wholeness* of the phenomenon of Dasein is now first of all integrated from this primal structure of the being of Dasein as care. The wholeness of Dasein cannot be combined from various ways of being and the coupling which then comes into play. On the contrary, with care we now find the phenomenon from which we can then understand the various ways of being as ways of *being*, that is, as care.

Care has the formal structure of being-ahead-of-itself-in-already-being-involved-in something. This being-ahead implies a structure whereby care is always a *being about* something, specifically such that Dasein in concern, in every performance, in every provision and production of something in particular, is at the same time concerned for its Dasein. This being-ahead-of-itself signifies precisely that care or Dasein in care has *thrust* its own being *ahead as existential facticity*. This being out for its own being, which is at issue for it, always takes place already in *being involved in* something, from a being-always-already-in-the-world-involved-in. (In-being is therefore constitutive for every kind of being of Dasein—even for authentic being!) The structure of 'being out for something' which I do not yet have, but being-out in an already-involved-in which *eo ipso* is being out for something, brings with it the phenomenon of not yet having something which I am out for. This phenomenon of not yet having something which I am out for is called *being in want*. It is not merely a pure and simple objective not-having but is always a not-having of something that I am out for. It is what first constitutes being-in-want, lack, need. Later, as the interpretation proceeds, this basic structure of care will lead us back to the constitution of being which we shall then come to understand as *time*. But first it is important to bring out a few more structures in care itself, specifically in relation to what we have learned in the preceding analysis of Dasein.

b) The phenomena of urge and propensity

In the two structural moments of being-ahead-of-itself and already-being-involved-in, there is a puzzling character which is peculiar to care and, as we shall see, is nothing other than *time*. This peculiar character of the *'before,'* of the 'ahead,' this *'fore-character,'* namely, that Dasein is always ahead of itself and always already involved in something—which displays a double phenomenon—now determines the concrete ways of being which we have already come to know. Before we proceed toward the understanding of one of these ways of being, namely, the interpretation of this character of the "before," we shall clarify the two phenomena which are closely associated with care— *urge* and *propensity*.

In the structure identified as being-ahead-of-itself-in-already-being-involved-in something, care is first and foremost the condition of possibility for urge and propensity, and not the other way around, where care would be pieced together from these two phenomena. Urge has the character of 'towards' something. In particular, this 'towards something' points to an element of compulsion which comes from the 'towards' itself. Urge is a 'towards' something which brings the drive into play from itself. When we view it against the background of care, urge brings out both the character of compulsion and being out for something. Care is modified in order to predominate in these two structural moments of care. Care as urge suppresses. The suppression here applies to the remaining structural moments also given in care. These do not fall away or fall out but are there in the urge as suppressed moments, where *suppressed* always means *covered up*, inasmuch as Dasein is defined by discoveredness. Insofar as the urge takes over the primary kind of being of Dasein, it suppresses the already-being-involved-in something along with that something, but it also suppresses the explicit being-ahead-of-itself. For in urge, care is now merely a concern for a 'towards and nothing else.' Urge as such blinds, it makes us blind. We are in the habit of saying that 'love is blind.' Here, love is regarded as an urge and so is replaced by an entirely different phenomenon. For love really gives us sight. Urge is a mode of the being of care, specifically *care which has not yet become free*, but care is not an urge. That care has not yet become free means that in urge the full structure of care does not yet come to its authentic being. For urge only cares about the 'towards,' and this at any price, in blind disregard of everything else. This blind state of only being 'towards and nothing else' is a modification of caring.

Propensity is distinguished from urge. It is likewise a modification of care. Care is also implied in propensity, but in its other structures, specifically in what urge pushes aside, in already-being-involved-in something. Just as there is in urge a specific exclusiveness in the impulsive 'only towards, at any price,' so also in propensity there is likewise such as 'only,' namely, 'always already only being involved in something.' Propensity is being out for Dasein's evasion of itself in being-involved-in. We must guard against confusing these two structures of urge and propensity. The 'always already only being involved in' in propensity is of course also a 'towards something.' But it is a 'towards' which is not defined by drive, but rather a 'towards' of letting itself be drawn by what it is involved in. And just as urge covers up the being of care in certain respects in the direction of suppression, so also does propensity cover up. For the care of 'being able to let itself only be drawn by something' deprives care of the possibility of an original and genuine being-ahead-of-itself.

Urge is care which has not yet become free, while propensity is care which is already bound in what it is involved in in its very being. Along with care, propensity as well as urge are constitutive of every Dasein. Propensity itself cannot be eradicated any more than urge can be annihilated. But certain possibilities of propensity and urge can be modified and guided by the genuine possibility of care. Against the care which has not yet become free in the urge, against the attachment of propensity, there is their liberation in the sense that they are not simply let go but are themselves fulfilled in their way of fulfillment in genuine care. When they are seen and understood, these two structures (propensity and urge) are always understood such that care is from the start co-intended in them. Care, however, is not a phenomenon composed of propensity and urge.

c) Care and discoveredness

To Dasein as being-in-the-world belongs *discoveredness*. The enactment of the being of this moment is *understanding*. Discoveredness is the determination of the being of Dasein whereby it is always involved in something, such that the involvement itself becomes *sighted* and so can see. This phenomenon of discoveredness also appears in a primary way in care. Care is characterized by discoveredness.

The moments of 'toward something,' of 'already being involved in,' and of 'being ahead' are all phenomena having the character of discoveredness. They are not sighted in the sense that they themselves could be the theme of seeing. Rather, they have a *sight* in themselves. As far as I can see, this peculiar constitution of Dasein provides the basis for understanding an old idea and interpretation of Dasein, whereby it is said that the *lumen naturale*, the "natural light," is inherent in human Dasein. Dasein by itself, by its nature, in what it is, has a light. It is intrinsically defined by a light. To take an example, this means that a mere thing, a stone, has no light within itself, which means that what it is and how it is toward its environs, if we can speak at all of an environment for the stone, is without sight. We cannot even say that it is dark, since darkness is in fact the negation of light. There is darkness only where there can be light. The manner of being of a mere thing stands beyond or before light and dark. By contrast, the idea that the *lumen naturale* belongs to the Dasein of man means that *it is lighted within itself*, that it is involved in something, has and sees this something and together with it is this very involvement. With the phenomenon of discoveredness, we have arrived at nothing other than the concept, as it were, the category of this structure of being, the phenomenon which was already manifestly seen in the old interpretation of Dasein as the *lumen naturale*.

Care has the character of discoveredness, which means that understanding is always sighted understanding. Here we must note that understanding as we defined it earlier can at the same time gain a new meaning in view of care itself. For in ordinary language, we also use 'understanding' in another sense when we say 'He understands how to handle men,' 'He knows how to talk.' Understanding here means 'knowing how' [*können*], 'being capable of.' And 'being capable of' means *having the possibility for something in oneself;* more accurately put, since we are dealing here with Dasein, it means nothing but *being the very possibility for something.* As care, as being-ahead-of-itself-in-already-being-involved-in, Dasein not only has possibilities for something which it could take up on occasion and cast aside again, so that it could also be without them. Dasein itself, insofar as it is, is nothing but *being-possible.* The Dasein which I myself am in each instance is defined in its being by my being able to say of it, *I am, that is, I can.* Only because this entity as Dasein is defined by the 'I can,' can it procure possibilities in the sense of opportunities, means, and the like, and be concerned about them. Every concern and every entity which is defined by care implies a priori the mode of being of the 'I can.' Specifically, this 'I can' as a constitutive state of the being of Dasein is always an understanding 'I can.' In concern, I can do the one and the other, which means I can do the one as well as the other, and furthermore, I can do either the one or the other. It should thus be noted that the phenomena of 'either-or,' 'as well as,' 'the-one-*and*-the-other-*and*-the-other' show a definite structural buildup, and that the 'and,' the one 'and' the other 'and' the other, is not primary, certainly not the 'and' in the sense of the purely theoretical enumerative 'and.' For example, when I say, 'I love my father *and* my mother,' the 'and' here in no sense has the meaning of counting them together, as when I say, 'the chair and the table.' Rather the 'and' here is a specific 'and'—the 'and' of loving. The 'and' thus first has an absolutely primary sense which is oriented towards care, towards the 'I can.' To put it more precisely, however, what is primary here is not the 'and' but the 'either-or.' It is only because there is an 'either-or' that there is an 'as well as' and an 'and' of concern. Unfortunately, I cannot deal with the more precise structures of these correlations here. Dasein is intrinsically being possible. It will now have to be shown in what way Dasein is itself its own possibility and its possibilities.

d) Care and the character of the 'before'
in understanding and interpretation
(prepossession, preview, preconception)

Understanding is not a primary phenomenon of knowledge but a way of primary being toward something, toward the world and toward itself. Furthermore, this being toward something is now first fully defined by the 'I can.' 'I can' necessarily corresponds as a correlative to the understandability of something. And conversely, what can be of concern as something understandable is what can be pursued in care and in concern. Understanding in the earlier sense, where it was taken solely as a way of being toward, now has, as a mode of being of Dasein, the character of care. But this implies that understanding and more so the way of enacting understanding, interpretation, are determined by this kind of being of Dasein, by care. This phenomenon of care as being-ahead-of-itself-in-already-being-involved-in includes the character of 'before.' It is precisely interpretation, as a mode of being of understanding and so of care, which is defined by this character of the 'before.'

All interpretation, *considering something as something*, interprets by laying out in an already-being-involved-in, namely, in intimacy with that about which the discourse is. That about which the discourse is from the start is always already discovered in some sense, anticipated as this or that for a primary preunderstanding. It necessarily stands in an understandability which is by and large preliminary. As a kind of being of Dasein, that is, of care and so of being ahead, interpretation at any given time has its *prepossession* in which, before it takes any further step—indeed as a basis for it—it already understands the about-which. To this prepossession, to the predetermination of that of which the discourse is, always belongs in its being—inasmuch as interpreting considers something *as something*—a certain *view* under which we place what is to be spoken about and talked over in the interpretation. In every speaking, in every interpretation, what is placed in prepossession is aligned in our sights in a certain way. That *toward which* what is placed in prepossession is thus sighted, that toward which it is regarded, with respect to which it comes into sight, is what we call the *preview*. These two constitutive moments determine in advance, prior to all discussion, how the theme is approached in interpretation as this or that, in this or that view. Prepossession and pre-view indicate in advance which of the possible correlations of meaning (should and can) be brought out in the thematic field. They point forward to the correlations of meaning which are taking conceptual shape in interpretive discourse and especially in scientific discourse. This means that the *conceptuality* which corresponds to this particular interpretation and this particular theme is thus prefigured. This prefiguration which is inherent in the structure of the interpretation is the *preconception*. We understand interpretation in these its fundamental structures only when we have understood that it is a kind of being of Dasein, a way of being-ahead-of-itself-in-already-being-involved-in.

The three structural moments—prepossession, pre-view, preconception—belong essentially to every interpretation, including scientific interpretation, specifically because interpretation is the mode of being of understanding, understanding has the mode of being of care, and care is intrinsically being-ahead-of-itself-in-already-being-involved-in something. Interpretation is consequently founded in the structure of Dasein. All hermeneutics, all elucidation of the various possibilities of interpreting must refer back to this basic structure and so to the constitution of the being of Dasein. Not only every hermeneutics in the sense of a theory of interpretation but every concrete historical interpretation requires, if it claims to be relevant to the subject matter, constant reflection on whether that which it has taken into prepossession, pre-view, and preconception at any given time as an interpretation is expressly suited for the purpose or is merely thrown together by chance. These phenomena, which accompany every interpretation as prepossession, pre-view, and preconception, are the well-known and familiar, but equally inconvenient, self-evident elements in every interpretation, which we think we can ignore for the time being. But it is precisely on this "self-evident" basis that the degree and kind of scientificity of each interpretation are decided, and not on whether and how much material is brought to bear on the proof of an interpretation.

As self-expressive, all discourse expresses *itself*, that is, Dasein *itself* as being-ahead-of-itself-in-already-being-involved-in something. In expressing itself about something, in thus speaking out, every discourse always already speaks out of this preunderstanding which is the about-which of the discourse, and which predetermines the toward-which as well as the potential presence of meaning. But we should not conclude from this that Dasein always says beforehand how it sees the things, so that every interpretation would from the outset be subjective. On the contrary, it implies that in expressing itself Dasein always already speaks out of a pregiven way in which things have been interpreted, and necessarily so. For Dasein itself, this is the necessity of *its foregoing discoveredness for itself*. It is only because Dasein is itself discovered that there can be a covering up by idle talk and by no longer being toward something in an original way. But this is also why there are also *rediscoveries* and *further discoveries*. The necessity of rediscovery is grounded in Dasein itself, specifically in its mode of being of falling.

When, for example within historical research, ingenious historians arrive at more original readings of what has already been interpreted earlier, it is not a matter of caprice on their part, as if they now had to be different and so make some changes in earlier ideas on the topic. Rather, it simply brings about the destruction of what was already discovered earlier in a certain way but then fell into obscurity. It is therefore absurd to think that historical research could arrive at a moment when it would be finished, so that we would then know once and for all how things were in history. This idea of objectivity is essentially excluded from history. But this makes it clear that research and science are themselves only possibilities of the being of Dasein and so are also necessarily subject to the modifications of the being of Dasein. For they are themselves in fact also necessarily more or less exposed to falling and so get absorbed in their undertakings or, where there is no apparatus and the like, in idle talk. If all science and every form of research includes this possibility of falling, and necessarily so, it also goes without saying that philosophy is always necessarily a bit of sophistry, and that, as a form of enactment of Dasein, it carries this danger within itself.

It has thus become clear in connection with a phenomenon, that of interpretation, how the structure of care, especially the character of the 'before,' extends to the individual forms of enactment of these kinds of being of Dasein itself. With the phenomenon of care, we have thus brought out the basic structure from which the hitherto explicated phenomena are now to be seen. The 'pre'-structure of care, particularly of understanding, has become visible, but it will be illuminated only when we answer this question: In this being-ahead-of-itself and in the being-already-involved-in, what is actually meant by *being*?

e) The 'Fable of *Cura*' as an illustration of an original self-interpretation of Dasein

The assertion, "The structure of the being of Dasein is care," is a *phenomenological and not a pre-scientific self-interpretation* such as, for example, an assertion like "Life is care and toil." The first proposition is concerned with a basic structure which the second assertion reproduces only in one of its immediate everyday aspects. But the first assertion can and must at the same time be taken as a definition of man, if Dasein is indeed our theme. Also, this interpretation of Dasein based upon the phenomenon of care is not an invention of mine. It does not come from a particular philosophical standpoint—I have no philosophy at all—, but is suggested simply by the analysis of the matters themselves. Nothing is being read into the matters (in this case Dasein); instead, everything is drawn from them (it); Dasein itself is a self-interpreting, self-articulating entity. It was seven years ago, while I was investigating these structures in conjunction with my attempts to arrive at the ontological foundations of Augustinian anthropology, that I first came across the phenomenon of care. Of course, Augustine and ancient Christian anthropology in general did not know the phenomenon explicitly, nor even directly as a term, although *cura*, care, already played a role in Seneca as well as in the New Testament, as is well-known. Later, however, I came across a self-interpretation of Dasein in an old fable, in which Dasein sees itself as care. Such interpretations have the primary advantage of being drawn from an originally naive view of Dasein itself and so of playing a particularly positive role for all interpretation, as Aristotle already knew.

This old fable is to be found among the fables of Hyginus. It is the 220th fable and bears the title *Cura*. I would like to share it with you:

> Cura cum fluvium transiret, videt cretosum lutum
> sustulitque cogitabunda atque coepit fingere.
> dum deliberat quid iam fecisset, Jovis intervenit.
> rogat eum Cura ut det illi spiritum, et facile impetrat.
> cui cum vellet Cura nomen ex sese ipsa imponere,
> Jovis prohibuit suumque nomen ei dandum esse dictitat.
> dum Cura et Jovis disceptant, Tellus surrexit simul
> suumque nomen esse volt cui corpus praebuerit suum.
> sumpserunt Saturnum iudicem, is sic aecus iudicat:
> "tu Jovis quia spiritum dedisti, in morte spiritum,
> tuque Tellus, quia dedisti corpus, corpus recipito,
> Cura enim quia prima finxit, teneat quamdiu vixerit.
> sed quae nunc de nomine eius vobis controversia est,
> homo vocetur, quia videtur esse factus ex humo."

In the translation:

> Once when 'Care' was crossing a river, she saw some clay. Thoughtfully, she took up a piece and began to shape it. While she was meditating on what she had made, Jupiter came by. 'Care' asked him to give it spirit, and this he gladly granted. But when she wanted her name to be bestowed upon it, he forbade this, and demanded that it be given his name instead. As they were arguing, Earth arose and requested that her name be conferred on the creature, since she had given it a part of her body. They asked Saturn to be the judge, and he made the following seemingly just decision: "Since you, Jupiter, gave it spirit, you shall have that spirit at its death. Since you, Earth, gave it the gift of a body, you shall receive its body. But since 'Care' first shaped this creature, she

shall possess it as long as it lives. But since there is a dispute among you about its name, let it be called '*homo*,' for it is made of *humus* (earth)."

In this naive interpretation of Dasein, we observe the astonishing fact that here the view is directed toward Dasein and that along with body and spirit something like 'care' is seen as that phenomenon which is attributed to this entity as long as it lives, to wit, as Dasein, which we have regarded here as being-in-the-world. Konrad Burdach, through whom I also came across this fable, has now worked out the details.[1] Burdach shows here that Goethe got the fable of Hyginus from Herder and adapted it in his *Faust*, in the second part. Burdach then gives, as always in a very reliable and scholarly way, a large amount of material relating to the history of this concept. Among other things, he says that the word in the New Testament for 'care' (*sollicitudo* in the Vulgate), μέριμνα (or as it probably was originally called, φροντίς), was already a technical term in the moral philosophy of the Stoics. It was used in Seneca's 90th letter, which was also known to Goethe, for the description of primitive man. The double sense of *cura* refers to care for something as concern, absorption in the world, but also care in the sense of devotion. This concurs with the structures which we have exposed. But does this not mean that in a certain way *cura* is already seen in the natural interpretation of Dasein, although not in the form of an explicit question regarding the very structure of the being of Dasein?

With the phenomenon of care, we have arrived at that structure of being from which the previously secured characters of the being of Dasein can now be made understandable, not only in their structure as such, but in the possible ways of being arising from it.[2]

f) Care and intentionality

Now that we have brought the various structures of Dasein into a certain correlation with the basic phenomenon of care, this stage in our consideration serves to provide us with the basis upon which we could critically repeat what we have heard about *intentionality* in our introductory considerations. It could be shown from the phenomenon of care as the basic structure of Dasein that what phenomenology took to be intentionality and how it took it is fragmentary, a phenomenon regarded merely from the outside. But what is meant by inten-

---

1. K. Burdach, "Faust und die Sorge," *Deutsche Vierteljahrsschrift für Literaturwissenschaft und Geistesgeschichte* I (1923), pp. 41f.

{2.} Editor's note: End of [Heidegger's handwritten] manuscript.

tionality—the bare and isolated directing-itself-towards—must still be set back into the unified basic structure of being-ahead-of-itself-in-already-being-involved-in. This alone is the authentic phenomenon which corresponds to what inauthentically and only in an isolated direction is meant by intentionality. I refer to this here only in passing in order to mark the place from which a fundamental critique of phenomenological inquiry finds its start.

SECOND DIVISION

The Exposition of Time Itself

---

§32. The result and the task of the fundamental analysis of Dasein: elaboration of the question of being itself

The time has come to raise some more exacting questions: What have we gained by these considerations, and what are we looking for? What aim do we have in mind in going through with the explication of Dasein?

The interpretation of Dasein in the everydayness of being opened the prospect for understanding the fundamental constitutive states of this entity. Structures like *being-in-the-world, in-being* and *being-with, the Anyone, discoveredness, understanding, falling,* and *care* came to light. The latter phenomenon at the same time reveals the unifying root of this manifold of structures. We have constantly reiterated that these structures are *co-original*. To say that they are co-original means that they always already belong with and to the phenomenon of care. They are ingrained in it even when they do not come to the fore-ground. These structures are therefore not optional additions to something which might from the start be akin to care without them. Nor do we have something which could be shaped into what we have called the phenomenon of care by putting these structures together. But if our inquiry is pointed toward the being of Dasein, as we have constantly done here, then whenever Dasein is interrogated, it is al-ways already meant in the co-originality of these structures. Thus, when I phenomenologically envisage discoveredness or the Anyone or falling, the unity of these structures is always co-intended.

Dasein is neither a combination of comportments nor a composite of body, soul, and spirit, so it is futile to search for the sense of the being of this unity of the composite. It is also *not* a subject or con-sciousness, which only incidentally provides itself with a world. Nor is it a center from which acts spring, where neither the being of this center nor the being of the acts is defined. The structures which we have exhibited are themselves ways of being of this entity and as such are understandable only from the being always already intended with them, namely, from care. Dasein understands itself from itself as care. Care is accordingly the primary *totality* of the constitution of the being of Dasein, which as this totality always adopts this or that particular way of its can-be. This totality of being is as such totally present in every way of being of Dasein. What has thus been secured with the phenomenon of care as the being of Dasein is not a derived universal concept which, as a genus, would underlie every way to be. Still less is it the concept resulting from the interplay of various ways to be and conceived by drawing an abstract universal out of them. The interplay of the various ways of being is what it is only as the playing out and playing apart, so to speak, at any given time of the primary structures of the totality of Dasein itself.

The question now is, what aim did we have in mind in undertaking this analysis of Dasein? The elaboration of the structures of the being of the entity which we ourselves are and which we called Dasein, was approached earlier as that investigation which has the task of *working out the formulation of the question of being as such.* The concrete fundament for any possible kind of research into being as such has to be secured. In other words, the fundament for the question, What is meant by being?, is to be made manifest. We want to come to an answer to this question which is not only formulated in a formal proposition but which prescribes concrete ways for the research into being itself. After what has been secured up to this point, we can formulate *the basic phenomenological question, What is meant by being?*, with greater methodological precision.

Phenomenological research is the interpretation of entities with regard to their being. For such an interpretation, what is put into prepossession is what it has in advance as its thematic matter: an entity or a particular region of being. This entity is interrogated with regard to its being. In other words, that *with regard to which* [*woraufhin*] what is put into prepossession is interrogated, the view *to which* [*woraufhin*] it is seen and to be seen, is being. Being is to be read off in the entity; that is to say, what phenomenological interpretation puts into pre-view is being. It has put a temporally particular entity into prepossession. It asks about the being of the entity. Such a question about the being of the entity is a clear and sure guide for the investigation only when that with regard to which the entity is interrogated, namely being, is adequately elaborated and conceptually determined. The more originally and the less prejudicially the elaboration of what is put into pre-view is brought about, the less one uses fortuitous, seemingly self-evident and worn-out concepts which are unclear in their origin, then all the more surely will concrete research into being attain its ground and stay rooted there in its native soil.

This phenomenon of 'being,' which takes the lead and so decides the way for all research into being, must be elaborated. As we showed earlier, this calls for the interpretation of the very questioning; what is needed here is the clarification of the very structure of research into being, of the interrogation of the entity with regard to its being. The formulation of the question can as such be clearly realized only when it has become clear what questioning, what understanding, what taking a view, what an experience of an entity is, what the being of an entity in general means, in short, when all that we mean by Dasein has been elaborated.

§33. Necessity for the thematic development of the phenomenological interpretation of Dasein as a whole. The phenomenon of death

The phenomenological interpretation of Dasein itself is a special task, inasmuch as it has a particular entity for its theme. Now this phenomenological interpretation is in its turn, again as an interpretation, guided by the clue given with the very structure of interpretation. If it wishes to proceed in an appropriate manner, such an interpretation of Dasein has to ask whether it has from the start brought into prepossession in an original and genuine manner that which it takes to be the theme of its analysis, namely Dasein. More precisely put, it has to ask whether Dasein at the onset of its analysis was taken in advance in such a way that the whole entity in its wholeness came into prepossession. For it is only when we make the entity as a whole our theme that we are assured of being able to read off the totality of its being in that entity. The success of the *preparatory* interpretation of Dasein in drawing out the structure of the being of Dasein in itself is based upon this, that in the thematic development of the analysis this very entity—Dasein in its totality—is secured.

We must therefore ask: Is Dasein itself, in our previous consideration of it, from the start brought into view in its wholeness and held in such a way that the totality of its being can be read off in this entity as a whole? This present consideration, which I prefer to call a transitional consideration, is of fundamental significance for what follows, and it is important for you to be able to carry out the individual steps of the deliberation for yourselves with phenomenological clarity.

On the basis of the foregoing, I could now leap ahead and relate all sorts of things to you about *time*. An understanding for what time means would in every case be lacking. You would be left merely with some propositions about time. I therefore choose the only possible way for maintaining a genuine continuity in our consideration, so as to lead you through these individual steps to the field from which time itself then becomes manifest in a certain way. It is not so much a matter of coming up with results in the form of propositions about time, but of having your eyes opened by this consideration, so that you may see and check for yourselves what we have gained thus far.

The question remains: in our considerations thus far, is Dasein approached as a whole, so that we can claim that the characters of being gained thus far as such fully define Dasein as such? If the being of Dasein is interpreted as care, we then ask: Does this phenomenon give us the totality of the structures of its being? Or does not the elaboration of this phenomenon of care lead us straight to the insight that Dasein as a whole was not put into prepossession in the consideration thus far? Indeed, does it not lead to the insight that the whole of Dasein is not only not in fact secured but in principle can *not* be secured, precisely because care constitutes the basic structure of its being? Formulated in another way, insofar as Dasein shows itself in this structure of being of care, it stands in direct opposition to the possibility of ever being grasped in its wholeness and so brought into prepossession.

Reading off the genuine totality of being requires that the entity as a whole be given. To the extent that care became manifest as the being of this entity, this means that the whole is in principle never given, and the purported reading is in principle impossible. In regard to Dasein itself and our previous elaboration, we have obtained full clarity on the following points: The being of this entity is care; among other things, care means being out for something; Dasein's concern includes a concern for its own being. As being out for something, it is out for *what it still is not*. As care, Dasein is essentially *underway towards something*; in caring it is toward itself as that which it still is not. Its own sense of being is to always have something before itself which it still is not, which is still outstanding. That something is always still outstanding means that the being of Dasein as care, insofar as it is, is *always incomplete*; it still lacks something so long as it is.

But when Dasein is complete, a conclusion which is called *death*, then Dasein is indeed at an end, nothing more is outstanding for it as an entity, but with this 'nothing more outstanding' for it, it is also no longer Dasein. Upon reaching its wholeness and precisely in it, it becomes no-longer-Dasein. Its wholeness makes it vanish. Accordingly, Dasein as a whole in principle can never be forced into prepossession. But even if that were in some way possible, this only means again, strictly speaking, that no use could be made of this prepossession. For we must adhere to the determination of Dasein given earlier, that in essence it is in each instance mine. This character—Dasein is mine at the time—is ineradicable in it. And it is only because Dasein in essence is in each instance my own that I can lose myself in the Anyone. When Dasein reaches wholeness in death, then it can no longer be experienced by me as mine. More accurately, in totality understanding self-finding is no longer possible. For the entity which was supposed to find *itself* when wholeness was reached in fact no longer is precisely because of wholeness. But first, entirely apart from whether it makes any sense at all to maintain the possibility that in dying Dasein might have an opportunity for a phenomenological investigation of its being, it would in fact always have to wait until it was completely at the end in order to grasp this wholeness. This points to an impossibility in principle to find oneself in the wholeness of Dasein, to experience it and thereupon to extricate the totality of this being from it. It should of course be noted that this impossibility is not grounded in the famed irrationality of lived experiences and their structures, nor in the limitation and insecurity of our cognitive faculty, nor in the inappropriateness of the moment of dying for phenomenological investigations. Rather, this impossibility is anchored solely in the kind of being of this very entity. If reaching wholeness means no-longer-being, a loss of any possible disposition, must we then forgo the possibility of exhibiting the corresponding totality and an adequate characterization of the being of Dasein on the basis of its own kind of being?

But there still seems to be a way to make Dasein in its wholeness the theme of a characterization of being, particularly if we do not lose sight of a character of Dasein which we have already demonstrated. Dasein as being-in-the-world, we said earlier, is at the same time being-with-one-another. Insofar as death for Dasein constitutes being-at-an-end in the sense of no longer being Dasein, death in fact prevents me from having and experiencing my own Dasein in its wholeness. But this possibility still remains for the others with whom this Dasein as being-with once was. The Dasein which still is for the time being as being-with others has the possibility of regarding the Dasein of others as concluded and, it seems, to read off in it the totality of the being of such an entity. But the reference to this alternative of taking the Dasein of others which has come to an end as a substitute theme is a dubious bit of information. And this is not because the apprehension of the connections of being, which in the Dasein of others constitute what is last of all still outstanding, runs into special difficulties in experiencing the dying of others in its authentic sense. It is not this chance difficulty which shows that this alternative is in principle inappropriate. The reasons which prohibit a reference to the Dasein of others as an alternative are of a more fundamental kind:

1) Upon dying, the Dasein of others is also a no-longer-Dasein in the sense of no-longer-being-in-the-world. When they have died,

their being-in-the-world is as such no more. Their being is no longer being 'in' a world, 'involved in' a disclosed world. Their still-being-in-the-world is that of merely being on hand as a corporeal thing. The unique change-over of an entity from the kind of being belonging to Dasein, whose character is being-in-the-world, to a bare something which is still only on hand is especially evident here. This bare "still being on hand" is the extreme counterinstance to the foregoing kind of being of this entity. Strictly speaking, we can no longer even say that something like a human body is still on hand. We must not deceive ourselves. For with the dying and the death of others, an entity is indeed still on hand, but certainly not their Dasein as such.

2) This sort of information not only mistakes the kind of being which belongs to Dasein. It even presupposes that the temporally particular Dasein can be arbitrarily replaced by another. If I perchance cannot observe something in myself, I can see it in the other. What then is the standing [Bewandtnis] of the presupposition that Dasein is an entity which in principle and always could replace an entity of its own kind of being, another Dasein? This possibility does in fact belong to being-with as being with one another in the world. I can replace the other precisely in the everyday kind of being of concerned absorption in the world. In what then?—in what he does, in the world in which he is concerned and in this very concern. It was shown earlier that Dasein in its everyday self-interpretation sees itself, interprets, considers, and names itself precisely in terms of what it in each case does. One is what one does. In this being of everyday absorption with one another in the world, we can in a certain way mutually replace one another, the one can within limits take over the Dasein of the other. But such a substitution always takes place only 'in' something, which means that it is oriented to a concern, to a specific what.

For all that, this possibility of replacing someone fails utterly when it comes to replacing the being of what constitutes the end of Dasein and thus gives it its wholeness in its time. That is to say: *no one can relieve the other of his own dying.* It is true that he can die for another, but this is always for the sake of a definite cause, in the sense of concern for the being-in-the-world of the other. Dying for the other does not mean that the other has thus had his own death taken away and abolished. Every Dasein must take dying upon itself as its very self, as Dasein. More precisely, *every Dasein, insofar as it is, has already taken this way of being upon itself. Death is in each instance and in its time my own death*; it belongs to me insofar as I am.

The information proposed above operates with the implicit assumption that a response to the question of arriving at the wholeness of Dasein is primarily and solely a matter of making Dasein available as an object for consideration. This is the secondary difficulty. The primary one is whether Dasein is the entity which one oneself is and which of *its essence* entails that it *be in each instance mine*, and whether this entity has the possibility *to be* its wholeness. It is only on the basis of this possibility of being that we could have the further possibility of experiencing this self-being of Dasein in its wholeness now also in an explicit fashion.

But now, insofar as the wholeness of Dasein is reached in the dying which of its essence is mine, this reaching of the whole is as usual again a no-longer-Dasein. And so the impossibility of being the wholeness of Dasein persists, and with it more than ever the impossibility of the experience of what constitutes the whole. This insight into such an impossibility is not deduced indirectly from contradictory propositions, but is taken directly from a positive look at the constitution of the being of Dasein itself. At the same time, however, it gives us something positive, namely, the understanding of a distinction in kind of the being of Dasein compared to that of the entity which we call a world-thing.

When Dasein reaches the mode of being in which nothing more in it is outstanding, that is, when it is finished as Dasein, then in its being-finished it no longer is what it is. *Being-finished, when asserted about Dasein, means no-longer-being.* By contrast, an entity encountered in concern can totally fulfill its function as something used or produced (table, book, equipment of every kind) only when it is finished, on hand. *Being-finished, asserted about a world-thing on hand, means precisely first being on hand and becoming available.* We have thus arrived at two different phenomena of reaching wholeness and of being whole. The difference refers to the bearing that reaching wholeness has on the being of what has in each case become whole. 'Finished' has a different sense in accordance with the fundamentally different kind of being of the entity—world-thing versus Dasein.

But this implies that the structure of the specific totality of Dasein nonetheless must have somehow become visible, and that this structure of totality became visible in a provisional consideration of the phenomenon of death as a phenomenon of Dasein. It is only when the impossibility of the experience of Dasein as a whole is exhibited expressly from the phenomenon of Dasein itself and from death as a mode of being of this being that this impossibility of determining the totality of Dasein receives its scientific justification. It is only when this demonstration has been conducted with phenomenological clarity that an insurmountable barrier is placed before the investigation of the being of Dasein. In order that we may scientifically ascertain the impossibility of whether Dasein can be experienced as a whole and thus whether its totality of being can be brought into structural relief, *the phenomenological concept of death must be elaborated.* But this means

that we need the genuine interpretation of death as a pure phenomenon of Dasein, which in turn means that we have to understand death
from what has previously been exhibited about Dasein in connection
with the structures of being. The phenomenologically pure accom-
plishment of this task brings out something remarkable: the purported impossibility is a mere semblance. Genuine phenomenological
interpretation of the phenomenon of death is rather the only way to
open the prospect for Dasein as such to implement a possibility of
being *to be itself* genuinely in its wholeness. The character of being of
this very possibility will then yield the phenomenal ground for securing the sense of being of Dasein's being-whole. Not only that. In Dasein's genuine totality, which manifests itself in the genuinely seen
phenomenon of death, and which is commensurate with its being, this
primary totality of being simultaneously shows itself. The elaboration
of death as a phenomenon of Dasein, its determination in strict conformity with the structures of being of the entity which we have as
our theme, *eo ipso* leads us to the being of the entity itself and indeed in such a way that the totality of the being of Dasein is thereby
understood.

§34. Phenomenological interpretation of death as a phenomenon of Dasein

We can start with the distinction between how tools and world-
things are finished and how Dasein is finished. Being-finished in the
first sense first and foremost means being on hand. Being-finished in
the second sense means no longer being on hand, first of all taken as
the occurrence of what up until now was still outstanding, what heretofore has not yet appeared in the entity. But how is Dasein seen here?
It is taken as a flowing continuity of comportments and processes
which at a certain moment reach a conclusion as a wholeness, which
first fully becomes what it is with the occurrence of the still missing
remainder. The totality of this wholeness has the sense of the *composite*. Totality, the being of the end taken as death, is here understood
in terms of the structure of the being of world-things, is here seen by
way of the world.

But *death* is neither constitutive of a totality for a whole understood
as a composite, nor even constitutive of a totality for a whole taken
as a composite such that it would no longer be when it is finished.
Rather, if death is indeed a character of the being of Dasein, it cannot
be conceived in its sense of being primarily in terms of the being-
on-hand and not-being-on-hand of world-things. As care, Dasein is
rather being toward something. Death is not something which is still

outstanding in Dasein. Death does not stand out in Dasein, but *stands before* [*bevorsteht*] Dasein in its being, and constantly at that, as long as it is Dasein. In other words, death is always already *impending* [*bevorstehend*]. As such, death belongs to Dasein itself even when it is not yet whole and not yet finished, even when it is not dying. Death is not a missing part of a whole taken as a composite. Rather it *constitutes the totality of Dasein from the start*, so that it is only on the basis of this totality that Dasein has the being of temporally particular parts, that is, of possible ways to be.

But even this sharper specification still does not give us an adequate conception of death. For the characterization 'something which is impending' does not belong to death solely and uniquely. There are many things in Dasein of which we can say, 'It is imminent,' 'It impends,' 'It stands before us.' It does not need to be death. Of course, it can be said that death too belongs to what stands before me. But there is an ambiguity in this. For it does not specify how death is now understood. To be sure, it is no longer an outstanding objective event which is paratactically attached to the series of states which have already expired; it is rather as something impending and inevitable that care is out for. But is this impending thing now an occurrence which encounters me, something alien which befalls me from the world? Or is it something which I will simply never encounter, but which I myself am in a certain way, as Dasein? In fact, it is only then that death is understood as a character of Dasein, although it is now not taken as an impending worldly encounter, as something which first runs into me. Death is understood as a character of Dasein only when it is conceived from the structure of the being of Dasein, from care, from its being-ahead-of-itself.

With death, which at its time is only *my* dying, *my ownmost being* stands before me, is imminent: I stand before my can-be at every moment. The being that I will be in the 'last' of my Dasein, that I can be at any moment, this possibility is that of my ownmost 'I am,' which means that I will be my ownmost I. I myself am this possibility, where death is my death. There is no such thing as death in general.

Care as being-ahead-of-itself is as such at the same time a being-possible. 'I can,' or more accurately, I am this 'I can' in a superlative sense. For I am this 'I can die at any moment.' This possibility is a possibility of being in which I always already am. It is a superlative possibility. For *I myself am this constant and utmost possibility of myself*, namely, to be no more. Care, which is essentially care about the being of Dasein, at its innermost is nothing but this being-ahead-of-itself in the uttermost possibility of its own can-be. Therefore Dasein is essentially its death. With death, the impending is not something worldly, but Dasein itself. Dasein stands before itself, not in a possibility of being of its choosing but in its no-longer-Dasein. Insofar as Dasein *qua* being-possible is essentially already its death, it is as Dasein always already a whole. Because Dasein means 'being-ahead-of-itself as care,' it can of itself be its being wholly in every moment of its being. The wholeness of Dasein will become phenomenally comprehensible in its structure with the elaboration of the way of being in which Dasein can be this its utmost possibility authentically. In connection with this way of being it now becomes evident how, in what kind of being Dasein is its very death. The elaboration of the way of being in which Dasein is its utmost possibility of being constitutes the sense of the phenomenological interpretation of the phenomenon of death, where death is taken as a constitutive determination of the being of Dasein. This at the same time indicates what this interpretation of death cannot take into account:

1) It cannot give an account of the factual content of death, whether it be the many causes of death or the various possible ways of dying, how human beings can and do comport themselves in dying. Aside from the fact that this theme does not devolve upon ours, we would in this way learn much less about death than about the life of the human beings in question. And in the end, such an interpretation of dying can be carried out only under the guidance of a rigorous concept of death itself, which we now wish to obtain.

2) But if the phenomenological explication of death does not prejudge any attitudes towards death, it makes no decision about whether there is anything after death or what that may be, or whether there is nothing at all. Nothing is decided about immortality and the beyond, the "other side," nor for that matter about "this side," as if to say how one is to comport oneself toward death and how not. Nevertheless it can be stated that the explication maintains the most radical orientation to "this side," specifically in regard to what the death of an entity, of the Dasein at its time, can be. Such a this-sided interpretation really does not prejudice the traditional questions of immortality and resurrection; in fact, it is only with such an interpretation of the structure of the being of death that the sense and the basis for such questions are given. As long as speculation operates with confused and mythically superficial popular concepts of death, then speculation and philosophizing about death remain baseless. As long as I have not asked about Dasein in its structure and as long as I have not defined death in what it is, I cannot even rightly ask what could come after Dasein in connection with its death. The phenomenological concept of Dasein and death is the presupposition for posing the question of immortality with any sort of sense at all. This question, however, does not belong in the framework of a philosophy which understands itself.

To secure the phenomenological concept of death means to make visible the way of being of Dasein in which it can be its utmost possibility. In this connection it should now be noted that the relationship of being to a possibility which an entity itself is—like Dasein here and its death—is itself a being-possible. Being a possibility essentially means being capable of this being-possible. But this implies that Dasein can—it is after all essentially an 'I can'—be this its utmost possibility either in this or that way. But it is at the same time constantly the possibility of its death, because death is constitutive of the being of Dasein. Dasein is this possibility even in its everydayness. Since we have drawn out the constitution of the being of Dasein first of all in its everydayness, we want to start from it in our subsequent investigation and ask how Dasein is its death in the immediate mode of being of its everydayness. This analysis becomes the proof of how death for the most part can be in everydayness. From this characterization we shall at the same time be able to read off certain structures of the mode of being of death. We shall consider two points: 1) the kind of being of Dasein as everydayness toward its utmost possibility, death; 2) we ask, as what does the being of death in this everyday-being show itself to him?

a) The utmost possibility of death in the mode of being of everydayness

The everydayness of Dasein is defined by absorption in the Everyone. In the public arena of being-with-one-another, death is an established everyday encounter. This encounter is interpreted as 'one also dies some day.' This 'Everyone dies' harbors an ambiguity in itself, for this Everyone is just what *never* dies and *never* can die. Dasein says 'Everyone dies' because this means 'No one dies,' namely, not I myself. Death is something in being-with-one-another for which the Everyone already has a suitable interpretation ready. In 'Everyone dies' death is from the start leveled to a possibility of being which in a sense is no one's possibility. Death, in terms of what it truly is, is thus from the start driven away. 'Everyone dies' is the interpretation in which Dasein re-labels its ownmost possibility for the public way of having things interpreted for everyday circulation, thereby driving its ownmost possibility away from itself.

There is a further ambiguity in thus driving it away. 'Everyone dies, but for the time being death won't come.' One speaks as if death first had to come from somewhere, while Dasein itself is in each instance already this its possibility. Driving away the authentic being of death at the same time has the character of *tranquilization*. The public self-interpretation of Dasein goes so far that in being-with-one-another one even cheers the dying person up by telling him that he will soon be up and around again, that is to say, back in the everydayness of Dasein. The average worldly self-interpretation of Dasein hopes thereby to console the other, to come into a genuine being-with-one-another with him, where however such consolations only serve to push Dasein back again into becoming absorbed in the world, so that the specific situation of its being now really remains concealed to it.

The same public way of having things interpreted now also from the start regulates the public kind of being toward death, in the way that it has also already decided about what is to be held in thinking about death. Thinking about death is publicly regarded as cowardly dread and a gloomy flight from the world. The public does not permit the courage for dread in the face of death to come up, but hastens to forget it while at the same time interpreting this action as a form of self-security and superiority of Dasein opposed to this ostensible gloominess of life. These are the characters which mark the way of being of the Everyone, and it should be clear that what appears here is once again the way of everydayness in its being, that is, in the mode of being of falling.

In making death ambiguous, the Everyone not only drives it away in regard to what it is. Driving it away is at the same time tranquilizing and has the character of *estrangement*, since not thinking about death now becomes a concern. In not wanting to think about death, the everydayness of Dasein is in constant *flight in the face of death*. But here is where it becomes phenomenally evident that death does not come from somewhere but has gained a hold in Dasein itself. In not wanting to think about it, Dasein bears witness to its being in death itself. Conversely, death is not first in Dasein because it by chance thinks about it. That before which Dasein flees in its falling flight in everydayness, even without expressly thinking about death, is nothing other than Dasein itself, specifically insofar as death is constitutive of it.

But the mode of being of falling is also a covering up. It operates by way of a reinterpretation, not letting itself see what death is. But this still implies a constant seeing beforehand, so that what it conceals in it is its own being. The inconspicuous concern of not thinking about death covers up a basic character in it, namely its *certainty*. This certainty is reinterpreted into uncertainty by means of the ambiguity of 'Everyone dies someday.' One takes the edge off this certainty in this public way of having death interpreted which says, 'Each of us will someday have to believe in this'—a statement about death which is really addressed to no one, where after all the sense of death is just that it is my own possibility of being. This certainty, that "I myself am in that I will die," is *the basic certainty of Dasein itself*. It is a genuine

§34. Phenomenon of death [437–439]   317

statement of Dasein, while *cogito sum* is only the semblance of such a statement. If such pointed formulations mean anything at all, then the appropriate statement pertaining to Dasein in its being would have to be *sum moribundus* ["I am in dying"], *moribundus* not as someone gravely ill or wounded, but insofar as I am, I am *moribundus*. *The* MORIBUNDUS *first gives the* SUM *its sense.*

The uncertainty with which Dasein covers up its original certainty of being is at the same time supported by the calculation and determination that now—according to a general estimate, which is the way one tends to see things—death in any case cannot be anticipated. One in a sense reckons that death can come and thereby overlooks that this *indefiniteness*, whereby death can come at any moment, belongs essentially to its certainty. This indefiniteness as to when death comes positively refers to the possibility that it can come at any moment. It in no way weakens the certainty of its coming, but rather gives it its sting and the character of an utmost and constant possibility which Dasein is. These two characters, that death is absolutely certain, and that this certainty is at the same time indefinite, constitute the manner of being of this possibility of death. *Death is the utmost, though indefinite, yet certain possibility* in which Dasein itself stands before itself, but at the same time the possibility before which Dasein flees in everydayness, so that it makes this possibility ambiguous. This means that everydayness does not have the most authentic and most original relationship to death, inasmuch as a character of the being of death is disregarded or covered up by it, namely, that death is in each instance my death.

b) The authentic relationship of the being of Dasein toward death

The authentic possibility of the being of death is grasped only when the relationship to this possibility is such that it is thereby understood as a certainty of my being, specifically a certainty having the character of something indefinite and a certainty of being which is my certainty. The question therefore arises, whether there is a possibility of being in Dasein itself in which Dasein can now acquire a relationship of being toward death in the authentic sense.

I have already indicated that the relationship of being to a possibility must be such that it lets the possibility stand as a possibility, and not such that the possibility becomes reality, perhaps by causing my own death in suicide. By suicide I surrender the possibility precisely as possibility; it is radically reversed, for it becomes a reality. The possibility is however just what it is only when it is left standing, that is, when it is left standing before us as impending. A relationship of being to it must be such that I am precisely the possibility itself. This

implies that in this being toward the possibility it cannot be a matter of
wanting to possess the possibility in the way that worldly concern appresents and makes available what is of concern, but rather the reverse. The being must *run forward* toward the possibility, which has to
remain what it is. It must not draw it near as a present but must let it
stand as a possibility and be toward it in this way. In thus forerunning
into the possibility, I come as it were into the nearest nearness to it.
But as I approach it in this way, the possibility does not become a
world, say, but becomes more and more a possibility and more authentically only a possibility. This possibility into which I can run is of
its essence and in an extreme sense my possibility. The possibility of
going out of the world by dying is, as being-in-the-world, defined by
the world as still only being on hand as the wherein which I am leaving. In dying, the world is only that which has nothing more to say for
my own being, which Dasein gives up precisely as being-in-the-world.
In dying, in this way of being-in-the-world, the world is that upon
which Dasein is no longer dependent, the world remains only the
pure wherein of still-being.

This implies that the utmost possibility of death is the way of being
of Dasein in which it is *purely and simply thrown back upon itself*, so absolutely that even being-with in its concretion of "to be with others" becomes irrelevant. Of course, even in dying, Dasein is of its essence
being-in-the-world and being-with with others, but the being is now
transposed authentically directly to the 'I am.' Only in dying can I to
some extent say absolutely, 'I am.'

The utmost possibility of death as the being of Dasein, in which it is
wholly by and of itself, has to be seized in Dasein itself. But insofar as
Dasein is in everydayness, that means that it must be called back from
this everydayness to the utmost possibility of the 'I am.' *Dasein's running forward toward death at every moment means Dasein's drawing back
from the Everyone by way of a self-choosing.*

§35. The phenomenon of willing to have a conscience and of being guilty

In choosing myself as my possibility I myself choose my being. But
this possibility which I choose in running forward toward death is a
certain possibility and as such at the same time an indefinite possibility. The self-choosing in forerunning into possibility must as authentic
self-choosing come into an appropriate relationship of being to the
characters of possibility. This means that the indefiniteness of death is
seized when I have understood the possibility as a possibility for every
moment, that is, when I am absolutely *resolute* in having chosen my-

self. The certainty of this possibility is seized when every other possible can-be of mine is set apart from it, that is, when the resoluteness toward itself is such that it is the source of the possibility of this or that action. If Dasein in forerunning can bring itself into such an absolute resoluteness, it means that in this running forward toward its death Dasein can make itself responsible in an absolute sense. It 'can' *choose the presupposition of being of itself*, that is, it can *choose itself*. What is chosen in this choice is nothing other than *willing to have conscience*. This choice of course does not have to take place only in this forerunning. Willing to have conscience can also be actuated otherwise, but insofar as the issue in Dasein is to choose itself in understanding the full transparency of Dasein as a whole, there is only this one possibility of forerunning toward death, in order to choose Dasein not for the next two days but to choose it in its very being. *Forerunning is the choice of willing to have conscience.* But he who acts, as Goethe already said, is always without conscience. I can truly be without conscience only when I have chosen to be willing to have conscience.

The actor is without conscience; that is, in being with one another he who acts necessarily becomes 'guilty,' not in the sense that he commits this or that blunder. As an active being-with with others and as such, Dasein is *eo ipso* guilty, even when—and precisely when—it does not know that it is injuring another or destroying him in his Dasein. With the choice of being willing to have conscience, I have at the same time chosen *to have become guilty*. The genuine kind of being of Dasein corresponding to its utmost and ownmost possibility (the ownmost being-ahead-of-itself enacted by itself) is what we have characterized as the forerunning of willing to have conscience, which at the same time means choosing the essential guilt of Dasein itself, insofar as it is.

§36. *Time as the being in which Dasein can be its totality*

But forerunning into my ownmost possibility of being is nothing but the being of my ownmost *coming to be being*. Being guilty, which is posited in it and with it, is the being of my ownmost *having been*. The being of having-been is the past, such that in such a being I am nothing but the *future* of Dasein and *with it its past*. The being, in which Dasein can be its wholeness authentically as being-ahead-of-itself, is *time*.

Not "time is" but "Dasein qua time temporalizes its being." Time is not something which is found outside somewhere as a framework for world events. Time is even less something which whirs away inside in consciousness. It is rather that which makes possible the being-ahead-of-itself-in-already-being-involved-in, that is, which makes possible the being of care.

The time which we know everyday and which we take into account is, more accurately viewed, nothing but the Everyone to which Dasein in its everydayness has fallen. The being in being-with-one-another in the world, and that also means in discovering with one another the one world in which we are, is being in the Everyone and a particular kind of *temporality*.

The movements of nature which we define spatio-temporally, these movements do not flow off 'in time' as 'in' a channel. They are as such completely *time-free*. They are encountered 'in' time only insofar as their being is discovered as pure nature. They are encountered 'in' the time which we ourselves are.

EDITOR'S EPILOGUE

Martin Heidegger gave the lecture course announced under the title "History of the Concept of Time" in the summer semester of 1925, meeting four hours a week at Marburg University. The subtitle was "Prolegomena to the Phenomenology of History and Nature." The plan called for the following outline (cf. §3):

First Part: Analysis of the phenomenon of time and derivation of the concept of time.

Second Part: Disclosure of the history of the concept of time.

Third Part: On the basis of the first and second part, the elaboration of the horizon for the question of being in general and of the being of history and nature in particular.

The actual course covered the introduction to the three main parts and the first part. Because of its size, the introduction was designated as the "Preliminary Part" in this edition. It includes the following three chapters:

Chapter One: Emergence and initial breakthrough of phenomenological research.

Chapter Two: The fundamental discoveries of phenomenology, its principle, and the clarification of its name.

Chapter Three: The early development of phenomenological research and the necessity of a radical reflection in and from itself.

The only Part presented was called the "Main Part" in the edition. In turn, only the first two divisions of it are worked out, the second division in fact in a very sketchy way:

First Division: Preparatory description of the field in which the phenomenon of time becomes manifest.

Second Division: The exposition of time itself.

Since Heidegger did not complete the presentation of the central thematic of *History of the Concept of Time* it seemed appropriate with the publication of the course to change the original title to "*Prolegomena to the History of the Time Concept*" for the German edition. For these "Prolegomena" are worked out and were delivered.

The range of themes of the lecture course is staked out by the subtitle, "Prolegomena to the Phenomenology of History and Nature." 'History' and 'Nature' can however be adequately treated only on the basis of the new guiding clue, discovered by Heidegger, of 'time' or 'temporality.' But 'time' means '*temporality of Dasein*.' This lecture course of 1925 is an early draft of *Being and Time*, even though the

322   Editor's Epilogue [444–445]

theme of temporality is not yet actually covered here. By examining this early draft, we can trace how the meaning of many concepts is definitely established for the first time in the course of the elaboration. In the manuscript, for example, Heidegger speaks of the "discoveredness of Dasein" and of the "disclosedness of the world." In Simon Moser's transcript, Heidegger crosses out 'discoveredness' in favor of 'disclosedness' in Dasein and notes in the margin: "Disclosedness as such does not first discover from discoveredness but rather co-constitutes discoveredness. Disclosedness can be cultivated, however, but because it is discoveredness—never free-floating—the being of research." (Moser, p. 329; cf. above, p. 254).

Heidegger's thematic deliberations begin with a characterization of the situation of philosophy and science in the second half of the nineteenth century. He exhibits what in his interpretation was the decisive event of that time, the breakthrough of phenomenology as philosophical research. He investigates its essential discoveries, defends it against misunderstandings, in order then to advance his own critique as to where phenomenology has not done justice to its own call to get back 'to the matters themselves.' Heidegger indicates that he is not satisfied with the exposition of its essential discoveries (intentionality, sense of the apriori, categorial intuition), and raises the question of their essential enabling dimension. The "Main Part" is just such an investigation of their condition of possibility. It would be a mistake to think that the "Preliminary Part" is merely a historical survey contributing to the pure characterization of phenomenology as such and of how it has been historically and temporally conditioned, or that it is even a disparagement of phenomenology in favor of Heidegger's own thinking, which would then appear at the center of all of the deliberations. Heidegger is always interested in letting the development of a (or better, his) problem become evident, in showing how the thematic of being and Dasein necessarily had to emerge from the phenomenology of Husserl and Scheler, how phenomenology harbored this tendency toward radicalization within itself. By taking phenomenological inquiry and its maxim, 'to the matters themselves,' at their word, he comes across ultimate and unposited, because unseen, presuppositions: the neglect of the question of the being of the intentional and of the question of being itself. In a 'preparatory fundamental analysis,' Heidegger makes the transition from Husserl's "position of consciousness" to the analytic of Dasein as it was published in *Being and Time*.

The documents at my disposal for this edition of the text were Heidegger's handwritten but not yet transcribed manuscript and Simon Moser's transcript of the actual lectures, authorized by Heidegger and supplemented with his remarks. I have taken it upon myself to make a typewritten transcription of the manuscript. The stenographic transcript typed by Moser was regularly delivered to Heidegger immediately upon completion, who looked it over, now and then corrected errors, and added his own remarks. In addition, I had at my disposal a set of handwritten notes focused on key-words made by his student at the time, Helene Weiss, which proved useful only with difficulties in deciphering and with citations.

The original manuscript comprises 88 numbered pages, along with inserts, notes, addenda, some of which are tied directly to a particular page, while some record leading concepts, leading ideas in the form of key-words. The horizontally written pages of the original manuscript in folio-format contain on the left side a text three-fourths of which is formulated in sentences, with many insertions standing between dashes and not always fully formulated. On the right side, there are a great number of marginalia, most of which are formulated in key-words.

In the preparation of the manuscript to be published, preference was given in every instance to the handwritten manuscript. The Moser transcript was used solely within the limits of the guidelines issued by Heidegger for such instances. Accordingly, it was followed 1) when the lecture amplified, supplemented, or developed the ideas beyond the handwritten manuscript, 2) when the pedagogical repetitions which summarize the previous day's lecture introduce new concepts and open new perspectives in the line of thought, and 3) in order to fill out the condensed formulations, schematized in the form of key-words, of the marginalia and supplementary remarks in the handwritten manuscript. One exception must be mentioned. The original manuscript does not comprise the entire text of the lecture course held then, but ends with the 'Fable of Care' (cf. §31e). But the transcripts of both Moser and Weiss bear witness to the fact that Heidegger's lecture course did not end there. The Second Division of the Main Part is therefore taken from the transcript of Simon Moser, which bears Heidegger's authorization.

To the extent that it corresponded to the actual content presented in the lecture course, I have adhered closely to the course outline given by Heidegger at the beginning. The Introduction, which turned out to be quite long, has been renamed simply "Preliminary Part," while the first part is now called "Main Part," since it was the only one which was worked out. The major division into chapters in the "Preliminary Part" is in its formulation also taken from Heidegger himself, as are the titles of the two divisions of the "Main Part." The division into paragraphs and their further differentiation were undertaken by the editor and in formulation are always tied to Heidegger's linguistic usage. This means that they rely on expressions which almost always appear word for word in the context in question.

In bringing this volume to fruition, I am particularly indebted to Professor Doctor Walter Biemel for his help, as well as to Professor Doctor Friedrich-Wilhelm von Herrmann, Mrs. Elfride Heidegger, and Mr. Fritz Heidegger, along with Mr. Bernd-Friedemann Schultze for his collaboration in collating the text. For their help in reading the proofs, I am thankful to Miss Eva-Maria Hollenkamp and Mr. Klaus Neugebauer.

Petra Jaeger

GLOSSARY OF GERMAN TERMS

This glossary is not intended to be exhaustive. It seeks primarily to list the most significant and problematic expressions in the vocabulary of Heidegger and Husserl, especially when their translation here deviates from the customary. For each expression, the most important and frequent translations appear before the semicolon, the infrequent or rare ones after the semicolon.

abheben: set off, contrast, bring into relief, bring out; highlight
abschatten: adumbrate, shade off
Abstand: spacing, spaced interval, interval; distance, being apart
Abständigkeit: apartness
abträglich: detrimental
alltäglich: everyday
angegangen: solicited, approached
angewiesen: dependent
Angst: dread
ansetzen: approach; begin with, put forward
ansprechen als: consider as
Anwesenheit: presence
Anzeige: indication
appräsentieren: appresent
Apriori: apriori[1]
aufdecken: uncover
Auffassung: conception, comprehension; apprehension, construal, 'reading,' point of view, view
Aufgehen: absorption
aufhalten: dwell
Aufnahme: adoption, assumption, admission, reception
Aufweis: exposition; exhibition
Ausarbeitung: elaboration; working out
Ausbildung: cultivation; development, formation
Ausdrücklichkeit: expressness, explicitness
Ausgedrücktheit: expressedness
Ausgelegtheit: way of being (having been) interpreted; way of interpretation
ausgezeichnet: distinctive; outstanding, superlative, principal
auslegen: interpret; expose, lay out
Auslegung: (expository) interpretation; exposition
Ausrichtung: directionality
ausschalten: suspend
Aussehen: outward appearance
Aussein auf: being out for
ausweisen: demonstrate; point out

bedeuten: mean; signify
Bedeutung: meaning; significance, import
Bedeutsamkeit: meaningfulness

(Sich)befinden: self-finding, finding oneself
befindliches: situated
Befindlichkeit: disposition, being disposed, disposedness
Befragtes: what is interrogated
begegnen: encounter; confront, meet with
Begegnenlassen: leeway of encounter
Begegnisstruktur: structure of encounter
bei: (intimately) involved with (in); in touch with, with
beiträglich: conducive
Besinnung: reflection
Besorgen: concern
besorgend: concerned; concernful
besorgt: under concern
Besorgtes: what is of concern
Besorgtheit: what is of concern; concernedness
Bestand: composition, subsistence; (compositive) existence, constellation
Bestände: constituents
bestimmen: determine, define, specify; analyze
bestimmtes: definite, specific, particular, certain
Betrachtung: consideration; reflection, contemplation, regard, observation, examination, etc.
Bewandtnis: standing (generic), deployment (of tools): cf. "On the Way to Being and Time"
Bewandtnisganzheit: deployment totality, stanced totality for orientation
Bewenden, in the phrase *hat ein Bewenden*: plays its part
bodenständig: autochthonous, rooted in native soil

Charakter: character, (distinguishing) feature; form, aspect

da: there, here; present (in a few idiomatic contexts)
Dasein: Dasein, being (t)here; existence
deuten: interpret, signify
Drang: urge

eigentlich: really, actually, truly, genuinely, authentically; properly, strictly
eigentümliches: peculiar; odd, special, particular, inherent, unique
Einklammerung: bracketing
entdecken: discover, uncover
Entdecktheit: discoveredness
Entfernung: remotion [versus *Ferne* (distance) and *Abstand* (spacing)]; remoted distance
Ent-fernen: re-moting (i.e., removing distance)
entfernt: removed
entweltlichen: unworld, deprive of its worldhood
erfahren: experience; undergo
Erfassung: apprehension
Erfragtes: what is asked for
Er-leben: living-through
Erlebnis: lived experience; experience (in contexts where it cannot be confused with *Erfahrung*)
Erscheinung: appearance
erschliessen: disclose
Erschlossenheit: disclosedness

faktisch: actually, factually, in fact; factically
Faktizität: facticity
Ferne: distance
Fragestellung: (line of) questioning (*or* inquiry), manner of inquiry, way of
    questioning, formulation (articulation) of the question
freilegen: lay open, lay out, expose; display, bring into the open
Fundierung: founding

Gefragtes: what is asked about
Gegend: region
gegenwärtigen: make present; present, presentify
gegenwärtiges: in the present, present
Geisteswissenschaften: human sciences
geistiges: spiritual, intellectual, mental
Gerede: idle talk
Geschichte: history (versus *Historie*, historiology)
gestuftes: multi-level, multi-layered, phased
gleichursprünglich: co-original

Hang: propensity
Hebung: accentuation, highlighting; bringing out
Heraushebung: drawing out, accentuation, highlighting
Historie: historiology

In-der-Welt-sein: being-in-the-world
In-Sein: in-being (versus *Sein-in*, being-in; cf. p. 157)

je: in each (particular) instance (*or* case); always
jeweilig: at the (that, its) time; in its time, for the time being, in each case
jeweiliges: (temporally) particular
Jeweiligkeit: temporal particularity; the particular while
jeweils: at any given (particular) time

Leermeinen: empty intending
leibhaft-da: bodily there
Leibhaftigkeit: bodily presence

man: one; everyone, we
das Man: the Anyone, the Everyone
meinen: intend; refer to
Mitdasein: co-Dasein[2]
Miteinandersein: being-with-one-another[3]
Mitsein: being-with
Mitwelt: with-world
Moment: moment, element; factor, feature, part

nächstes: nearest, closest, (most) immediate, (most) proximate; intimate, next
Nähe: nearness, neighborhood

offenbar: manifest
Öffentlichkeit: (the) public; public arena, public character, publicity
originär: originarily

präsentieren: present
Präsenz: presence

Rede: discourse; talk
reelles: immanently real (versus *reales*, transcendently real)
(Sich-)richten-auf: directing-itself-toward

Sache: subject matter, matter; issue, 'thing'
Sachgehalt, Sachhaltigkeit: material content
Sachverhalt: state of affairs
Schein: semblance; seeming
schlichtes: simple
Seiendes: entity[4]
Sein: being[4]
Sein-bei: being-(intimately-) involved-with (*or* -in); being-with, being-in-touch-with
Seinkönnen: can-be
Sein zu: being toward(s)
selbstverständliches: obvious, self-evident; matter-of-course, taken for granted
Sinn: sense
Sorge: care; concern (in one idiomatic context)

Tatbestand: state of affairs; composition, status, sort of case
Tatbestände: matters of fact, actual elements; component elements

Umgang: preoccupation, occupation
Umhaftes: aroundness
Umsicht: circumspection
Umwelt: environing world, environment, world around us
ursprüngliches: primordial, original

verbergen: conceal
verdecken: cover up, conceal
Verfallen: falling
Verfassung: constitution, constitutive state
vergegenwärtigen: envisage, bring to mind, bring home, recall
Verhalt: (comportmental) relation
(sich) verhalten: comport oneself
Verhältnis: relationship; bearing
Vermeinen: presuming; intending
vernehmen: apprehend, perceive; come to awareness
Verstand: intellect, (intellectual) understanding
verständliches: understandable, comprehensible; intelligible
Verständnis: understanding; comprehension
Verweisung: reference
vollziehen: perform; accomplish, consummate, carry out, go through, fulfill, realize
Vollzug: performance, enactment; execution, fulfillment, realization
Vorgriff: preconception
Vorhabe: prepossession
vorhanden: on hand, extant; available, present, existent
Vorlaufen: running forward, forerunning

Vor-sicht: pre-view
Vorstellung: representation
(*Sich-*)*vorweg-sein*: being-ahead-of-itself
vorzeichnen: prefigure; prescribe, trace, outline, draw

Wahrgenommenheit: perceivedness
Weise zu sein: way to be; manner of being
Weltding: world-thing, thing of (in) the world; worldly thing
weltlich: worldly
Weltlichkeit: worldhood
Werkwelt: work-world, world of work
Werkzeug: tool
Wesen: essence; being (in compounds such as *Lebewesen*, living being, and *organisches Wesen*, organic being)
Wiederholung: repetition
Wobei: involvements, (intimate) with-which
Woran: whereat
Worinheit: the wherein

zeitigen: temporalize; bring to fruition, evoke
Zeitigung: temporalization; maturation
Zeug: equipment, tool
Zugehörigkeit: belonging (together); affinity
zuhanden: handy
Zusammenhang: context, correlation, connection, interconnection, interrelation; nexus (of relations), continuity, coherence, contexture
Zu-sein: to-be

NOTES TO THE GLOSSARY

1. Here I am following a growing, and to me sensible, trend of taking 'apriori' as a single word, given its overwhelming use in philosophical contexts as a noun. Cf. for example Dorion Cairns, *Guide for Translating Husserl* (The Hague: Nijhoff, 1973), p. 9. The only exception I have made is its rare use as an adverb.

2. One can read 'coexistence' here, though this is not adequate for our purposes.

3. Here and with other such expressions, I have omitted the hyphens when no ambiguity is interjected by doing so.

4. The reader should note that I have adhered strictly to this convention in order to reflect the ontological difference between *Sein* and *Seiendes* in the translation, in view of the large number of passages in the German text in which Heidegger speaks of being in the singular *dieses Sein* and indefinite *ein Sein*. Note however that *Wesen* is also translated as 'being' in combinations such as *Lebewesen*, living being, and *organisches Wesen*, organic being.